Western Hemisphere Economic Integration

Central America, the Caribbean, and South America

Gary Clyde Hufbauer
Jeffrey J. Schott
assisted by Diana Clark

Western Hemisphere Economic Integration

Institute for International Economics
Washington, DC
July 1994

With the support of
the Tinker Foundation

Gary Clyde Hufbauer is the Reginald Jones Senior Fellow. He was formerly Marcus Wallenberg Professor of International Finance Diplomacy at Georgetown University (1985–92), Deputy Director of the International Law Institute at Georgetown University (1979–81); Deputy Assistant Secretary for International Trade and Investment Policy of the US Treasury (1977–79); and Director of the International Tax Staff at the Treasury (1974–76). He has written extensively on international trade, investment, and tax issues, including *NAFTA: An Assessment* (rev. 1993), *US Taxation of International Income* (1992), *North American Free Trade* (1992), *Economic Sanctions Reconsidered* (second edition 1990), *Trade Policy for Troubled Industries* (1986), and *Subsidies in International Trade* (1984).

Jeffrey J. Schott, Senior Fellow, was a Senior Associate at the Carnegie Endowment for International Peace (1982–83) and an International Economist at the US Treasury (1974–82). He is coauthor of *NAFTA: An Assessment* (rev. 1993), *North American Free Trade: Issues and Recommendations* (1992), *Completing the Uruguay Round* (1990), *Economic Sanctions Reconsidered* (Second edition 1990), *Free Trade Areas and US Trade Policy* (1989), *The Canada-United States Free Trade Agreement: The Global Impact* (1988), *Auction Quotas and US Trade Policy* (1987), and *Trading for Growth: The Next Round of Trade Negotiations* (1985).

INSTITUTE FOR INTERNATIONAL ECONOMICS
11 Dupont Circle, NW
Washington, DC 20036–1207
(202) 328–9000 FAX: (202) 328–5432

C. Fred Bergsten, *Director*
Christine F. Lowry, *Director of Publications*

Cover design by Naylor Design, Inc.
Typesetting by BG Composition
Printing by Automated Graphic Systems

Printed in the United States of America
97 96 95   8 7 6 5 4

Library of Congress Cataloging-in-Publication Data

Hufbauer, Gary Clyde.
    Western Hemisphere economic integration / Gary Clyde Hufbauer, Jeffrey J. Schott.
        p.   cm.
    Includes bibliographical references and index.

    1. America—Economic integration.
I. Schott, Jeffrey J., 1949–   . II. Title.
HC94.H84   1994
337.1'7—dc20   94-3985
                                                    CIP

ISBN 0–88132–159–1

Marketed and Distributed outside the USA and Canada by Longman Group UK Limited, London

TO DAVID ROCKEFELLER

For his lifelong devotion to promoting economic development in Latin America and to improving relations among the countries of the Western Hemisphere.

His wisdom has been an enormous source of encouragement to the work of the Institute and inspired us to explore the important ties that unite the Americas.

Contents

Preface   **xi**

Acknowledgments   **xv**

1   Overview   **1**
Elements of Integration   3
Sequencing the Elements of Integration   11
Plan of the Book   13

2   US–Latin American Economic Relations   **15**
Latin American Debt and US Interests   16
US–Latin American Trade Relations   17
US Investment Interests in Latin America   17
Changing Economic Relations   17
Summary   23

3   WHFTA: Feasible and Desirable   **25**
Unrealized Trade Potential: Scope for Trade Creation   25
Regional Economic Ties   27

4   Regional Implications of a WHFTA   **51**
Regional Implications for Latin America   51
Impact on the United States   60

5   Latin American Reforms and Readiness Indicators   **63**
Readiness Indicators   66

6   Subregional Integration and Readiness Assessment   **97**
North American Free Trade Agreement   97
Chile   103
Mercosur   106
Andean Group   113
Central American Common Market (CACM)   120
Caribbean Community (Caricom)   124
Caribbean Basin Initiative (CBI)   127
Cuba   128

7   Hemispheric Negotiations   **131**
Paths to Integration   131
Content of the Negotiations   134
Traditional Issues   134
New Issues   143
Collateral Issues   146

8   The Hemisphere and the World   **159**
Implications of WHFTA for the World Trading System   160
Trade Diversion   162
Investment Diversion   164
GATT Surveillance of Trade Diversion   166
Concerns of Asia and Europe   169
Conclusion   170

9   Toward a WHFTA   **173**
Economic Rationale for a WHFTA   174
The Widening Process   176
Links between the Western Hemisphere and Asia   182

APPENDIX A: Trade Deficiency in Latin America   **185**
APPENDIX B: Impact on Latin America and the
**   United States**   **191**
APPENDIX C: Chronologies of Regional Agreements   **219**
APPENDIX D: Trade and Investment Diversion   **251**

References   **263**

Index   **269**

Tables

1.1	Achievement scores on economic integration	6
2.1	Latin America: economic indicators, 1980–92	18
3.1	Merchandise trade by region of destination, 1992	29
3.2	Good customers: shares of destination regions in total exports of regions of origin, 1992	31
3.3	Strong-neighbor index: ratio of export shares of destination regions by region of origin to destination regions' shares of world GDP, 1992	32
3.4	Major trading partners from good customer and strong neighbor perspectives	33
3.5	Trade values, 1992	36
3.6	Good-customer indexes, 1992	38
3.7	Strong-neighbor indexes, 1992	40
3.8	Direct investment stock on a historical cost basis by countries of origin, 1990	44
3.9	Direct investment stock shares by countries of origin, 1990	45
3.10	Ratio between a destination's share of direct investment by country of origin and its share of world GDP, 1990	46
3.11	Regional diversity as measured by per capita GDP levels	49
4.1	Gross domestic investment as a share of GDP, 1980–90	55
4.2	Direct and portfolio investment inflows for selected Latin American countries, 1982–92	56
5.1	Public and private resource flows to Central and South America, net of principal repayments, 1985–92	68
5.2	Consumer prices, 1981–92	80
5.3	Latin America: range of budget deficits by annual inflation rate ranges, 1981–90	82
5.4	Consolidated surplus or deficit of central government budgets, 1981–92	83
5.5	Latin America: current account balances, 1981–92	85
5.6	Total disbursed external debt as a percentage of exports of goods and services, 1985–92	88
5.7	Secondary loan prices, fourth quarter 1989–93	90
5.8	Net interest payments as a percentage of exports of goods and services, 1982–92	91
5.9	Latin America: market exchange rates, 1984–92	92
5.10	Real effective exchange rates, 1981–92	93
5.11	International trade taxes as a percentage of current revenue, 1981–91	95
6.1	Performance scores on readiness indicators	102
7.1	Latin America: average tariffs applied on world imports, 1991 and 1993	136
7.2	US trade barriers most relevant to Latin America: tariff plus tariff equivalents of quotas, 1990	138

7.3	US trade barriers specifically imposed on imports from Latin American countries, 1990	142
7.4	Emissions performance, 1989	151
7.5	Latin America: average hourly compensation in manufacturing	155
7.6	Latin America: real average wages, 1984–92	156
8.1	Hypothetical calculation of trade compensation to be paid by NAFTA	167
A1	Actual and predicted trade-to-GDP ratios and values, 1990	186
B1	Export and import performance, 1980–90	193
B2	GDP and trade growth projected under two scenarios	197
B3	US exports to Latin America, by commodity group, annual average 1989–91, and projected for 1997 and 2002	198
B4	US imports from Latin America, by commodity group, annual average 1989–91, and projected for 1997 and 2002	206
B5	US jobs supported by US exports and dislocated by imports associated with worker groups sorted by median weekly wage levels, under two scenarios	214
B6	US exports and imports by product group, sorted by US median weekly wage levels, under two scenarios	216
B7	Impact on total US jobs and median weekly wage levels, per worker group, under two scenarios, 2002	217
D1	Projected merchandise trade diversion from South Asia, East Asia, and Western Europe by WHFTA, 1997 and 2002	253
D2	Investment diversion from third countries resulting from WHFTA	259

Preface

The Institute for International Economics has conducted major studies of each step in the evolving process of regional economic integration involving the United States. Starting with the Canada–United States Free Trade Agreement, Paul Wonnacott prepared *The United States and Canada: The Quest for Free Trade* in 1987 prior to the negotiations, and Jeffrey J. Schott and Murray G. Smith edited *The Canada–United States Free Trade Agreement: The Global Impact* in 1988 to assess its results. Turning to the NAFTA, Gary Clyde Hufbauer and Jeffrey J. Schott authored *North American Free Trade: Issues and Recommendations* in 1992 as a guide to the subsequent talks. The same authors appraised the results in *NAFTA: An Assessment* (1993).

This volume attempts to provide a similarly comprehensive analysis of proposals for extending the NAFTA throughout the Western Hemisphere. Its goal is to assess both the economics and the politics of the overall concept and of the several possible avenues that might be followed. Following their completion of this study, the authors have launched an analysis of *Economic Cooperation in the Asia Pacific*, the other potential venue for major regional trade liberalization involving the United States in the foreseeable future.

An important aspect of all these regional liberalization efforts is their impact on the global trading system. Here the authors will draw on their extensive earlier analyses of the Uruguay Round and the GATT as a whole: *Trading for Growth: The Next Round of Trade Negotiations*, which produced one of the original blueprints for the round (in 1985); Schott's *Completing the Uruguay Round: A Results-Oriented Approach to the GATT Trade Negotiations* (1990), which suggested a course of action to meet the original target date for completing the GATT talks; and Schott's *The Uruguay Round: An Assessment* (forthcoming 1994) that analyzes the actual results. The current volume also draws on Schott's *Free Trade*

Areas and U.S. Trade Policy (1989), which examined the overall relationship between the global system and regional trading arrangements.

The Institute for International Economics is a private nonprofit institution for the study and discussion of international economic policy. Its purpose is to analyze important issues in that area and to develop and communicate practical new approaches for dealing with them. The Institute is completely nonpartisan.

The Institute is funded largely by philanthropic foundations. Major institutional grants are now being received from the German Marshall Fund of the United States, which created the Institute with a generous commitment of funds in 1981, and from the Ford Foundation, the William and Flora Hewlett Foundation, the William M. Keck, Jr. Foundation, the C. V. Starr Foundation, and the United States–Japan Foundation. A number of other foundations and private corporations also contribute to the highly diversified financial resources of the Institute. The Tinker Foundation, Inc., the Andrew Mellon Foundation, and the Inter-American Development Bank provided support for the research underlying this project and the bank sponsored seminars for the discussion of its preliminary results. The Dayton Hudson Foundation provides support for the Institute's program of studies on trade policy. About 16 percent of the Institute's resources in our latest fiscal year were provided by contributors outside the United States, including about 7 percent from Japan.

The Board of Directors bears overall responsibility for the Institute and gives general guidance and approval to its research program—including identification of topics that are likely to become important to international economic policymakers over the medium run (generally, one to three years), and which thus should be addressed by the Institute. The Director, working closely with the staff and outside Advisory Committee, is responsible for the development of particular projects and makes the final decision to publish an individual study.

The Institute hopes that its studies and other activities will contribute to building a stronger foundation for international economic policy around the world. We invite readers of these publications to let us know how they think we can best accomplish this objective.

C. FRED BERGSTEN
Director
June 1994

Acknowledgments

The authors would like to thank C. Fred Bergsten, Paul Boeker, Richard N. Cooper, Harry Kopp, Riordan Roett, and Sidney Weintraub for their insightful comments on earlier drafts of the entire manuscript. Special thanks are also due to Johanna Buurman, Jonathan Coleman, Tammany Hobbs, Anup Malani, Patricia Martin, and Rosa Moreira for their valuable research assistance. Professional staff at the Inter-American Development Bank gave useful criticisms as the research was under way; we are especially grateful to Carolyn Beetz, Fred Jaspersen, Muni Figueres Jimenez, Nohra Rey de Marulanda, Willy van Ryckeghem, and Daniel Szabo. We appreciate the work of Angela Barnes, who typed numerous drafts of the manuscript, Valerie Norville, who carefully edited the text, and Brigitte Coulton and Christine Lowry, who ensured rapid publication.

1

Overview

The 1980s have been labeled the lost decade for Latin America.[1] Tremendous debt burdens, shrinking investment, and poor economic performance plagued the region. At the same time, US economic relations with Latin American slipped off the policy radar screen as the United States and Europe focused on integration in their own neighborhoods and on the fast-growing markets of East Asia.

In June 1990, President George Bush responded to Latin America's difficult economic situation by announcing a new framework for relations between the United States and Latin America: the Enterprise for the Americas Initiative (EAI). Latin American countries enthusiastically welcomed the proposal.[2] The EAI made economic reform the cornerstone of US relationships with Latin America. In the short run, the program called for debt relief and trade and investment liberalization. In the long run, Bush envisaged a Western Hemisphere Free Trade Area (WHFTA).

Economic integration in the Western Hemisphere will not be fully accomplished in the tenure of any government in office today, nor perhaps even in the career of young civil servants now entering ministries of trade and finance. After four decades of dedicated effort, Western Europe has just arrived at the threshold of internal free trade and invest-

---

1. In this context, and throughout the book, the term Latin America includes Central America, South America, and the Caribbean region, but excludes Mexico. This definition also applies to data on Latin America unless otherwise specified.

2. In a 10 May 1992 *Los Angeles Times* editorial, Henry Kissinger even declared that the EAI ''replaces interventionism with reciprocal obligations.''

ment, monetary union, and fiscal coordination. It seems likely that trade and investment integration will proceed at a faster pace within the Western Hemisphere, but fiscal and monetary coordination and labor mobility are likely to take far longer in the Western Hemisphere than in Europe.

If historical parallels are to be drawn, the North American Free Trade Agreement (NAFTA) comes as close to the 1957 Treaty of Rome, which established the European Economic Community (EEC), as the Western Hemisphere is likely to see. Henceforth, Western Hemisphere economic integration will likely be characterized by variable geometry, as is happening in Europe. Over the past three decades, the European Community has expanded its scope in stepwise fashion, with numerous association agreements (the countries of the European Free Trade Association, Turkey, Central Europe, and others) and with flexible arrangements for membership in the Exchange Rate Mechanism and Economic and Monetary Union (Henning, Hochreiter, and Hufbauer 1994). Economic integration in the Western Hemisphere will probably go forward in a similar way. However, the US debate over the NAFTA suggests that labor and environmental standards will occupy a higher place on the Western Hemisphere agenda than in Europe.

The broad direction of events in Western Hemisphere economic integration should, however, be clear. In the first stage, now largely but not entirely accomplished, one country after another has met or is meeting the preconditions for closer economic ties.[3] In the second stage, which is under way in most Latin American countries, barriers to trade and investment are coming down. The third and subsequent stages—the creation of a hemispheric free trade area with its own institutional structure, the reconciliation of differing national laws that regulate competition practices, and workplace, safety, and environmental standards—lie well in the future.

When the EAI was announced in June 1990, the second stage had just started in some countries. The EAI has done little more than reinforce ongoing trade and investment reforms and accelerate subregional efforts toward integration.[4] Since its inception, the EAI has taken a back seat to the NAFTA. Efforts to elaborate a broader vision of Western Hemisphere economic integration necessarily awaited the results of that negotiation. Now President Clinton and the other hemispheric leaders

---

3. The major exception is Brazil, which represents almost half of Latin American population and GDP.

4. Under EAI auspices, as of December 1992, $1.1 billion in Inter-American Development Bank investment-sector loans to eight countries and $303 million of debt reduction to five countries had been approved. In addition, by providing an umbrella for trade and investment agreements, the EAI has helped lock in place the broad Latin American reform process (US Department of Commerce, "Enterprise for the Americas Fact Sheet," 15 January 1993).

are pressing ahead with a summit meeting, and the United States, Canada, and Mexico have clearly indicated that negotiations will soon open for Chilean accession to NAFTA.

Meanwhile, Latin American countries have gone forward with their own reforms and integration efforts. Several overlapping free trade agreements (FTAs) are being negotiated among Latin American regions. These negotiations are loosely linked under the Latin American Integration Association (LAIA) umbrella.

Elements of Integration

The integration process has five elements: the liberalization of barriers to trade in goods and services; the elimination of restraints on investment; the provision of freer labor movement, at least for specialized workers; the harmonization of monetary and tax policies; and the establishment of supraregional institutions to administer the arrangements and to resolve disputes among the partner countries. Not every element is addressed at each stage of integration, and based on European experience, progress in each element is likely to occur in fits and starts (see, e.g., Hufbauer 1990, chapter 1; Jovanović 1992).

Once a group of countries liberalizes its trade in goods and services, the logic of economics and politics inevitably points to other elements of the integration agenda. For example, the right to invest in a partner country can be essential in marketing goods and providing services to the local population. Free trade in goods and services and free mobility of capital in turn reinforce the case for allowing migration of people with special qualifications. Radical exchange rate fluctuations are usually inimical to free trade (one side or the other seems to have an unfair advantage), and at a later stage, the fear of a tilted playing field serves to push the concept of tax harmonization. Finally, the more countries that participate in integration and the wider its scope, the greater the need for some institutional mechanism to administer the arrangements and to resolve the inevitable disputes, and the stronger the case for a common legal framework.

Where does a prospective WHFTA fit in? Compared with a customs union or an economic community, FTAs represent integration of a lesser kind. In an FTA, countries reciprocally extend preferences to their trading partners. The focus is on trade liberalization, especially merchandise trade, and on border measures rather than behind-the-border policies. However, FTAs also need to ensure that investment barriers do not become surrogates for trade barriers: either capital mobility should already have been established (as in the EC-EFTA context under the auspices of OECD work on capital liberalization), or the FTA needs to provide national treatment and establishment rights (as does the

Canada-US FTA).[5] FTAs require a modicum of institutional support, but rarely do these special bodies preempt national laws and regulations. Mobility of labor plays only a minor role, if at all, and few demands or disciplines are imposed on monetary and fiscal policies.

This stage of integration is illustrated by the FTAs between the European Community and individual EFTA members in the early 1970s and US agreements with Israel, Canada, and Mexico since 1985. In Europe, the FTAs represent the next step toward European integration—one that is beyond the limited trade preferences in the association arrangements and precedes membership in the European Union. In North America, the FTAs represent the culmination of a series of bilateral arrangements (e.g., the US-Canada Auto Pact and, less formally, the maquiladora program between the United States and Mexico and the 1985 US-Mexico agreement on subsidies) and framework agreements on trade and investment issues.

Integration in the Western Hemisphere has been substantially revitalized since the mid-1980s within each of the existing subregional groups[6] and through the creation of the Mercosur[7] and NAFTA. In addition, individual countries that were not part of any group have signed agreements or have started negotiations toward integration with other countries in the region.[8] FTAs in the Western Hemisphere usually go well beyond the traditional concepts and cover many areas besides merchandise trade. In fact, Latin America's main interest in negotiating an FTA with the United States is from an investment perspective (see chapters 4 and 7).

Even though efforts at economic integration have in some instances just begun, the achievements of each subregional group can already be

---

5. In the postwar period, most FTAs contained significant sectoral exemptions (especially agriculture) that skirted GATT requirements that preferential trading arrangements cover ''substantially all'' the trade between the partner countries if the pact was to qualify for exemption from the most-favored nation obligation of GATT Article I. Moreover, most FTAs ducked investment issues, on which GATT rules are relatively silent. More recently, the Australia–New Zealand arrangement, the Canada-US FTA, and the NAFTA went further down the integration path by including provisions on services trade and investment and intellectual property rights.

6. The Latin American Integration Association (LAIA), the Rio Group (Central and South American countries), the Andean Group, the Central American Common Market (CACM), and the Caribbean Community (Caricom).

7. Including Argentina, Brazil, Paraguay, and Uruguay.

8. Thus, Chile signed a free trade agreement with Mexico in September 1991, one with Venezuela in April 1993, and one with Colombia in December 1993. Cuba signed an agreement in mid-1993 establishing a Joint Commission for Technical Cooperation agreement with Caricom. In addition, several bilateral and trilateral agreements have been signed: Colombia, Venezuela, and CACM (February 1993); Mexico and Costa Rica (March 1994); El Salvador, Guatemala, and Honduras (May 1992); G-3—Mexico, Colombia, and Venezuela (May 1994).

assessed.[9] To do this, we employ a rating system to assess each group's progress. As a comparative yardstick, we use the experience of the European Union. We rate the Union, based on a scale of 0 (lowest) to 5 (highest), across the elements of economic integration: free movement of goods and services (4), free movement of capital (4), free movement of labor (3), supraregional institutions (5), monetary coordination (3), and fiscal coordination (1) (table 1.1). The European Union has worked on reducing barriers and meshing policies for a long time—between three and four decades, depending on the subject. Even so, its achievement scores are often less than the highest value in our scorecard. The rationale for the EU achievement scores is briefly described below. These explanations should provide a useful baseline for our assessment of achievements in the Western Hemisphere.

We start with free trade in goods and services. The Union long ago removed internal tariffs and the vast majority of quotas. Some internal quotas still remain on automotive and textile and apparel trade. Moreover, border checks are still used to enforce different rates of value-added taxation and excise taxation. For technical standards, the respective realms of the mutual recognition principle (for most goods and services) and the harmonization principle (for environmental, safety, and telecommunications standards) have not yet been fully worked out, and trade in professional services (e.g., accounting, law, and medicine) is still encumbered. These barriers will be substantially dismantled by the Europe 1992 program, which when fully implemented in the mid-1990s should raise the EU's score in this category from 4 to 5.

In the case of capital movement, complete freedom of portfolio capital movement was achieved in 1992 (excluding Greece and Portugal). Moreover, greenfield industrial plants can be established throughout Europe by firms of practically any nationality. However, when it comes to the takeover of established firms, many member states still favor bids from their own national firms on a de facto basis. Hence we award a score of 4 for the free movement of capital.

In the case of labor mobility, a score of 3 is explained by significant remaining barriers, in the form of professional and vocational qualifications, and the limited portability of pension rights and other fringe benefits.[10]

In the area of supraregional institutions, the European Union has achieved far more than most regional groups might reasonably expect. The European Commission, Council, Parliament, and Court of Justice have many of the powers of comparable institutions in federal states. On this subject, we score Europe with a 5.

---

9. The declared objectives of most subregional groups are far more ambitious than their achievements.

10. The limited portability of pensions and health insurance coverage also hinders labor mobility in the United States.

Table 1.1   Achievement scores on economic integration

Subject	EU	NAFTA	Mercosur	Andean Group	CACM	CARICOM
Free trade in goods and services	4	4	2	3	2	4
Free movement of capital	4	4	1	3	0	3
Free movement of labor	3	2	1	1	1	2
Supraregional institutions	5	3	2	3	2	2
Monetary coordination	3	1	0	0	0	2
Fiscal coordination	1	0	0	0	0	0
Average	**3.3**	**2.3**	**1**	**1.7**	**0.8**	**2.2**

In the area of monetary coordination, the European Union has gone a long distance—some would say too far—toward a single currency. Under the Exchange Rate Mechanism (ERM), most members pledged to maintain their exchange rate fluctuations within a band of ± 2.25 percent around the European Currency Unit (ECU), and under the Maastricht Treaty, the member states are still headed toward a common currency at the end of the century. In late 1992, the ERM broke down, and the Maastricht Treaty was badly battered in the Danish and French polls, losing the first referendum and narrowly winning the second. For the time being, tight coordination of exchange rates has been abandoned, and fluctuations of ± 15 percent are permitted, giving scope to divergent national interest rates. All this adds up to a score of 3 on monetary coordination.

In comparison with significant progress on monetary coordination (even though a single currency is years away), the European Union has made little headway in the area of fiscal coordination. The Union's own budget absorbs just over 1 percent of European GNP. Member states still have considerable latitude with respect to their own public finances. The Maastricht Treaty calls for member states to maintain public deficits under 3 percent of GNP and to bring their public debt-to-GNP ratios under 60 percent, but so far these numbers are at best distant targets. At this juncture, EU fiscal coordination rates a score of just 1.

Economic integration in the Western Hemisphere will be a long-term project, as it has been in Europe. In the near term, progress toward Western Hemisphere economic integration will likely proceed via measured steps within subregional (and sometimes overlapping) groupings in Latin America. To date, progress in Latin America has been most pronounced in liberalizing trade in goods and services[11] and in building supraregional institutions.[12] By contrast, coordination of monetary and fiscal policies has not advanced, which is not surprising given the limited European and North American achievements in these realms. Within each subregion, there has been some progress toward free movement of labor. However, a hemispherewide provision will be far down the agenda of integration issues (table 1.1).

Supraregional Institutions

The NAFTA group has had some success in the area of supraregional institutions. The Canada-US FTA of 1988 established an innovative dispute settlement procedure administered by a US-Canadian trade commission. This procedure is replicated and amplified in the NAFTA and merits a score of 3. The NAFTA creates a Free Trade Commission, eight committees, and six working groups.[13] In addition, the supplemental agreements on environment and labor created a North American Commission for Environmental Cooperation (NAEC) and a parallel North American Commission on Labor Cooperation (NALC).

The most noteworthy progress to date of the Mercosur has been the creation of supraregional institutions. The member countries have established two administrative bodies comprising representatives from each government to oversee the functioning of the group. In addition, Mercosur has adopted a dispute settlement mechanism, modeled after the Canada-US FTA, and a special procedure for resolving dumping and subsidy disputes during the transition period to the common market. For these initial achievements, we awarded a score of 2.

In the Andean Group,[14] the idea of regional institutions dates back to 1969 (with the creation of the Andean Commission, the Andean Junta, and the Andean Development Corporation) and was reinvigorated in 1980 under the umbrella of the LAIA. In 1979 three organizations were created: the Justice Tribunal of the Cartagena Agreement, the Andean

---

11. The rest of chapter 1 deals with other measures of integration; Latin America's progress in liberalizing trade in goods and services is detailed in chapter 6.

12. By comparison with the supraregional institutions in the European Union, those in the Western Hemisphere are comparatively small and weak. However, the NAFTA countries, the Andean countries, and to a lesser extent the Caricom countries have created regional commissions dealing with special issues.

13. The committees deal with trade in goods, trade in worn clothing, agricultural trade, sanitary and phytosanitary measures, standards-related measures, small business, financial services, and private commercial disputes. Working groups will address rules of origin, agricultural subsidies, Mexico-US issues, Canada-Mexico issues, trade and competition, and temporary entry provisions.

14. Including Bolivia, Colombia, Ecuador, Peru, and Venezuela.

Parliament (to supervise political aspects of the Cartagena Agreement), and the Andean Council of foreign relations ministers (to provide guidance toward achieving economic integration and political cooperation). While ambitious on paper, these organizations have not yet performed their assigned functions (CEPAL 1992b, 21 and 69).

The Central American Common Market[15] has made limited advances toward establishing supraregional institutions, free trade in goods and services, and free movement of labor. The CACM established its first administrative body, the Permanent Secretariat of the General Treaty for Central American Economic Integration, or SIECA, at its inception 33 years ago. It also created the Central American Bank for Economic Integration, the Central American Monetary Union, the Central American Compensation Chamber, and later on, the Central American Stabilization Fund. Since 1986, CACM presidents and ministers have met on a regular, scheduled basis every June and December. These meetings have produced concrete agreements on intraregional trade liberalization. For these efforts at creating supraregional institutions, we believe the CACM merits a score of 2.

The Caribbean Community[16] has a fairly long list of supraregional institutions. Caricom organizations include the Caribbean Development Bank, the Caribbean Environmental Health Institute, the Caribbean Regional Drug Testing Laboratory, and the Caribbean Meteorological Organization (weather watch and warning system), among others.[17] But these are mainly technical organizations, and there has been opposition to the creation of a Caricom Commission (proposed at its October 1992 meeting) because it evokes images of the powerful European Commission based in Brussels.[18]

Free Movement of Labor

In free movement of labor, the NAFTA countries have formally done little or nothing. On an informal basis, there is a great deal of migration

---

15. Including Costa Rica, El Salvador, Guatemala, Honduras, and Nicaragua.

16. Includes Antigua and Barbuda, Bahamas, Barbados, Belize, Dominica, Grenada, Guyana, Jamaica, Montserrat, St. Kitts and Nevis, St. Lucia, St. Vincent and the Grenadines, and Trinidad and Tobago.

17. There is also an established system of regional censuses that coordinates uniformity in data collection with a centralized processing and analysis of the data that facilitates data comparability (Rainford 1991, 44).

18. "Rather than create a Caricom Commission, the Caricom Secretariat should be restructured and provided with increased resources," say representatives from the Caribbean Policy Development Centre (1992, 2). The article goes on to say that those who oppose the commission do not oppose the companion proposal for a broad-based assembly of Caribbean Community parliamentarians.

between Mexico and the United States (Martin 1993); on a formal basis, Canada and the United States made special provision in the FTA for work visas for managerial and technical employees and for entertainers. Likewise the NAFTA includes provisions for the entry of business and professional personnel.[19] As a result, we score the NAFTA a 2 for labor mobility.

The Mercosur agreement provides for free movement of people by January 1995. Citizens of Mercosur countries can travel within the region with only a national identity card instead of a passport (*Washington Post*, 19 January 1994, A15; *International Trade Reporter*, 12 January 1994, 59).

Free movement of labor is, in practical terms, not yet on the Andean agenda. The Act of La Paz (November 1990), stated that "within six months, visa requirements will be dropped for nationals of the Andean Pact to visit another member country for less than 90 days." Later, the Act of Caracas (May 1991) committed Andean nations to coordinate their approach to educational issues such as transferability of degrees, professional certification, and mutual recognition of credentials, for example, in medicine and engineering.[20]

The CACM has started to drop restrictions on the free movement of labor. Progress has been made to eliminate tourist and commercial visas for Central American and Panamanian nationals, and the adoption of a single migratory control card (Joint Economic Committee, US Congress 1993, 286), meriting a score of 1.

Caricom has also made some progress in facilitating the free movement of labor within the region, and the steps taken merit a score of 2. Progress began in 1972 on integration in education. A system of regional examinations, operated through the Caribbean Examinations Council (CXC), has been "one of the outstanding outcomes of the working of Caricom integration arrangements." Moreover, many Caricom students attend a common university, the University of the West Indies, located in Kingston, Jamaica. During the 1980s there was also considerable effort to introduce a regional system of nursing examinations, but no agreement was reached (Rainford 1991, 44). In 1983, in response to public demand, Caricom called for action to make intraregional travel by Caricom nationals easier and specifically agreed that passports should not be needed for such travel. The Organization of Eastern Caribbean States (OECS) resolved to introduce free movement of OECS nationals within the organization by December 1991 (Rainford 1991, 9).

---

19. Intracompany transferees will be allowed to enter a NAFTA partner country if they have been with the company for at least one year out of the previous three years; 5,500 Mexican professionals will also be allowed to enter the United States annually in addition to those admitted under global immigration limits (NAFTA Annex 1608, Schedule III).

20. One ambitious objective is to standardize university degree requirements, as promised in the Act of Baharona (December 1991).

Monetary and Fiscal Coordination

In terms of monetary coordination, the United States and Canada can boast only minor success. In 1962 both nations became charter members of the Group of Ten. Further, in the early 1960s, when the United States instituted the Interest Equalization Tax, there was a special carve-out for Canada, which in turn prompted closer collaboration on monetary policy. Since then, there has been less formal collaboration, but in setting monetary policy, the Bank of Canada pays close attention to maintaining stability in the Canadian dollar–US dollar exchange rate. Accordingly, we felt NAFTA deserved a 1 in this category.

Nor has much progress been made on monetary and fiscal coordination within the Mercosur. Mercosur has created a working group comprising economic and finance ministers, under the direction of the Common Market Group, to supervise monetary and fiscal measures that affect trade. However, Mercosur has not achieved monetary and fiscal convergence to any discernible degree. This is not surprising since even the European Community took many years, and experienced many setbacks, in achieving a degree of monetary coordination and has made virtually no progress on fiscal coordination. Mercosur receives a 0 on our scale for both its monetary and fiscal achievements.

Monetary and fiscal coordination likewise remain for future Andean consideration. While the ministers of finance and central bank presidents have often met, the progress made so far on price and currency stability and on budget discipline has been the result of national initiatives rather than regional coordination.

The CACM has done relatively little in the realm of monetary and fiscal coordination. Indeed, at this stage, coordination would be premature. One year after its creation in 1960, the group did create the Central American Compensation Chamber (CACC), which organized a multilateral payments system. In 1964, this organization planned to create a monetary union in the region (CEPAL 1991, 27–29). Those efforts died in the civil and military strife of the 1970s and 1980s. Monetary coordination in the region will probably be put off until free trade in goods and services is achieved.

In 1983, eight of the smallest Caricom countries created the Organization of Eastern Caribbean States and adopted a common currency, the Eastern Caribbean dollar, which is pegged to the US dollar. Three of the largest Caricom countries—Bahamas, Barbados, and Trinidad and Tobago—also have effectively tied their currencies to the US dollar. With their mutual links to the dollar, most Caricom countries have established a de facto common monetary policy. In terms of details, the countries have tried to introduce a Caricom travelers check (with limited success), and the Treaty of Chaguaramas raises the idea of allowing the national currencies within Caricom to be exchanged directly against one another rather than intermediated through the US dollar (Rainford 1991, 21). With regard to monetary coordination, Caricom leads the pack among regions in the Western Hemisphere. Indeed, it is the only region to show any progress at all. Thus, Caricom rates a score of 2 for monetary coordination. However, parallel progress on the fiscal side is lacking, and on this subject, Caricom merits a score of 0.

Sequencing the Elements of Integration

The varied experience of North America and Europe in the postwar period, as well as the integration episodes documented by the World Bank (Michaely, Papageorgiou, and Choksi 1991, vol. 7), can be used to illustrate the staging and sequencing of each element of integration.

The North American and European experiences in the postwar period illustrate the tempered pace and long-term nature of integration. In North America, the United States and Canada engaged in more than 20 years of sectoral negotiations (starting with the Auto Pact of 1965) before entering into an FTA in 1988. Integration of the US and Mexican economies has been under way for several decades, starting with the Bracero program (1942–64), which was succeeded by the maquiladora industrial program, launched in 1965. Maquiladora plants linked the northern cities of Mexico with the US industrial economy, which in turn led to bilateral trade and investment framework agreements in the late 1980s and culminated in the NAFTA, ratified in 1993.

In Europe, geopolitical considerations have given economic integration a distinct and powerful thrust throughout the postwar period. The formation of an economic community served the dual role of speeding postwar recovery and uniting historically quarrelsome neighbors against the escalating threat from the Soviet Union. Yet European integration has proceeded in incremental steps over the past four decades. Although the approach has been step-by-step, each initiative has been taken in the context of more ambitious long-term goals.

The formation of the Benelux Union (1948), the European Payments Union (1950), and the European Coal and Steel Community (1951) provided the foundation for the Treaty of Rome, signed in 1957, which in turn established the European Economic Community and provided the long-term vision of European integration. Thereafter, the central organs of the EEC (the Council, Commission, and Court of Justice) expanded into supraregional institutions with responsibilities over a broad range of regional economic activity.

In the trade area, the Treaty of Rome projected the elimination of barriers to cross-border trade in goods and services within 12 years. In fact, the EEC did move relatively quickly in its first 12 years to eliminate cross-border tariffs on merchandise trade, to harmonize agricultural policies, and to establish a common external tariff. However, liberalization of nontariff barriers and services trade lagged significantly, with some key intra-EC barriers still intact in the early 1990s (for example, differing rates of value-added taxation, differing product standards, natural restrictions on life insurance and mutual fund companies). The Single European Act of 1987 sought to overcome the remaining barriers and fulfill the vision set by the Treaty of Rome for a unified European market by launching the Europe 1992 process.

In similar fashion, the Treaty of Rome noted the importance over time of coordinating monetary and fiscal policies. However, the first concrete steps toward coordination of monetary policies only surfaced in the Werner Plan of 1970, whose short-lived ''currency snake'' presaged the more durable European Monetary System of 1979. Owing to its excessive rigidities, the EMS broke down in 1992. However, the Maastricht Treaty, ratified in 1993, rechristened the European Community (EC) as the European Union (EU) and pointed toward full Economic and Monetary Union by the year 2000.

The World Bank case studies of successful and partially successful episodes of liberalization (Michaely, Papageorgiou, and Choksi 1991, vol. 7) confirm the European experience regarding the timing and sequencing of reforms. Eight specific conclusions were derived from their extensive analyses. These conclusions yield important insights on the readiness of Latin American countries to engage in integration episodes:

- Trade reforms should complement and follow the implementation of macroeconomic stabilization.

- Trade liberalization should be phased in gradually, say over six to seven years, but not so long as to build up political coalitions against adjustment.

- Liberalization programs should begin with slashing reductions in quantitative restraints (QRs); ''creeping'' liberalization of quotas is usually unsuccessful.

- Tariffs should be reduced according to a fixed schedule.

- Initial trade reforms should be accompanied by a significant devaluation to stimulate export-led growth, to compensate import-competing industries for the reduction in border protection, and to preserve foreign exchange reserves.

- Specific export promotion measures are generally not needed; exchange rate devaluation provides the requisite export stimulus.

- Liberalization of capital markets should proceed after trade reforms are well under way; otherwise the country runs the risk of either excessive capital inflows that push up the real exchange rate or excessive capital outflows that erode confidence in the economic reforms.

- A stable political climate is needed to sustain the trade reform program.

Plan of the Book

In the first part of the book (chapters 1 to 4), a brief review of US–Latin American relations over the last decade (focusing on the Enterprise for the Americas Initiative) is followed by an analysis of the economic foundations for regional integration. We attempt to measure first the unrealized trade potential that can be released with hemispheric integration; we then examine the strength of existing regional economic ties (measured by trade and investment ties) and the extent of economic distance (measured by regional diversity). Finally, we estimate the impact of a WHFTA on Latin America and the United States. We conclude that a WHFTA would add to efficiency and prosperity in both parts of the hemisphere.

In chapter 5, drawing on integration episodes in both developed and developing countries, we develop readiness criteria for embarking on hemispheric economic integration. The broad areas are macroeconomic stability, market-oriented policies, and a reduced reliance on trade taxes and a functioning democracy.

Based on the criteria laid out in chapter 5, chapter 6 evaluates accomplishments toward subregional integration in the Western Hemisphere. While considerable progress has been made by Latin American countries in shifting economies toward stable market-oriented systems, in most countries further reforms are needed before hemispheric negotiations (or negotiations with NAFTA countries) can be contemplated.

In chapter 7, we examine the likely content of the negotiating agenda. We discuss traditional items on the trade agenda (the phaseout of tariffs and quotas), those that have become part of trade negotiations in recent years (intellectual property rights, trade-related investment measures, and trade in services), and those that burst upon the trade scene during the NAFTA debate (labor and environmental issues).

In chapter 8, we discuss the implications of hemispheric economic integration for third countries and for the world trading system. We conclude that hemispheric initiatives can complement and reinforce the world trading system, if the negotiations are conducted in conformity with the letter and spirit of the multilateral obligations of member countries. Nonetheless, we estimate that a hemispheric accord would divert some trade and investment from other regions, though not significant amounts, and we suggest a new approach for addressing concerns about trade diversion resulting from regional pacts.

Finally, in chapter 9 we summarize the economic rationale for a Western Hemisphere Free Trade Area and describe the alternative paths to integration. In closing, we emphasize the importance of the links between a WHFTA and the Asia-Pacific region and the different approaches needed in negotiations with each region.

2

US–Latin American Economic Relations

Economic relations between the United States and Latin America have a long and rich history. In the 1980s, however, the debt crisis dominated the economic agenda and led to a sharp contraction in trade and investment ties between the developed and developing countries in the hemisphere. Building on the Brady Plan and other debt initiatives,[1] the Enterprise for the Americas Initiative (EAI) in 1990 sought to address four specific concerns.

First, Latin American countries desperately needed new and larger inflows of foreign capital if the debt crisis was to be resolved without a long period of economic stagnation. At the same time, the risk of default on Latin debt represented an additional threat to US banks already suffering from heavy losses from domestic energy and real estate loans. Second, the United States wanted to support market-based reforms that were emerging across the region. Third, the United States wanted to highlight the continued importance of Latin America at a time when events in Eastern Europe and the Soviet Union had become a focus of world attention. Finally, the launch of the EAI shortly after the announcement of US-Mexico trade talks was designed to show that the United States would not forget Latin America as it entered into free trade negotiations with Mexico.

Basic economic conditions have changed since 1990, when President Bush announced the EAI. But overall, developments have reinforced the desirability and viability of the EAI.

---

1. For an appraisal of these initiatives, see Cline (1994).

Latin American Debt and US Interests

In retrospect, it is clear that by 1990 the most acute phase of the debt crisis had passed. Each Latin American country had passed its peak in terms of debt as a percentage of GNP, debt as a percentage of exports, and interest payments as a percentage of exports. But in 1990 it was still unclear whether the improvements registered in the late 1980s could be sustained or whether Latin nations would sink back into a new round of debt restructuring. Importantly, 1992 data showed that debt as a percentage of exports remained staggeringly high for many Latin American countries: Argentina's debt, for example, was 454 percent of its export earnings (World Bank, *World Debt Tables 1993–94*, 14).

By 1990, the US Treasury had concluded that belt tightening alone would not solve the Latin American debt problem. If net financial resources continued to flow from Latin America to its creditors—i.e., if principal and interest payments continued to exceed new loans and direct investment—it would be difficult to achieve renewed growth in the region.[2] Without growth, widespread economic reforms might be reversed. Another round of debt rescheduling might then be unavoidable.

In Treasury's opinion, dismantling barriers to trade and investment, coupled with privatization, provided the best road out of the economic impasse. The Brady Plan, which Treasury introduced with Mexican debt restructuring in 1989, provided a strong indication of the commitment to improving the financial predicament of Latin America (Iglesias 1990, 349).[3] The Treasury hoped that the EAI would build on the Brady Plan and help attract both new private foreign capital and the return of Latin American "flight" capital to the region.

However, the massive US budget deficit, coupled with pent-up pressure for social spending, precluded any solution that called for a large-scale transfer of financial assistance from the United States to Latin America, either directly or indirectly through the International Monetary Fund or the multilateral development banks. The United States had to encourage Latin American economic performance with a minimum US financial contribution. The EAI provided the vehicle: its trade and investment pillars encouraged microeconomic reforms, while the debt

---

2. The US Treasury argued that reducing the debt burden would build confidence, thereby spurring investment and growth (Under Secretary of the Treasury for International Affairs David C. Mulford, statement before the subcommittees on the Western Hemisphere, Human Rights, and International Organizations, and International Economic Policy and Trade Committee on Foreign Affairs, US House of Representatives, as reported in *Treasury News*, 18 July 1990, 4–5).

3. To date, the Latin American countries that have negotiated a Brady plan include Mexico (February 1990), Costa Rica (May 1990), Venezuela (December 1990), Uruguay (February 1991), and Argentina (July 1993). Two other countries are in the process: Brazil and the Dominican Republic (World Bank, *World Debt Tables 1993–94* and *1992–93*, 35 and 88).

pillar offered modest relief of US official debt for those countries that first agreed on stabilization and structural adjustment programs with the IMF and the World Bank.

US–Latin American Trade Relations

During the 1980s, US trade with Latin America declined relative to US trade with other regions. As table 2.1 shows, Latin America's share of worldwide US exports fell from 10.7 percent in 1980 to 6.6 percent in 1989.[4] If Latin America had maintained its 1980 position as an export destination, US shipments would have been about $16 billion higher in 1989. Through the EAI, the United States hoped to recapture some of these "lost" exports. Chapter 3 and appendix A provide a more detailed analysis of the unrealized trade potential between countries in the Western Hemisphere that has been constrained by import barriers and debt problems.

US Investment Interests in Latin America

Despite poor economic performance in the region, US foreign direct investment in Latin America did not fall drastically. In 1980, the share of worldwide US direct investment placed in Latin America was 12.1 percent; by 1986 this figure rose slightly to 13.0 percent before it returned to 11.5 percent in 1989 and 10.6 percent in 1992. Expressed at book value, US direct investment in Latin America actually increased: from $26 billion in 1980 to $34 billion in 1986 and then to $52 billion in 1992 (table 2.1).

The US investment position gave additional support to the EAI concept. The initiative was designed not only to provide a better climate for attracting new direct investment to Latin America; it was also intended to safeguard US investment already committed to the region.

Changing Economic Relations

Between 1989 and 1993, the conditions that gave rise to the EAI vision changed, some of them dramatically. The economic outlook in Latin America improved far more rapidly than most observers expected in early 1990.

The changes are illustrated in table 2.1, which presents trade, investment, and debt figures for 1980, 1982, 1986, 1989, and 1992. These years were selected to represent the situation well before the debt crisis, the

---

4. We cite 1989 data because that was the latest data available when Treasury was formulating the EAI.

Table 2.1   Latin America: economic indicators, 1980–92[a]

	1980	1982	1986	1989	1992
Trade					
United States					
Exports to Latin America (billions of dollars)	23.6	21.8	18.7	24.1	35.1
Imports from Latin America (billions of dollars)	26.1	23.8	26.6	32.5	36.0
Latin America					
Trade balance with the United States (billions of dollars)	2.5	2.1	7.9	8.4	0.8
Share of US exports (percentages)	10.7	10.3	8.6	6.6	7.9
Foreign direct investment[b]					
US stock in Latin America (billions of dollars)	26.1	31.4	33.8	44.0	51.7
Latin American share of US FDI stock (percentages)	12.1	15.1	13.0	11.5	10.6
Latin American debt					
External debt (billions of dollars)	200	247	333	357	383
External debt-to-export ratio	195	257	384	302	282
External debt-to-GNP ratio	40	45	63	52	44

a. Figures for Latin America include the Caribbean and exclude Mexico.
b. This figure excludes Bermuda and the Netherlands Antilles, where US firms place large amounts of investment in their financial affiliates for debt transactions on a global basis. The stock of US investment in Bermuda reached $26 billion in 1992. The Netherlands Antilles position in 1982 was a negative $19.8 billion due to borrowing in the Eurobond market by US parent companies through their Antilles affiliates. In 1992 the Netherlands Antilles position was a negative $1.9 billion, reflecting repayments by US parents.

Sources: International Monetary Fund, Direction of Trade Statistics Yearbook, 1987 and 1993; World Bank, World Debt Tables, 1989–90 and 1993–94; US Department of Commerce, Statistical Abstract of the United States 1988, p. 761; and Survey of Current Business, August 1986, August 1989, and July 1993.

situation at the onset of crisis, at the peak of the crisis, information available at the time the EAI was formulated, and the most current information now available.

Debt

In designing the EAI, the US Treasury was primarily concerned with Latin America's economic solvency. From a Treasury perspective, growth was the best way for countries in the region to maintain their debt service payments. After 1989, belt tightening in Latin America would probably not have succeeded in reducing the nominal amount of external debt. By contrast, renewed growth might shrink the various debt service ratios and thereby improve the credit of Latin America. The crisis reached a peak with respect to the debt-to-GNP ratio in 1985 and with respect to the debt-to-export ratio in 1986.[5] The ratios dropped sharply by 1989 and declined further by 1992. Most of the improvement since 1989 has resulted from renewed economic growth rather than reduction of nominal debt levels (table 2.1).

Under the EAI, seven Latin American countries have benefited from debt reduction: Chile, Bolivia, Jamaica, Colombia, El Salvador, Uruguay, and Argentina. From original levels of $648 million (assistance provided via PL 480) and $942 million (loans through the Agency for International Development), these countries reduced their PL 480 debt by 77.7 percent and their AID debt by 36.4 percent (World Bank, *World Debt Tables 1993–94*, 36).

After 1989, net flows of nonguaranteed private debt (i.e., new loans, less repayments of principal and interest) showed an improvement. For the Latin American region as a whole, net outflows reached a high of $2.3 billion in 1984 and only became positive again in 1990.

Another debt indicator, secondary loan prices for sovereign debt, shows that only Chile's prices are near par, reaching 91 percent of face value. Secondary loan prices for other countries have risen, sometimes dramatically in percentage terms, but they are still well below par. Investors still attach a high risk premium to much of Latin American debt (see table 5.7).

Trade

Reflecting growth in the region, US merchandise exports to Latin America have picked up over the past three years. US exports in 1992 were $35.1 billion against $24.1 billion in 1989, and Latin America now accounts for 7.9 percent of total US merchandise exports, up from 6.6 percent in 1989. The numbers continued to improve in 1993.[6]

However, while trade gains have already been achieved, even greater gains remain to be realized with dramatic reforms of Latin American trade policy. A rough analysis of untapped Latin American trade potential indicates that, in 1990, the Latin American merchandise export

---

5. Chapter 5, on readiness indicators, discusses the debt experience of Latin America in greater detail.

6. US merchandise exports to Latin America totaled $37 billion and accounted for 8 percent of total US merchandise exports (US Department of Commerce, *Commerce News*, December 1993, 18 and January 1994, 24; US Department of Commerce, *Direction of Trade Statistics*, March 1994).

shortfall was $56 billion while the region's merchandise import shortfall was $92 billion (appendix A). By adopting market-oriented policies, Latin American countries could eliminate a large part of the calculated trade deficiency. Assuming that they recover only half of the calculated trade deficiency, the resulting expansion of imports ($46 billion) would result in an additional $14 billion in US exports to Latin America, an increase of more than 50 percent over actual US merchandise exports to Latin America in 1990.[7]

Because a hemispheric free trade area would require the elimination of tariffs on substantially all trade between countries, Latin American countries might lower their tariffs by about 24 percentage points on average from the 1990 levels.[8] This decline would far exceed US tariff reductions, considering that the 1990 average tariff for the United States was 3.3 percent on total imports.[9] The asymmetrical magnitude of potential tariff cuts indicates that incremental market opening could be much greater for US exports than for Latin American exports.

But it should be stressed that many tariffs will be cut unilaterally and multilaterally rather than in the context of hemispheric negotiations (First Boston 1993, 6; see chapter 5 for more information on recent reforms on trade). Some Latin American countries have already lowered their tariffs sharply from 1990 levels. By 1992, for example, Chile had a uniform import tariff of 11 percent, Colombia had an average rate of 12 percent, and Venezuela had an average rate just under 10 percent. In July 1993, Brazil lowered its average tariff to 14 percent. Moreover, following full implementation of the Uruguay Round tariff cuts shortly after the year 2000, we forecast that the average Latin American tariff should fall to below 10 percent, and the average US tariff to just over 2 percent.

Investment

By reducing the debt burden of Latin American countries, the EAI aimed to encourage private capital flows to the region. In addition, the debt reduction pillar of the program called for domestic investment reform. Both actions were intended to stabilize the foreign investment climate in Latin America.

---

7. In 1990, Latin America imported $26 billion from the United States, or 30.9 percent of Latin America's total imports ($84 billion).

8. The figure of 24 percent represents the trade-weighted average tariff for all sectors for the countries included in Erzan and Yeats (1992, 37). For a detailed discussion of anticipated tariff reductions, see chapter 6.

9. In 1990, total US imports were $490.6 billion, and dutiable imports were $329.4 billion. Tariffs collected were $16.3 billion. The average tariff on dutiable imports was 5.0 percent, but the average on total imports was just 3.3 percent (*Statistical Abstract of the United States 1992*).

In terms of broad magnitudes, however, the US investment picture in Latin America has not changed significantly since the announcement of the EAI in 1990. The stock of US foreign direct investment in Latin America increased from $44 billion in 1989 to $52 billion in 1992, yet Latin America's share of the US investment stock remained about 11 percent in both years (table 2.1).

But investment conditions in Latin America have changed dramatically since the mid-1980s, and nearly all reforms have been implemented unilaterally. Argentina, for example, has made considerable progress in reforming foreign investment rules and regulations. Limits have been abolished on foreign equity or debt participation and on profit and dividend remittances. Colombia has also implemented investment reforms that abolish limits on equity participation and restrictions on remittances but has retained its local-content requirements. With the exception of the finance, petroleum, and mining sectors, Colombia is generally open to investors. However, despite extensive investment, unstable macroeconomic conditions have constrained foreign direct investment in some other countries (First Boston 1993, 6; see chapter 5 for more information on recent reforms on investment).

New Issues

Several new elements have entered the global economic picture since June 1990. These new elements will influence whether the EAI vision is pursued and in what shape it is implemented.

First, as a by-product of the NAFTA debate, two big new issues have been added to the US trade agenda: labor and environment standards. The procedures and commitments negotiated in the NAFTA supplementary agreements will serve as a benchmark, and to the extent that Latin American countries are unable to accept parallel procedures and commitments, there will be strong opposition within the United States against further steps toward forming a Western Hemisphere Free Trade Area (WHFTA).[10]

Secondly, the United States is increasingly attracted to trade opportunities in the Pacific Rim. Whereas Latin America is certainly a "strong neighbor," Asia (excluding Japan) is both a "strong neighbor" and a very "good customer" (technical definitions of these terms are given in chapter 5). Relative to their respective GDP levels, both Latin America and Asia (excluding Japan, Australia, and New Zealand) import substantially from the United States. Based on experience during the 1980s, a $1 billion increase in Asian real GDP (excluding Japan, Australia, and New Zealand) creates a $65 million increase in nominal US exports to

---

10. For a detailed discussion of these trade policy questions, see chapter 6.

the region. The same increase in Latin America's GDP prompts an increase of $54 million in nominal US exports. Moreover, given its much larger and faster growing economies, the Asian region imports much more from the United States than does Latin America. In 1993, Latin America imported $36 billion from the United States, whereas Asia (excluding Japan, Australia, and New Zealand) imported $71 billion.

Obviously the United States wants to enhance its trade ties with the fast-growing economies of Asia. Growing US attention on the Asia Pacific Economic Cooperation (APEC) group will likely proceed in parallel with the WHFTA initiative.[11] To emphasize this tandem forward motion, President Clinton followed his APEC meeting in Seattle in November 1993 with a proposal to host a Western Hemisphere summit in 1994.[12] The United States has further sought to coordinate its WHFTA and APEC ventures by promoting Mexico (in 1993) and Chile (in 1994) for APEC membership.

The Clinton administration is determined to pursue trade agreements with other Latin American countries. Early in May 1994, the US Trade Representative (USTR) delivered to Congress a list of nations (including Latin American countries) that might be considered for trade negotiations.[13] The administration will then determine with which countries the United States should seek negotiations. In addition, a range of economic and cultural issues will be discussed at the Western Hemisphere summit in Miami on 9–10 December 1994.

In May 1993, Secretary of State Warren Christopher pointed out that human rights are at the core of US policy toward Latin America.[14] When the time comes for serious negotiation, human rights and labor and environmental standards are sure to be high on the US agenda. The fact that Secretary Christopher doggedly pursued human rights issues during his visit to China in March 1994, despite rebuffs from Premier Li Peng, underscores the importance that Washington attaches to these questions (*Washington Post*, 13 March 1994, A1).

---

11. 993, the APEC member countries included Australia, Brunei, Canada, China, Hong Kong, Indonesia, Japan, Korea, Malaysia, Mexico, New Zealand, Papua New Guinea, the Philippines, Singapore, Chinese Taipei, Thailand, and the United States.

12. In December 1993, Vice President Al Gore first proposed a 1994 summit of Western Hemisphere democracies. The summit has been scheduled for 9–10 December 1994.

13. This report was required by the Danforth amendment to the NAFTA implementing legislation. The report was intended to be a list of those foreign countries that currently provide fair and equitable market access beyond what is required by existing multilateral trade agreements or that have made significant progress in opening their markets to US exports.

14. Speech by Deputy Secretary of State Clifton R. Wharton on behalf of Secretary of State at Council of the Americas conference on Latin America and the United States, 3–4 May 1993.

Summary

For most of the factors that will influence a US decision to move forward with hemispheric free trade, recent changes improve the readiness of Latin American countries for hemispheric negotiations. A falling debt burden, positive private capital inflows, and significant trade and investment reforms have already improved Latin America's economic prospects and have significantly narrowed the ''negotiating distance'' between economic systems in North and South America.[15]

Ironically, as Latin American reforms have made WHFTA negotiations more realistic, they also have made them less urgent. The very fact that the debt crisis has passed, that private capital is now flowing to Latin America, and that Latin America has unilaterally implemented trade reforms has taken some of the edge from US concerns about the region. Meanwhile, the post-NAFTA paradigm ensures that human rights, labor, and environmental issues have become an integral part of trade negotiations, and this decidedly raises the readiness threshold confronting Latin America in WHFTA talks. All in all, it seems that the United States is more likely to embark on country-by-country negotiations in the next few years (starting with Chile) and encourage unilateral reform and subregional arrangements within Latin America, rather than mount a major hemispherewide trade initiative.

---

15. These changes are reflected as well in the standing of Latin American countries on the readiness criteria set out in chapter 5.

3

WHFTA: Feasible and Desirable

While a grand hemispheric arrangement may not be launched in the next few years, economic integration is clearly the lead item on the hemispheric political agenda. The North American Free Trade Agreement (NAFTA) has now been ratified, Mercosur has survived its birth pangs, the Andean Group shows new life, and US-Chilean talks have already started on an informal basis.

This momentum raises an important question. For a given quantum of policy effort, what rewards can be reaped by forming a regional group within the Western Hemisphere? Should a Western Hemisphere Free Trade Area (WHFTA) be given priority over arrangements with other regions?

Our approach to this broad question is to answer it in two parts. First, do the data indicate considerable room for export and import expansion by Latin American countries? Second, are economic ties more intense within the region than with other regions of the global economy? If the answer to both questions is yes, then a policy of regional integration can arguably yield a disproportionate expansion of trade.

Unrealized Trade Potential: Scope for Trade Creation

To the extent that unrealized trade potential exists, it seems plausible to expect that economic liberalization by Latin American nations will unleash faster export and import growth. In turn, trade expansion could make a significant contribution to overall economic growth by harnessing comparative advantage to boost economic efficiency. In the section that follows, we use a set of cross-sectional data to illuminate untapped trade potential in Latin America.

We examine the ratio of merchandise exports to GDP and that of merchandise imports to GDP to assess trade intensity for 58 market-oriented countries in Europe, Asia, and the Western Hemisphere for a single year, 1990. This analysis permits us to measure the extent to which Latin American trade ratios were depressed from world norms in that year. Depressed Latin American trade ratios in 1990 reflect the aftereffects of the import substitution policies of the 1960s and 1970s and new restrictions introduced in the 1980s in response to the debt crisis. In our view, these policies and their effects are reversible, and outward-looking economic reforms in the 1990s should cause an expansion of both imports and exports, allowing Latin American trade ratios to reach world norms.

In our analytic work, the trade figures refer only to merchandise trade because data on trade in business services are not widely available. We assume, however, that the same overall relationships between trade policy and trade ratios would hold if business services were included in the analysis.

The model is explained in appendix A. Based on this model, we calculate the difference between actual and predicted trade levels, expressed both in ratio terms and in dollar terms. Several interesting points concerning Latin America emerge from the analysis.[1]

Most countries and subregions in Latin America are trade-deficient, in the sense that the model predicts larger export and import ratios than the observed 1990 ratios. The difference between actual and predicted 1990 exports for all of Latin America was a shortfall of $56 billion; the difference for imports was a shortfall of $92 billion. Interestingly, these figures imply that Latin America should have had a merchandise trade deficit of about $9 billion in 1990 rather than the realized merchandise trade surplus of $27 billion. This implication is consistent with the idea that, in normal times, Latin America should be a capital-importing region, not a capital-exporting region.

Most of the trade shortfalls in Latin America are attributable to Mercosur countries: their estimated combined export deficiency was $52 billion, while their estimated combined import deficiency was $72 billion. The Andean Group exhibited a combined export deficiency of $3 billion (with above-average exports from oil-rich Venezuela counterbalancing below-average exports from the other countries) and a combined import deficiency of $19 billion. CACM showed an export deficiency of $1.4 billion and an import deficiency of $0.5 billion. Despite extensive trade reforms in the late 1980s, Mexico was still trade-deficient to the extent of about $7.0 billion in exports and $7.3 billion in imports.

---

1. The implications of the model for other regions are also summarized in appendix A.

Only the Caribbean Community (Caricom) and Chile showed normal levels of trade intensity (appendix A, table A1).

Regional Economic Ties

The harvest of potential gains portrayed in the previous section could be realized through unilateral or multilateral trade liberalization accompanied by domestic policy reforms. There is no logical requirement that the gains be achieved through regional trade initiatives. Unilateral and multilateral liberalization are logical alternatives. But as a practical matter, it is difficult to enlist political support for the unilateral reduction of tariff and nontariff barriers below levels of 10 or 20 percent ad valorem.[2] And multilateral liberalization takes a long time: the Tokyo Round required six years from political start to finish; the Uruguay Round required twelve years (beginning with the failed ministerial meeting of 1982). Bearing these obstacles in mind, regional liberalization is surely worthwhile—if it commands political support within the hemisphere, if circumstances do not permit unilateral liberalization, and if further multilateral liberalization would require a decade or more to accomplish. The second-best case for regional initiatives is further strengthened if subregional and hemispheric arrangements are negotiated on an all-or-nothing basis: either total free trade within the group on a reasonable timetable or no agreement. This test serves to ensure the greatest amount of trade created among the member countries relative to the trade diverted from outsiders. Thus, a second-best case can readily be made for regional initiatives.

Beyond the basic rationale for regional integration—faster and more extensive free trade than under other political arrangements—a further question should be asked. Is there any reason to expect that Latin American trade expansion would occur more briskly within the Western Hemisphere rather than with other regions of the global economy, for example, with Europe or Asia? This question can be put another way. Does a natural economic "neighborliness" exist within the Western Hemisphere—by comparison with trade ties between the hemisphere and other regions of the global economy—that would justify regional integration on economic as well as political grounds?

First, a definition: two countries can be considered strong neighbors if economic expansion in one increases trade between them at a faster rate than trade with other countries.[3] Suppose countries A and B are strong economic neighbors. If country B takes policy measures that increase its

---

2. Unilateral liberalization to roughly this extent has been achieved by Chile, Mexico, Colombia, Venezuela, and Argentina.

3. We use the term "strong neighbor" with the same meaning that other authors give to the term "natural trading partner."

GDP by $1 billion, country A can expect more growth in demand for its own exports than if country B was not a strong economic neighbor. In turn, this prospect should make country A more willing to embark on a program of economic integration that sparks prosperity in country B, simply because prosperity in B will attract exports from A.

Applying this logic to the Western Hemisphere, we need to examine whether economic data supports the proposition that countries within the hemisphere, or subregions of the hemisphere, are in fact strong economic neighbors. We also need to contrast the extent of potential friction arising from economic diversity within the hemisphere by comparison with economic diversity within other regions.[4]

The major geographic regions in the global economy are North America, Latin America, Western Europe, Central Europe and the former Soviet Union, Japan, Australia and New Zealand, other South and East Asia and Pacific,[5] Africa, and the Middle East. At a subregional level, leading trade groups include the NAFTA, Mercosur, the Andean Group, the European Union (EU), EFTA, ASEAN, and the Australia–New Zealand arrangement. To what extent are these geographic regions and trade groups natural economic neighbors? While many indicators could be examined, we concentrate on three: trade ties, investment ties, and diversity in per capita GDP (as a measure of potential friction).

For reasons of space, we focus the exposition on regions and subregions of immediate interest to the Western Hemisphere. Basically, we want to know whether ties within the hemisphere are any stronger than ties with the outside world. We start by examining trade ties that are easily measured and usually serve as the point of departure for regional analysis. We then look at investment ties. Finally, we examine diversity in per capita GDP, using this data as an indicator of potential obstacles to economic integration.

Regional Trade Ties

Table 3.1 gives 1992 merchandise trade figures, expressed in billions of US dollars, by origin and destination for the major geographic areas.

---

4. When a group of countries are strong economic neighbors, that does not imply that they should ignore other regions. Rather, they can view closer economic ties within the region as a solid first step toward further integration.

5. In tables 3.1 to 3.4, "Developing Asia" includes all Asia and Pacific countries except for Japan, Australia, New Zealand, Mongolia, and North Korea. In tables 3.8 to 3.10, we group Asian and Pacific countries as follows: Japan, Australia and New Zealand; centrally planned Asia (China, Mongolia, Vietnam, North Korea); and South and East Asia (Asia minus Japan, Australia, New Zealand, and centrally planned Asia). In tables A.1 and B.1, we group Asian countries as follows: Australia and New Zealand; Japan; ASEAN; Korea, Taiwan, China, Hong Kong; and Bangladesh, India, Nepal, Pakistan, and Sri Lanka. The different groupings reflect data in the original sources.

Table 3.1   Merchandise trade by region of destination, 1992 (billions of dollars)

Region of origin	North America[a]	Western Europe[b]	Latin America[c]	Developing Asia[d]	Japan, Australia, New Zealand	Africa	Middle East	World total[e]
North America[a]	270	131	39	81	66	7	21	624
Western Europe[b]	133	1,203	29	85	43	46	63	1,699
Latin America[c]	33	29	23	8	6	2	3	107
Developing Asia[d]	130	95	8	215	82	10	18	573
Japan, Australia, New Zealand	114	79	12	135	24	6	16	392
Africa	14	42	2	6	3	6	2	90
Middle East	17	41	3	27	28	2	12	144
World total[e]	714	1,682	117	566	256	81	139	3,687

a. Includes United States, Canada, and Mexico.
b. Includes the European Union, European Free Trade Association countries, and Turkey.
c. Latin America does not include Mexico.
d. As defined by *Direction of Trade Statistics Yearbook*.
e. Includes regions not specified.

Source: International Monetary Fund, *Direction of Trade Statistics Yearbook*, 1993.

The first step toward examining trade intensity within and between regions is to express the dollar trade figures as a percentage of the total exports of the region of origin, which is done in table 3.2. The rationale for this calculation is simple: each region, in its own self-interest, will put much of its commercial policy efforts into bettering relations with its good customers—that is, countries or regions that absorb a sizable share of the exporting region's total shipments. We label this approach to regional analysis the "good-customer" approach.

While the good-customer approach has compelling descriptive and prescriptive merit, it is not the total story. A major goal of economic integration is for each partner to enhance the prosperity of the other partners. A distinguishing feature of economic groups is that each member normally exhibits more practical concern about the prosperity of other members than about the prosperity of the world at large. In turn, it is important that this mutual concern be reinforced by disproportionately strong trade ties among the partners.

Disproportionately strong trade ties imply the following relationship. Suppose country A trades with two other countries, B and C. Country C is much larger than country B (they have GDP levels of $200 billion and $50 billion, respectively) and because of its larger size, country C buys more goods and services from country A than does country B. However, country B could still be a stronger economic neighbor. This would be true, for example, if for each $1 billion increment in country B's GDP, country B would buy twice as many goods and services from country A as country C would buy for each $1 billion increment in its GDP. Suppose, by its own policy actions, country A can help induce a $1 billion increment in the GDP of either country B or country C, but not both. Then, in terms of enhancing its own export sales, country A would do better to concentrate on country B.

To identify strong neighbors, the trade destination shares for exporting country A should be adjusted by the GDP levels of the destination countries (countries B and C) in order to assess the intensity of trade relations per unit of GDP. Thus, we calculate a "strong-neighbor" index in table 3.3 by dividing export destination shares from table 3.2 by the percentage of world GDP accounted for by each of the destination regions. A ratio greater than 1.0 indicates that the export percentage exceeds the GDP percentage of the destination country or region, and it is hence a stronger neighbor; a ratio of less than 1.0 indicates the converse, a weaker neighbor. The strong-neighbor indexes reflect the average propensity of a destination country or region to import from a source country or region. We assume that the average propensities also apply to marginal GDP growth in the destination area.

Several important insights emerge from tables 3.2 and 3.3. These insights are summarized for several regions in table 3.4, which identifies the top three partner regions both from a good-customer perspec-

Table 3.2 Good customers: shares of destination regions in total exports of regions of origin, 1992[a]
(percentages)

Region of origin	North America	Western Europe	Latin America	Developing Asia	Japan, Australia, New Zealand	Africa	Middle East
North America	43.3	21.0	6.2	13.0	10.6	1.2	3.4
Western Europe	7.8	70.8	1.7	5.0	2.6	2.7	3.7
Latin America	31.4	27.0	21.8	7.0	5.7	1.4	2.4
Developing Asia	22.7	16.6	1.5	37.4	14.3	1.7	3.2
Japan, Australia, New Zealand	29.0	20.1	3.0	34.5	6.2	1.6	4.2
Africa	15.6	46.6	2.3	6.5	3.6	7.1	1.8
Middle East	11.7	28.7	2.3	18.5	19.5	1.7	8.6
World	19.4	45.6	3.2	15.3	7.0	2.2	3.8

a. Regional groups are the same as in table 3.1.

Source: Table 3.1.

Table 3.3 Strong-neighbor index: ratio of export shares of destination regions by region of origin to destination regions' shares of world GDP, 1992[a] (world total = 1.0)

Region of origin	North America	Western Europe	Latin America	Developing Asia	Japan, Australia, New Zealand	Africa	Middle East
North America	1.5	0.7	1.7	1.7	0.6	0.9	1.8
Western Europe	0.3	2.3	0.5	0.7	0.2	2.0	2.0
Latin America	1.1	0.9	6.1	0.9	0.3	1.1	1.3
Developing Asia	0.8	0.5	0.4	5.0	0.9	1.3	1.7
Japan, Australia, New Zealand	1.0	0.6	0.8	4.6	0.4	1.2	2.3
Africa	0.5	1.5	0.7	0.9	0.2	5.4	1.0
Middle East	0.4	0.9	0.6	2.5	1.2	1.3	4.7
World	0.7	1.5	0.9	2.1	0.4	1.7	2.1

a. Regional groups are the same as in table 3.1.

Source: Table 3.2, The World Bank, *World Development Report 1993*; International Monetary Fund, *World Economic Outlook*, October 1993; and Central Intelligence Agency, *Handbook of Economic Statistics*, 1990.

Table 3.4   Major trading partners from good customer and strong neighbor perpectives

Region	Top three partner regions from a good customer perspective	Top three partner regions from a strong neighbor perspective
North America	North America Western Europe Developing Asia	Middle East Latin America/Developing Asia North America
Japan, Australia, and New Zealand	Developing Asia North America Western Europe	Developing Asia Middle East Africa
Western Europe	Western Europe North America Developing Asia	Western Europe Africa/Middle East Developing Asia
Latin America	North America Western Europe Latin America	Latin America Middle East North America/Africa
Developing Asia	Developing Asia North America Western Europe	Developing Asia Middle East Africa

Sources: Tables 3.2 and 3.3.

tive based on table 3.2 and a strong-neighbor perspective based on table 3.3.

For North America, based on the good-customer perspective, its best partners are North America, Western Europe, and developing Asia. From a North American perspective, viewed solely in trade terms, the case for economic integration with Latin America is not overwhelming. Latin America appears only on the North American strong-neighbor list. By contrast, developing Asia appears on both North American lists. Moreover, North America appears on the good-customer list of all regions listed; hence, North America is likely to be pursued as a potential trade partner by other areas besides Latin America.[6]

For Western Europe, a happy coincidence exists between the good-customer and strong-neighbor perspectives. Using each test, Western Europe is its own best partner. Developing Asia also appears in both lists.

For Japan, Australia, and New Zealand, the best partner based on both lists is developing Asia. North America and Western Europe appear only on the good-customer list.

---

6. The Middle East appears as North America's best partner from a strong-neighbor perspective. It also appears in the strong-neighbor lists of other regions. However, the results for this region are heavily influenced by trade in a single commodity, petroleum, and therefore do not point to extensive benefits from wider economic integration.

For Latin America, the picture is also simple. The most desirable partner regions, both from a good-customer perspective and a strong-neighbor perspective, include Latin America and North America.

Finally, developing Asia, arguably the world's most dynamic trading region, is a highly desirable partner for many regions. It appears on both lists for all regions except Latin America. For developing Asia, there is no doubt that it is its own best partner (tables 3.2 and 3.3).

These findings can be recapitulated as they apply to the Western Hemisphere (table 3.4). North America's good-customer list is headed by North America. Latin America appears among the top three North American strong neighbors, but not among the top three North American good customers. Not surprisingly, developing Asia appears among the top three on both North American lists, suggesting that, ignoring political and geographic factors, North America would be more interested in enhancing economic ties with developing Asia than with Latin America.

Latin America and North America appear at the top of both Latin American lists, indicating that Western Hemisphere integration is definitely Latin America's best first step toward economic integration on a global basis. From a trade perspective, Latin America must inevitably play the role of demandeur partner vis-à-vis North America.

We turn now to a closer examination of several subregions, concentrating on the hemisphere and starting with North America (tables 3.5, 3.6, and 3.7). North America's best customers are North America and Western Europe. Of those two, only North America is also a strong neighbor. Among the Latin American subregions, the Andean Group, Caricom, and the Central American Common Market (CACM) are all strong neighbors for North America.

Within North America, it is clear that the United States is the most desirable partner for both Canada and Mexico, whatever the test. For the United States, Canada and Mexico taken together are also best partners on both tests. Commercial links between Mexico and Canada are too weak for those countries to be considered strong neighbors; in a trade sense they are linked by their common interest in the US market.

Chile's best customer is Western Europe, followed distantly by North America (mainly due to the United States) and "Other Latin America" (mainly due to the Mercosur). For Chile, Japan appears as a stronger neighbor than the United States and as good a customer as the United States. From a strong-neighbor perspective, other Latin America is the most desirable partner for Chile. At a subregional level, the Andean Group and Mercosur are the best partners for Chile as measured by the strong-neighbor index.

The Mercosur's best customers are Western Europe and North America, and its strongest neighbor is Latin America. Among the Latin American subregions, Mercosur is its own best customer, but all Latin regions are promising partners under the strong-neighbor test. The same analysis generally holds for each individual Mercosur country. However, for Argentina, other Latin America is as good a customer as Mercosur.

For the Andean Group, the discordance between the calculus of good customer and strong neighbor is sharp. North America and Western Europe are very good customers, but they are not strong neighbors. The Latin American subregions are not good customers, but CACM, Caricom, and the Andean Group itself are strong neighbors. The same pattern applies to each Andean Country with a few exceptions: Caricom is not a strong neighbor for Bolivia and Ecuador, neither is CACM for Bolivia, and the Mercosur is a very good customer for Bolivia.

Inside the Andean region, all good-customer indexes are low. In addition, Bolivia is a strong neighbor only for Peru and to a lesser extent for Colombia. In terms of the good-customer perspective, Bolivia still sells more to Argentina, Ecuador to Chile, and Peru to Brazil and Canada, than each sells to other Andean countries.

CACM presents a very different picture from the Andean Group. For CACM as a group and also for each individual country, North America and CACM itself are good partners measured by both indexes.

Intraregional good-customer ties with Central America are low (except for trade between El Salvador and Guatemala), but strong-neighbor indexes are very high.[7] The slow pace of integration in this region testifies to the power of political strife to overwhelm sensible economic policies.

Finally, for the Caricom countries, North America, Western Europe, and to a lesser extent other Latin America are good customers. North America and other Latin America are strong neighbors.[8] By far the strongest neighbor, however, is Caricom itself: the Caricom nations exhibit double-digit and even triple-digit strong-neighbor index values.

For individual Caribbean countries, the picture is somewhat different. North America is a good customer and a strong neighbor for every country except for Barbados. Western Europe is a good customer for each member except for Trinidad and Tobago. The best partners (measured by both indexes) for Barbados and Trinidad and Tobago are in the Caribbean while the best partners for the Bahamas are outside Latin America.

To summarize our findings, existing subregional arrangements generally make sense in terms of the strong-neighbor index, but in most cases the groups are not first-choice arrangements in terms of the good-customer test. We conclude that subregional integration can continue to

---

7. The only exception: Guatemala is not a strong neighbor for Nicaragua.

8. In this case, other Latin America includes Caribbean countries such as the Netherlands Antilles, Leeward Islands, Windward Islands, Grenada, and Martinique.

Table 3.5 Trade values, 1992 (millions of dollars)

Origin	Subregional member countries					Japan	Western Europe
	US	Canada	Mexico				
North America	136,484	92,363	41,211			54,967	131,149
US	--	90,156	40,598			47,764	116,417
Canada	103,860	--	613			6,073	11,233
Mexico ᶜ	32,624	2,207	--			1,130	3,499
Chile	1,650	75	93			1,588	3,047
	Argentina	Brazil	Paraguay	Uruguay			
Mercosur	3,365	2,050	752	840		2,814	16,120
Argentina	--	1,598	201	314		468	4,090
Brazil	3,070	--	541	517		2,324	11,378
Paraguay	45	168	--	9		2	211
Uruguay	250	284	10	--		20	441
	Bolivia	Colombia	Ecuador	Peru	Venezuela		
Andean Group	43	454	256	538	594	1,044	5,789
Bolivia	--	25	3	58	5	1	290
Colombia	7	--	133	304	473	208	2,131
Ecuador	1	35	--	48	9	89	606
Peru	34	88	40	--	107	343	1,011
Venezuela	1	306	79	128	--	403	1,752
	Costa Rica	El Salvador	Guatemala	Honduras	Nicaragua		
CACM	146	257	197	62	133	93	1,261
Costa Rica	--	53	70	12	47	20	531
El Salvador	50	--	119	16	26	5	99
Guatemala	84	170	--	29	55	33	243
Honduras	2	17	8	--	5	13	166
Nicaragua	11	18	--	5	--	21	122
	Bahamas	Barbados	Guyana	Jamaica	Trinidad and Tobago		
CARICOM	7	81	45	40	53	70	1,091
Bahamas	--	--	--	--	--	18	333
Barbados	1	--	2	3	19	3	45
Guyana	1	0	--	4	6	12	166
Jamaica	1	16	3	--	29	18	429
Trinidad and Tobago	4	66	40	33	--	19	118

a. For each region/country of origin, "Other Latin America" includes all Latin America minus that region/country (e.g., exports from Mercosur to "Other Latin America" does not include intra-Mercosur trade).

			Destination			
North America	Mercosur	Andean Group	CACM	CARICOM	Other Latin America [a]	Total exports [b]
270,058	10,711	12,103	4,738	2,582	38,800	623,547
130,754	9,608	10,943	4,293	2,344	34,941	447,400
104,473	600	722	66	139	1,888	133,447
34,831	503	438	379	99	1,971	42,700
1,817	991	538	43	1	1,633	9,956
10,516	7,007	2,201	254	104	4,681	50,786
1,597	2,113	707	46	25	1,662	12,366
8,656	4,128	1,458	207	79	2,927	36,207
34	222	0	0	0	0	593
229	544	36	1	1	92	1,620
13,779	1,087	1,884	593	159	5,167	30,363
120	166	91	0	0	190	705
2,954	103	917	119	13	692	7,226
1,417	31	92	44	0	364	3,237
952	195	270	14	2	265	3,484
8,335	592	514	416	144	3,656	15,710
3,304	6	40	796	17	209	5,836
1,350	4	15	183	8	109	2,234
391	1	1	211	0	23	739
1,177	0	23	338	8	71	2,002
274	0	1	32	0	6	515
111	0	0	33	1	2	346
2,454	54	80	18	227	674	4,803
599	12	0	0	0	35	995
34	0	1	0	25	45	222
147	0	0	0	11	15	367
729	21	0	1	48	56	1,371
945	21	79	17	143	524	1,847

b. Total exports includes destinations not specified.
c. Mexican figures do not include maquiladora trade.

Table 3.6 Good-customer indexes, 1992[a]

	Destination					
Origin	**Subregional member countries**					**Japan**
	US	Canada	Mexico			
North America	21.9	14.8	6.6			8.8
US	--	20.2	9.1			10.7
Canada	77.8	--	0.5			4.6
Mexico	76.4	5.2	--			2.6
Chile	16.9	0.8	0.9			15.9
	Argentina	Brazil	Paraguay	Uruguay		
Mercosur	6.6	4.0	1.5	1.7		5.5
Argentina	--	12.9	1.6	2.5		3.8
Brazil	8.5	--	1.5	1.4		6.4
Paraguay	7.6	28.3	--	1.5		0.4
Uruguay	15.4	17.5	0.6	--		1.2
	Bolivia	Colombia	Ecuador	Peru	Venezuela	
Andean Group	0.1	1.5	0.8	1.8	2.0	3.4
Bolivia	--	3.6	0.4	8.2	0.7	0.2
Colombia	0.1	--	1.8	4.2	6.5	2.9
Ecuador	0.0	1.1	--	1.5	0.3	2.8
Peru	1.0	2.5	1.2	--	3.1	9.9
Venezuela	0.0	1.9	0.5	0.8	--	2.6
	Costa Rica	El Salvador	Guatemala	Honduras	Nicaragua	
CACM	2.5	4.4	3.4	1.1	2.3	1.6
Costa Rica	--	2.4	3.1	0.6	2.1	0.9
El Salvador	6.7	--	16.1	2.2	3.5	0.7
Guatemala	4.2	8.5	--	1.4	2.8	1.7
Honduras	0.3	3.3	1.6	--	1.0	2.5
Nicaragua	3.2	5.1	0.0	1.4	--	6.2
	Bahamas	Barbados	Guyana	Jamaica	Trinidad and Tobago	
CARICOM	0.1	1.7	0.9	0.8	1.1	1.5
Bahamas	--	0.0	0.0	0.0	0.0	1.8
Barbados	0.5	--	1.0	1.3	8.4	1.3
Guyana	0.4	0.0	--	1.0	1.7	3.2
Jamaica	0.0	1.2	0.2	--	2.1	1.3
Trinidad and Tobago	0.2	3.5	2.2	1.8	--	1.0

a. Based on table 3.5. Calculated as share of destination country/region in total exports of region of origin.

Destination						
Western Europe	North America	Mercosur	Andean Group	CACM	CARICOM	Other Latin America
21.0	43.3	1.7	1.9	0.8	0.4	6.2
26.0	29.2	2.1	2.4	1.0	0.5	7.8
8.4	78.3	0.4	0.5	0.0	0.1	1.4
8.2	81.6	1.2	1.0	0.9	0.2	4.6
30.6	18.3	10.0	5.4	0.4	0.0	16.4
31.7	20.7	13.8	4.3	0.5	0.2	9.2
33.1	12.9	17.1	5.7	0.4	0.2	13.4
31.4	23.9	11.4	4.0	0.6	0.2	8.1
35.6	5.7	37.4	0.0	0.0	0.0	0.0
27.2	14.1	33.6	2.2	0.1	0.0	5.7
19.1	45.4	3.6	6.2	2.0	0.5	17.0
41.1	17.0	23.6	12.9	0.0	0.0	26.9
29.5	40.9	1.4	12.7	1.6	0.2	9.6
18.7	43.8	1.0	2.8	1.3	0.0	11.2
29.0	27.3	5.6	7.7	0.4	0.1	7.6
11.2	53.1	3.8	3.3	2.6	0.9	23.3
19.9	56.6	0.1	0.7	13.6	0.3	3.6
23.8	60.4	0.2	0.7	8.2	0.4	4.9
13.3	52.9	0.2	0.1	28.5	0.0	3.1
12.2	58.8	0.0	1.2	16.9	0.4	3.5
32.2	53.2	0.0	0.1	6.2	0.1	1.1
35.4	32.2	0.0	0.0	9.6	0.2	0.5
22.7	51.1	1.1	1.7	0.4	4.7	14.0
33.5	60.2	1.2	0.0	0.0	0.0	3.5
20.2	15.2	0.0	0.4	0.0	11.2	20.0
45.2	40.1	0.0	0.0	0.0	3.1	4.0
31.3	53.2	1.6	0.0	0.1	3.5	4.1
6.4	51.2	1.1	4.3	0.9	7.7	28.4

Table 3.7   Strong-neighbor indexes, 1992[a]

Origin	Destination — Subregional member countries					Japan
	US	Canada	Mexico			
North America	0.9	6.6	5.2			0.6
US	--	8.9	7.1			0.7
Canada	3.1	--	0.4			0.3
Mexico	3.0	2.3	--			0.2
Chile	0.7	0.3	0.7			1.1
	Argentina	Brazil	Paraguay	Uruguay		
Mercosur	12.1	2.2	53.0	37.0		0.4
Argentina	--	7.2	58.1	56.9		0.3
Brazil	15.5	--	53.5	32.0		0.4
Paraguay	14.0	15.7	--	33.6		0.0
Uruguay	28.2	9.7	22.8	--		0.1
	Bolivia	Colombia	Ecuador	Peru	Venezuela	
Andean Group	6.1	7.9	15.9	8.6	7.8	0.2
Bolivia	--	18.8	8.1	39.8	2.8	0.0
Colombia	4.1	--	34.9	20.4	26.0	0.2
Ecuador	0.8	5.6	--	7.1	1.2	0.2
Peru	43.0	13.4	22	--	12.2	0.7
Venezuela	0.3	10.3	9.5	3.9	--	0.2
	Costa Rica	El Salvador	Guatemala	Honduras	Nicaragua	
CACM	95.4	162.4	78.6	86.8	74.2	0.1
Costa Rica	--	87.0	73.0	45.3	68.7	0.1
El Salvador	256.8	--	373.9	180.0	112.6	0.0
Guatemala	159.5	313.1	--	116.6	89.7	0.1
Honduras	11.9	121.2	37.7	--	33.0	0.2
Nicaragua	120.7	186.5	0.0	112.5	--	0.4
	Bahamas	Barbados	Guyana	Jamaica	Trinidad and Tobago	
CARICOM	10.8	236.0	576.5	54.0	51.2	0.1
Bahamas	--	--	0.0	0.0	0.0	0.1
Barbados	38.8	0.0	600.7	84.9	386.7	0.1
Guyana	28.9	2.3	--	67.0	77.1	0.2
Jamaica	3.3	160.6	116.2	--	96.1	0.1
Trinidad and Tobago	15.2	494.0	1340.2	116.9	--	0.1

a. Calculated as the ratio between share destination of exports (from table 3.6) and share of world GDP by region of destination.

Destination						
Western Europe	North America	Mercosur	Andean Group	CACM	CARICOM	Other Latin America
0.7	1.5	0.7	2.7	5.5	7.0	1.7
0.8	8.3	0.9	3.4	6.9	8.9	2.2
0.3	2.9	0.2	0.7	0.4	1.8	0.4
0.3	3.0	0.5	1.4	6.4	3.9	1.3
1.0	0.6	4.1	7.5	3.1	0.1	4.8
1.0	0.7	5.7	6.0	3.6	3.5	8.0
1.1	0.4	9.1	7.9	2.7	3.4	10.1
1.0	0.8	18.4	5.6	4.1	3.7	11.0
1.1	0.2	15.7	0.0	0.0	0.0	10.5
0.9	0.5	14.1	3.1	0.6	0.7	11.1
0.6	1.6	1.5	8.6	14.0	8.9	6.0
1.3	0.6	9.7	18.4	0.1	0.0	11.2
0.9	1.4	0.6	23.8	11.8	3.1	6.6
0.6	1.5	0.4	4.2	9.7	0.0	4.0
0.9	0.9	2.3	15.0	2.9	1.1	4.6
0.4	1.8	1.6	6.9	19.0	15.5	8.0
0.6	2.0	0.0	1.0	97.9	5.0	1.0
0.8	2.1	0.1	0.9	72.2	6.1	3.7
0.4	1.8	0.1	0.1	253.8	0.0	8.9
0.4	2.0	0.0	1.6	175.1	6.8	5.8
1.0	1.8	0.0	0.2	49.1	1.2	2.1
1.1	1.1	0.0	0.0	88.4	3.3	2.8
0.7	1.8	0.5	2.3	2.6	79.8	4.0
1.1	2.1	0.5	0.0	0.0	0.0	1.0
0.6	0.5	0.0	0.5	0.0	215.1	8.7
1.4	1.4	0.0	0.0	0.0	54.0	2.0
1.0	1.8	0.6	0.0	0.4	79.4	2.1
0.2	1.8	0.5	5.9	6.6	206.5	10.2

make progress, driven by the logic of neighborhood integration. However, after a certain point, good-customer considerations will compel each of the Latin American subregions to seek closer ties with North America. Moreover, the same good-customer logic will prompt the United States, Brazil, Chile, and other hemispheric countries to avoid measures that would damage their trade links with Europe and Asia.

Regional Investment Ties

In the realm of portfolio capital, it makes little sense to speak either of strong or weak ties between countries or regions. Unlike circumstances 30 years ago, portfolio capital is now highly mobile across international borders. Once portfolio capital passes through financial intermediaries, its origin becomes practically anonymous. Furthermore, "units" of portfolio capital—that is, units defined as to currency of denomination, interest rate, and maturity—are highly substitutable whatever the origin.[9]

The same anonymity does not apply to direct investment and to the activities of multinational enterprises (MNEs). One MNE is not perfectly substitutable for another, even if they both operate in the same industry. Instead, each multinational firm commands a unique range of products, processes, and distribution networks. Moreover, while the rootless multinational, with no strong ties to any home country, was long ago heralded by Vernon (1971), and while nationality-neutral MNEs can be found (for example, Nestlé and Honda), such firms are far from typical. Instead, most MNEs remain closely identified with a home country in terms of corporate headquarters, R&D activity, and the preponderance of manufacturing plants. Moreover, most MNEs concentrate their operations in a few geographic areas; their sales and production are not dispersed across the globe proportional to national or regional GDP (see investment section in next chapter).

Working individually and through business groups, MNEs can shape the evolution of economic policy, especially once market-oriented policies are widely espoused by political leaders. As a general rule, multinationals favor the reduction of trade and investment barriers, the harmonization of technical standards (or the mutual recognition of standards), and progress toward monetary union. Hence most MNEs are natural and effective proponents of the first and last stages

---

9. This observation is not meant to diminish the importance of portfolio capital in economic integration. By bringing real interest rates for a given type of debt risk closer to world levels and by facilitating the convergence of price-earnings ratios for shares with equivalent investment characteristics, portfolio capital flows enable rival companies to compete on a more level playing field, so far as capital costs are concerned. In turn, this makes economic integration politically easier. The point of our observation is that portfolio capital has "stateless" origins and is not susceptible to regional analysis.

of economic integration, at least in regions where their business interests are focused.[10]

Hence, it is worth applying the analysis used earlier in evaluating trade ties to examine the strength of investment ties in various economic regions. Unfortunately, far fewer data are available on the origin and destination of direct investment than on the origin and destination of merchandise trade. In particular, hardly any information exists on direct investment flows or stocks between advanced developing countries, for example, within the Mercosur region or within the Association of Southeast Asian Nations (ASEAN). Instead, origin and destination data are only available for the major industrialized home countries. The available information is summarized in tables 3.8, 3.9, and 3.10.

From a "good destination" perspective, the United States concentrates its direct investment in Western Europe (EU plus EFTA; 50 percent), North America (18 percent), and Latin America (10 percent) (table 3.9). Canada concentrates its direct investment in North America (63 percent), the European Union (22 percent), and Latin America (10 percent).

As with trade, a strong-neighbor index can be calculated for direct investment. The index is calculated by dividing each country's direct investment stocks abroad by the share of world GDP accounted for in each destination region (table 3.10). For the United States, from a strong-neighbor perspective the most desirable partners are Canada and Latin America. Hence, for the United States, there is some coincidence between the good-destination and strong-neighbor investment perspectives: Latin America shows up among the top three on both lists. Canada's preferred partners from the strong-neighbor standpoint are Latin America and the United States.

The top three destination regions for Japan's direct investment are the United States, the European Union, and South and East Asia.[11] Latin America is fifth on Japan's list, claiming four-fifths the stock of direct investment that Japan has placed in South and East Asia (table 3.9). From a strong-neighbor perspective, Japan's preferred investment partners are Latin America, Australia and New Zealand, and South and East Asia.

---

10. Multinational firms adopt a less clear-cut stance when it comes to the intermediate stages of economic integration—policy convergence in areas such as corporate taxation, mandated employee benefits, labor standards, and environmental controls. In these areas, if the choice is between policy differentiation and upward convergence, multinationals often prefer policy differentiation. See the chapter 1 discussion on elements of integration. Moreover, those multinationals that have a favored position in certain markets may actively lobby against trade liberalization.

11. Official Japanese and US sources show a large discrepancy in the amount of Japanese direct investment in the United States. Ministry of International Trade and Industry data show Japanese foreign direct investment stock in the United States of about $130.5 billion for 1990; US Department of Commerce figures show $83.5 billion.

Table 3.8 Direct investment stock on a historical cost basis by countries of origin, 1990 (billions of dollars)

Destination for direct investment	North America	United States	Canada	Japan[a]	Germany[b]	United Kingdom[c]	France[d]	Italy[e]
North America[f]	120.4	77.8	42.1	138.1	33.8	98.4	21.4	4.2
United States	42.5	—	42.0	130.5	29.6	86.9	n.a.	n.a.
Canada[g]	68.4	67.0	—	5.7	2.9	11.0	n.a.	n.a.
Mexico[h]	9.5	9.4	0.1	1.9	1.2	0.5	n.a.	n.a.
Japan	21.6	21.0	0.7	—	2.1	2.3	n.a.	n.a.
European Union	187.4	177.6	14.4	55.3	44.7	48.9	33.2	21.2
European Free Trade Association	31.3	32.1	1.1	3.4	9.4	6.4	4.6	5.3
Australia, New Zealand, and South Africa	20.6	18.9	2.0	17.0	2.5	22.3	n.a.	n.a.
South and East Asia[i]	27.6	22.9	2.8	45.3	2.5	10.1	0.5	n.a.
Middle East	4.9	4.0	0.1	3.4	0.5	0.6	0.3	n.a.
Africa	3.9	3.9	0.1	5.8	1.0	3.7	0.3	0.4
Latin America[j]	47.8	42.7	6.9	36.9	7.7	3.4	1.7	4.8
Andean Group	4.7	4.0	0.1	1.2	0.1	2.6	n.a.	n.a.
Mercosur	19.6	17.9	1.3	7.0	5.6	0.1	n.a.	n.a.
China and centrally planned Asia[k]	n.a.	n.a.	n.a.	2.9	n.a.	n.a.	n.a.	n.a.
World Total	488.6	424.1	67.1	310.8	109.5	207.5	67.9	39.6

n.a. = not available.
a. US data show Japanese direct investment in United States as $83.5 billion.
b. Translated to dollars using *International Financial Statistics 1989* period average ($0.53 = DM1.00).
c. Translated to dollars using *International Financial Statistics 1989* period average ($1.64 = £1.00).
d. Translated to dollars using *International Financial Statistics 1989* period average ($1.00 = 6.38 francs).
e. Translated to dollars using *International Financial Statistics 1989* period average ($1.00 = 1372.1 lire)
f. North American and US totals include $0.6 billion in Mexican direct investment in Canada and the United States.
g. Translated to dollars using *International Financial Statistics 1990* period average ($0.85 = C$1).
h. Mexican data show Canadian FDI in Mexico as $0.4 billion. *Survey of Current Business*, October 1991, cites official US figure of current value of US FDI in Mexico at the end of 1989 as $21.0 billion.
i. Based on GATT classification: roughly Asia other than enumerated countries.
j. Includes unspecified countries in Western Hemisphere, other than North America.
k. Centrally planned Asia includes China, North Korea, Mongolia, and Vietnam.

Sources: US Department of Commerce, *Survey of Current Business*, June 1992; Japan, Ministry of Trade and Industry, *Japanese Direct Investment Abroad*, June 1991; Statistics Canada, *Canada's International Investment Position, 1991*; Mexican Secretariat of Commerce and Industrial Development, *General Directorate of Foreign Investment*, 1990; *German Statistical Yearbook, 1990*; United Kingdom, Central Statistics Office, *Business Monitor*, May 1990; United Nations, Transnational Corporations and Management Division, Department of Economic and Social Development.

Table 3.9   Direct investment stock shares by countries of origin 1990 (percentages)

Destination for direct investment	North America	United States	Canada	Japan	Germany	United Kingdom	France	Italy
North America	24.6	18.3	62.7	44.4	30.9	47.4	31.5	10.6
United States	8.7	—	62.6	42.0	27.0	41.9	n.a.	n.a.
Canada	14.0	15.8	—	1.8	2.6	5.3	n.a.	n.a.
Mexico	1.9	2.2	0.1	0.6	1.1	0.2	n.a.	n.a.
Japan	4.4	5.0	1.0	—	1.9	1.1	n.a.	n.a.
European Union	38.4	41.9	21.5	17.8	40.8	23.6	48.9	53.5
European Free Trade Association	6.4	7.6	1.6	1.1	8.6	3.1	6.8	13.4
Australia, New Zealand, and South Africa	4.2	4.5	3.0	5.5	2.3	10.7	n.a.	n.a.
South and East Asia	5.6	5.4	4.2	14.6	2.3	4.9	0.7	n.a.
Middle East	1.0	0.9	0.1	1.1	0.5	0.3	n.a.	n.a.
Africa	0.8	0.9	0.1	1.9	0.9	1.8	0.4	1.0
Latin America	9.8	10.1	10.3	11.9	7.0	1.6	2.5	12.1
Andean Group	1.0	0.9	0.1	0.4	0.1	1.3	n.a.	n.a.
Mercosur	4.0	4.2	1.9	2.3	5.1	0.0	n.a.	n.a.
China and centrally planned Asia[a]	n.a.	n.a.	n.a.	0.9	n.a.	n.a.	n.a.	n.a.

n.a. = not available.
a. Centrally planned Asia includes China, North Korea, Mongolia, and Vietnam.

Source: Derived from table 3.8.

Table 3.10 Ratio between a destination's share of direct investment by country of origin and its share of world GDP, 1990 (world total = 1.0)

Destination	North America	United States	Canada	Japan	Germany	United Kingdom	France	Italy
North America	0.9	0.7	2.3	1.6	1.1	1.7	1.1	0.4
United States	0.4	—	2.6	1.7	1.1	1.7	n.a.	n.a.
Canada	5.5	6.2	—	0.7	1.0	2.1	n.a.	n.a.
Mexico	1.8	2.1	0.1	0.6	1.0	0.2	n.a.	n.a.
Japan	0.3	0.4	0.1	—	0.1	0.1	n.a.	n.a.
European Union	1.4	1.6	0.8	0.7	1.5	0.9	1.8	2.0
European Free Trade Association	1.7	2.0	0.4	0.3	2.2	0.8	1.8	3.5
Australia, New Zealand, and South Africa	2.2	2.3	1.5	2.8	1.2	5.6	n.a.	n.a.
South and East Asia	1.1	1.0	0.8	2.8	0.4	0.9	0.1	n.a.
Middle East	0.7	0.6	0.1	0.7	0.3	0.2	n.a.	n.a.
Africa	0.7	0.8	0.1	1.7	0.8	1.6	0.4	0.9
Latin America	2.9	3.0	3.1	3.6	2.1	0.5	0.8	3.6
Andean Group	1.5	1.5	0.2	0.6	0.1	2.0	n.a.	n.a.
Mercosur	1.7	1.8	0.8	1.0	2.2	0.0	n.a.	n.a.
China and centrally planned Asia[a]	n.a.	n.a.	n.a.	0.3	n.a.	n.a.	n.a.	n.a.

n.a. = not available.
a. Centrally planned Asia includes China, North Korea, Mongolia, and Vietnam.
Source: Table 3.9 and World Bank, *World Development Report, 1992.*

Figures for direct investment placements by the major Western European countries are difficult to find. From a good-destination perspective, Germany has concentrated its direct investment within Western Europe (EU and EFTA) and North America, and to a lesser extent in Latin America. The United Kingdom has invested primarily in North America, Western Europe (EU and EFTA), and Australia, New Zealand, and South Africa. Data on investment flows for France suggest that North America and the European Union plus EFTA receive the overwhelming majority of French direct investment, with Latin America a distant third destination. The German, British, and French data suggest that Latin America is not among the major recipients of direct investment from Europe.[12]

The major source of direct investment in Latin America is the United States, followed by Japan. Of the regional trading groups within Latin America, Mercosur has been the most successful in enticing foreign direct investment. The Andean Group has also received a considerable amount of direct investment, particularly from the United States. In some respects, the investment data support the analysis based on trade statistics. Latin America is among the top three regions for both the United States and Japan, seen both from a good-destination standpoint and from a strong-neighbor perspective. Building on these ties, Latin America should probably concentrate its efforts to attract direct investment from North America and Japan.

For the industrial countries, the conclusions are more ambiguous. When viewed from a strong-neighbor perspective, Latin America is a significant region for investors in the industrial countries. But Latin America is only the third destination region for US direct investment, far behind Western Europe and North America. Likewise, Japan's direct investment is concentrated in the United States, Western Europe, and South and East Asia. In the case of the large European countries for which data are available, Latin America appears to be a minor destination for direct investment. Hence, for the industrial countries, improved direct investment relations with Latin America may be important, but they are not more important than improved relations with a number of other regions.

This conclusion, based on investment analysis, reinforces the earlier suggestion, based on trade analysis, that neither the United States nor Canada would want to improve its commercial ties with Latin America at the expense of ties with other regions. However, hemispheric arrangements need not compel an either-or choice (see discussion in chapter 9). Properly designed, trade and investment liberalization within the hemisphere can point the way toward global trade and investment liberalization.

---

12. Italy is an exception. It invests about as much in Latin America as it does in North America and EFTA.

Regional Diversity

A third way to assess the prospects for hemispheric economic integration is to examine potential friction within the regional group. The variable we use to measure potential friction is diversity in per capita GDP between partner countries.[13] Per capita GDP serves as a proxy for many variables that reflect the "tilt" of business playing fields, such as wage costs, health and safety conditions, and environmental controls. The greater the difference in these background conditions between any two countries, the larger the scope for disagreement as they enter into a free trade arrangement.

In addition, per capita GDP is highly correlated with physical and human capital endowments. When capital endowment conditions are similar, countries are likely to expand their intra-industry trade faster than their interindustry trade. Both forms of trade expansion yield significant economic benefits, but intra-industry trade usually creates less political friction, for a given quantum of commerce, than interindustry trade. This is because intra-industry trade implies that many firms can sort themselves out into niches of specialization, whereas interindustry trade often entails the wholesale contraction of firms and sectors.

Table 3.11 gives per capita GDP data for 13 regional groups. The 1988 per capita GDP figures are taken from Summers and Heston (1991) and reflect the purchasing power of different national currencies rather than prevailing exchange rates. For each group, the table also gives an income diversity index. The index can take values of zero and higher; the larger the index, the more diverse the region. The income diversity index is a weighted coefficient of variation, calculated as explained in the table notes.

North America, with an income diversity index of 0.38, ranks among the more disparate regional groups from the standpoint of per capita GDP. The high NAFTA index reflects large differences between per capita GDP in the United States ($19,851) and Canada ($17,681), on the one hand, and Mexico ($5,323) on the other hand (on a purchasing power basis, the Mexican per capita GDP figure is much larger than when measured on a current exchange rate basis).

Income diversity indexes for the Latin American groups range from a practically homogeneous value of 0.08 for Mercosur to a highly diverse value of 0.61 for Caricom. Measured by per capita GNP differences, the Mercosur is the most homogenous of all 13 regional groups because Argentina and Brazil, with per capita incomes of $4,363 and $4,621, respectively, account for about 97 percent of the group's population.

---

13. This measure does not reflect the disparity of income within a country, only between countries. Highly unequal income distribution within a country may hinder economic integration if opponents can persuasively argue that freer trade and investment will only worsen the distribution of income.

Table 3.11 Regional diversity as measured by per capita GDP levels

Region	Diversity index[a]
North America	0.38
European Union	0.31
EFTA	0.13
Australia–New Zealand Closer Economic Cooperation	0.09
ASEAN	0.48
Other East Asia[b]	0.41
West Asia[c]	0.34
Mercosur	0.08
Andean Group	0.32
CACM[d]	0.36
CARICOM[e]	0.61
Other Latin America[f]	0.45
Western Hemisphere	0.73

a. The diversity index is roughly a weighted coefficient of variation. The weights are each country's share of its region's total population. The squared difference between the country's and region's average per capita income is multiplied by the population share weight. These population-weighted squared differences are then summed, and the square root is taken of the summed value. The coefficient is obtained by dividing the resulting figure by the average per capita income figure for the region.
b. Korea, Taiwan, China, and Hong Kong.
c. Bangladesh, India, Nepal, Pakistan, and Sri Lanka.
d. CACM countries and Panama.
e. Includes only Bahamas, Barbados, Guyana, Jamaica, and Trinidad and Tobago.
f. Dominican Republic, Haiti, and Surinam.

Sources: Robert Summers and Alan Heston, "The Penn World Table (Mark 5): An Expanded Set of International Comparisons, 1950–1988," The Quarterly Journal of Economics, May 1991; World Bank, World Development Report 1992; Inter-American Development Bank, Economic and Social Progress in Latin America, 1991 Report; Council for Economic Planning and Development, Republic of China, Taiwan Statistical Data Book, 1991.

The Andean Group is the second most homogenous region in Latin America, after Mercosur, but with a much higher diversity index of 0.32, reflecting the gap between impoverished Bolivia ($1,481) and oil-rich Venezuela ($5,648). CACM comes in third, with an index of 0.36, reflecting per capita GNP differences ranging from Honduras ($1,491) to Costa Rica ($4,317). The most diverse Latin group is Caricom, with an index of 0.61. At one extreme, the Bahamas ($11,004) has a flourishing tourist industry; at the other extreme, Guyana ($1,542) has a battered agricultural economy.

The Western Hemisphere has an income diversity index of 0.73, larger than that for any other regional group. This figure is very high compared to the European Union and EFTA (indexes of 0.31 and 0.13, respectively). Even ASEAN has a lower index (0.48) than the Western Hemisphere. Diversity in Western Hemisphere per capita GDP translates into huge differences in labor conditions and other social indicators. While not insurmountable, income diversity perhaps constitutes the greatest barrier to economic integration in the hemisphere.

4

Regional Implications of a WHFTA

In chapter 3, we examined the unrealized trade potential in Latin America and concluded that liberalization could unleash faster export and import growth. This chapter first examines how trade and investment expansion could contribute to overall economic growth in Latin America. It then looks at the impact of a Western Hemisphere Free Trade Area (WHFTA) on the United States.

Regional Implications for Latin America

For the growth assessment exercise, we use a set of cross-sectional data to examine the association between economic growth and trade growth for 58 market-oriented countries in Europe, Asia, and the Western Hemisphere for the decade 1980–90. Our working hypothesis is that improved Latin American trade performance in the 1990s, inspired by policy liberalization, will help induce higher rates of GDP growth; in turn, higher GDP growth will bring a second round of trade expansion. Based on relationships estimated for the panel of 58 market-oriented countries, we can then calculate potential Latin American GDP growth and total trade expansion resulting from the new approach to economic policy.

GDP Growth and Trade Expansion

To calculate the implied difference trade liberalization has made on Latin American GDP growth during the 1990s, we assume that the overall trade deficiencies for Latin America are eliminated over a 10–year period as a result of reform policies.

To carry out the calculations for Latin America as a whole,[1] we need to know the association between GDP growth and trade expansion. The growth of GDP and the associated expansion of trade entails a two-way process. GDP growth stimulates trade through macroeconomic mechanisms, both of a supply-side character and of a demand side (or Keynesian) character. As an economy grows, its capability of selling into export markets is enhanced (supply-side mechanics), while its appetite for imports expands (demand-side mechanics).

Looking at the two-way process from another angle, the balanced expansion of exports and imports stimulates GDP growth through microeconomic mechanisms. Expanded export opportunities enable a country to specialize in producing those goods and services in which it has a comparative advantage. This mechanism boosts GDP by shifting employees, capital, and other resources from low-earning pursuits to high-earning pursuits. At the same time, import expansion forces domestic firms to become more efficient and to shed uncompetitive operations.

The two-way association between GDP growth and trade expansion can be assessed by examining cross-sectional data for 58 market-oriented countries for 1980–90 (see appendix B for details). Here we focus on the contribution that faster trade growth makes to GDP growth.

The analysis in appendix B suggests that, when both exports and imports grow at the rate of 5 percent per year in real terms, rather than staying constant, real GDP growth is increased by 2.3 percentage points annually over its baseline level. Specifically, an annual 5 percent real growth in exports contributes 1.3 percentage points to annual real GDP growth, while an annual 5 percent real growth in imports contributes 1.0 percentage point to real GDP growth (1.3 plus 1.0 equals 2.3).[2]

From 1980 to 1990, Latin American merchandise exports declined by $27 billion in real terms, while Latin American merchandise imports declined by a staggering $60 billion. Not surprisingly, many Latin American nations suffered declining GDP, and only Colombia, Costa Rica, and Chile experienced annual real GDP growth of 3.0 percent or more.

From the trade deficiency analysis set forth in appendix A, we conclude that broad economic reform, including trade liberalization, can spur Latin countries to achieve higher export and import levels. From the growth analysis set forth in appendix B, we conclude that trade

---

1. We do not attempt to make estimates for individual countries or subregions because we do not think the approach can be carried to that level of detail.

2. A study by the University of Michigan estimates the economic effects of extending the North American Free Trade Agreement to Argentina, Brazil, Chile, and Colombia. It suggests that as each Latin country joins the NAFTA, all countries win. The gains range from 0.1 percent of GDP up to 2.2 percent (Brown et al. 1993).

expansion can raise GDP growth rates. The next step is to use the estimated relationships between GDP growth and trade expansion to calculate the magnitude of potential gains from trade liberalization.

Latin American Growth and Trade Prospects

The trade deficiency analysis suggests that if Latin American nations liberalize their economies and adopt outward-looking policies, higher trade-to-GDP ratios could potentially add $56 billion to total Latin American exports and boost import levels by $92 billion during the 1990s (appendix A, table A1).[3] Policy-induced trade expansion of these magnitudes would powerfully stimulate Latin American GDP growth, bringing a second round of trade growth.

Our scenarios do not assume total elimination of the Latin American trade deficiency by the year 2002. Instead, the WHFTA scenario assumes that market-oriented policies reduce the Latin American trade deficiency in comparison with other market-oriented countries by one-third. This reduction by the year 2000 would mean a policy-induced expansion of $19 billion in real exports and $31 billion in real imports (19 is one-third of 56, and 31 is one-third of 92).

Based on the analysis in appendix B, we calculate that this degree of trade liberalization, complemented by other reforms (the WHFTA scenario), could enable Latin America to increase its annual real GDP growth rate by 1.5 percentage points in the 1990s as compared with our baseline scenario, which we label the continuing-reform scenario (described below). The additional real GDP growth on account of policy liberalization would yield an annual increment in Latin American GDP of about $273 billion in the year 2002, or about $525 per capita.[4]

Owing to the interaction between trade growth and GDP growth, the real level of Latin American exports would be $87 billion higher in the year 2002, and real imports would be $104 billion greater than in the continuing-reform scenario. The ambitious course of economic policy reform envisaged in the WHFTA scenario would thus add about $191 billion to the level of two-way Latin American trade by the year 2002.

The baseline continuing-reform scenario assumes gradual implementation of policy reforms beyond the changes achieved by 1990, resulting in a modest reduction in Latin America's trade deficiency over the next several

---

3. The real amount of policy-induced trade expansion measured in 2002 should be larger than these estimates made in terms of 1990 base-level trade because, with a growing Latin American economy over 1990–2002, the base levels of imports and exports will be larger. Additionally, the nominal levels will be larger because a small annual amount of inflation in dollar prices, say by 3 percent per year, will cumulatively add about 43 percent to nominal values over 12 years.

4. In 1991, total population in Latin America was 433 million. By the year 2002, we assume it will be 520 million.

years. Specifically, the continuing-reform scenario contemplates a policy-induced elimination of the trade deficiency that is just one-half of the WHFTA scenario levels. Thus, in the continuing-reform scenario, policy-induced expansion is $9.5 billion for real exports and $15.5 billion for real imports. This scenario envisages unilateral trade reforms and small trade groups, but not an umbrella WHFTA. In rough terms, the continuing-reform scenario estimates what would happen under the present trend of Latin American reforms. However, without a WHFTA, there is less assurance that Latin American countries will continue along their present path.

Latin American Investment Prospects

Latin American investment ties are particularly strong with the United States and with Japan. In 1992 the stock of US direct investment in Latin America reached $75.5 billion, up from $62.2 billion in 1990; the Japanese direct investment stock reached $44.4 billion, up from $38.6 billion in 1990.[5] Leaving aside the Caribbean, the main destination of US and Japanese investment is Brazil: $16.1 billion from the United States and $7.2 billion from Japan (mainly in the manufacturing sector).[6] Although investment inflows in Latin America have been increasing, Latin countries are still far from achieving the overall investment rates found in Asian countries. In 1990, for example, Argentina's gross domestic investment as a percentage of gross domestic product was 8.4 percent, the Venezuelan figure was 10.2 percent, and the Chilean figure was 20.2 percent (table 4.1).[7] In comparison, Asian countries have gross investment rates that average 35 percent of GDP.

In sharp contrast with their perceptions 20 years ago, Latin American countries now see expanded investment inflows as a complement, not a competitor, to domestic investment. More investment by foreign firms is thus perceived as a major benefit of economic integration. Correspondingly, in the aftermath of NAFTA, the potential investment diversion in

---

5. The Japanese figures represent "planned" transactions, which may differ from actual completed transactions.

6. Foreign investment in the Caribbean is heavily influenced by transactions in which the Caribbean country is a financial intermediary (usually for tax reasons). Since parent companies use their Caribbean affiliates for debt transactions on a global scale, the investment figures for all of Latin America, including the Caribbean, are overstated. Important Caribbean intermediaries for US financial investment are Bermuda ($25.8 billion), Panama ($11.5 billion), the Bahamas ($4.6 billion), and other British Islands ($5.0 billion). Japanese firms use some of the same intermediaries: Panama ($18.8 billion) and Cayman Islands ($8.1 billion) (*Survey of Current Business*, June 1992 and July 1993; Rutter 1993, appendix table 12).

7. By 1992, the estimated figure for Argentina rose to 14 percent.

Table 4.1   Gross domestic investment as a share of GDP, 1980–90

Country	1980	1985	1990
North America	20.6	20.2	17.6
United States	19.9	20.2	17.1
Canada	23.6	20.2	20.5
Mexico	27.4	21.2	21.8
Chile	22.7	13.7	20.2
Mercosur	23.1	16.2	18.1
Argentina	22.2	8.5	8.4
Brazil	23.3	19.2	21.7
Paraguay	31.7	22.0	22.9
Uruguay	24.2	11.4	11.5
Andean Group	24.7	18.3	14.1
Bolivia	14.8	10.2	12.7
Colombia	19.1	19.0	18.2
Ecuador	26.1	18.2	17.9
Peru	29.0	18.4	14.6
Venezuela	26.4	18.5	10.2
CACM	18.5	16.1	17.5
Costa Rica	26.6	25.9	27.1
El Salvador	13.3	10.8	11.8
Guatemala	15.9	11.5	13.2
Honduras	24.8	17.1	21.0
Nicaragua	16.8	23.1	19.2
CARICOM[a]	26.5	21.2	17.4
Barbados	25.3	15.4	18.3
Guyana	32.8	35.8	29.4
Jamaica	15.9	25.3	20.9
Trinidad and Tobago	30.6	19.4	13.7

a. Also part of CARICOM: Antigua and Barbuda, Belize, Dominica, Grenada, Monserrat, St. Kitts, St. Lucia, and St. Vincent.

Sources: World Bank, *World Tables,* 1993, p. 53; and International Monetary Fund, *International Financial Statistics,* Yearbook 1993.

favor of Mexico has become a major concern among Latin American countries. Some Latin American countries are eager to join an expanding NAFTA to improve their standing in the "investment beauty contest."

But economic integration does not offer a unique magic key for increasing the flow of inward investment. East Asian countries, for example, succeeded in drawing foreign capital without trade agreements. The connection between a hemispheric free trade agreement and attracting substantial investment is that, to achieve either objective, a country must undergo the same reforms.

This lesson has not been ignored. Many Latin American nations have taken great strides unilaterally to improve their local investment climates. In fact, the main drama of the last five years has been the reforms taken by individual countries and subregional groups. As a result, Latin countries have successfully attracted foreign capital on a large scale. Table 4.2 compares portfolio and direct investment inflows for five large Latin countries. Between 1982 and 1992, the five countries received $42

Table 4.2 Direct and portfolio investment inflows for selected Latin American countries, 1982–92
(millions of dollars)

Country	1982	1983	1984	1985	1986	1987	1988	1989	1990	1991	1992	Accumulated 1982–92
Chile												
Direct	426	135	78	64	116	230	141	184	249	563	737	2,923
Portfolio	negl.	negl.	negl.	50	199	701	886	1,408	774	190	412	4,620
Argentina												
Direct	239	185	268	919	574	–19	1,147	1,028	1,836	2,439	4,179	12,795
Portfolio	313	649	372	–617	–542	–572	–718	–1,098	–1,105	6,257	4,821	7,760
Brazil												
Direct	3,105	1,560	1,598	1,348	320	1,225	2,969	1,267	901	972	1,454	16,719
Portfolio	negl.	–278	–268	–234	–451	–428	–498	–391	98	3,808	14,466	15,824
Colombia												
Direct	389	618	584	1,023	674	319	203	576	500	457	790	6,133
Portfolio	–7	–2	–3	–1	30	48	n.a.	179	–4	81	60	381
Venezuela												
Direct	273	86	18	68	16	21	89	213	451	1,916	629	3,780
Portfolio	1,692	208	n.a.	n.a.	n.a.	n.a.	n.a.	–158	15,529	167	15	17,453
Total												
Direct	4,433	2,584	2,546	3,422	1,700	1,776	4,549	3,268	3,937	6,347	7,789	42,351
Portfolio	1,998	577	101	–802	–764	–251	–330	–60	15,292	10,503	19,774	46,038

n.a. = not available.
negl. = negligible.

Source: International Monetary Fund, *Balance of Payments Yearbook*, 1989 (part 2, C-14 and C-15), 1990 (part 2, C-14 and C-15), and 1993 (part 2, C-17 and C-18).

billion of direct investment and $46 billion of portfolio investment. Portfolio inflows soared over the decade, from low levels in the early and mid-1980s to huge amounts in the 1990s. Meanwhile, direct investment to these five countries increased significantly, reaching $7.8 billion in 1992, up from a figure of $1.7 billion in 1986.

Whether rising capital inflows are a mixed blessing depends on the circumstances. Investment that is accompanied by technology transfer and labor training will almost always enhance the long-term growth of a country.[8] On the other hand, inward financial flows that merely compensate for low domestic saving can only act as a short-term fix. Market-oriented policies and macroeconomic stability can improve a country's credit rating and help attract portfolio capital. But in some circumstances, such as Chile and Colombia have discovered, high domestic interest rates designed to slow the pace of inflation have attracted large amounts of "hot" foreign portfolio capital, leading to an appreciation of the exchange rate and a squeeze on nontraditional exports. The benefits of this policy outcome can be questioned (Michaely, Papageorgiou, and Choksi 1991, vol. 7, 277).

In light of the recent reform trend, we project additional inward direct investment flows linked to a hemispheric agreement of $60 billion over the 12 years between 1990 and 2002. We sketch out two scenarios. Under the continuing-reform scenario, inward direct investment will be $5 billion per year higher than otherwise (from a late 1980s base). Under the WHFTA scenario, inward investment will be $10 billion per year higher than otherwise (appendix D).

The additional inflows envisaged under these two scenarios can be compared with actual figures for foreign investment into Latin America. As table 4.2 shows, direct investment in Latin America doubled between 1990 and 1992, from $3.9 billion to $7.8 billion. Over the next several years, with a modest extension of the reforms already implemented, the new, higher level should be maintained. Roughly, this corresponds to our continuing-reform scenario. By contrast, a WHFTA scenario would entail even deeper reforms, accompanied by guaranteed access to the huge North American market. In this circumstance, we project a much larger increment of direct investment inflows, totaling $10 billion annually over 12 years. This projection is not outlandish, since direct investment in Mexico rose from less than $1.0 billion in 1988 to $5.4 billion in 1992.

Latin American Investment Regulations

The areas of greatest concern for foreign investors in Latin America include national treatment, restrictions on the repatriation of capital, res-

---

8. A recent example: Compaq's decision to make personal computers in Brazil. In 1994, Compaq will build a $15 million factory in Brazil employing 400 people (*New York Times*, 23 March 1994, D5).

ervation of certain sectors to nationals (e.g., telecommunications, mining, airlines), performance requirements, and local-content requirements. As in most areas, Chile was the first Latin American country to implement favorable investment reforms. In recent years, aggressive reforms have also been implemented in Argentina, Colombia, and Venezuela.

Chile permits foreign ownership in almost all sectors of its economy. In addition, since the late 1970s, Chile's investment regime has provided almost complete equality of treatment between foreign and domestic investors (USITC 1992, 5–14). However, foreign investors still cannot repatriate their profits before three years, all foreign investment is subject to pro forma screening by the government, and foreign banks and securities companies are not permitted to enter via branch operations (USTR 1993, 45). Foreign loans with less than a one-year duration are subject to a 20 percent reserve requirement (USITC 1992, 5–14).

In 1989, Argentina significantly liberalized its foreign investment regime by abolishing performance requirements, freeing capital movement, and providing national treatment to foreign investors in most instances (USITC 1992, 7–8). In September 1993, Argentina adopted a new decree designed to encourage foreign investment. Based on these reforms, Argentina signed a bilateral investment agreement with the United States in 1993 (approved by the US Senate in November 1993). The accord guarantees national treatment or most-favored nation (MFN) terms, whichever are better; it guarantees the free transfer of capital, profits, and royalties; it abolishes performance requirements; it allows international arbitration; and it guarantees adequate compensation in case of expropriation (*International Trade Reporter*, 1 September 1993, 1464). Argentina still retains restrictions on foreign participation in the broadcasting industry (Price 1994, 75).

In the late 1980s, Andean countries decided to make their investment procedures more flexible. Decision 24, which regulated and restricted foreign investment in the Andean Group, was repealed in April 1991. Even before that landmark change, individual Andean countries had relaxed their restrictions on foreign investment: Ecuador abolished its capital import restrictions in November 1989.[9] Venezuela enacted a more liberal foreign investment code in January 1990. Peru allowed restrictions on profit remittances to expire in August 1990. Colombia allowed foreign firms in some situations to hold more than 49 percent of domestic financial companies. And Bolivia signed commitments for investment insurance with a number of bilateral and multilateral organizations (The Institute of International Finance 1990; Cariaga 1990).

---

9. In addition, Ecuador signed a bilateral investment treaty (BIT) with the United States in 1993. The accord is similar to that between the United States and Argentina. In addition to Ecuador and Argentina, only Jamaica and Panama have such treaties with the United States.

In 1989, Colombia introduced a plan that virtually eliminated all import licensing requirements and foreign investment restrictions (USITC 1992, 6–10; USTR 1992, 56). Colombia has liberalized investment by granting equal treatment to foreign and local investors in most sectors; the main exceptions are petroleum, mining, and finance (USITC 1992, 6–9). There are no limits on equity participation, and no restrictions on remittances (First Boston 1993, 6). However, Colombia's automotive sector continues to be protected by a combination of fees, taxes, import performance requirements and local-content rules.[10] Cooperation agreements between the stock exchanges of Colombia, Paraguay, and Argentina were signed on July 1993. The plan is to coordinate rules covering the securities markets in each country and eventually create a group of Latin American countries with linked stock markets (*International Trade Reporter*, 21 August 1993, 1220).

Venezuela still enforces some local-content requirements (USITC 1992, 6–16; First Boston 1993). However, Venezuela now offers unrestricted capital movements, unlimited profit remittances, and full capital repatriation. Venezuela has partially opened investment access to foreign firms, with notable exceptions in the auto, iron ore, petroleum, banking, and media sectors. In addition, Venezuela retains some restrictions on foreign ownership of equity in Venezuelan companies.

A country that significantly lags its neighbors in introducing investment reforms is Brazil. Constitutional limitations on private-sector participation in certain sectors, statutory limits on profit and capital repatriation, performance requirements, and restricted access to local capital markets are major barriers. Foreign investment is proscribed in the mining and petroleum industries and in telecommunications, the use of price controls is a barrier to foreign investment in some sectors, and investment in many service industries is discouraged by local-content requirements (USITC 1992, 7–16; USTR 1992, 23).

A revision to Brazil's 1988 constitution, designed to remove discriminatory provisions, is scheduled for passage in 1994. This revision is significant because, among a list of 27 countries, Brazil now imposes the most severe restrictions on foreign capital.[11] In November 1993, President Franco made a start by sending Congress a bill to exempt all royalty payments remitted to foreign firms from the financial operations tax. The purpose of this measure is to encourage Brazilian companies to spend more on acquiring patent rights, either from their parent companies abroad or from third parties (*Gazeta Mercantil*, 15 November 1993, 5).

---

10. Colombia and Peru each signed a tax treaty with the United States in 1993 (*International Trade Reporter*, 11 August 1993, 1341).

11. This ranking is based on a Price Waterhouse study cited in the *International Trade Reporter* (17 November 1993, 1945). The study ranked 27 countries in Asia, Europe, and Latin America, focusing on legal and bureaucratic barriers to foreign investment.

Aggressive investment reforms are also needed in other Latin American countries. In Costa Rica, for example, foreign investment is forbidden in newspapers, communications, customs brokerage firms, public utilities, insurance, and some energy sectors. In addition, the government does not allow repatriation of foreign capital for two years after investment (USITC 1992, 8–5).

Impact on the United States

To assess the impact of Western Hemisphere economic integration on the United States, it is first necessary to project future trade between the United States and Latin America (excluding Mexico). We attempt to predict the level of US exports to Latin America and US imports from Latin America in 1997 and 2002, under the two scenarios: the continuing-reform scenario and the WHFTA scenario. We also calculate the impact of the changes in trade levels on US jobs and on the average wage levels associated with jobs dislocated by imports and jobs created by exports (see appendix B for details).

US Export and Import Gains

The base-year level (average 1989–91) of US exports to Latin America was $24 billion. By 2002, US exports to Latin America are projected to reach a level of $70 billion (expressed in 1990 prices) under the continuing-reform scenario and $106 billion under the WHFTA scenario. The WHFTA scenario would thus increase US exports to Latin America in the year 2002 by about $36 billion above the levels that might be reached under the continuing-reform scenario.

On the import side, the base-year level (average 1989–91) of US imports from Latin America was $30 billion. By 2002, US imports from Latin America are projected to reach $65 billion (expressed in 1990 prices) under the continuing-reform scenario and $92 billion under the WHFTA scenario. Thus, the WHFTA scenario entails an annual level of US imports from Latin America in 2002 that is about $28 billion greater than might be reached under the continuing-reform scenario. A WHFTA would enable the United States to reach a merchandise trade surplus with Latin America by the year 2002 that would be about $9 billion higher than under the continuing-reform scenario. In our view, this number represents a responsibly high estimate of the balance of trade impact of a successful Western Hemisphere Free Trade Area.

Job Effects and Wage Levels

Because the US trade balance with Latin America improves in both scenarios, the calculated net impact on US jobs will be positive. The

WHFTA scenario shows a net increase of 60,800 US jobs in the year 2002 by comparison with the continuing-reform scenario.

Within the overall totals, the composition of job effects by worker group is interesting.[12] In the year 2002, the two groups of higher-wage workers are responsible for the positive net effect on total US jobs. Under the WHFTA scenario, for example, 325,000 more net jobs are created in the two higher-wage worker groups by comparison with the continuing-reform scenario. By contrast, in the two lower-wage groups the WHFTA scenario entails the dislocation of 264,000 more US jobs by comparison with the continuing-reform scenario. It must be emphasized that these calculations assume that incremental US imports from Latin America are concentrated in low-wage products and that incremental US exports are proportional to base-level exports.

In net terms, a WHFTA coupled with accelerated reform in Latin America could cause a modest rotation of the US job market in favor of high-skill industries and against low-skill industries. Over the long run, the United States should welcome the implied upgrading in the skill characteristics of the labor market. In the short run, however, the potential dislocation of lower-skilled workers is a political liability, and it would need to be addressed within the broader context of training and relocation programs.

The effect of trade changes under the various scenarios on the wage levels associated with each worker group will be small. Other scholars assert that trade flows played only a minor role in US wage changes over the past decade.[13] Our analysis suggests that the prospective expansion of US trade with Latin America under a WHFTA umbrella will have a similarly modest impact, even if import growth is biased toward low-wage products to a far greater extent than historical experience would predict (appendix B).

Based on our calculations, the impact of different trade scenarios on US wage rates by worker groups is as follows. In the year 2002, wages for the highest-wage group with by far the larger number of employees—63.5 million members, making up more than half the US work force—are calculated to rise under a continuing-reform scenario by 0.52 percent as a result of expanded trade with Latin America. Under the WHFTA scenario, the rise would be 1.03 percent. In terms of weekly

---

12. We divide US workers into four groups according to their median weekly wages. For a median weekly wage between $493 and $451, there are 62.5 million workers; for a median weekly wage between $450 and $422, 10 million workers; for a median weekly wage between $421 and $396, 29.7 million workers; and for a median weekly wage between $395 and $271, 6.7 million workers (US Department of Labor, Bureau of Labor Statistics).

13. For example, Borjas, Freeman, and Katz (1991) argue that only 1.9 percentage points of the 12.4 percent increase in the differential between college graduate and high school graduate wages between 1980 and 1988 can be explained by trade effects.

wages, the difference between the two scenarios (0.51 percent) translates into weekly wage gains of about $2.41, or annual wage gains of about $125, for more than half the US work force. However, the two lowest-wage groups lose ground. The hardest hit is the fourth group, with 6.7 million workers. This group suffers a wage loss of 8.71 percent in the WHFTA scenario, by comparison with a loss of 3.69 percent in the continuing-reform scenario. The additional loss (5.02 percent) translates into $16.70 per week, or about $868 per year, for this 6 percent of the US work force (table B7).

These wage and job calculations can be summarized in the following way. By adopting counterfactual and pessimistic—but not outlandish—assumptions, it is possible to project small job losses and somewhat lower wages for lower skilled US workers as a consequence of expanded trade with Latin America. Net job losses for these workers are not significant relative to the size of the US work force (about 120 million) or the number of US employees dislocated annually for all reasons (nearly 2 million). For the US work force as a whole, expanded trade with Latin America implies slightly more jobs and slightly higher wages.

5

Latin American Reforms and Readiness Indicators

Economic integration has been a theme of Latin American economic policy since the 1960s. Regional economic integration in Latin America began with the formation in 1960 of the Latin American Free Trade Area (LAFTA) between Argentina, Brazil, Chile, Mexico, Paraguay, Peru, and Uruguay. In 1960, Costa Rica, El Salvador, Honduras, Guatemala, and Nicaragua formed the Central American Common Market (CACM). In 1969, the Andean Group was created, comprising Bolivia, Chile (which left in 1976), Colombia, Ecuador, and Peru; Venezuela joined later in 1973. But this first wave of regional arrangements enjoyed none of the success of contemporary efforts in Europe (the European Community and the European Free Trade Association). To understand the failures in Latin America, it is necessary to revisit the 1940s.

At the end of the Second World War, many countries throughout the world feared a return to the dismal conditions of the Great Depression. The common response was a huge dose of state intervention. The British voted out Winston Churchill, electing instead Clement Attlee, with Labor Party promises of nationalized industry and public health care. Germany, France, and Italy likewise enlarged their public sectors. Even under conservative governments, Australia and New Zealand created numerous parastatal corporations and promoted monolithic trade unions. The United States took a more cautious approach, but under Presidents Truman and Eisenhower, the United States expanded its Depression-era programs for agriculture, home mortgages, rural electrification, and social security.

Latin America was both swept along and contributed to these intellectual tides. Most Latin countries extended the reach of their parastatal enterprises to cover electric power, air transportation, telecommunications, steel, petroleum, petrochemicals, and other goods and services. As in Europe, many Latin countries ran large budget deficits and pursued easy money policies. But in the case of Latin America, macroeconomic excesses guaranteed high inflation and permanent balance of payments crises. Finally, there was a specific Latin American contribution to the postwar policy mix: import substitution. While the industrial countries used the umbrella of GATT to reverse their Depression-era tariffs and quotas, Latin America took a very different direction.

In the 1930s, Latin American export earnings were drastically slashed as prices of primary products tumbled in the Great Depression. Export earnings fell faster than import costs, and most countries defaulted on their external debt (Colombia was a notable exception). During the 1940s, Latin American access to foreign manufactured goods was severely restricted because production in the United States and Europe was skewed toward war needs. As a pragmatic response to hard times (the 1930s) and war shortages (the 1940s), most Latin American nations adopted import substitution policies (Balassa et al. 1986, 55).

After the war, under the intellectual stewardship of Raúl Prebisch, import substitution acquired new respectability as a long-term answer to the perceived inequality of economic relations between developing countries on the one hand (including Latin America) and the United States and Europe on the other hand. According to Prebisch's center-periphery thesis, the terms of trade for Latin American countries were destined to deteriorate decade after decade. Ever-worsening terms of trade for Latin America were ordained by a combination of competitive markets and relatively slow demand growth for primary products, contrasted with oligopolistic markets and relatively fast demand growth for manufactured goods. The answer was to make a virtue of import substitution by promoting local production of manufactured goods via protective trade barriers. Not coincidentally, import substitution achieved two important political goals: it generated relatively well-paid manufacturing jobs, and it enriched a new class of rising entrepreneurs.

Initially, when Latin America was producing nondurable consumer goods using labor-intensive techniques, import substitution worked rather well because these industries could thrive with modest levels of protection. Later, as Latin countries attempted to produce a broader range of intermediate goods and capital equipment, the requisite levels of protection, and the ensuing extent of economic inefficiency rose rapidly (Balassa et al. 1986, 55–57). The combination of statist industrial policies, highly expansionary fiscal and monetary policy, and import substitution practically ensured the failure of attempts made in the 1960s to launch Latin American economic integration. Economic integration was simply irreconcilable with the broader direction of economic policy.

By the mid-1960s, two decades of state intervention had created nationalized industries that were overstaffed and inefficient and private companies that enjoyed the comforts of a regulated economy. Parastatal firms and private oligopolists were simply not receptive to the challenges and opportunities that normally result from trade liberalization. Moreover, import substitution was only one element in a broader state effort to promote growth by insulating the economy from market forces. As Enrique Iglesias (1992, 29) explained:

> Almost all of the countries created national planning systems, development financial institutions, national savings and loan systems. . . . This robust institutional development growth was linked to the role the state played in the implementation of the development strategy. . . . A burgeoning, inefficient bureaucracy began to appear, whose job was to impose a series of frequently contradictory regulations aimed at monitoring the level of protectionism and the management of the exchange rates.

Policies of import substitution and state capitalism implied that, in any regional trade arrangement, the partners would be buying from each other at far higher prices than they would pay for the same goods imported from the industrial nations. Customs tariffs that were once collected by the public treasury, and quota rents that were once appropriated by favored local firms, would now be captured by the new regional trading partners. Politically and economically, this was a significant drawback to regional integration, and it meant that each country wanted freer trade with its customers but not with its suppliers. Finally, chronic debtor countries with overvalued currencies were reluctant to liberalize at all, for fear of worsening already bad current account deficits.

Finally, regulation and statism were basically hostile to foreign direct investment. When allowed to operate, foreign multinational enterprises would collect part of the economic rents created by "hothouse" policies, and if allowed to operate freely, foreign multinationals would eventually challenge parastatal enterprises and favor local firms. In an attempt to reconcile the costs and benefits of multinational investment, one regional initiative, the Andean Group, tried to disperse new development projects across the region (Fontaine 1977). In practice, the Andean policy discouraged both foreign and local investors, since the designated locations for investment were seldom the most attractive places to do business.

This thumbnail history illustrates how dramatically conditions in Latin America have changed since the mid-1980s. Parastatal firms have been sold. Inflationary macroeconomic policies have been widely discredited. The doctrine of import substitution has been abandoned. Excessive bureaucracy is being trimmed.

In addition, two major political changes have dramatically altered the trade and investment environment. First, the United States is no longer widely perceived as an economic and political adversary. Indeed, the Enterprise for the Americas Initiative was enthusiastically received in many Latin American capitals.

Second, Latin America has seen the end of most armed conflicts, the general rejection of military officers as political leaders, and a widespread embrace of democracy. These political changes have given new prominence to the economic agenda, and the command-and-control structures that once permeated economic life have been replaced by the greater flexibility of market-oriented arrangements.

From here on, the success of the reform process will largely depend on the ability of individual governments to win public support by ensuring that the process of change is accompanied by social fairness (Iglesias 1994, 498). If reform prevails, both economic policies and political conditions will remain far more favorable to economic integration in the 1990s than they were in the 1960s and the 1970s.

Readiness Indicators

History holds few examples of developed and developing countries successfully entering reciprocal free trade agreements; hence the the North American Free Trade Agreement (NAFTA) sets a notable precedent. Before it could embark on free trade negotiations with the United States and Canada, Mexico had to undergo a rigorous reform and adjustment process to prepare Mexican industries and workers for intense competition with their northern neighbors. And the United States and Canada had to think through the problems of economic integration with a country that has much less-developed social and environmental conditions.

The prospect of Western Hemisphere economic integration poses a similar challenge for the countries of North and South America. Within the Western Hemisphere, language differences are great, and more importantly, income disparities are huge. Large income disparities between North and South America do not foreclose the possibility of future integration, but they greatly complicate the process. Competitiveness in poor countries suffers from weak economic infrastructure, which for some industries may completely offset any cost advantage derived from lower wages. But for other industries, the comparative advantage of low wages may be decisive. Under these circumstances, the result of freer trade can be a dramatic contraction or expansion of certain firms and industries both in the poorer countries and in the richer countries.

Moreover, low income closely correlates with poor social conditions: for example, weak minimum wage legislation, inadequate health and safety rules for the workplace, missing social safety nets (old age, health, and welfare assistance), poor environmental controls, and low educational standards. Yawning differences in social conditions between the United States and Canada on the one hand and Latin America on the other are sure to create political resistance in North America as the process of hemispheric economic integration goes forward. Even with a smaller gap, differing social conditions within Europe led some Northern Europeans to resist the accession of Greece, Portugal, and Spain as members of the European Community in the mid-1980s and reinforced subsequent efforts to craft an EC Social Charter to even up work conditions throughout Europe.

In short, when income disparities and social conditions between trade partners are great, the trauma of economic integration is bound to be large. The economic playing field looks distinctly slanted, and for different reasons each country feels threatened by the economic standing of its partner.

In Europe, pronounced social disparities between members of the European Union are to some extent addressed through fiscal transfers from richer partners to poorer partners—sometimes as high as 3 percent of the receiving nation's GDP (*Official Journal of the European Communities*, December 1991).[1] These transfers are part of the glue of the expanding Union, since they go hand-in-hand with an upgrading of economic infrastructure in the poorer member states, and they implicitly provide a quid pro quo for the ceding of sovereignty over trade and monetary policy to supraregional bodies.[2]

However, the situation in the Western Hemisphere is not closely analogous to that of Europe. Integration between North and South America is likely to proceed much more slowly and is unlikely to include large-scale financial assistance programs to bridge the social disparities. To be sure, the Inter-American Development Bank (IDB) and the World Bank will continue to contribute importantly to economic development in the South, providing official finance of at least 1 percent of Central and South American GNP annually (table 5.1).[3] As in the case of NAFTA,

---

1. At various stages in EC history, the Common Agricultural Policy (CAP) has also acted as a fiscal transfer mechanism, redistributing income from richer urban areas to poorer rural areas.

2. This rationale was evident in the positive vote on the Maastricht Treaty in the Irish referendum held in June 1992. Ireland, along with Greece, Spain, and Portugal, have all received massive regional development funds, particularly for infrastructure investments, since their accession to the Community (these countries also benefit from high prices under the Common Agricultural Policy, or CAP). Similarly, when the German Democratic Republic was reunited with the Federal Republic, the Federal Republic committed huge amounts of money to a broad reconstruction program (DM170 billion in 1991 and DM218 billion in 1992), and the agrarian districts of the former German Democratic Republic will certainly benefit from the CAP.

3. In 1992, Central and South America's GNP was 916.5 billion. Official development finance from bilateral and multilateral sources amounted to 10.2 billion (OECD 1992, 42; World Bank, *World Debt Tables*, 1993–94).

Table 5.1 Public and private resource flows to Central and South America, net of principal repayments, 1985–92ᵃ (annual averages)

Year	Official development financeᵇ	Official export credits	Private flows FDIᶜ	Private flows Bank lending	Private flows Other	Private flows Total	Total	GNP (Central and South America, billions of dollars)
1985–87								
Billions of dollars	9.2	1.2	6.6	3.8	-1.3	9.1	19.6	
Share of total flows	46.9	6.1	33.7	19.4	-6.6	46.4	100.0	
Share of GNP	1.8	0.2	1.3	0.8	-0.3	1.8	3.9	504.7
1988								
Billions of dollars	8.2	1.3	9.7	1.5	0.1	11.3	20.8	
Share of total flows	39.4	6.3	46.6	7.2	0.5	54.3	100.0	
Share of GNP	1.4	0.2	1.6	0.3	0.0	1.9	3.5	590.8
1989								
Billions of dollars	8.2	2.0	9.7	6.0	-0.6	15.1	25.3	
Share of total flows	32.4	7.9	38.3	23.7	-2.4	59.7	100.0	
Share of GNP	1.2	0.3	1.4	0.9	-0.1	2.3	3.8	669.1
1990								
Billions of dollars	13.4	1.3	8.8	-7.7	6.9	8.0	22.7	
Share of total flows	59.0	5.7	38.8	-33.9	30.4	35.2	100.0	
Share of GNP	1.8	0.2	1.2	-1.0	0.9	1.1	3.0	760.6
1991								
Billions of dollars	10.8	1.6	12.0	-2.0	7.9	17.9	30.3	
Share of total flows	35.6	5.3	39.6	-6.6	26.1	59.1	100.0	
Share of GNP	1.4	0.2	1.5	-0.3	1.0	2.3	3.8	787.2
1992ᵈ								
Billions of dollars	10.2	3.8	13.4	11.0	13.2	37.6	51.6	
Share of total flows	19.8	7.4	26.0	21.3	25.6	72.9	100.0	
Share of GNP	1.2	0.4	1.6	1.3	1.6	4.4	6.1	849.6

a. These figures are "net" in terms of new extensions of credit and repayments of principal. They do not reflect interest payments.
b. Official development finance (ODF) comprises flows from official bilateral and multilateral institutions, including official development assistance and other less concessional or nonconcessional flows (including World Bank and the Inter-American Development Bank).
c. Direct investment from OECD countries.
d. Preliminary.

Source: OECD, Financing and External Debt of Developing Countries, 1992 Survey, p. 42, 1993.

the IDB may administer special regional funds for environmental projects. But in the foreseeable future, as in the past, at least half of financial resources flowing to Latin America will arrive as private rather than public investment.

Even with large-scale inflows of public and private capital, accounting for 3 to 4 percent of Latin American GDP annually, it will take decades before income disparities are significantly narrowed within the hemisphere. Hence, it is doubly important that the Western Hemisphere partners become compatible in other dimensions of their economic and political life before North-South integration proceeds.

There is no simple test that indicates when a country is ready to pursue closer economic integration with its neighbors. Strong trade and investment linkages provide the obvious starting point. Trade and investment interdependence determine a "natural region" for integration efforts and establish the raison d'être for the negotiations—that is, to expand access in the known markets of the partner country and to boost investment.[4] These linkages were detailed in chapter 3. Our analysis indicated that the prerequisite trade and investment linkages exist for integration efforts within subregions of Latin America and, to a lesser extent, for integration of the Western Hemisphere as a whole.

In addition, much depends on the political will to accept the "creative destruction" of local industries and jobs, the sort of destruction that Schumpeter (1942) identified as the lifeblood of a capitalist economy. Each country has a different threshold of economic pain and different means of sharing that pain across social groups. Those thresholds and mechanisms will inevitably govern the inauguration and the pace of economic integration.

The postwar experience of integration episodes yields some useful guideposts with regard to economic and political conditions in the prospective partner countries. This history suggests certain indicators of readiness for economic integration. Macroeconomic indicators include price stability, budget deficits, external debt, and exchange rate variability. Microeconomic indicators include market-oriented policies and fiscal reliance on trade taxes. The final indicator is the presence of a functioning democracy. While necessarily qualitative, this attribute is becoming increasingly important.

The NAFTA debate points to collateral issues that will feature prominently in assessments of readiness. Different levels of development between the integrating countries usually imply differing environmental and labor laws and differing degrees of enforcement of these laws (see the section in chapter 7 on environment, labor, and human rights). A

---

4. The clearest examples of this point are in North America, where both Canada and Mexico rely on the US market for the preponderant share of their trade and draw on US firms and banks for most of their inward foreign investment (tables 3.5 and 3.8).

clear shift toward stronger laws and enforcement on the part of the poorer countries will increase their readiness as perceived by the richer partners. While we do not include these issues in our readiness indicators, we are aware that they will play an important role in determining a country's readiness.

Readiness Indicator Scales

We rely on the data given in tables 5.2 through 5.11 (see end of chapter pp. 80–96), and on our impressions of the political economy in each country, to scale the countries within each subregional group according to their readiness for economic integration. Generally, we use three-year averages of numerical data (usually 1990, 1991, and 1992) to evaluate readiness. Some countries demonstrated dramatic improvement in 1992 or 1993, but their indicators are burdened by poor performance in 1990 and 1991. Recent progress, if sustained, could significantly improve their readiness indicator scores when recalculated using data for 1991, 1992, and 1993.

The seven indicators are price stability, budget discipline, external debt, currency stability, market-oriented policies, reliance on trade taxes, and functioning democracy.

For the price stability indicator, a score of 5 was awarded to countries that maintained average inflation rates between zero and 5 percent over the three-year evaluation period (table 5.2). Other scores were awarded as follows: a score of 4 for inflation between 5 and 20 percent, a score of 3 for 20–50 percent, a score of 2 for 50–100 percent, a score of 1 for 100–200 percent, and a score of zero for inflation greater than 200 percent.

Budget discipline was evaluated in terms of the public deficit (or surplus) as a percentage of GDP (table 5.4). A score of 5 for the public deficit ratio was awarded to countries with a 1990–92 average deficit of less than 2.5 percent of GDP or a surplus. A score of 4 was awarded for a deficit of 2.5–4 percent, a score of 3 for a deficit of 4–6 percent, a score of 2 for a deficit of 6–8 percent, a score of 1 for a deficit of 8–10 percent, and a score of zero for a deficit greater than 10 percent.

The total external debt (public and private) was assessed as a percentage of exports of goods and services (table 5.6). A score of 5 was awarded if external debt in 1992 (or the most recent year) was below 150 percent of total exports of goods and services. A score of 4 was awarded for a debt ratio between 150 and 220 percent, a score of 3 for a 220–290 percent debt ratio, a score of 2 for a 290–360 percent debt ratio, a score of 1 for a 360–430 percent debt ratio, and a score of 0 for a debt ratio greater than 430 percent.

For currency stability, our focus is on real exchange rates (table 5.10). High variability in a country's real exchange rate rapidly changes the competitive position of the traded goods sector, alternately creating conditions of boom and bust. For each nation, we calculated the standard deviation of the real exchange rate index over 1990–92. Using this measure of variability, real exchange rate fluctuations of less than 10 percent were scored a 5, fluctuations of 10–30 percent were scored 3, and fluctuations greater than 30 percent were scored 0.

Scoring the extent of market-oriented policies requires a far more qualitative approach. This indicator seeks to measure the extent to which countries have privatized and deregulated. Scores of 5 were assigned to both Canada and the United States, both long-established practitioners of market-oriented economic policies. In Latin America, it is hard to measure in absolute terms whether one economy is more or less market-oriented than another. Instead the scores for Latin countries reflect reports of recent privatization, deregulation, and liberalization efforts. Each country's overall score for market-oriented policies represents an average of three judgmental scores for privatization, deregulation, and tariff reform.[5]

Countries were divided into three categories according to their privatization efforts: the best were countries with operational privatization programs, next best were countries with plans that are not yet implemented, and the poorest were countries with no plans. Likewise, countries received high scores for deregulation if they had, or were starting to undertake, measures to loosen restrictions. Those with no reported deregulation measures received low scores. Most of the larger Latin American countries have initiated tariff reforms since the mid-1980s. Countries that have made efforts to reduce their peak and average tariff rates received higher scores.

The fifth readiness indicator measures each country's reliance on trade taxes (table 5.11). To receive a score of 5, a country has to derive less than 5 percent of its public revenue from taxes on international trade on a three-year average (1989–91). Reliance of 5 to 10 percent merits a score of 4; 10–15 percent, a score of 3; 15–20 percent, a score of 2; 20–25 percent, a score of 1; and greater than 25 percent, a score of 0.

The last readiness indicator, functioning democracy, again requires a highly subjective judgment. Broadly speaking, a functioning democracy should observe two principles: majority rule and minority rights. Elections should obviously reflect the will of the majority; hard evidence of the majority rule principle comes when opposition parties win an open election. A peaceful transition of power, without the military involvement or sporadic coups that have long plagued Latin America, demonstrates majority rule at work. The minority rights principle is observed

---

5. Information on privatization was taken from the *Financial Times* and the *Journal of Commerce*; data on deregulation were taken mainly from Williamson (1990 and 1994); and data on tariff reforms were based on CEPAL (1992a), USTR (1992 and 1993), IDB (1992, 248), and USITC (1992).

when ethnic minorities and those in the political opposition can participate both in public life and the private economy without persecution. To
assess the degree to which governments in Latin America respect these
principles, we used the 1994 Freedom House rankings (Karatnycky and
Ryan 1994) of civil and political rights in Latin American countries
in recent years. We converted the average Freedom House values
(rounded to the nearest whole digit) to our own 0 to 5 scale. The worst
score on the Freedom House scale, a 7, corresponds to a 0 in our scale, a
6 corresponds to a 1, a 5 corresponds to a 2, both a 4 and a 3 correspond
to a 3, both a 2 and a 2.5 correspond to a 4, and the best score on their
scale, a 1, corresponds to a 5 in our scale.

Macroeconomic Stability

Above all, a country must put its economic house in order. Trade and
investment reforms will not take root in a climate of fiscal and monetary
excess. Volatile and high inflation, hemorrhaging budget deficits, and
wildly fluctuating exchange rates are incompatible with any sustained
program of international economic liberalization.[6]

What this suggests is that economic integration requires participating
countries to achieve a minimum degree of discipline over their macroeconomic policies. In Europe, the ambitious goal of economic and monetary union led to agreement on formal criteria for the convergence of
macroeconomic policies in the Maastricht Treaty in December 1991. The
formal criteria address price stability, the convergence of long-term
interest rates, budgetary discipline, and exchange rate stability. But the
Maastricht criteria were long ago preceded by the informal convergence
of member-state monetary policies, beginning in the 1960s.

Monetary union is clearly a remote aspect of Western Hemisphere economic integration. Monetary union requires a higher degree of economic
convergence than free trade and investment; nonetheless, free trade and
investment do require some degree of macroeconomic convergence, and
the Maastricht criteria have considerable relevance for the ambitious integration elements among the Western Hemisphere nations.

First Indicator: Price Stability

Experience teaches that high average inflation rates, year-to-year, are also
highly variable rates, year-to-year. Highly variable inflation wrenches and
twists the economy; not all prices and wages rise at the same fast but
changing rate. In particular, with high and variable inflation, enormous

---

6. Reinforcing the findings of the World Bank studies (Michaely, Papageorgiou, and
Choksi 1991, vol. 7), Rodrik (1992, 39) concludes that ''nothing will help sustain open
trade policies more than a stable macroeconomic environment.''

shifts in the real exchange rate are bound to occur, which alternately expose the traded goods sector to mania and depression. Moreover, when inflation exceeds 20 percent, real interest rates will be highly variable, prompting large swings of portfolio capital. This is another reason that real exchange rates will be subject to episodes of acute overvaluation and undervaluation.[7]

In manic episodes, when the domestic currency is undervalued, partner countries will usually complain about unfair trade subsidized by a cheap exchange rate; in depressive moods, when the domestic currency is overvalued, home-country industries will certainly seek and often obtain protection against imports.

This was the experience of the United States in the first half of the 1980s, when a rapid fall in inflation and a superstrong dollar led to a wave of protection in automobiles, steel, and other products. It is a recurring experience in Latin America. The data in tables 5.2, 5.9, and 5.10 document the roller coaster movement of Latin American consumer prices and exchange rates over the last decade. Inflation often proceeded at very different rates than nominal exchange rate devaluation. For example, even in relatively stable Chile, inflation in 1990 and 1991 exceeded 20 percent per annum, whereas the peso depreciated by less than 15 percent per annum against the dollar. The result was to put a significant price-cost squeeze on Chilean producers of tradeable goods.

It would seem that inflation rates much above 20 percent per annum call into question sustained progress on trade and capital liberalization. The inflation target espoused and achieved by Mexico and Chile—single-digit inflation—commends itself to other Latin American countries.[8]

Second Indicator: Budget Discipline

Large public deficits are hostile to economic integration for two main reasons.[9] First, in the face of large budget deficits, governments often

---

7. A chi square test indicates a statistically significant correspondence, at a 95 percent confidence level, between higher inflation rates and larger absolute changes in the real effective exchange rate. At the extreme, in 8 out of 16 country-years when individual Latin American countries experienced absolute real effective exchange rate changes in excess of 20 percent, they also experienced inflation rates of more than 100 percent (Hufbauer and Schott 1994). Despite dizzying inflation, Brazil kept its exchange rate depreciation moving more or less in accord with escalating domestic prices during most of the 1980s and early 1990s. However, like other currencies with high inflation, the Brazilian cruzeiro was subject both to overvaluation and undervaluation.

8. In 1993, Mexico achieved the single-digit goal with a 9.7 percent inflation, and Chile reached a 12.6 percent rate, both measured by the CPI.

9. In a monetary union, excessive public deficits by one country (e.g., Germany in 1991 and 1992) can push up real interest rates paid by all members (e.g., the rest of Europe),

put pressure on the central bank to purchase government debt and thus to expand the monetary base, with inevitable inflationary consequences. Table 5.3 gives a matrix of annual budget deficits and inflation rates for Latin American countries during the 1980s. The chi square test indicates a highly significant association between the two variables, at a confidence level of 99.9 percent. Budget deficits in excess of 5 percent of GDP are a root cause of devastating inflation in Latin America. In 32 out of 62 country-year episodes of inflation greater than 50 percent, budget deficits exceeded 5 percent of GDP.

The second reason that large public deficits are troublesome is that they tend to enlarge the current account deficit. To be sure, other components of the national saving-investment balance can offset the impact of budget deficits on the current account position. Other things being equal, however, a growing public deficit tends to soak up goods and services, thereby enlarging the trade deficit. A string of current account deficits in turn worsens the external debt position of the country, and as part of the inevitable economic correction, the country may impose controls on imports and impede the free flow of capital.

Based on a statistical analysis of the data in tables 5.4 and 5.5, the association between current account balance and fiscal stance is fairly robust for the smaller and traditionally more open Latin American countries. These countries on average experience about $0.69 of current account improvement for each $1.00 reduction in the fiscal deficit (and vice versa).[10] By contrast, for the large Latin American countries (Mexico, Brazil, Chile, Argentina, Colombia, and Venezuela), there was practically no statistical correspondence between the fiscal stance and the current account deficit in the 1980s. The most likely explanation is that trade and capital controls were generally so tight that an upward shift in the fiscal deficit either ''crowded out'' private investment (through punitive interest rates) or ''crowded in'' private saving (through unexpected inflation)[11] and that the converse was true for a downward shift in the fiscal deficit. As the large Latin American countries adopt more open trade and investment policies, they, too, can expect that changes in the fiscal stance will, to a greater extent, produce counterpart changes in the current account.

---

possibly visiting them with economic stagnation. In the Western Hemisphere, however, this sort of transmission effect is likely to be small simply because monetary union and even exchange rate targets are many years away.

10. Although the R^2 is low (0.27), implying that less than a third of the variation in the current account is explained by changes in the fiscal deficit, the standard error of the estimated coefficient linking the budget swings and current account changes is small (Hufbauer and Schott 1994).

11. By suddenly raising consumer prices, unexpected inflation can cut real wages and increase profits and thereby add to businesses' savings.

Because of the adverse links between public deficits, inflation, and current account balances, Western Hemisphere countries should consider a commitment to limit their own central government deficits. Budget deficits in excess of 5 percent of GDP would appear to put countries in a danger zone.

In Latin America, a general tendency toward declining budget deficits is evident and welcome. Some Latin countries are paragons of fiscal virtue. From 1987 to 1992, Chile ran budget surpluses, Mexico improved its budget deficit from negative 14.2 percent to positive 2.7 percent, Argentina improved from negative 5.7 percent to negative 0.3 percent, Ecuador improved from negative 6.2 percent to negative 0.5 percent, and Colombia kept its budget deficit at less than negative 2.0 percent.[12] Notable exceptions are a few high-deficit countries such as Brazil, Nicaragua, Guyana, and Surinam (table 5.4).

Third Indicator: External Debt

In the Latin America context, early warning signs of excessive debt are the ratio of external debt (both public and private) to GDP and the ratio of external debt service payments to total exports. By these tests, in most Latin countries external debt is much less troublesome now than it was in 1987 (tables 5.6 and 5.8). However, private investors still attach high risk premiums to most of Latin American debt issues (table 5.7; Cline 1994). While it is clear that there was significant progress in 1987–92, it is not clear that the debt crisis is over. A prolonged recession or sustained high interest rates could reverse this trend. Furthermore, in Brazil sustained improvement in the external debt position will depend on a resolution of severe domestic economic conflicts (Cline 1994).

Fourth Indicator: Exchange Rate Stability

Tight limits on exchange rate movements would be infeasible and inappropriate in the Western Hemisphere context. Exchange rate stability is infeasible because price stability has not been attained even in the pioneer reform countries, Mexico and Chile. Moreover, exchange rate stability is inappropriate because the underlying networks of goods and services trade are not nearly so dense and the movement of capital and labor are not nearly so free within the Western Hemisphere as they are within Western Europe. For the foreseeable future, nominal and real exchange rate changes will remain an essential adjustment mechanism (tables 5.9 and 5.10).

---

12. In some cases, improved fiscal performance resulted in part from the extensive privatization of state-owned enterprises. Mexican privatization, which yielded over $22 billion in revenues, is well known, but not isolated.

Nevertheless, some limits on the extent of exchange rate variability should be considered. Dramatic exchange rate devaluation can worsen an already bad rate of inflation, and in the short run severe devaluation can make a country supercompetitive, to the annoyance of its trading partners. Many Latin countries, such as Mexico, Chile, and Brazil, have addressed these problems by adopting a crawling peg for their exchange rates, where the rate of crawl is periodically modified to reflect past and anticipated rates of inflation.[13] Within the context of Western Hemisphere arrangements, we think that countries should first concentrate on achieving single-digit inflation and the rely on crawling pegs for exchange rate adjustment.

Fifth Indicator: Market-Oriented Policies

The core microeconomic precondition for economic integration is a willingness to accept the tenets of a market economy and to reject the teachings of statism. Possibly the most important effect of lowered trade barriers and relaxed restrictions on inward investment is to enlarge the number of firms in each market niche, thereby driving down profit margins and putting competitive pressure on domestic industry to cut costs and innovate. Such pressure is stoutly resisted both by state-run firms and by highly regulated industries, which are usually the victim of two forces.

First, employees and managers come to think of themselves as tenured workers. In turn, this makes it necessary to maintain output, even when the goods or services are rejected by the market, and it makes it hard to introduce efficiencies that entail staff layoffs. Second, cozy relations often develop with domestic supplying industries, and these relations virtually equate to buy-national preferences. When a large part of industry operates under state control, free trade is at best a nuisance. Neither on the production side nor on the purchasing side do state enterprises or highly regulated firms wish to respond to market signals, and their first line of defense is to block those signals by undermining trade agreements.

In recent years, most Latin nations have turned away from statist policies; in some cases the reform has matched the achievements of Eastern Europe. Chile and Mexico are notable for the wholesale disposal of state-run enterprises and the deregulation of other industries. More recently, Argentina, Colombia, and Venezuela have all embarked on extensive privatization campaigns. Privatization plans in Brazil, on the other hand, have not been very successful (First Boston 1993, 8).

---

13. Argentina has gone one step further and pegged its currency to the dollar. Note, however, that the fixed rate for the peso has contributed to increased trade friction with its main trading partner, Brazil. It remains to be seen whether this bold experiment succeeds.

This wave of privatization and deregulation has decisively closed the policy gap between Latin America on the one hand and the United States and Canada on the other. Pockets of statism and regulated industry exist in every country. But once major strides in a market-oriented direction have been taken, the remaining areas of regulation and state ownership can become appropriate subjects of international negotiation. This is true, for example, of trucking regulations in the United States and Mexico, the extent to which energy remains a public preserve in Mexico and Venezuela, and the conditions of access to and investment in financial services and telecommunications industries throughout the hemisphere.

Sixth Indicator: Reduced Reliance on Trade Taxes

Countries need to rationalize their fiscal structure so that trade liberalization can be accommodated without disrupting macroeconomic stability.[14] When import tariffs and export taxes form a large part of government revenues, say 15 percent or more, it will be difficult for governments to accept the phaseout of these charges. Thus, another indicator of readiness to engage in integration efforts is the willingness of the government to look to other revenue sources besides duties on international transactions.

Until the late 1980s, most Latin American countries relied on trade taxes for 15 percent or more of their revenue. Brazil and Chile were among the few exceptions. In the past few years, many countries have reduced their reliance on trade taxes, but most still need a greater degree of unilateral tariff reduction before they can accept the fiscal consequences of economic integration (table 5.11).

Seventh Indicator: Functioning Democracy

To build a successful WHFTA, governments must be able to implement and then sustain a program of trade and investment reforms. This involves a two-stage process: first, to gain adequate domestic support to spark the reform program and then to manage the political difficulties that inevitably arise from the resulting redistribution of income within the country. Political stability and political pluralism are both key ingredients in sustaining trade reforms.

In some instances, political change may be necessary in the initial phase to alter the status quo and create a window of opportunity for dramatic economic reform. In 4 of the 15 cases of sustained liberalization

---

14. Reduction of international trade taxes can raise the more fundamental issue of basic tax reform. Many developing countries are burdened by inefficient and regressive tax systems; integration may yield an important benefit by spurring national efforts to rethink the fiscal structure.

documented by the World Bank, the reform programs followed a change in regime (Michaely, Papageorgiou, and Choksi 1991, vol. 7). But continuous political instability can be a leading indicator of erratic economic policies. Erratic economic policies in turn discourage investment and inhibit growth, making it more difficult to inaugurate a policy of trade and investment reform.

The sustainability of trade reforms is a separate and usually more difficult problem than the initial inauguration. Trade liberalization often increases the income gap between rich and poor. Reforms can shift a larger share of income to capital, making capital assets more valuable and thus enriching the wealthy elite and perhaps (with the sale of public enterprises) furthering the concentration of asset holdings among a few large groups. At the same time, reforms will often create new employment opportunities for high-skilled workers, bidding up their wages. Meanwhile, the ranks of low-skilled workers may be swollen by migration from rural to urban sectors, thus dampening wage gains at the low end of the wage scale. This last tendency is particularly pronounced when trade reform liberalizes an agricultural sector that had long enjoyed protection from world markets.[15]

Trade liberalization thus poses a stark political challenge to government leaders. If trade and investment reforms are to be sustained, government needs to balance the business demands for stable policies with the public demands for more equitable income distribution.

What type of regime is best suited to manage this tightrope act? The World Bank study of liberalization episodes in the postwar era gives an ambiguous answer for the launching of reforms. Chile, Korea, and Taiwan, for example, all embarked on the path of economic reform while military or authoritarian governments were in power. But the World Bank study shows that successful episodes *that were sustained over time* have been associated with complementary political reforms. Among the 15 countries that experienced sustained or partially sustained liberalization episodes, a large majority started with authoritarian regimes, but almost all subsequently adopted democratic reforms. In short, economic liberalization breeds political pluralism. Among the Latin American countries, every successful episode studied by the Bank (Chile, Colombia, Uruguay) eventually produced democratic elections, although political reform lagged economic liberalization by several years.

Mexico was not included in the World Bank study, but interestingly, Mexico seems to fit the study's success profile. Mexican politics have

---

15. On 31 December 1993, an insurrection claimed four municipalities in the State of Chiapas (San Cristobal, Ocosingo, Las Margaritas, and Altamiro). This region has traditionally been one of the poorest of the country. While the insurrection essentially represents a protest against concentrated land ownership, extensive political corruption, and limited public spending on roads and other infrastructure, it also posts a warning against the possible adverse effects of NAFTA on the impoverished rural economy.

long been dominated by a single party, the PRI; only in recent years have the opposition parties effectively engaged in competitive elections. Since the economic reform program gained momentum in the late 1980s, the PRI has negotiated extensive electoral reforms with the main opposition parties and has even conceded questionable elections to opposition candidates. While democratic traditions are not strong or deep in Mexico, they seem to be taking root.[16]

In sum, the readiness of a country to engage in Western Hemisphere free trade talks will depend importantly on the degree to which it has developed a stable and pluralistic political regime. Autocratic regimes may be well-suited to force the inauguration of trade reforms, but a democratic regime seems better able to manage the political differences that inevitably arise from the resulting redistribution of income and dislocation of industries within the country and thus to sustain those reforms over time. Moreover, democratic regimes are inherently more appealing to the United States and Canada, and increasingly to all members of the Organization of American States. The Clinton administration has explicitly stated that respect for democracy will be an important factor in the US decision to open negotiations with a prospective partner.

A democratic regime is important for another reason. Economic integration in the Western Hemisphere will necessarily be based on a commitment to a body of rules and to the protection of property rights. As Stephan Haggard notes, ''The absence of law and clearly enforced property rights reduces predictability, increases transactions costs, and negatively affects the propensity of firms and individuals to take risks regardless of the nature of the economic system'' (Haggard 1992, 50). Each participant in a prospective hemispheric trade pact will thus need to ensure that its administrative and legal systems can extend the rights and benefits of the agreement to other countries and offer protection of those rights in its own territory.

---

16. The August 1994 presidential election will be a good test of this thesis.

Table 5.2 Consumer prices, 1981–92 (percentage increase)

Country	1981	1982	1983	1984	1985	1986	1987	1988	1989	1990	1991	1992	1990–92 average	Price stability score
North America														
United States	13.5	10.3	6.2	3.2	4.3	3.6	1.9	3.7	4.8	5.4	4.2	3.0	4.2	5
Canada	10.2	12.5	10.8	5.8	4.3	4.0	4.2	4.4	5.0	4.8	5.6	1.5	4.0	5
Mexico	27.9	58.9	101.6	65.5	57.7	86.2	131.8	114.2	20.0	26.7	22.7	15.5	21.6	3
Chile	19.7	9.9	28.0	20.3	29.9	19.0	20.2	14.7	17.1	26.0	21.8	15.4	21.1	3
Mercosur														
Argentina	104.0	165.2	345.0	627.5	672.2	90.1	131.3	343.0	3,079.2	2,314.0	172.8	23.0	836.6	0
Brazil	106.0	97.6	142.0	196.7	226.9	145.3	229.7	682.3	1,287.0	2,938.0	440.8	1,000.0	1,459.6	0
Paraguay	13.9	6.8	13.5	20.3	25.2	31.7	21.9	22.7	26.2	38.2	24.3	15.1	25.9	3
Uruguay	34.1	19.0	48.0	56.8	72.4	76.0	64.2	61.9	80.3	112.6	102.0	68.5	94.4	2
Andean Group														
Bolivia	29.0	132.6	200.0	1,300.0	11,804.8	276.4	14.6	16.0	15.2	17.1	21.4	12.1	16.9	4
Colombia	27.5	24.5	19.8	16.1	24.0	18.9	23.3	28.1	25.8	29.1	30.4	27.0	28.8	3
Ecuador	16.4	16.3	48.4	31.3	28.0	23.0	29.5	58.3	75.6	48.5	48.7	54.6	50.6	2
Peru	75.4	64.4	111.2	110.2	163.4	77.9	85.8	667.1	3,398.7	7,482.6	409.5	73.5	2,655.2	0
Venezuela	16.2	9.6	6.2	12.2	11.4	11.5	28.2	29.5	84.3	40.8	34.2	31.4	35.5	3
CACM														
Costa Rica	37.1	90.1	32.6	12.0	15.1	11.8	16.9	20.8	16.5	19.0	28.7	21.8	23.2	3
El Salvador	14.8	11.7	13.3	11.5	22.4	31.9	24.9	19.8	17.6	24.0	14.4	11.3	16.6	4
Guatemala	11.4	0.3	4.6	3.4	18.6	36.9	12.3	10.9	11.4	41.2	33.2	10.1	28.2	3
Honduras	9.4	9.0	7.8	4.7	3.4	4.4	2.4	4.6	9.8	23.3	33.9	8.8	22.0	3
Nicaragua	23.9	24.8	31.1	35.4	219.5	681.5	911.9	14,295.3	4,770.4	7,485.2	2,742.3	20.0	3,415.8	0
Panama[a]	7.3	4.2	2.1	1.6	1.0	-0.1	1.0	0.0	0.0	1.0	1.0	1.9	1.3	5

CARICOMᵇ													
Bahamas	11.1	6.0	4.0	4.0	4.6	5.4	5.8	4.4	5.4	4.6	7.1	5.7	5.8	4
Barbados	14.6	10.3	5.1	4.7	3.4	1.3	3.4	4.9	6.2	3.1	6.2	6.0	5.1	4
Guyana	24.7	20.3	14.9	25.2	15.0	7.9	28.7	39.9	90.0	65.0	80.0	26.3	57.1	3
Jamaica	12.7	6.6	11.6	27.8	25.7	15.1	6.6	8.3	14.3	22.0	51.1	77.3	50.1	3
Trinidad and Tobago	14.3	11.5	15.2	13.3	7.6	7.7	10.8	1.7	11.4	11.0	3.0	6.5	6.8	4
Other Latin America														
Dominican Republic	7.5	7.6	4.8	27.1	37.6	9.7	16.0	44.4	45.4	59.4	53.9	5.0	39.4	3
Haiti	10.9	7.4	10.3	6.5	10.6	3.3	−11.4	4.0	6.9	21.5	15.4	20.1	19.0	4
Surinam	8.7	7.3	4.4	3.7	11.3	17.9	53.3	7.3	0.8	21.7	26.0	43.7	30.5	3

a. Panama is an active member of the CACM but has not yet fully joined in plans for regional economic integration.
b. Also part of CARICOM: Antigua and Barbuda, Belize, Dominica, Grenada, Monserrat, St. Kitts, St. Lucia, and St. Vincent.

Sources: Inter-American Development Bank, *Economic and Social Progress in Latin America: 1993 Report*, October 1993, table F-2; and International Monetary Fund, *International Financial Statistics*, October 1993, p. 59.

Table 5.3   Latin America: range of budget deficits by annual inflation rate ranges, 1981–90[a] (number of cases)

Public fiscal stance	0–10 percent	10–20 percent	20–50 percent	50–100 percent	>100 percent	Total
Surplus to −2.5 percent	22	26	31	8	4	91
−2.5 to −5.0 percent	15	18	11	8	10	62
−5.0 to −7.5 percent	19	2	5	2	6	34
−7.5 to −10.0 percent	3	6	1	2	3	15
Greater than −10 percent	6	11	8	5	14	44
Total	65	63	56	25	37	246

a. Numbers in the grid are country year observations. For example, in the cell corresponding to an inflation rate of 10 to 20 percent and a government budget deficit of 2.5 to 5 percent, there were 18 cases of Latin American countries having this combination of annual inflation and a public budget deficit during 1981–90.

Chi square test: there is a significant association between the fiscal stance and the annual inflation rate at the 99.9 percent confidence level.

Table 5.4 Consolidated surplus or deficit of central government budgets, 1981–92[a] (percentage of GDP)

Country	1981	1982	1983	1984	1985	1986	1987	1988	1989	1990	1991	1992	Average 1990–92	Budget discipline score
North America														
United States	-2.7	-4.1	-6.2	-4.9	-5.4	-5.0	-3.3	-3.2	-2.8	-4.0	-4.8	-5.7	-4.9	3
Canada	-1.5	-5.9	-6.9	-6.5	-6.8	-5.4	-3.8	-2.5	-3.0	-4.1	-6.1	-6.4	-5.5	3
Mexico	-6.7	-15.4	-8.2	-7.2	-7.6	-13.0	-14.2	-9.6	-5.0	-2.8	3.3	4.5	1.7	5
Chile	3.1	-2.6	-3.7	-2.9	-1.8	-0.5	2.4	3.7	5.2	1.4	1.6	2.7	1.9	5
Mercosur														
Argentina	-9.1	-7.5	-10.1	-5.7	-3.1	-3.2	-5.7	-4.0	-2.7	-1.4	-1.1	-0.3	-0.9	5
Brazil	-2.4	-2.6	-4.3	-5.0	-11.1	-13.3	-11.2	-21.5	-24.9	-14.3	n.a.	n.a.	-20.2[e]	0
Paraguay	-2.8	-1.5	-2.6	-2.9	-2.3	0.0	0.4	0.6	2.4	3.2	-0.2	-1.0	0.7	5
Uruguay	-0.1	-8.7	-4.2	-5.8	-3.1	-1.3	-1.3	-2.0	-3.4	-0.1	0.4	0.3	0.2	5
Andean Group														
Bolivia[b]	-6.7	-13.7	-17.0	-19.1	-9.7	-1.7	-3.9	-4.7	-1.8	-1.2	0.6	-1.0	-0.5	5
Colombia	-1.2	-2.0	-1.0	-4.3	-2.7	-1.3	-0.5	-1.4	-1.7	-0.1	-0.8	-1.5	-0.8	5
Ecuador	-4.8	-4.4	-3.0	-0.6	1.9	-2.2	-6.2	-2.0	0.4	3.5	1.4	-0.5	1.5	5
Peru	-3.9	-3.1	-7.3	-4.4	-3.0	-4.3	-6.9	-3.9	-6.3	-5.4	-1.9	-2.0	-3.1	4
Venezuela	2.2	-2.1	-0.6	2.8	2.0	-0.4	-1.6	-7.4	-1.0	-2.1	2.8	-3.4	-0.9	5
CACM														
Costa Rica	-4.6	-3.2	-3.4	-3.1	-2.0	-3.3	-2.0	-2.5	-4.1	-4.4	-3.1	-2.0	-3.2	4
El Salvador	-8.2	-5.9	-4.1	-3.2	-2.0	-3.2	-0.8	-2.7	-3.3	-1.4	-2.8	-3.0	-2.4	5
Guatemala	-7.4	-4.7	-3.6	-3.7	-1.8	-1.5	-1.3	-1.7	-2.9	-2.1	0.0	0.0	-0.7	5
Honduras	-7.3	-9.7	-9.0	-9.7	-8.6	-7.8	-7.6	-7.4	-7.6	-7.7	-4.4	-5.4	-5.8	3
Nicaragua	-9.8	-13.3	-30.0	-22.5	-21.3	-14.5	-16.0	-26.1	-3.4	-25.3	4.4	-2.1	-7.7	2
Panama[c]	-5.0	-11.4	-6.2	-7.4	-3.4	-4.5	-4.2	-5.2	-6.9	6.8	-0.1	n.a.	-0.1[f]	5

(Table continues next page)

Table 5.4 Consolidated surplus or deficit of central government budgets, 1981–92ª (percentage of GDP) (Continued)

Country	1981	1982	1983	1984	1985	1986	1987	1988	1989	1990	1991	1992	Average 1990–92	Budget discipline score
CARICOMᵈ														
Bahamas	0.3	−5.2	−4.1	−0.9	−1.4	−0.5	−0.8	−3.1	−4.3	−3.1	−2.9	−2.2	−2.7	4
Barbados	−9.6	−5.0	−4.1	−4.2	−4.2	−5.3	−5.3	−2.3	−0.8	−6.7	−2.1	−1.1	−3.3	4
Guyana	−37.0	−34.3	−40.1	−43.0	−51.9	−51.3	−49.6	−35.8	−7.0	−21.7	−17.0	−12.8	−17.2	0
Jamaica	−15.9	−14.8	−14.6	−5.4	−3.6	0.7	1.5	−1.6	1.3	1.5	3.9	3.2	2.9	5
Trinidad and Tobago	2.6	−12.0	−11.9	−8.9	−5.1	−5.9	−5.9	−5.7	−4.2	−1.2	−0.2	−2.5	−1.3	5
Other Latin America														
Dominican Republic	−2.2	−2.7	−2.5	−0.3	1.1	0.0	−1.3	−0.8	1.2	1.0	1.2	3.4	1.9	5
Haiti	−9.2	−5.6	−4.0	−5.5	−3.1	−1.3	−2.1	−2.6	−2.2	−2.7	−2.4	n.a.	−2.4ᶠ	5
Surinam	−1.1	−1.7	−17.6	−16.9	−21.4	−24.8	−24.3	−21.1	−13.7	−6.7	−19.2	−13.8	−13.2	0

n.a. = not available.

a. A positive sign indicates a surplus; a negative sign indicates a deficit.

b. Data from 1989 are not comparable with those of earlier years.

c. Panama is an active member of the CACM but has not yet fully joined in plans for regional economic integration.

d. Also part of CARICOM: Antigua and Barbuda, Belize, Dominica, Grenada, Montserrat, St. Kitts, St. Lucia, and St. Vincent.

e. Average 1988–90.

f. Average 1989–91.

Source: Inter-American Development Bank, *Economic and Social Progress in Latin America: 1993 Report*, October 1993, table C-4; International Monetary Fund, *International Financial Statistics*, Yearbook 1993, p. 142–43; and OECD, *OECD Economic Outlook*, various issues.

Table 5.5 Latin America: current account balances, 1981–92[a]

Country	1981 Millions of dollars	1981 Percent of GNP	1982 Millions of dollars	1982 Percent of GNP	1983 Millions of dollars	1983 Percent of GNP	1984 Millions of dollars	1984 Percent of GNP
Mexico	−16,061	−6.7	−6,307	−3.9	5,403	3.9	4,194	2.5
Chile	−4,733	−15.1	−2,304	−10.2	−1,117	−6.2	−2,111	−12.2
Mercosur								
Argentina	−4,712	−8.4	−2,353	−4.5	−2,436	−4.3	−2,495	−3.4
Brazil	−11,751	−4.6	−16,312	−6.3	−6,837	−3.5	42	0.0
Paraguay	−374	−6.4	−375	−6.7	−248	−4.4	−317	−7.1
Uruguay	−461	−4.1	−235	−2.6	−60	−1.2	−129	−2.7
Andean Group								
Bolivia	−466	−15.1	−174	−5.6	−139	−5.2	−175	−6.7
Colombia	−1,961	−5.4	−3,054	−8.0	−3,003	−7.9	−1,401	−3.8
Ecuador	−998	−7.6	−1,196	−10.4	−134	−1.4	−264	−2.8
Peru	−1,733	−7.1	−1,612	−6.5	−875	−4.6	−223	−1.1
Venezuela	4,000	5.1	−4,246	−5.5	4,427	5.6	4,651	8.0
CACM								
Costa Rica	−409	−17.6	−272	−12.5	−313	−11.1	−251	−7.5
El Salvador	−250	−7.4	−120	−3.6	−148	−4.1	−189	−4.7
Guatemala	−573	−6.7	−399	−4.6	−224	−2.5	−377	−4.1
Honduras	−303	−11.5	−228	−8.5	−232	−8.1	−374	−12.3
Nicaragua	−592	−25.8	−514	−22.6	−507	−21.5	−597	−21.8
Panama	56	1.5	−51	−1.3	416	10.4	218	5.1
Other Latin America								
Dominican Republic	−389	−6.0	−443	−6.7	−418	−6.3	−163	−3.4
Haiti	−149	−10.2	−99	−6.7	−111	−6.9	−103	−5.7

(Table continues next page)

Table 5.5 Latin America: current account balances, 1981–92ᵃ (Continued)

Country	1985 Millions of dollars	1985 Percent of GNP	1986 Millions of dollars	1986 Percent of GNP	1987 Millions of dollars	1987 Percent of GNP	1988 Millions of dollars	1988 Percent of GNP
Mexico	1,130	0.6	−1,673	−1.4	3,968	3.0	−2,443	−1.5
Chile	−1,328	−9.3	−1,137	−7.6	−808	−4.7	−167	−0.8
Mercosur								
Argentina	−952	−1.6	−2,859	−3.8	−4,235	−5.5	−1,572	−1.8
Brazil	−273	−0.1	−5,304	−2.0	−1,450	−0.5	4,159	1.2
Paraguay	−252	−8.0	−365	−10.4	−490	−13.3	−210	−5.4
Uruguay	−120	−2.7	45	0.8	−161	−2.3	16	−0.2
Andean Group								
Bolivia	−282	−10.4	−384	−10.7	−427	−10.5	−303	−7.3
Colombia	−1,809	−5.4	383	1.1	336	1.0	−216	−0.6
Ecuador	114	1.0	−553	−5.3	1,124	11.5	−536	−5.7
Peru	135	0.9	−1,077	−4.7	−1,640	−6.3	−1,246	−6.8
Venezuela	3,327	5.6	−2,245	−3.8	−1,390	−3.0	−5,809	−9.9
CACM								
Costa Rica	−291	−8.0	−161	−3.9	−376	−8.9	−304	−7.1
El Salvador	189	5.0	−17	−0.4	−68	−1.5	−129	−2.4
Guatemala	−246	−2.6	−18	−0.3	−443	−6.4	−414	−5.4
Honduras	−293	−8.8	−255	−7.2	−245	−6.4	−161	−4.5
Nicaragua	−726	−27.8	−688	−27.8	−679	−21.3	−715	−26.2
Panama	286	6.4	355	7.4	318	6.4	611	14.8
Other Latin America								
Dominican Republic	−108	−2.6	−186	−3.6	−364	−7.6	−19	−0.4
Haiti	−95	−4.7	−45	−2.0	−31	−1.5	−40	−1.8

Table 5.5 (Continued)

Country	1989 Millions of dollars	1989 Percent of GNP	1990 Millions of dollars	1990 Percent of GNP	1991 Millions of dollars	1991 Percent of GNP	1992 Millions of dollars	1992 Percent of GNP
Mexico	-3,958	-2.0	-7,117	-3.1	-13,785	-5.0	22,811	-7.1
Chile	-767	-3.3	-598	-2.3	142	0.5	-583	-1.5
Mercosur								
Argentina	-1,305	-2.4	1,903	1.9	-2,810	-2.2	-8,381	-3.7
Brazil	1,025	0.2	-3,788	-0.7	-1,408	-0.3	6,275	1.6
Paraguay	256	6.3	-172	-3.1	-466	-7.5	n.a.	n.a.
Uruguay	121	1.6	170	2.2	43	0.5	-207	-1.8
Andean Group								
Bolivia	-264	-6.2	-198	-4.7	-262	-5.5	-533	-10.5
Colombia	-201	-0.5	542	1.4	2,349	5.9	912	1.9
Ecuador	-514	-5.5	-166	-1.7	-467	-4.3	n.a.	n.a.
Peru	94	0.3	-1,092	-3.1	-1,632	-3.4	-2,080	-9.8
Venezuela	2,161	5.2	8,279	17.6	1,736	3.3	-3,365	-5.7
CACM								
Costa Rica	-480	-9.9	-494	-9.1	-99	-1.4	-371	-5.9
El Salvador	-330	-5.9	-235	-4.5	-213	-2.8	n.a.	n.a.
Guatemala	-367	-4.5	-233	-3.1	-184	-2.0	-706	-6.9
Honduras	-180	-5.9	-186	-7.5	-231	-8.3	-264	-8.4
Nicaragua	-362	-13.6	-305	-12.0	-5	-0.3	-695	-51.4
Panama	155	3.8	47	1.1	-192	-3.7	-143	-2.5
Other Latin America								
Dominican Republic	-199	-3.1	-9	-0.1	-58	-0.8	-393	-5.2
Haiti	-63	-2.7	-39	-1.6	-11	-0.4	n.a.	n.a.

n.a. = not available.
a. Minus signs indicate debits.

Sources: International Monetary Fund, *International Financial Statistics*, Yearbook 1993 and April 1994; The World Bank, *World Debt Tables*, 1989–90, 1991–92, 1992–93, and 1993–94.

Table 5.6 Total disbursed external debt as a percentage of exports of goods and services, 1985–92

Country	1985	1986	1987	1988	1989	1990	1991	1992	External debt score
North America									
United States[a]	85	92	89	83	81	80	90	98	5
Canada[b]	161	172	180	176	190	203	218	n.a.	4
Mexico	326	423	364	308	249	243	254	243	3
Chile	434	387	331	232	183	180	154	149	5
Mercosur									
Argentina	491	610	717	525	538	412	443	454	0
Brazil	362	452	431	314	290	321	327	311	2
Paraguay	252	249	282	192	143	107	124	114	5
Uruguay	295	245	253	201	191	181	195	196	4
Andean Group									
Bolivia	651	814	875	711	464	429	433	536	0
Colombia	302	220	223	228	209	181	167	162	4
Ecuador	261	351	424	424	392	370	363	339	2
Peru	328	430	478	489	417	485	484	453	0
Venezuela	206	305	268	273	207	155	183	220	3

CACM									
Costa Rica	347	318	316	274	236	180	178	150	4
El Salvador	172	155	176	171	199	174	156	130	5
Guatemala	223	232	239	196	173	167	149	150	4
Honduras	297	291	338	324	328	371	350	334	2
Nicaragua	1,683	2,368	2,447	3,176	2,804	2,647	2,928	3,466	0
Panama	75	79	98	138	135	122	106	223	3
CARICOMc									
Bahamas	14	16	14	12	n.a.	n.a.	n.a.	n.a.	5
Barbados	58	76	84	88	70	82	78	n.a.	5
Guyana	567	688	639	754	778	785	676	n.a.	0
Jamaica	300	286	278	246	213	188	187	154	4
Trinidad and Tobago	56	106	110	122	117	99	105	110	5
Other Latin America									
Haiti	164	178	192	202	220	242	187	n.a.	4
Dominican Republic	221	223	212	181	170	188	193	185	4

n.a. = not available.

a. Calculated as foreign official assets in the United States, plus US liabilities to unaffiliated foreigners, plus US Treasury bills as a percentage of exports of goods and services.

b. Calculated as foreign investment in Canada, other than direct investment, as a percentage of exports of goods and services.

c. Also part of CARICOM: Antigua and Barbuda, Belize, Dominica, Grenada, Monserrat, St. Kitts, St. Lucia, and St. Vincent.

Sources: The World Bank, *World Debt Tables 1993–94*; *Statistics Canada—Canada's International Investment Position, 1991*; *Statistical Abstract of the United States 1992*, tables 1314 and 1317.

Table 5.7 Secondary loan prices, fourth quarter 1989–93
(percentage of face value)

	1989	1990	1991	1992	1993
Mexico[a]	36	46	62	65	84
Chile	59	74	90	91	95
Mercosur					
Argentina[b]	13	20	38	48	69
Brazil[c]	22	25	31	30	53
Uruguay[d]	50	57	75	75	80
Andean Group					
Bolivia	11	11	11	16	n.a.
Ecuador[e]	14	20	24	28	52
Peru	6	4	13	19	68
Venezuela[f]	34	50	68	57	74
CACM					
Costa Rica[g]	17	34	51	60	82
Honduras	20	19	27	35	31
Nicaragua	1	4	8	7	10
Panama	13	13	21	29	61
Other Latin America					
Jamaica	42	42	76	71	76

n.a. = not available.
a. Prices after February 1990 refer to par bonds offered under Brady initiative.
b. 1987 Guaranteed Refinancing Agreement (GRA).
c. Multi-Year Deposit Facility Agreement (MYDFA). 1993 figure is for the third quarter.
d. Prices after December 1990 refer to par bonds offered under Brady initiative.
e. Multi-Year Refinancing Agreement (MYRA).
f. Prices after August 1990 refer to par bonds offered under Brady initiative.
g. Prices after May 1990 refer to series A par bonds offered under Brady initiative.

Source: The World Bank, Financial Flows and the Developing Countries, Quarterly Review, April 1993 and May 1994, 43 and 34.

Table 5.8 Net interest payments as a percentage of exports of goods and services, 1982–92

Country	1982	1983	1984	1985	1986	1987	1988	1989	1990	1991	1992
Mexico	46.3	32.1	30.7	30.6	31.6	23.3	21.4	20.4	12.0	12.5	12.1
Chile	40.5	32.9	46.7	38.8	27.9	23.5	13.1	14.5	17.5	25.4	11.1
Argentina	33.3	62.8	55.6	48.0	46.8	47.1	41.9	44.8	26.5	35.1	25.6
Brazil	47.1	38.7	28.5	28.5	29.1	35.8	34.7	20.2	19.5	14.1	19.4
Uruguay	4.8	15.0	20.5	22.6	17.0	16.0	13.4	7.5	7.5	2.1	2.1[a]
Bolivia	10.5	38.5	52.4	40.1	22.5	20.8	15.7	12.0	14.3	13.6	21.6
Colombia	12.5	18.8	16.0	25.5	22.7	17.0	16.8	19.5	13.6	12.7	15.9
Ecuador	34.9	21.5	28.8	24.4	28.6	33.1	26.6	25.9	27.4	24.8	19.8
Peru[b]	22.2	20.1	30.9	27.6	30.6	30.0	33.8	30.0	40.5	34.5	29.9
Venezuela	5.5	9.6	4.6	9.1	14.0	11.3	14.0	11.7	4.3	3.5	5.4
Costa Rica	28.9	45.4	21.9	25.9	20.6	20.2	15.5	9.1	4.7	6.4	6.4
Jamaica	14.6	16.6	23.9	23.9	22.7	18.2	16.0	14.9	11.1	10.6	10.6[a]

a. Assumes that the 1992 figure is the same as in 1991.
b. Net interest payments from central bank.

Sources: World Bank, *World Debt Tables*, various issues; International Monetary Fund, *International Financial Statistics*, various issues; and IMF, *Balance of Payments Statistics*, various issues.

Table 5.9 Latin America: market exchange rates, 1984–92[a] (annual percentage change against the dollar)

Country	1984	1985	1986	1987	1988	1989	1990	1991	1992
Mexico	39.6	53.1	138.1	125.3	64.9	8.3	14.3	7.3	2.5
Chile	25.3	63.2	19.8	13.7	11.6	9.1	14.2	14.5	3.8
Mercosur									
Argentina	518.2	785.3	56.6	127.4	308.3	4,736.1	1,051.9	95.6	4.9
Brazil	216.7	226.3	121.0	186.1	665.3	833.3	2,339.3	495.3	1,009.9
Paraguay	59.5	52.6	10.6	62.1	0.0	92.0	16.4	7.8	13.2
Uruguay	62.6	80.7	49.9	49.1	58.5	68.5	93.4	72.4	49.9
Andean Group									
Bolivia	1,254.0	12,655.5	300.0	31.2	14.3	12.5	18.5	12.5	8.3
Colombia	27.8	41.2	36.5	24.9	23.3	27.9	31.3	26.0	20.0
Ecuador	41.7	11.4	76.4	38.8	76.9	74.5	45.9	36.3	45.9
Peru	118.8	214.3	26.4	20.9	666.7	1,969.9	−93.0	311.1	61.3
Venezuela	62.8	7.1	8.0	79.0	0.0	139.3	35.2	21.1	20.4
CACM									
Costa Rica	8.3	13.5	10.9	12.1	20.7	7.5	12.4	33.6	9.9
El Salvador	0.0	0.0	96.0	2.0	0.0	0.0	36.0	17.6	5.0
Guatemala	0.0	0.0	90.0	31.6	4.0	7.7	60.7	11.1	4.0
Honduras	0.0	0.0	0.0	0.0	0.0	0.0	100.0	35.0	1.9
Nicaragua	0.0	165.0	137.7	11.1	379,185.7	5,738.0	4,445.2	733.3	16.3
Panama	0.0	0.0	0.0	0.0	0.0	0.0	0.0	0.0	0.0
CARICOM[b]									
Bahamas	0.0	0.0	0.0	0.0	0.0	0.0	0.0	0.0	0.0
Barbados	0.0	0.0	0.0	0.0	0.0	0.0	0.0	0.0	0.0
Guyana	26.7	13.2	0.0	127.9	2.0	172.0	45.2	183.0	11.8
Jamaica	105.3	43.6	−1.8	0.0	0.0	3.6	26.3	68.1	90.1
Trinidad and Tobago	0.0	4.2	44.0	0.0	5.6	13.2	0.0	0.0	0.0
Other Latin America									
Dominican Republic	0.0	210.0	−6.5	31.0	60.5	3.3	34.9	49.4	0.8
Haiti	0.0	0.0	0.0	12.0	7.1	10.0	13.6	0.0	27.3
Surinam	0.0	0.0	0.0	0.0	0.0	0.0	0.0	0.0	0.0

a. Period average rates. A positive number indicates depreciation against the dollar; a negative number indicates appreciation against the dollar.
b. Also part of CARICOM but not listed here: Antigua and Barbuda, Belize, Dominica, Grenada, Monserrat, St. Kitts, St. Lucia, and St. Vincent.
c. Official rate from 1983–86, and market rate from 1987 thereafter.

Sources: Inter-American Development Bank, *Economic and Social Progress in Latin America: 1993 Report*, table F-1; and International Monetary Fund, *International Financial Statistics*, Yearbook 1993.

Table 5.10 Real effective exchange rates, 1981–92 (1985=100)

Country	1981	1982	1983	1984	1985	1986	1987	1988	1989	1990	1991	1992	Standard deviation, 1990–92	Currency stability score
North America														
United States[a]	83.9	90.3	92.9	98.9	100.0	79.8	71.8	69.0	73.5	69.6	68.0	65.6	2.0	5
Canada[a]	94.8	101.2	105.6	103.7	100.0	92.9	96.1	102.5	105.8	102.2	102.3	96.5	3.3	5
Mexico[b]	76.7	115.4	120.0	101.0	100.0	131.0	133.0	112.0	107.0	107.0	96.0	90.0	8.6	5
Chile[a]	171.5	155.0	126.3	124.1	100.0	84.5	78.4	73.3	75.0	72.9	75.1	79.5	3.3	5
Mercosur														
Argentina[b]	90.0	102.0	99.0	91.0	100.0	122.0	155.0	138.0	131.0	134.0	139.0	156.0	11.5	3
Brazil[b]	93.0	89.0	108.0	99.0	100.0	105.0	109.0	98.0	75.0	70.0	88.0	99.0	14.6	3
Paraguay[a]	149.5	132.0	123.1	115.9	100.0	100.7	81.0	83.9	63.9	62.1	71.8	70.7	5.3	5
Uruguay[a]	168.3	176.0	108.2	103.7	100.0	98.6	96.3	90.7	94.7	85.5	97.2	104.4	9.5	5
Andean Group														
Bolivia[a]	45.1	48.9	45.0	58.4	100.0	29.5	28.4	27.0	25.9	21.8	22.5	22.0	0.4	5
Colombia[a]	117.9	125.7	125.2	114.7	100.0	74.5	66.5	64.1	61.8	54.5	56.3	61.4	3.6	5
Ecuador[a]	125.2	122.5	116.7	96.3	100.0	80.5	61.9	46.5	53.8	49.5	51.9	52.3	1.5	5
Peru[c]	82.0	74.0	85.0	83.0	100.0	89.0	81.0	84.0	52.0	42.0	35.0	33.0	4.7	5
Venezuela[a]	124.8	135.0	122.9	104.2	100.0	83.5	59.8	66.7	56.8	51.0	54.5	57.0	3.0	5

(Table continues next page)

Table 5.10 Real effective exchange rates, 1981–92 (1985=100) (Continued)

Country	1981	1982	1983	1984	1985	1986	1987	1988	1989	1990	1991	1992	Standard deviation, 1990–92	Currency stability score
CACM														
Costa Rica[a]	78.5	89.7	103.2	101.4	100.0	89.9	81.6	74.7	77.5	76.0	69.3	70.7	3.6	5
El Salvador[c]	169.0	152.0	135.0	117.0	100.0	162.0	139.0	122.0	105.0	141.0	134.0	135.0	3.8	5
Guatemala[c]	118.0	120.0	118.0	113.0	100.0	142.0	185.0	186.0	188.0	220.0	192.0	193.0	15.9	3
Honduras[c]	128.0	117.0	108.0	101.0	100.0	109.0	117.0	118.0	109.0	195.0	200.0	197.0	2.5	5
Nicaragua[a]	49.8	50.5	61.5	70.6	100.0	118.8	173.1	173.3	103.5	157.1	141.7	133.3	12.1	3
CARICOM[d]														
Bahamas[a]	90.4	92.8	95.5	98.0	100.0	96.8	94.8	93.4	95.2	91.8	94.6	96.7	2.5	5
Guyana[a]	71.4	80.9	94.9	96.8	100.0	94.8	48.8	61.3	48.6	34.3	29.6	32.7	2.4	5
Jamaica[b]	58.1	55.7	54.8	89.6	100.0	83.1	80.1	77.0	74.0	78.6	87.9	n.a.	7.1	5
Other Latin America														
Dominican Republic[a]	130.6	132.4	125.3	91.5	100.0	93.6	78.1	65.4	81.6	84.2	90.0	90.6	3.5	5
Haiti[c]	135.0	127.0	117.0	107.0	100.0	103.0	123.0	123.0	150.0	156.0	145.0	139.0	8.6	5

n.a. = not available.

a. *International Financial Statistics* figures. Includes selected trade partners.
b. Economic Commission for Latin America and the Caribbean figures. Includes main trading partners and uses wholesale price index.
c. Economic Commission for Latin America and the Caribbean figures. Includes main trading partners and uses consumer price index.
d. Also part of CARICOM: Antigua and Barbuda, Belize, Dominica, Grenada, Monserrat, St. Kitts, St. Lucia, and St. Vincent.

Source: International Monetary Fund, *International Financial Statistics,* Yearbook 1993; Economic Commission for Latin America and the Caribbean, *Preliminary Overview of the Economy of Latin America and the Caribbean,* 1991 and 1992, p. 47.

Table 5.11 International trade taxes as a percentage of current revenue, 1981–91[a]

	1981	1982	1983	1984	1985	1986	1987	1988	1989	1990	1991	Average 1989–91	Score for trade tax reliance
North America													
United States	1.3	1.4	1.3	1.6	1.6	1.7	1.7	1.72	1.59	1.57	1.46	1.5	5
Canada	6.1	4.4	4.8	5.3	4.7	4.2	4.0	3.81	3.5	n.a.	n.a.	3.8[f]	5
Mexico	32.1	32.9	24.1	19.3	20.0	15.9	17.8	12.2	12.5	14.8	12.8	13.4	3
Chile	17.9	13.0	18.0	23.5	25.3	7.7	8.6	7.9	6.9	8.9	8.6	8.1	4
Mercosur[b]	3.8	5.2	11.9	11.8	7.8	5.5	4.8	6.4	5.9	5.3	3.1		
Mercosur[c]	15.7	13.9	18.8	16.0	13.6	11.6	11.9	11.1	16.2	17.2	11.7		
Argentina	15.8	16.0	37.6	32.5	26.2	15.2	15.1	16.4	33.2	21.9	7.6	20.9	1
Brazil	n.a.	2.4	4.2	4.2	2.4	2.3	1.6	3.4	2.3	1.5	1.9	1.9	5
Paraguay	30.2	22.8	17.4	11.6	12.0	12.9	16.1	10.7	17.3	17.3	16.7	17.1	2
Uruguay	16.7	14.4	16.1	15.6	14.0	16.2	14.7	13.8	12.2	12.5	10.9	11.9	3
Andean Group[b]	15.8	16.3	19.4	19.1	18.3	23.2	23.1	16.5	14.4	12.6	9.7		
Andean Group[c]	22.0	20.2	20.2	21.2	19.2	20.5	20.9	15.8	13.8	12.2	10.8		
Bolivia	n.a.	n.a.	n.a.	28.6	20.6	12.6	15.4	10.4	8.7	7.3	6.0	7.3	4
Colombia	23.4	22.8	17.6	16.9	18.8	20.6	21.2	21.6	19.4	16.1	12.2	15.9	2
Ecuador	29.4	23.7	21.1	21.4	17.3	22.0	19.9	14.5	14.9	13.2	14.0	14.0	3
Peru	28.7	23.9	21.8	19.5	22.1	20.8	21.5	19.0	18.3	18.7	9.1	15.4	2
Venezuela	6.6	10.3	20.1	19.6	17.2	26.5	26.7	13.3	7.7	5.8	7.8	7.1	4

Table continues next page

Table 5.11 International trade taxes as a percentage of current revenue, 1981–91a (Continued)

	1981	1982	1983	1984	1985	1986	1987	1988	1989	1990	1991	Average 1989–91	Score for trade tax reliance
CACMb	25.5	21.4	19.7	19.9	21.1	26.1	22.8	21.2	20.7	25.1	21.5		
CACMc	26.7	23.6	21.1	20.9	22.0	26.4	23.0	20.4	19.7	23.0	22.2		
Costa Rica	40.3	41.2	34.3	29.8	32.9	33.1	32.3	27.5	29.1	26.8	28.7	28.2	0
El Salvador	29.6	25.0	22.0	24.1	27.5	41.3	26.1	21.1	16.8	21.8	20.6	19.7	2
Guatemala	24.0	18.2	15.8	16.6	16.1	26.8	25.5	23.6	20.6	34.3	28.1	27.7	0
Honduras	41.9	35.1	34.8	35.4	37.5	34.3	33.4	28.7	29.7	26.2	n.a.	28.2g	0
Nicaragua	11.9	9.8	6.9	6.4	5.1	8.0	7.1	12.4	10.6	14.2	18.6	14.5	3
Panama	12.5	12.5	12.7	13.2	12.9	14.7	13.6	9.0	11.4	14.9	13.3	13.2	3
CARICOMb,d	n.a.	n.a.	n.a.	n.a.	n.a.	n.a.	n.a.	13.3	14.0	12.4	12.2		
CARICOMc,e	20.4	19.6	21.7	20.7	23.0	23.6	24.5	23.1	23.9	22.1	21.3		
Bahamas	53.2	55.8	59.3	57.7	61.1	58.7	62.5	63.4	64.4	59.0	55.5	59.6	0
Barbados	20.6	15.1	16.6	15.0	15.2	16.5	16.8	14.4	13.0	12.1	9.9	11.7	3
Guyana	12.0	8.4	13.0	12.4	10.9	11.5	12.2	9.2	12.9	13.4	13.1	13.1	3
Jamaica	9.5	10.8	11.2	11.2	18.1	22.0	23.3	21.4	21.5	18.0	19.9	19.8	2
Trinidad and Tobago	6.6	7.7	8.6	7.3	9.7	9.2	7.5	7.3	7.8	8.2	8.2	8.1	4
Other Latin America													
Dominican Republic	9.8	24.9	26.1	25.0	46.3	32.1	37.0	33.9	32.7	33.5	35.8	34.0	0
Haiti	43.2	38.7	34.9	32.0	27.1	28.3	22.0	18.1	19.7	19.4	20.9	20.0	1

n.a. = not available.

a. Includes all taxes on international trade and commercial transactions in the form of both specific and ad valorem import and export duties raised for purposes of revenue mobilization and for protectionism. Also included are taxes that are levied on foreign exchange transactions.

b. Indicates weighted average using GNP figures as the weights.

c. Indicates simple average.

d. The weighted average for CARICOM does not include the Bahamas.

e. Also part of CARICOM: Antigua and Barbuda, Belize, Dominica, Grenada, Monserrat, St. Kitts, St. Lucia, and St. Vincent.

f. Average 1987–89.

g. Average 1988–90.

Sources: Inter-American Development Bank, Economic and Social Progress in Latin America: 1992 Report, 1992, table C-13; figures for Brazil, Bolivia, El Salvador, the United States, and Canada were taken from International Monetary Fund, Government Finance Statistics Yearbook, 1992, 58–59 and 1988, 54.

6

Subregional Integration and Readiness Assessment

The Danforth amendment to the NAFTA implementing legislation requires that, by 1 May 1994 and then again by 1 May 1997, the US Trade Representative should submit a list of countries that "provide fair and equitable market access to US exports . . . or have made significant progress in opening their markets . . . and the further opening of those markets has the greatest potential to increase US exports. . . ." Based on this report, the president should determine prospective partners for free trade area negotiations.[1]

In light of the previous discussion and using the scale described in chapter 5, we assess the level of readiness of each subregion in Latin America for further hemispheric integration. At the same time, we survey economic reforms within each country and achievements toward subregional integration. The summary material in this chapter is supplemented by extensive chronological surveys of each subregion in appendix C.

North American Free Trade Agreement

The United States and Canada have a long history of bilateral trade talks. In the 19th and early 20th century, abortive attempts were made to establish freer trade between the two countries. The underlying tension, which persists to this day, is between the mutual benefits of trade liberalization and Canada's historic preoccupation with maintaining its distinct identity from the United States.

---

1. This language is contained in the NAFTA implementing legislation (HR 3450), Section 108, on "congressional intent regarding future accessions."

A bilateral trade agreement between the United States and Canada was negotiated under the authority of the Reciprocal Trade Agreements Act of 1934. The accord provided for reciprocal reductions of tariffs on bilateral trade and began unwinding the protectionism of the Depression era.

However, notable steps toward US-Canada economic integration did not unfold until well after the Second World War. Two important liberalization measures were reached in the 1950s and 1960s, both of a sectoral nature. The first was the Defense Production Sharing Agreement of 1958, which opened up US military procurement to Canadian firms. The second was the Auto Pact of 1965, which substantially eliminated tariffs on bilateral trade in the auto sector. In addition to these sectoral initiatives, both countries reduced their barriers on a multilateral basis in successive negotiating rounds of the General Agreement on Tariffs and Trade.

While trade barriers between industrialized nations were being lowered under GATT auspices, Canada tried to selectively avert the dominance of US multinational firms by restricting investment in key sectors of its economy. In essence, Canada attempted to distinguish between free trade and free investment. In 1967, Canada revised its Bank Act, prohibiting all foreign residents combined from holding more than a 25 percent share in the equity of a financial institution. In 1973, Canada created the Foreign Investment Review Agency (FIRA) to screen incoming direct investment. A particularly sensitive issue for Canadians has been control of the energy sector. In the early 1980s, the Trudeau government instituted a National Energy Program to promote Canadian self-sufficiency and ownership in the sector. By restricting investment, Canada felt it could maintain better control of its economy and limit the balance of payments costs resulting from the repatriation of profits by foreign firms.

During the 1980s, the United States, Canada, and later Mexico revived their interest in broad-gauge trade liberalization in North America. Indeed, US interest in free trade talks dates back to the 1970s, when the US Congress, in Section 612 of the Trade Act of 1974, granted the president authority to negotiate a free trade agreement with Canada. The Congress went further in Section 1104 of the Trade Agreements Act of 1979, authorizing an executive-branch study on the desirability of entering into trade agreements with North American countries. In his 1980 campaign, candidate Ronald Reagan painted the vision of a North American free trade area.

While the political will for free trade negotiations was apparent in the United States as early as 1974, Canada was slow to welcome negotiations. However, two influential national commissions, the Trade Policy Review in 1983 and the Macdonald Commission in 1985 came out in favor of free trade with the United States, providing the first Canadian stirrings for FTA talks. The commissions' reports were influential in assuaging Canadian fears about loss of autonomy to the United States. Not coincidentally, the creation of Investment Canada in 1985 (replacing FIRA) signified a policy shift, and Canada began to welcome foreign investment. The failure of ongoing US-Canada sectoral trade talks led both countries to agree in late 1985 to broaden the agenda to a wide-ranging free trade agreement, and FTA negotiations commenced in May 1986.

The changing Canadian attitudes toward trade liberalization, followed by 20 months of bilateral negotiations, led to the Canada-US FTA, signed in January 1988, with implementation started in January 1989. The agreement requires the phaseout of all tariffs within 10 years, the elimination of most nontariff barriers, and the relaxation of investment controls between the two countries (with notable exceptions in the energy sector). In addition, the FTA contains path-breaking rights and obligations on services, trade, and investment.

One of the most important achievements of the Canada-US FTA was the dispute settlement procedures established under chapters 18 and 19 of the pact. Disputes concerning the interpretation of the FTA are heard under chapter 18 by a panel of experts, with recourse to a governing body (the Canada-US Trade Commission) for review. The chapter 18 procedures are similar to the GATT process. Disputes concerning anti-dumping and countervailing duty actions are heard under chapter 19 by a panel of experts. Unlike GATT procedures, chapter 19 panel rulings are binding on the parties.[2]

Despite the FTA accomplishments, various sticking points remained unresolved, most notably in subsidies, government procurement, energy sector investment, transportation services, and intellectual property rights. Many of these topics were revisited in NAFTA talks, and some still remain on the post-NAFTA agenda (e.g., possible reform of the antidumping laws among the NAFTA partners).

Prior to the NAFTA talks, the United States and Mexico had a limited and issue-specific record of negotiation on economic integration. In 1942, the two countries signed a bilateral trade agreement that was later dropped. In 1945 at Chapultepec, the United States proposed the Economic Charter of the Americas, which envisaged a reduction of trade barriers. Mexico and other Latin American countries demurred.

While broad trade agreements ran counter to Mexican concerns about sovereignty and Mexican preference for import substitution policies,

---

2. With the new dispute settlement procedures of the World Trade Organization (WTO), disputes under the GATT and the General Agreement on Trade in Services (GATS) will be resolved more quickly than before. However, the final decisions will be given effect by a combination of moral suasion and threatened retaliation rather than by direct application under the domestic laws of the contracting party (the situation under the Canada-US FTA and the NAFTA).

progress was made on specific issues. In 1942, the United States instituted the Bracero Program, seeking to eliminate a wartime labor shortage by recruiting Mexican agricultural workers. The explicit recruitment of Mexican workers lasted until 1964. Afterward, the United States implicitly allowed Mexican workers into the country by maintaining a relaxed level of surveillance at the border and by not enacting laws that would prohibit the hiring of undocumented aliens. The elimination of the Bracero Program in 1964 provided the impetus for Mexican border industrialization programs designed to create manufacturing jobs for Mexicans (Weintraub 1990, 157). In 1965, Mexico established the maquiladora ("twin plant") program that involved the secondary assembly of duty-free, imported components for eventual reexport. This program stimulated both bilateral trade and direct investment in Mexico by US companies. By 1992 there were over 2,075 maquiladora plants, employing 505,000 workers (Hufbauer and Schott 1993a, 172).

Meanwhile, Mexican workers continued to emigrate to the United States on a large scale. By 1986, the US Congress had become so concerned with illegal immigration that it passed the US Immigration Reform and Control Act to curtail undocumented migration from Mexico by applying sanctions against US employers that hire illegal immigrants. In the late 1980s, possibly in response to the IRCA sanctions, border apprehensions dropped, but by 1992 they once again exceeded 1 million annually. Most experts agree that over the long term the only way to slow illegal immigration is to create better jobs in Mexico.

Movement toward US-Mexico economic integration proceeded slowly in the 1960s and 1970s, reflecting Mexico's preference for semiautonomous economic policies. The debt crisis in the early 1980s led to a dramatic reorientation of Mexican economic priorities, including trade policies. Starting in 1985, Mexico unilaterally reduced tariffs, phased out most licensing regulations, and eliminated the use of official prices for customs valuation purposes. Mexico complemented these unilateral actions with trade pacts. It joined the GATT in 1986 and signed three bilateral trade agreements with the United States: the Understanding on Subsidies and Countervailing Duties (1985), the Framework of Principles and Procedures for Consultation Regarding Trade and Investment Relations (1987), and the Understanding Regarding Trade and Investment Facilitation Talks (1989).

To this point, the respective bilateral trade relationships of Canada and Mexico with the United States had progressed rapidly. However, the two countries had done little to enhance economic relations between themselves. In March 1990, Mexico and Canada took a first step, signing 10 accords on trade and nontrade issues. In June 1990, President Carlos Salinas of Mexico proposed free trade negotiations with the United States; this initiative soon prompted Canada to join the talks as well. In June 1991, trilateral negotiations for a free trade area in North America began in Toronto. The NAFTA negotiators sought to augment the Canada-US FTA, among other things addressing services trade and intellectual property rights, which were not resolved in the FTA (Hufbauer and Schott 1993a).

Not surprisingly, the United States, Canada, and Mexico score well on the seven readiness indicators. Overall, the group received a high average score of 4.4 on our scale. The United States and Canada received the highest scores, 4.7 and 4.6, respectively, while Mexico scored a 3.9 (table 6.1).

The United States received a score of 5 in every category except budgetary discipline, for which it received a 3. The large US federal deficit averaged 4.9 percent of GDP over 1990–92.

Canada also received a score of 5 in all categories except in budget discipline, for which it scored a 3 and external debt, a 4. Canada's budget deficit has averaged 5.5 percent over the last three years. External debt as a percentage of exports of goods and services amounted to 218 percent, resulting in a score worse than some Latin American countries.[3]

Mexico received a 5 for budget discipline, currency stability, and market-oriented policies, and a score of 3 in the other categories. Mexico has dramatically reduced its public deficit, its real exchange rate fluctuated an average of only 8.6 percent per annum in the last three years, and it has substantially deregulated and privatized its economy since 1985. Also, average tariff levels were reduced to about 10 percent before NAFTA (Banco de Mexico, *The Mexican Economy 1992*, 12).

By contrast, Mexico still has room for improvement in other areas. Mexico's triple-digit inflation of the mid-1980s has been sharply curtailed and continues to fall. The inflation figure was still a high 16 percent in 1992, dropping to less than 10 percent in 1993. If this figure is sustained, Mexico's price stability score will rise from 3 to 4. Mexico still has a high external debt ratio: 243 percent of its exports of goods and services.[4]

Recent developments in Mexico helped increase its score for functioning democracy. After the 1988 presidential election that was widely viewed as fraudulent, the ruling Institutional Revolutionary Party (PRI) negotiated an electoral reform law with the opposition parties. The legislation created a supposedly impartial bureaucracy, the Federal Electoral Institute, to oversee future presidential elections. In 1991, President Salinas forced the resignation of two PRI state governors whose

---

3. Canada's external debt is calculated as foreign investment in Canada other than direct investment. Therefore, the external debt Canadian figure includes portfolio investment in stocks and bonds and other debt.

4. On the positive side, William Cline (1994, table 5–1) rates Mexico third in terms of "debt cooperativeness."

Table 6.1 Performance scores on readiness indicators[a]

Region/Country	Price stability	Budget discipline	External debt	Currency stability	Market-oriented policies	Reliance on trade taxes	Functioning democracy	Average
North America	4.3	3.7	4.0	5.0	5.0	4.3	4.3	4.4
US	5	3	5	5	5	5	5	4.7
Canada	5	3	4	5	5	5	5	4.6
Mexico	3	5	3	5	5	3	3	3.9
Chile	3	5	5	5	5	4	4	4.4
Mercosur	1.3	3.8	2.8	4.0	3.5	2.8	3.5	3.1
Argentina	0	5	0	3	5	1	4	2.6
Brazil	3	0	2	3	3	5	3	2.3
Paraguay	3	5	5	5	3	2	3	3.7
Uruguay	2	5	4	5	3	3	4	3.7
Andean Group	2.4	4.8	1.8	5.0	3.0	3.0	3.2	3.4
Bolivia	4	5	0	5	4	4	4	3.7
Colombia	3	5	4	5	4	2	3	3.7
Ecuador	2	5	2	5	3	3	4	3.4
Peru	0	4	0	5	2	2	2	2.1
Venezuela	3	5	3	5	4	4	3	3.9
CACM	2.6	3.8	3.0	4.2	1.8	1.0	2.8	2.7
Costa Rica	3	4	4	5	3	0	4	3.3
El Salvador	4	5	5	5	2	2	3	3.7
Guatemala	3	5	4	3	1	0	2	2.6
Honduras	3	3	2	5	2	0	3	2.6
Nicaragua	0	2	0	3	1	3	2	1.6
CARICOM	3.6	3.6	3.8	5.0	2.8	2.4	4.4	3.7
Bahamas	4	4	5	5	3	0	4	3.6
Barbados	4	4	5	5	3	3	5	4.1
Guyana	3	0	0	5	2	3	4	2.4
Jamaica	3	5	4	5	3	2	4	3.7
Trinidad and Tobago	4	5	5	5	3	4	5	4.4

a. Scores for price stability are taken from table 5.2; scores for budget discipline are taken from table 5.4; scores for external debt are taken from table 5.6; scores for currency stability are taken from table 5.10; scores for market-oriented policies are based on the discussion in chapter 5; scores for international trade taxes are taken from table 5.11; and scores for functioning democracy are taken from the Freedom House rankings.

electoral victories had been tainted with charges of vote fraud (Baer 1991, 15–16). Continuing its process of political liberalization, the once-hegemonic PRI conceded defeat to an opposition party, the Partido Acción Nacionalista (PAN) in the governor's race in Chihuahua state in 1992.

But the most significant achievement was the 27 January 1994 signing of the Pact for Peace, Democracy, and Justice by seven of the eight registered political parties. The pact calls for "the appointment of impartial representatives to election boards, open access to the country's voter registration data base and an outside audit of the voter list, a more even distribution of media campaign coverage, a revision of campaign financing laws once the 1994 election is complete, and prohibition of the use of public programs and funding for a candidate or party" (*New York Times*, 28 January 1994, A1; *El Financiero*, 7–13 February 1994, 16). The critical test for the reform process is whether the presidential elections in August 1994 are broadly regarded as fair.

Overall, the NAFTA region received very high scores across the board on the readiness indicators. The weakest area is budget discipline. Even here, the region received an average score of 3.7.

Chile

The Chilean case is noteworthy in two respects. First, economic liberalization preceded political liberalization by more than a decade. In this respect, Chile was like Korea, Taiwan, and Thailand. By contrast, economic liberalization was contemporaneous with, or even led by, political liberalization in other Latin countries. The second noteworthy aspect is that, while not yet a member of any trade group, Chile has been a pioneer advocate of freer trade and a textbook practitioner of unilateral liberalization.

Chile began modest market reforms in the 1960s under President Eduardo Frei and became an original signatory of the Cartagena Declaration that created the Andean Group in 1969. In 1970, Chilean policy reversed course under newly elected President Salvador Allende, who embarked on a program of nationalization and drastic import substitution. In 1973, General Augusto Pinochet seized control from President Allende in a bloody coup. Chile instituted an economic stabilization and liberalization program the next year, reversing both the macro and the microeconomic policies of the Allende regime.

In 1976, Chile dropped out of the Andean Group. By 1980, the new Chilean policies resulted in the privatization of more than 460 companies and the reduction of tariffs from an average of 105 to 10 percent ("Privatization in Latin America," *Latin Finance*, Supplement, March 1991, 47).

The move toward liberalization stalled temporarily in early 1982 when Chile faced severe internal and external pressures. To avoid a financial sector collapse, the banking industry was nationalized in 1983. Tariff levels were initially raised to 35 percent to stimulate the manufacturing sector but later were gradually cut to 15 percent by 1988 (Edwards and Edwards 1992, 205–06).

In 1985, Pinochet refocused economic policy. His new minister of finance, Hernan Büchi, concentrated on stimulating public investment, reprivatizing the financial sector, using monetary policy to target interest rates, and devaluing the exchange rate via a crawling peg. These measures spurred economic growth, which averaged 6.3 percent annually from 1985 to 1989 (Edwards and Edwards 1992, 204–09).

In contrast to its Latin American neighbors, Chile was at least moderately successful in dealing with external debt during the mid-1980s. In 1985, the Pinochet regime instituted a debt conversion program and a debt-equity swap program, both administered by the Chilean Central Bank. The conversion program allowed Chilean investors to buy their own foreign liabilities in the secondary market. The swap program allowed foreign creditors to obtain equity stakes in Chilean companies in return for the reduction of foreign-currency debt. Critics argued that the debt-equity swap program implied a subsidy of some 30 percent to foreign investors. Nevertheless, the two programs together enabled Chile to cut its external debt in half from 1985 to 1990 (Edwards and Edwards 1992, 210–12).

General Pinochet relinquished control of the government, while remaining chief of the army, when Patricio Aylwin was elected president in March 1990. In his initial economic program, Aylwin sought to allay the fears of foreign observers that a democratically elected government would succumb to internal redistributive pressures. In the first two years of his administration, Aylwin successfully balanced macroeconomic stability against social demands. His economic program continued the process of price liberalization. It also stressed a stable real exchange rate and low tariff levels. In early 1991, Aylwin unilaterally cut tariffs by a further 27 percent, to a uniform rate of 11 percent (Edwards and Edwards 1992, 214–16).

While keeping spending and inflation under control, Aylwin was successful in implementing a more liberal social policy. The Tax Reform of 1990, designed to fund social expenditures, temporarily increased corporate taxes and made the individual tax system more progressive. A labor reform act was passed in 1991, limiting the power of employers to discharge and lock out employees (Edwards and Edwards 1992, 216–17).

Under Aylwin, Chile complemented active participation in the Uruguay Round of GATT negotiations with a spate of new bilateral trade initiatives designed to cement internal reforms and to position Chile as a Latin American and Pacific nerve center. The first two bilateral agreements were signed in October 1990: a framework agreement with the United States under the Enterprise for the Americas Initiative (EAI) and a pact with Venezuela pledging to negotiate a free trade agreement.

In August 1991, Chile signed a framework agreement with Argentina to facilitate trade and promote investment between the two countries. In September 1991, Chile signed a bilateral agreement with Mexico; in April 1993, one with Venezuela; and in December 1993, one with Colombia. In their free trade agreement, Chile and Mexico pledged to reduce and eventually eliminate tariffs, starting in January 1992, on some 94 percent of the bilateral trade between the two countries by 1996. The agreements with Venezuela and Colombia will phase out tariffs by 1999. At the same time, Chile explored possible ties with the Mercosur group but did not go forward, judging that Mercosur's prospective common external tariff would likely be too high.

In February 1992, Chile signed an agreement with the United States to establish an EAI Environmental Fund. In May, Chile and Argentina began to integrate their mining sectors, allowing freer exchange of people, goods, and services in the industry. Also in May, Presidents Bush and Aylwin agreed to inaugurate free trade negotiations once the United States completed its negotiations with Canada and Mexico on a North American FTA. The Clinton administration has recently confirmed that it intends to negotiate Chile's accession to NAFTA by late 1995 (*New York Times*, 4 February 1994, D1).

Late in 1992, Chile signed four bilateral agreements with Malaysia. Under the agreements, the maximum duty will be 11 percent, and all tariffs on bilateral trade will be eliminated after five years (*Journal of Commerce*, 17 November 1992, 5A).

Chile implemented a patent and trademark law in September 1991. The new law provides protection for pharmaceuticals, but it provides neither ''pipeline'' protection nor protection for plant and animal varieties.[5] Patent protection lasts for 15 years, and copyright protection (revised in 1992) extends for the life of the author plus 50 years.

Chile is relatively open to foreign investment (see section on investment in chapter 4). However, foreign investors want a still better regime, and current restrictions are all targets of negotiations.

Chile's overall score for the readiness indicators is 4.4, with figures of 5 on budgetary discipline, external debt, currency stability, and market orientation. In fact, Chile has enjoyed budget surpluses since 1987. Chile's lowest score, 3, is for price stability: in 1992, inflation was still 15 percent.

---

5. ''Pipeline'' protection broadly refers to protection for products whose patent applications are being evaluated by the national patent office (which can take several years), products that are in the development stage, and products that are not yet sold in countries that are updating their intellectual property laws (*Journal of Commerce*, 20 August 1992; Industry Functional Advisory Committee for Trade in Intellectual Property Rights 1992, 17).

In terms of overall readiness, Chile's scores come closer to those of the United States and Canada than the scores of any other Latin American country. In terms of political willingness, Chile is fully committed to strike a free trade deal with its northern neighbors as soon as possible.

Mercosur

In March 1991, the presidents of Brazil, Argentina, Paraguay, and Uruguay signed the Treaty of Asunción, forming the Mercado Común del Sur (Mercosur). The treaty established a progressive, automatic tariff reduction schedule, with a common external tariff (CET) to be instituted by 1995. The countries also agreed to attempt to harmonize laws and regulations concerning rules of origin and dispute settlement and to consult regularly on macroeconomic policies.

The treaty created two administrative bodies: the Common Market Council and the Common Market Group. The Common Market Council is an executive body that supervises the implementation and operation of the agreement. The Common Market Group oversees the operation of 10 working groups on trade, regulatory, and macroeconomic issues between the countries. The administrative secretariat of the Common Market Group is located in Montevideo, Uruguay.

In the months following the formation of the Mercosur, the participating countries, both individually and as a group, continued to liberalize trade with third countries. Uruguay and Argentina signed separate pacts with Chile concerning trade and investment matters. In June 1991, the Mercosur countries signed a framework agreement with the United States under the EAI.

The first ministerial meeting of the Mercosur, held in December 1991, resulted in the adoption of a dispute settlement mechanism patterned after chapters 18 and 19 of the Canada-US Free Trade Agreement. The process stressed quick resolution of disputes by an arbitration panel. In February 1992, Brazil accelerated the pace of its tariff reductions and committed to implement tariff cuts that were originally slated for January 1994 by January 1993. The Mercosur summit at Las Leñas, Argentina, in June 1992 then adopted 10 decisions to facilitate the transition to the common market (including a special dispute settlement procedure for the transition period to 1995) and to plan the post-1995 agenda.

At the December 1992 Mercosur summit, the CET for imported products was set at a maximum of 20 percent. However, some items will be charged 35 percent until 2001, when the top rate for all goods will be 20 percent (*Journal of Commerce*, 8 January 1993, 4A). The CET rates are still expected to be effective in January 1995. As of December 1993, the four countries had agreed on CETs for about 85 percent of the goods. However, there are still disagreements concerning extraregional imports of capital goods, computers, and telecommunications. A decision on those CETs was postponed until June 1994 (*Inside NAFTA*, 12 January 1994; and *International Trade Reporter*, 12 January 1994, 59; and 26 January 1994, 135).[6]

The timetable for eliminating tariff and nontariff barriers within the Mercosur, culminating in zero tariffs by January 1995, has not yet run into fatal political trouble. The number of products on the lists of exceptions has been reduced in line with the agreement. Effective January 1994, for example, Argentina reduced its exceptions from 162 to 81 products. However, pressure to alter the schedule has come from the Argentine Industrial Union, the largest association of industrial enterprises in the country. The union requested a delay in the startup date from January 1995 to January 1997 (*International Trade Reporter*, 17 November 1993, 1925). In addition, the Argentine decision to impose dumping duties and quotas on important Brazilian exports, including auto parts and steel, has created difficulties (*International Trade Reporter*, 4 August 1993, 1304). Meanwhile, it seems likely that the deadline for macroeconomic coordination may have to be extended.[7] Brazilians argue that the macroeconomic problems that have slowed the Mercosur process are attributable to Argentina's dollarization and subsequent overvaluation of the peso, not to Brazilian inflation or undervaluation of the cruzeiro. Naturally, most Argentine commentators see the problem in reverse.

The Mercosur received an average score of 3.1 on our readiness scale.[8] Individually, Paraguay and Uruguay received the highest scores, 3.7. Brazil and Argentina scored much lower, 2.3 and 2.6, respectively (table 6.1).

Argentina

Argentina received its highest scores for budget discipline, a 5; market-oriented policies, a 5; and functioning democracy, 4. Argentina has run a public budget deficit averaging 0.9 percent of GDP annually for the

---

6. The EC Commission approved a $17 million grant and the Inter-American Development Bank a $4 million grant toward Mercosur's expenditure in drawing up its common external tariff, its rules on competition, and its cooperation mechanisms for agriculture, customs, and technical standards (*Gazeta Mercantil*, 1 November 1993, 12).

7. There is a disagreement on this issue. For example, Argentine Economic Minister Domingo Cavallo said in November 1992 that a revision of the agreed Mercosur timetable for macroeconomic coordination was inevitable. Rubens Barbosa, undersecretary for trade and integration in Brazil's foreign ministry, agreed with Cavallo, but Fernando Cardoso, then Brazil's foreign minister, insisted that there would be no change ("Latin American Regional Reports–Brazil," Latin American Newsletters, 7 January 1993, 4).

8. Note that our scores are not weighted. Since Brazil received the lowest score of the group and is the largest economy, our grade for the region overstates their readiness as a region.

past three years. In 1992, assisted by privatization sales, Argentina ran a budget deficit of only 0.3 percent of GDP.[9] In recent years, Argentina has begun to privatize and deregulate its economy. Through 1992, Argentina had privatized 33 companies, raising $5.3 billion in cash and retiring $6.8 billion face value of debt.[10] In addition, the maximum tariff was reduced to 22 percent and the average tariff to 9.6 percent (CEPAL 1992c).[11]

In September 1993, Argentina adopted a new decree designed to encourage foreign investment. Based on these reforms, Argentina signed a bilateral investment agreement with the United States in November 1993 (*International Trade Reporter*, 10 and 24 November 1993, 1909 and 1990; see investment section on chapter 4). In April 1993, USTR named Argentina to the ''priority watch list'' of countries because of its failure to enact patent legislation in October 1991 (*International Trade Reporter*, 9 March 1994, 380).

Argentina did not fare as well in the indicators of price stability, with a score of 0, external debt, also a 0, and reliance on trade taxes, a 1. Over 1990–92, Argentina maintained an average annual inflation rate close to 800 percent. Inflation has dramatically subsided under the Menem government—from 2,314 percent in 1990 to 23 percent in 1992. If the Menem policies are sustained, Argentina could become a model of recovery from hyperinflation. Argentina continues to carry a large external debt, amounting to 454 percent of exports of goods and services in 1992. However, in April 1992, Argentina reached a debt accord with its creditors under the auspices of the Brady Plan that should accelerate its return to international capital markets.[12]

Brazil

Brazil received its only high grade (a 5) for low reliance on trade taxes: on average, between 1989 and 1991, Brazil derived only 0.9 percent of its

---

9. The Argentinean Ministry of Economy reports that in 1992 the total budget surplus was $1,412 million and total privatization revenue was $1,865 million (*Annual Economic Report 1992*, February 1993, 58).

10. Privatizations include telecommunications, airlines, 2 TV channels, parts of petrochemical firms, an electric power station, a steel mill, a shipyard, a hotel, 372 buildings and concessions for roads, railways, and 256 oilfields (Fundación Mediterránea Newsletter, ''Argentina: Fundación Mediterránea,'' June 1992, 3; First Boston 1993).

11. In November 1992, however, Argentina raised the ''statistical tax'' on imports from 3 to 10 percent ad valorem as part of a broader economic policy initiative. The higher rate is expected to be temporary (USTR 1993, 21).

12. William Cline (1994) ranks the seven most heavily indebted countries on their ''cooperativeness.'' In his scoring, Argentina ranks fifth and Brazil sixth.

current revenue from international trade taxes. Brazil earned scores of 3 for the stability of the cruzeiro, market-oriented reforms, and functioning democracy. In the early 1990s, Brazil made strong strides toward market-oriented policies.[13]

Under President Franco, however, reforms have proceeded in fits and starts.[14] For example, in December 1992 Franco suspended the privatization program for three months to allow for a "review of the rules."[15] A few large companies have subsequently been sold, but several privatization deals were postponed for one reason or another (First Boston 1993). A program that listed 36 companies for privatization during 1994 was announced by President Franco in December 1993 (*Gazeta Mercantil*, 20 December 1993, 4). As of May 1994, the Brazilian government had auctioned off 25 state-controlled companies (mainly steel, chemical, and fertilizer enterprises), raising $7 billion. In addition, private buyers assumed $3 billion in government debt. Foreign buyers purchased only 3 percent of total capital. Thirty-one additional firms are scheduled to be auctioned in 1994, including electric utilities, a bank, a railway, and an aircraft manufacturer (*International Trade Reporter*, 4 May 1994, 701). In November 1993, the 40 percent ceiling on foreign investor stockholdings in privatized companies was abolished; foreign investors may now bid for as much as 100 percent (*Gazeta Mercantil*, 1 November 1993, 5).

Despite US pressure, reforms regarding intellectual property rights proceeded at a snail's pace. The United States threatened in the spring of 1993 to invoke Section 301 procedures if Brazil did not pass legislation improving intellectual property rights protection by February 1994. At the end of that month, the USTR terminated the case because Brazil committed to pass improved patent protection legislation by 15 June 1994 and a new copyright law by 1 January 1995. Brazil's new legislation will bring its laws into compliance with the Uruguay Round accord and even go beyond the obligations of the Trade-Related Aspects of Intellectual Property Rights Agreement (TRIPs) by implementing them immediately rather than waiting the five years permitted for less-developed

---

13. For example, import licensing is now automatic within five days of requesting a license (except for computers), the balance of payments–based restrictions were terminated in June 1991, and the Law of Similars was rescinded in 1990 (under which import licenses were denied to products "similar" to competing products already produced or capable of being produced in Brazil). See USITC (1992, 7–14).

14. Symbolic of its difficulties, Brazil had three different finance ministers during 1993.

15. The Franco government originally said that it was going to continue with the planned privatizations but that "strategic" companies (that is, Petrobras, Telebras, and Companhia Vale Do Rio Doce) would not be sold (*Financial Times*, 12 November 1992, 4; "Latin American Regional Reports–Brazil", Latin American Newsletters, 7 January 1993, 3; *Latin Finance*, December 1992, 27).

countries and by providing limited pipeline protection.[16] According to the International Intellectual Property Rights Alliance, US companies lost about $125 million in 1991 due to inadequate protection of intellectual property in Brazil (*US/Latin Trade*, February 1994, 11). Brazilian software companies have higher estimates. Just in the software industry, they estimate a loss of $2 billion over 1990–93 (*International Trade Reporter*, 6 April 1994, 552).

Investment reforms are also awaited. A revision to the 1988 constitution, which will remove discriminatory provisions, is scheduled for 1994. This revision would be significant, since among a list of 27 countries, Brazil imposes the most severe restrictions on foreign capital. The main restrictions are on foreign participation in the telecommunications and mining sectors. Unfortunately, it seems that those restrictions will be maintained (*International Trade Reporter*, 4 May 1994, 702).[17] However, in November 1993, President Franco sent Congress a bill designed to exempt all royalty payments remitted to foreign firms from the financial operations tax. The purpose of this measure is to encourage Brazilian companies to spend more on acquiring patent rights, either from their parent companies abroad or from third parties (*Gazeta Mercantil*, 15 November 1993, 5).

Brazil has made good progress at trade liberalization. In July 1993, the average tariff rate was lowered to 14.2 percent, although autos, like some other sectors, remain heavily protected, with a 35 percent tariff.[18] Brazil has steadily abolished its nontariff trade barriers, including its notorious informatics law.[19] At the same time, Brazil has activated its antidumping law, a favorite tool of discretionary protection in other countries, and perhaps now in Brazil as well. New regulations are expected to permit easier filing and quicker processing of dumping complaints (*International Trade Reporter*, 1 September 1993, 1466).

---

16. The TRIPs allows Brazil 5 years to implement most of the required intellectual property reforms. Brazil will offer pipeline protection, but only if the product has not yet been marketed in any country (*Inside U.S. Trade*, 4 March 1994, 11; and *International Trade Reporter*, 2 March 1994, 345).

17. This ranking is based on a Price Waterhouse study cited in the *International Trade Reporter* (17 November 1993, 1945). The study ranked 27 countries in Asia, Europe, and Latin America, focusing on legal and bureaucratic barriers to foreign investment.

18. Tariffs on computers are also 35 percent. Tariffs on videocassette recorders, stereo equipment, and fine chemicals are 30 percent; trucks, machine tools, clothing, and toys are 20 percent; and tariffs on textiles are 10 percent (*International Trade Reporter*, 14 September 1993, 1167).

19. "Local computer manufacturers have benefited for the last 16 years from the computer market reserve, which until October 1992 closed the Brazilian market to foreign computer goods. However, the manufacturers continue to benefit from reduced state and federal taxes on locally produced computer products" (*International Trade Reporter*, 14 July 1993, 1167; see also First Boston 1993).

Trade liberalization has already taken the blame for the poor performance of some sectors. In 1993, for example, Brazil became the world's second largest cotton importer. Until 1989, Brazil had a cotton import tariff of 55 percent. The tariff was slashed to 10 percent in 1990 and completely abolished in 1992 (*Gazeta Mercantil*, 20 December 1993, 12). While the tariff cuts are welcomed by cotton textile manufacturers, they are blamed by cotton buyers for reducing domestic-cotton prices and demand.

In March 1994, Brazil proposed the creation of a South American Free Trade Area. Its goal would be to accelerate regional integration between all South American countries (*International Trade Reporter*, 23 March 1994, 471).[20]

Not surprisingly, Brazil received the lowest scores for price stability and budget discipline. Brazil's three-year average inflation rate is almost 1,500 percent per year. In contrast with most other Latin American countries, Brazil's inflation significantly increased from 441 percent in 1991 to 1,000 percent in 1992. Brazil has run a public budget deficit averaging 20 percent of GDP annually during 1988–90. The crux of the problem is the 1988 constitutional mandate that transfers many revenue sources to states and municipalities, while retaining most expenditure responsibilities at the central government level. In addition, the 1988 constitution guarantees lifetime employment for public-sector employees. Without constitutional reform, Brazil will not be able to restore budget discipline and bring inflation under control.

At the federal level, Brazil appears to have a functioning democracy, with two presidential elections held since 1985. A strange proof of political pluralism is the fact that the legislature managed to impeach President Fernando Collor for corruption and replace him using established institutional procedures. Yet corruption remains pervasive, not only at the federal level but also in state and municipal governments. The problem in Brazil is not the absence of effective political opposition but the failure of accountability among political institutions at all levels.

Paraguay

Paraguay's budget discipline, external debt, and currency stability resulted in high scores in our rankings. On average, between 1990 and 1992 Paraguay ran a budget surplus of 0.7 percent of GDP. Its external

---

20. In 1993, President Franco proposed the Amazonian Initiative, with plans to negotiate trade and investment agreements with Peru, Bolivia, Guyana, Surinam, Colombia, Ecuador, and Venezuela. In late 1993, Brazil signed two frame-work agreements (one with Peru and another with Bolivia) as part of this initiative. The agreements cover trade liberalization in some sectors, rules of origin, and trade rules (*International Trade Reporter*, 8 December 1993, 2072; *New York Times*, 29 December 1993, D2).

debt is only 114 percent of exports of goods and services, and the guaraní fluctuated (in real terms) by just 5.3 percent annually over 1990–92.

Paraguay received only moderate scores for price stability, market-oriented policies, and functioning democracy, and a low score of 2 for heavy reliance on trade taxes. Over 1989–90, Paraguay derived 17 percent of its budget receipts from taxes on international trade.[21] During 1990 and 1992, inflation averaged 25.9 percent annually. In July 1993, Paraguay joined the GATT, presaging important steps toward lower tariffs and other trade reforms once the World Trade Organization enters into force in 1995. Concerning intellectual property rights, a component of market-oriented reforms, Paraguay's problem is not only to revise the current law (revisions to the patent law are under consideration) but also to enforce its present laws (Paraguay is a "subregional hub for counterfeit trademark products"; USTR 1993, 213).

Uruguay

Uruguay received a score of 3 or higher in every category except price stability, where it merited only a 2. Inflation has averaged 94 percent annually between 1990 and 1992. The high rate of inflation is surprising since Uruguay has a good record of budget discipline. In fact, Uruguay received scores of 5 for budget discipline and currency stability. The country had a small budget surplus, averaging 0.2 percent of GNP for 1990–92. The Uruguayan nuevo peso showed an average fluctuation of only 9.5 percent annually over 1990–92. Uruguay obtained a score of 4 on external debt; in 1992, its total external debt was 196 percent of exports of goods and services.

On market-oriented policies, Uruguay merited a 3. Uruguay's average tariff is 21.5 percent. Of the 7,745 items on Uruguay's tariff schedule, 0.2 percent enter the country duty-free, 28.2 percent are subject to a 10 percent tariff, 28.2 percent are subject to a 17 percent tariff, 43.4 percent are subject to 24 percent, and a few products are subject to 40 percent (Laird 1994, 5; GATT 1992c, vol. 1, 92).

Mercosur Summary

Readiness scores for Mercosur countries as a group are low for three indicators: price stability, external debt, and reliance on trade taxes. The average scores for those three readiness indicators—1.3, 2.8, and 2.8, respectively—suggest that the region has important obstacles to over-

---

21. Paraguay is a conduit for smuggling large volumes of imports into Argentina and Brazil. With trade reforms in those countries, this source of economic activity could dry up.

come before it can achieve further integration. Perhaps most alarming is the fact that Brazil and Argentina, the dominant economic powers of the region, scored the lowest of the four countries. The Mercosur countries need to control inflation and exchange rate swings better in order to enhance the possibilities for economic integration both in the subregion and more broadly in the Western Hemisphere.

Andean Group

In the second half of the 1980s, Andean economic policy embarked on a radical new course. Recognizing the failure of past policies that promoted parastatal enterprises, industrial planning, and import substitution, Andean countries adopted market-oriented policies and sought closer integration with world markets. Individual countries within the Andean Group undertook unilateral trade reforms, pursued competitive real exchange rate policies, sold off public enterprises, and allowed greater scope for the operation of market forces. The first Andean country to implement market-oriented reforms was Bolivia in 1985. Venezuela followed in 1989, Colombia in 1990, and Peru in 1992. In Ecuador, a more gradual economic reform process has begun, including trade liberalization and deregulation of the foreign exchange market (Williamson 1990; Gitli and Ryd 1991, 12; Pascó-Font 1992). Reflecting the new economic thinking, members of the Andean Group met in 1987 to reshape the original agreement and to set a timetable for economic integration.[22] During 1990, plans for economic integration accelerated. The Act of La Paz, signed in November 1990, promised that regional free trade would be achieved by 1992. In January 1992, Colombia and Venezuela eliminated their tariffs for the other Andean countries,[23] Bolivia joined them in October 1992,[24] and Ecuador fol-

---

22. The Quito Protocol (signed in 1987 and adopted in 1988) attempted to adapt the idea of integration to the new realities, but it did not accomplish much.

23. However, Colombia and Venezuela later signed a trade accord in August 1993 covering agricultural produce, oil, electrical power cooperation, and the auto industry that ran counter to trade reforms in several respects. For example, the two countries agreed to a common external tariff for auto imports from third countries at 35 percent. Colombia's tariffs were already 30 to 35 percent, but Venezuela had to increase its tariffs to establish a common level. Other provisions of the accord included measures to limit the massive influx of Venezuelan rice into Colombia and Colombian potatoes into Venezuela (*International Trade Reporter*, 25 August 1993, 1420).

24. Imports from Andean countries were scheduled to enter Bolivia duty-free as of January 1993. There were 11 exceptions, including a few industrial goods. In addition, Bolivia signed a bilateral agreement with Peru under which Peruvian exports will enter Bolivia duty-free (GATT 1993, vol. 1, 83).

lowed in December 1992 (each country with its own list of exceptions).[25] On the other hand, Peru withdrew from the Andean Group in August 1992.[26]

The Andean Group has reached beyond trade liberalization within the region to seek partners elsewhere. Separately, each of the Andean countries has signed a bilateral framework agreement with the United States. These agreements represent a first step toward closer economic relations with the hemisphere's major market. In addition, Venezuela and the Caribbean Community (Caricom) signed a one-way free trade agreement in October 1992.[27]

In February 1993, Colombia and Venezuela signed a free trade agreement with El Salvador, Guatemala, Honduras, Nicaragua, and Costa Rica. This agreement gives duty-free access during the first five years for 500 Central American Common Market (CACM) products destined for the Colombian and Venezuelan markets. A maximum tariff of 20 percent will be applied to most other products shipped in both directions by the seven countries (Nicaragua will be allowed to apply a maximum tariff of 40 percent). Starting in year 6, duty-free treatment will be reciprocal on the identified items. By year 10, all trade barriers, except those on "sensitive" goods, will be eliminated ("Latin American Regional Reports–Caribbean and Central America," Latin American Newsletters, 25 February 1993, 1). By June 1993, however, Colombia and Venezuela had reduced the number of products on which they were offering an immediate elimination of tariffs while the Central American republics had expanded theirs ("Latin American Weekly Report," Latin American Newsletters, 16 December 1993, 579).

In May 1994, Colombia and Venezuela finalized a free trade agreement with Mexico—the group is known as the G-3. The most difficult areas of negotiation were rules of origin for textiles and chemical products. In the end, no decision on rules of origin for polyester was included in the agreement. The formal signing will be 14–15 June (*Journal of Commerce*,

---

25. Another step toward integration is an agreement, signed by the Andean transport ministers, for a "multimodal" transport project expected to decrease freight charges by up to 40 percent (*Financial Times*, 28 August 1992, 5; and "Latin American Regional Reports–Andean Group," Latin American Newsletters, 2 November 1992, 1).

26. President Fujimori assumed dictatorial powers in April 1992. In August 1992, Peru withdrew from the Andean Group and assumed observer status, expecting to resume full membership by the end of 1993 (*Financial Times*, 28 August 1992, 4). After December 1993, Peru requested an extension to continue its observer status.

27. Under the pact, 1,300 Caricom products will enter Venezuela duty-free by 1997. After the initial five-year "one-way" period, a reciprocal arrangement will give Venezuelan products duty-free access to Caricom countries ("Latin American Regional Reports–Andean Group," Latin American Newsletters, 12 November 1992, 5).

17 May 1994, 5A).[28] In addition, both Colombia and Venezuela have signed bilateral agreements with Chile.[29] In November 1993, Peru and Brazil finalized an agreement to reduce tariffs on bilateral trade by 50 percent (*International Trade Reporter*, 8 December 1993, 2072). Because Bolivia's trade relations are more extensive with the Mercosur than with its Andean partners, Bolivia has considered negotiating bilateral agreements with Brazil and Argentina.[30]

The best performers of the Andean Group were Venezuela, Colombia, and Bolivia with scores of 3.9, 3.7, and 3.7, respectively. Ecuador followed closely with a 3.4, but Peru scored only a 2.1 (the second lowest of all Latin American countries).

Venezuela

Venezuela's top scores were for budget discipline and for stability of the bolivar. Venezuela received scores of 4 for market-oriented policies and low reliance on trade taxes and scores of 3 for other indicators.

Venezuela began its *apertura* in early 1989 and joined the GATT in September 1990. By 1992, Venezuela had reduced its tariffs to an average of about 10 to 12 percent,[31] and it has liberalized investment (see investment section in chapter 4). Venezuela began privatization programs in 1990. In 1991 the list of privatizations included the airline Viasa, three banks, and companies in the telecommunications industry. Other companies scheduled for privatization were in the tourism and sugar industries.[32] Privatization efforts stalled during 1993, but the new administration has committed to try to restart the process.

---

28. According to early press reports, tariffs on about 70 percent of the items traded between the three countries will be immediately eliminated, tariffs on 25 percent of the items will be phased out over four years, and tariffs on 5 percent of the products will be phased out over eight years ("Latin American Regional Reports–Mexico & NAFTA Report," Latin American Newsletters, 14 January 1993, 4). According to information from the Colombian Ministry of Trade, the agreement covers rules of origin, safeguards, investment rules, government procurement, dispute settlement, trade in services, intellectual property, and phytosanitary standards. The agreement includes all industrial sectors and some agricultural sectors (República de Colombia, Ministerio de Comercio Exterior, *Tratado de Libre Comercio entre Colombia, Mexico, y Venezuela*, summary sheets).

29. Chile and Mexico signed a free trade agreement in September 1991, Chile and Venezuela in April 1993, and Chile and Colombia in December 1993.

30. In December 1993, Brazil proposed a series of bilateral agreements with its Amazon neighbors. Peru will be the first, but negotiations with Bolivia are already planned. In January 1994, Bolivia was officially recognized as an observer in all future Mercosur meetings (*International Trade Reporter*, 26 January 1994, 135).

31. Reynolds, Thoumi, and Wettmann (1993, 68) suggest a figure of 12 percent. Laird (1994, 5) indicates a figure of 10 percent.

32. For more details, see *Latin Finance Supplement*, "Privatization in Latin America," March 1991; Salomon Brothers 1992.

Colombia

Colombia's scores were almost the same as Venezuela's. The only differences were external debt, on which Colombia scored better than Venezuela, and reliance on trade taxes, where its performance was lower. Colombia was the only Latin American country that avoided formal rescheduling of its debt. Its total external debt in 1992 was 162 percent of exports of goods and services.[33] On the other hand, trade liberalization in Colombia can create a serious fiscal problem because import taxes averaged 16 percent of revenues during 1989–91. In 1991, the government adopted a tax reform designed in part to compensate for the prospective loss of tariff revenues.[34]

In terms of market-oriented policies, Colombia has made good progress. Colombia liberalized its foreign exchange regime and in September 1991 reduced its tariffs to an average of 14.3 percent. Tariffs were set at 15 percent for finished consumer goods, between 5 and 10 percent for certain goods produced in Colombia, and duty-free for some raw materials, intermediate goods, and goods not produced in Colombia (the duty-free category accounts for 45 percent of total tariff lines). The surcharge on imports, which also applies to duty-free items, was reduced from 13 to 5 percent in early 1992. By May 1992, the tariff average (inclusive of surcharge) had been cut to 11.8 percent. Colombia also retains some local-content requirements (see investment section in chapter 4).

Bolivia

As with Venezuela and Colombia, Bolivia rates top scores for its budget discipline and the stability of the boliviano. The major difference is external debt, where Bolivia merited a score of 0. In 1992, Bolivia's total external debt amounted to 536 percent of exports of goods and services.

Market-oriented policy reform started early and traveled far in Bolivia, for which we award a score of 4. By 1990, Bolivia had lowered its tariffs to 5 percent for capital goods and 10 percent for all other goods (the resulting average tariff is 9.8 percent). Most nontariff barriers were also eliminated (except import licensing requirements for sugar, wheat, and national security items). In the same year, Bolivia liberalized foreign investment by permitting full foreign ownership with no screening pro-

---

33. William Cline (1994) ranks Colombia at the top of the list in terms of debt cooperativeness.

34. According to Miguel Urrutia (1994, 308), in 1989 trade taxes amounted to 25 percent of total central government revenues. The 1991 tax reform included an increase in income taxes, in the value-added tax, and in taxes on oil exports.

cedures and granting national treatment to foreign investors.[35] The country sold 30 state-owned companies (transferring another eight and closing seven) for $30 million between January 1992 and July 1993 ("Latin American Economy and Business," Latin American Newsletters, August 1993, 16).

Ecuador

Ecuador received scores of 5 for budget discipline and the stability of the sucre and a 4 for functioning democracy. Its scores are lower for reliance on trade taxes and market-oriented policies (scores of 3) and for price stability and external debt (scores of 2).

Ecuador experienced some difficulty meeting the deadline to join the Andean Group. However, its average tariff is now only 11.9 percent (Reynolds, Thoumi, and Wettmann 1993, 68). In August 1992, President Sixto Durán-Ballen introduced a reform program comprising spending cuts (including reduced subsidies), tax increases, and investment liberalization in the petroleum sector. In March 1993, Durán-Ballen sent a bill to Congress that called for the privatization of Ecuatoriana Airline, the telecommunications company Emetel, oil firm Petroecuador, and several ports and hotels ("Latin American Weekly Reports," Latin American Newsletters, 18 March 1993, 129). A privatization law was finally passed in November 1994, but implementation is still slow. Ecuatoriana Airline will be the first to be privatized.[36] In addition, Ecuador signed a bilateral investment treaty with the United States in August 1993 (see investment section in chapter 4). Finally, Ecuador also signed an intellectual property agreement with the United States that guarantees "comprehensive protection for intellectual property rights at a very high level" (International Trade Reporter, 17 November 1993, 1948).[37]

Peru

Faced with economic and political instability, Peru has made less progress than other Andean members. In fact, Peru obtained one of the lowest overall scores in the hemisphere: 2.1. Its good scores were for budget discipline, a 4, and for stability of the nuevo sol, a 5. All other indicators had scores of 2 or 0.

---

35. Some exceptions remain in the mining and hydrocarbons sectors and in telecommunications services (USITC 1992, 6–6; Reynolds, Thoumi, and Wettmann 1993, 68).

36. The government plans to retain a 25 percent share in the airline (International Trade Reporter, 19 January 1994, 87).

37. Ecuador is also applying for GATT membership (International Trade Reporter, 20 October 1993, 1780).

Peru has been overwhelmed with economic, political, and social problems that feed on each other. According to Reynolds, Thoumi, and Wettmann (1993, 139), macroeconomic policy remains an obstacle to integration:

> Current adjustment policies have produced very high interest rates and have attracted large capital inflows that have overvaluated the Peruvian currency. Because of this, the Peruvian government finds it difficult to yield to the Colombian and Venezuelan pressures to lower tariffs and face international competition.

The Peruvian average tariff had been reduced to about 16 percent as of June 1993.

Despite its efforts, the government has not been very successful in liberalizing trade (*International Trade Reporter*, 9 February 1994, 224). However, improvements are expected in 1994 and 1995. The Andean Group announced in April 1994 that it would gradually reincorporate Peru. Peru plans in 1994 to privatize Centromin (a mining/smelting complex), Electrolima and Electroperu (electric utilities), Petroperu (petroleum monopoly), Percaperu (fishing company), and several ports, hotels, and train lines (*International Trade Reporter*, 27 April 1994, 654). Fujimori plans to privatize all state-owned companies by the end of 1995.

Andean Group Summary

The success of market-oriented reform within the Andean Group is evidenced by the accomplishments toward integration. By January 1994, all Andean countries except Peru had succeeded in implementing the free trade agreement. The Andean countries had also agreed to improve intellectual property protection: notably, patent protection was extended from 15 to 20 years (*Inside NAFTA*, 12 January 1994, 9).[38] In addition, Colombia and Venezuela had succeeded in negotiating the G-3 free trade agreement with Mexico.

Overall, we assign the Andean Group a score of 3.4 (table 6.1). The Andean countries do well in terms of budget discipline and currency stability and moderately well in terms of market-oriented policies, reliance on trade taxes, and functioning democracy. They turn in a poor performance on price stability (except for Bolivia) and external debt (except for Colombia).[39]

Two severe and related problems stand in the way of closer economic association between the Andean countries and other nations in the

---

38. Pharmaceutical patents were previously limited to 10 years.

39. In William Cline's (1994) cooperativeness ratings of the seven indebted countries (Chile, Colombia, Venezuela, Mexico, Brazil, Argentina, and Peru), Venezuela is the forth most cooperative.

hemisphere: drug traffic and guerrilla violence.[40] In Colombia, drug traffic has created a wave of violence that continues to terrorize the population. The notorious drug dealer Pablo Escobar was killed in December 1993, but unfortunately, many others remain in the Cali and Medellín cartels who are ready and able to pursue the lucrative drug trade.

Based on past evidence, these difficult problems will have to be solved by the affected countries with limited outside assistance. The Andean Trade Preference Act (ATPA), passed by the US Congress with an authorized life of 10 years, underscores the limits of outside help. The ATPA is ambitiously designed to help overcome coca dependence.[41] But while Andean export revenue from the coca crop is estimated at $5 billion annually, the trade benefits from ATPA initially affected only $300 million worth of goods (*Journal of Commerce*, 16 January 1992, 1A).[42] There is however, room for export growth. In Peru, for example, the ATPA seems to have attracted additional investment. According to official sources, about $100 million of current Peruvian exports will see tariff duties removed under the auspices of the ATPA (*International Trade Reporter*, 22 December 1993, 2126).

With respect to guerrilla activity, Colombia has problems, but Peru has more problems.[43] In late 1992, Colombian President César Gaviria decided to end the frustrating peace negotiations and declared war against the guerrilla movement ("Latin American Regional Reports–Andean Group," Latin American Newsletters, 17 December 1992, 4). When President Alberto Fujimori assumed dictatorial powers in Peru in April 1992, he promised to eliminate the Shining Path movement by 1995. In September 1992, Abimael Guzmán, the leader of Shining Path, was captured and sentenced to life imprisonment. Since then, the Shin-

---

40. A few years ago, Venezuela was the only Andean country where these were not major problems. However, Venezuela has recently become an important route for shipping drugs to the United States and Europe (*Journal of Commerce*, 8 June 1992, 5B; *Time*, 29 November 1993, 35).

41. Cocaine production in the region has continued to grow strongly, despite increased US military assistance for drug interdiction in the Andean countries—from $5 million in 1988 to $140 million in 1990 (Sewell, Storm et al. 1992, 17).

42. Key excluded products are canned tuna, rum, most textiles and apparel, footwear, and petroleum. In addition, sugar remains subject to US tariff rate quotas. ATPA requires that each country first be reviewed by the administration to determine its eligibility based on criteria set forth in the act. Bolivia and Colombia (July 1992), Ecuador (April 1993), and Peru (August 1993) are formally designated as beneficiaries of the ATPA (Magill 1992, 987–1007; US Department of Commerce 1992, 4; *International Trade Reporter*, 8 July 1992, 21 April 1993, and 18 August 1993).

43. Violence in Colombia is a very serious problem. However, only about 15 percent of the violent deaths are associated with guerrilla actions ("Latin American Weekly Report," Latin American Newsletters, 6 May 1993, 203).

ing Path's influence appears to be declining. However, both Colombia and Peru face many difficult years before the causes and consequences of guerilla insurrection are satisfactorily addressed.

Central American Common Market (CACM)

After years of civil strife, the members of the Central American Common Market began to revive, if slowly, in the late 1980s. The five countries agreed on a "Plan for Immediate Action," creating an emergency fund to help reactivate regional trade. By April 1990, the CACM had secured a $165 million contribution from the European Community to stimulate intraregional trade. In June 1990, Central American presidents met in Guatemala, approving an economic plan providing for the free movement of people and goods. In December 1990, the Central American presidents signed the Puntarenas Declaration, establishing the goal of a common Central American customs and tariff policy. In January 1991, the CACM signed a framework agreement with Mexico to create a free trade zone by 1997.

The next CACM meeting in December 1991 resulted in the reactivation of the Organization of Central American States.[44] The move was designed both to accelerate economic integration and promote political stability in the region. Earlier, in June 1991, the CACM countries had agreed both to drop duties on regional trade in agricultural products by June 1992 and to impose a common external tariff (CET) with a ceiling of 20 percent by December 1992. However, at the end of 1992, the maximum external tariff of the Central American countries still varied from 20 to 40 percent. Early in 1993, the new CET ceiling was expected to be set at 20 percent, with exceptions for a few products (Joint Economic Committee 1993, 279 and 286).

Traditionally, Panama has not been part of key regional organizations—for example, the Central American Bank for Economic Integration and the Organization of Central American States. Its strong services sector coupled with its small agricultural and industrial sectors set Panama apart from its neighbors. Slowly, Panama has changed its commercial diplomacy and has started to participate in regional plans. In July 1991, Panama joined the CACM as an active member, although it did not fully join in economic integration plans (*Financial Times*, 18 July 1991, 7). In December 1992, Panama proposed, together with the other Central American countries, the development of a regional transportation network (*Journal of Commerce*, 4 December 1992, 1A). Panama was also included in the recent IDB agreement, Programa de Apoyo al Desar-

---

44. The Charter of the Organization of Central American States (ODECA) was signed by the five Central American countries in 1951. It represented an attempt at institutionalized cooperation among the Central American countries (Caribbean Community 1992).

rollo y la Integración de Centroamérica (PRADIC), signed 7 April 1992 and designed to reinforce Central American efforts for economic integration.

While the CACM was making progress as a group, its individual members were pursuing bilateral and trilateral negotiations within the region and beyond. Honduras and Costa Rica signed separate framework trade agreements with the United States in the context of the EAI in November 1990. El Salvador, Nicaragua, and Panama were not far behind, each signing framework agreements with the United States in May and June 1991. Guatemala followed suit in October 1991. In addition, Costa Rica signed separate bilateral trade agreements with Mexico and Venezuela in early 1991. Finally, CACM countries signed a free trade agreement with Colombia and Venezuela on February 1993; Panama is expected to join this pact as well. ("Latin American Regional Reports–Caribbean and Central America," Latin American Newsletters, 25 February 1993, 1).

The CACM countries have also begun to deepen their own integration efforts. In March 1991, El Salvador and Guatemala pledged to eliminate obstacles to trade and to expand infrastructure investments (e.g., highways, rails, ports) linking the two countries. In April 1991, Honduras and Guatemala signed a similar trade agreement. Those three countries signed a trilateral trade agreement in May 1992, establishing new import tariffs to take effect at the start of 1993.

We applied our analysis of the feasibility of increased economic integration within CACM by grading each country according to the seven readiness indicators. El Salvador and Costa Rica received the highest scores, 3.7 and 3.3, respectively. Honduras and Guatemala received scores of 2.6 each, while Nicaragua lagged with only a 1.6 on our readiness scale—the lowest of any country we graded (table 6.1).

El Salvador

El Salvador received good scores in every category except market-oriented policies and reliance on trade taxes, for which it received scores of 2, and functioning democracy, a score of 3.

El Salvador's best performance came in price stability (a 4), and it received scores of 5 for budget discipline, external debt, and stability of the colón.[45] During 1990–92, inflation averaged 16.6 percent, and the budget deficit averaged 2.4 percent of GDP.

---

45. One explanation for El Salvador's strong external position is the level of remittances. Private transfers from Salvadorans working in the United States exceeded $700 million in 1992 ("El Salvador: The Peace Dividend," US/Latin Trade, November/December 1993, 104–08).

In 1991, President Alfredo Cristiani introduced the Economic and Social Development Program to address macroeconomic imbalances and increase reliance on market forces (Joint Economic Committee 1993, 202). However, the government has done little to privatize state-owned companies beyond partial moves in the banking sector. In addition, like most of Central America, El Salvador does not provide adequate intellectual property protection.[46] According to the International Intellectual Property Alliance, piracy in El Salvador (mostly of music cassettes) cost the industry $7.4 million in 1992.

In August 1992, El Salvador imposed sanitary measures designed to eliminate imports of US poultry.[47] In addition, in 1990 and 1991, El Salvador implemented a price-band mechanism for corn, sorghum, soybeans and rice. Imports with prices below the band are charged higher tariffs (USTR 1993, 76).

Costa Rica

Costa Rica received high or moderate scores in every area except reliance on trade taxes, where its score is 0. Over the past two years, Costa Rica has derived over 28 percent of its public revenues from taxes on international trade. Costa Rica's highest score, a 5, is for the stability of the colón. It received scores of 4 for budget discipline, external debt, and functioning democracy.

Costa Rica partly redressed its external debt problems by negotiating a Brady Plan agreement in May 1990. Costa Rica is the only Central American country that received a score of 4 for functioning democracy. Its continuous democratic rule since 1948 and the absence of a permanent, standing army are remarkable achievements.

Costa Rica earns moderate scores of 3 for price stability and market-oriented policies. Costa Rica's average annual inflation during 1990–92 was 23.2 percent. In 1992, the uniform tariff was 11 percent, but there were over 200 exceptions. In March 1992, Costa Rica eliminated the central bank surcharge of 2 percent on all imports. However, Costa Rica still has high import-related restrictions: a selective consumption tax of 5 to 75 percent on certain imports, border fees, and a required 30 percent foreign exchange deposit prior to importation. Privatization has gone forward: of the more than 40 state-owned companies held in the early 1980s, all but 2 have been sold (Joint Economic Committee 1993, 198).

---

46. El Salvador's intellectual property laws are dated, and even limited revisions have not been enacted by the Salvadoran National Assembly.

47. The restrictions call for zero tolerance of three diseases (including salmonella), a standard that goes well beyond standards in the United States, Canada, Japan, and the European Union. Domestic production is not subject to the same requirements. US poultry exports to El Salvador ($3 million per year) have stopped.

However, Costa Rica still maintains some restrictions on foreign investment (see investment section in chapter 4).

Guatemala

Guatemala received high scores for budget discipline (5), and external debt (4); medium scores of 3 for price stability and for stability of the quetzal, and low scores for market-oriented policies (1), reliance on trade taxes (0), and functioning democracy (2). The exchange rate system has become more transparent, with free currency convertibility allowed between Guatemala, El Salvador, and Honduras (Joint Economic Committee 1993, 279). The government has done little to deregulate the economy, preferring sporadic changes rather than sweeping reform. It has no program to privatize public enterprises. However, parastatal enterprises play a smaller role in Guatemala than in most of Latin America.

As was the case in El Salvador, rapid increases of US poultry exports to Guatemala prompted the government to adopt measures to protect local poultry producers. Currently, there is a quota of 300 metric tons per month with an in-quota tariff of 20 percent and an above-quota tariff of 45 percent.[48] As in El Salvador, Guatemala set price bands for basic grains in 1992, charging higher tariffs on imports entering at prices below the band (USTR 1993, 103).

Honduras

Honduras received the highest score for the stability of the lempira and moderate scores of 3 for price stability, budget discipline, and functioning democracy. The inflation rate during 1990–92 averaged 22 percent, while the budget deficit averaged 5.8 percent of GDP. Low scores of 2 were awarded for external debt and market-oriented policies, and the score for reliance on trade taxes was 0. International trade taxes, for example, provided on average nearly 30 percent of the Honduran government's revenue during 1988–90.

Honduras recently devalued the lempira to better reflect its market value. Over the next three years, Honduras will phase out all customs privileges and exemptions and restructure its import tariffs from a range of 1 to 90 percent to a range of 5 to 20 percent (*International Trade Reporter*, 28 July 1993, 1258).

---

48. The difference between in-quota and above-quota tariffs does not violate GATT bindings. However, the amount of tariff collected is based on a reference price rather than the transaction value. The reference price used is the US published price for whole chickens, which is double the cost, insurance, and freight (CIF) value of the chicken legs and thighs that are actually imported. This procedure may violate the GATT understanding on custom procedures (USTR 1993, 103).

Nicaragua

Nicaragua trailed the other CACM countries, receiving very low scores in all indicators except for the stability on the nuevo córdoba (in terms of the real exchange rate) and reliance on trade taxes, where it received moderate scores. Runaway inflation and high budget deficits have been alarming. Fortunately, Nicaragua appears to have passed its bloody years of civil war. In 1990, the Sandinistas left office peacefully, paving the way for the new president, Violeta Chamorro. However, Nicaragua still receives a low score of 2 for functioning democracy.

CACM Summary

Overall, CACM received an average score of only 2.7 on our scale. The CACM score was burdened by the region's high reliance on trade taxes and by the slow pace of market-oriented reforms. Except for Nicaragua, scores for price stability, budget discipline, external debt, and currency stability are moderate to good.

Caribbean Community (Caricom)

After 15 years of relative stagnation, the Caribbean Community began a new spurt of activity in the late 1980s. In 1988, Caricom agreed on the System of Rules for Enterprises, a pact designed to promote investment in certain sectors. This agreement reversed an earlier policy, which, while never implemented, would have assigned certain types of investment to specific countries (similar to Andean Group Decision 24).

In July 1989, Caricom began to take bold steps toward economic integration, signing the Grand Anse Declaration. It proposed a new CET and an agreement on rules of origin by January 1991. In addition, Caricom sought to establish a regional stock exchange (which started in July 1991), to create a monetary union by 1995, and ultimately to allow for the free movement of labor.

At its summit in August 1990, in a move that would often be repeated, Caricom decided to postpone implementation of the CET. The deadline for the largest countries was set for April 1991, and the deadline for the smaller countries was extended until December 1991. In April 1991, when the new deadline for larger countries passed unfulfilled, Caricom decided to reduce the tariff rate at the upper end of the CET schedule.

This new schedule ranged from 5 to 45 percent, replacing the older structure of 5 to 70 percent. Within this schedule, low rates of duty are applied to imports that do not compete with goods produced by Caricom members, and higher rates are assessed on imports that might compete with industries in the region.

Caricom delayed implementation of the CET several more times. The recurrent postponement of the CET illustrates a major obstacle preventing full integration within Caricom. The largest countries have now implemented the common tariff schedule. However, the smaller countries (Belize, St. Kitts, St. Lucia, Antigua, Monserrat) have not, preferring to maintain their generally lower tariff schedules. The smaller countries worry about the possible inflationary impact of the CET and the sheer economic burden of buying high-cost goods from their larger neighbors. Responding to this concern, in October 1992 Caricom agreed to reduce the maximum 45 percent CET rate. The newest schedule will lower the maximum CET to 20 percent by 1998 (*Inside U.S. Trade*, 6 November 1992, 16).

In May 1992, concerned about the impending NAFTA and the small size of their own economies, four of Caricom's smallest members agreed on a plan to create a political union. Yet it remains unclear whether the smallest Caribbean countries will enact the common external tariff within Caricom.

Caricom has enjoyed good relations with other countries in the Western Hemisphere. Continuing its history of warm trade relations with the United States, Caricom signed a framework agreement on trade and investment with the United States in July 1991 under EAI auspices. The agreement established the US-Caricom Trade and Investment Council. In its first year, the council began to address debt relief and investment issues. These efforts quickly resulted in US forgiveness of $217 million of Jamaica's external debt in August 1991.

At about the same time, Caricom began to attract attention from other Latin American countries. In July 1991, Venezuela offered Caricom unilateral preferential access to its market for five years with the stipulation that Caricom member states would progressively lower their duties on Venezuelan exports during a subsequent five-year period. This agreement with Venezuela was finally signed in October 1992 ("Latin American Regional Reports–Andean Group," Latin American Newsletters, 12 November 1992, 5).

In July 1991, Cuba expressed an interest in joining the trading group. In July 1993, Caricom and Cuba signed an agreement establishing the Joint Commission on Technical Cooperation. In October 1991, citing its proximity to the region, Venezuela applied to become a member.

We applied our analysis of the feasibility of increased economic integration in Caricom by grading the largest countries (Bahamas, Barbados, Guyana, Jamaica, and Trinidad and Tobago) on the seven readiness indicators. The largest Caricom members may be relatively well-positioned for future integration. However, the smaller countries have consistently postponed adoption of the CET and may slow the pace of integration efforts. Recognizing the partial nature of the data, the following assessment of readiness in the largest countries can be found in table 6.1.

Trinidad and Tobago

Trinidad and Tobago, the best performer of all Latin American countries, received scores of 4 and 5, except for its market-oriented policies, for which it merits a 3. Trinidad and Tobago has just started to pursue privatization measures but to this point has made little progess (*Financial Times*, 6 April 1992; Worrell 1990, 272; "Latin American Regional Reports–Caribbean and Central America," Latin American Newsletters, 25 February 1993, 3).

Barbados

Barbados received the second highest score of all Latin American countries. It received moderate scores for market-oriented policies and reliance on trade taxes. Over the past three years, Barbados's inflation rate has averaged 5.1 percent annually; its currency, pegged to the US dollar, has not fluctuated. The US Senate ratified, in November 1993, a bilateral tax treaty with Barbados (*International Trade Reporter*, 1 December 1993, 2023).

Jamaica

Jamaica scored either a 4 or 5 in every category except price stability, market-oriented policies, and reliance on trade taxes; in these three areas, Jamaica merited a 3, a 3, and a 2, respectively. Jamaica received a 5 in budget discipline and currency stability. Except for 1988, Jamaica has run a surplus since 1986, and its real exchange rate has fluctuated an average of 7.1 percent in the last three years. In terms of market-oriented policies, Jamaica has made significant progress. Early in 1994, Jamaica signed both a bilateral investment treaty and an intellectual property rights agreement with the United States (*Inside U.S. Trade*, 11 February 1994, 7).

Bahamas

The Bahamas received high scores in every category except on market-oriented policies and reliance on trade taxes, where it received scores of 3 and 0, respectively. Annual inflation over the last three years was under 6 percent. The Bahamas dollar has been pegged to the US dollar, eliminating any fluctuation in the nominal rate. However, over the past two years, international trade taxes have provided 60 percent of revenues.

Guyana

Guyana received the lowest readiness score (2.4) of all the Caricom countries surveyed. Its lowest indicators are budget discipline and external debt. Over 1990–92, the government ran an average annual deficit equal to 17 percent of GDP, and in 1991 its total external debt as a percentage of exports of goods and services was almost 700 percent. Guyana also scores low in terms of a functioning democracy. The People's National Congress (PNC), which had been in power since 1964, lost an election in October 1992, allowing Cheddi Jagan from the People's Progressive Party (PPP) to become the new president. Prior to that election, opposition parties were subject to harassment by police and the armed forces.[49]

Caricom Summary

Based on the available data, Caricom received a relatively high overall score of 3.7, but this rating reflects the position of the larger countries, not the smaller members. The region performed best on currency stability. All Caricom countries have pegged their currencies to the US dollar, except for Guyana and Jamaica, and even these countries have stable currencies (IMF, *International Financial Statistics*, March 1993, 6).

Market-oriented policies for Caricom countries are hard to judge. In general, the Caribbean nations have relatively open economies, and they rely heavily on imports to augment the limited range of local production. Jamaica seems to have done more to open its economy than the other large Caricom members. In terms of privatization, Jamaica is ahead of most countries in the hemisphere: it has divested 201 state-owned companies since 1981. Guyana has done less to open its economy. Its privatization program was suspended early in 1993 because it lacked transparency and credibility (*Journal of Commerce*, 4 December 1992, 3A; and 8 January 1993, 3A). Trinidad and Tobago recently announced the total or partial privatization of 24 public companies. Of the 83 enterprises in which the state has an interest, 35 are wholly owned and 46 are partially owned by the government ("'Latin American Regional Reports–Caribbean and Central America,'' Latin American Newsletters, 25 February 1993, 3). With the exception of Guyana, the five largest Caricom members have well-established parliamentary democracies with effective opposition parties.

Caribbean Basin Initiative (CBI)

A total of 28 countries are eligible for Caribbean Basin Initiative benefits. They include all 13 Caricom countries and all 5 CACM countries, plus

---

49. The two parties do not differ much on economic policy; both used to be socialist, and both now favor market-oriented policies. Instead, the parties are divided along racial lines: PNC is supported by the Afro-Guyanese voters and the PPP by the Indo-Guyanese voters, who are the majority (Freedom House 1990 and 1992; *The Economist*, 19 September 1992, 53; *New York Times*, 3 November 1992, A4).

Panama, the Dominican Republic, Aruba, the British Virgin Islands, the Netherlands Antilles, and Haiti. Haiti's benefits, however, were temporarily suspended in November 1991. Although the CBI countries are not a group formed to accomplish integration, they are now working to secure NAFTA parity.[50] Under prior US legislation, CBI countries received unilateral preferential access to the US market (Hufbauer and Schott 1992, 273). However, with the passage of NAFTA, Mexico's access will soon be superior to the access they have enjoyed.

Separately from the NAFTA parity bill, in January 1994 the Clinton administration stated that it would try to help CBI countries in areas hurt by NAFTA (such as the assembly of cut parts into finished apparel). The administration is also interested in negotiating bilateral agreements with CBI countries dealing with investment and intellectual property rights or possibly NAFTA-style agreements but with scaled-back obligations (*Inside U.S. Trade*, 28 January 1994, 8).

Cuba

Cuba has been isolated from the rest of the hemisphere for more than 30 years. After Soviet economic support to Cuba was slashed in 1989, the country's economy started to worsen drastically. Cuba is now in the midst of a serious economic crisis. In response, President Fidel Castro has put an emphasis on restructuring the economy toward economic self-sufficiency and has tried to encourage foreign private investment (Preeg 1993).[51] More recently, he has also allowed Cubans to hold foreign currency ("Latin American Weekly Report," Latin American Newsletters, 29 July 1993, 339).

As trade with the former Soviet Union and East European countries diminished, Cuba's trade with Latin America, the Middle East, some Western European countries, and China increased. For example, at the end of 1990, Cuba reached a trade agreement with China providing for $500 million in two-way trade in sugar, citrus, and light industrial goods for bicycles, industrial spare parts, and textiles.

President Castro has participated in Ibero-American summits, where he was strongly encouraged by Latin and Iberian leaders to permit political and economic liberalization. At a meeting in late 1991 with presidents from Mexico, Colombia, and Venezuela, Castro was again pres-

---

50. A CBI parity bill (HR 1403), introduced in March 1993, would extend some NAFTA benefits to CBI countries for three years.

51. In the past, foreign investors were limited to 49 percent shareholdings. Early in 1991, the president of the Cuban Chamber of Commerce said that Cuba would consider offers up to 100 percent investment (Joint Economic Committee 1993, 138). Fidel Castro has already allowed more than 100 state enterprises to enter into joint ventures with foreign investors (*US/Latin Trade*, May 1994, 44).

sured to reform. The United States continues to oppose any enlargement of economic ties between Cuba and other hemispheric nations. In October 1992, the Cuban Democracy Act (the Torricelli bill), prohibiting overseas subsidiaries of US firms from trading with Cuba, was signed into law. Most other countries, however, have been willing to expand economic ties with Cuba (*International Trade Reporter*, 1 and 22 September 1993, 1464 and 1574). The EU parliament has called on EU members to ignore the Torricelli law. The United Kingdom and Canada adopted measures preventing locally based firms from yielding to the measure. Cuba has signed textile agreements with firms in Canada, India, Italy, the Netherlands, Panama, and Spain. Despite US criticism, Caricom established a Joint Commission for technical cooperation with Cuba in July 1993 (*Financial Times*, 18 August 1993, 5).

According to a study by Ernest Preeg (1993, table 5–1), if Cuba were to implement a free market economy and the United States were to end its embargo, foreign exchange earnings would double in two years, from $2.7 billion in 1992 to $5.5 billion in 1994, and would reach $9.5 billion by 1997. The largest increase would be expected in the service sector, mainly tourism. More than 600,000 tourists visited Cuba in 1993. The revenues reached $700 million (a 32 percent increase over 1992).

Several European and Latin American countries are interested in trading with and investing in Cuba. Spanish companies have taken over the management of a few hotels and formed joint ventures with others, Israel has invested on a citrus project and in tourism, and Canada has invested in mining (*US/Latin Trade*, February 1994, 12 and 18; May 1994, 38–45).

7

Hemispheric Negotiations

Building on the previous analysis of subregional integration and readiness indicators, we now return to an examination of the modalities and content of prospective hemispheric free trade talks. We start with a discussion of the alternative paths to Western Hemisphere economic integration. We then turn to an analysis of the key issues likely to be on the agenda of prospective hemispheric trade negotiations.

Paths to Integration

In the past, when the world economy primarily involved merchandise trade on the sea lanes of the Mediterranean, all roads led to Rome. The center of the Roman Empire served as the magnet for commerce from the periphery. Economic integration was less a matter of sharing than of subservience.

Today, the world economy is much more complex, and the Roman model of economic integration through military coercion is distinctly out of fashion. Yet other historical models do provide insights for countries seeking to integrate more closely on a regional or hemispheric level. While recognizing that there are numerous variants of each approach, we examine two models of economic integration: the ''big bang'' model and the hub-and-spoke model.

The Big Bang Model

Economic integration can occur when an overarching political event leads to the spontaneous integration of geographically proximate states.

Military conflict often has been the catalyst of such unions—for example, the American Revolution for the United States, the Franco-Prussian War for Germany, and the Second World War for the former Soviet bloc. In other instances, the catalyst for economic integration has been the release from colonial rule and the subsequent formation of a confederation of states or provinces, as in Canada in 1867, Australia in 1901, and India in 1947.

More recently, the big bang model has taken on new meaning in light of the dominant role played by the nuclear superpowers. Military coercion is primarily the domain of a few countries, but the fact that military conflict poses great risk has meant that it is less likely to serve as an integrating force. To be sure, the threat of superpower conflict was enough to hasten the creation of the European Community in the 1950s. In the post–Cold War era, however, the scope for "big bang" integration is much reduced and may be confined to cases of national unification (Korea) and subregional conflict (the Balkans).

It is important to note that, where it worked, the big bang approach only began a process of economic integration. In each case, the initial economic area created by the big bang was later deepened and enlarged. Deepening required the elimination of numerous internal barriers and a vigilant legal system to defend the principle of open markets. Accretion was pursued through either annexation, cooption, or negotiation, which often followed the hub-and-spoke model.

The Hub-and-Spoke Model

The hub-and-spoke model posits a country-by-country approach to a common objective: integration with the principal market by smaller countries in the neighborhood and the periphery. The country with the major market is the center or "hub" of interest for integration efforts. Smaller economies link up with the hub while remaining delinked from each other, much like spokes of a wheel without an outer rim. In retrospect, the British and French Empires of the 19th century can be seen as precursors of hub-and-spoke integration. More recently, the concept has been rediscovered in the context of EC and US commercial diplomacy, and the economic and political implications of such relationships have been examined in great depth by Park and Yoo (1989) and Wonnacott (1991).

The hub benefits from enhanced access to small markets; the spokes benefit from better access to a major market.[1] In addition, the hub's

---

1. A variant of the hub-and-spoke approach is the integration of a spoke country with different hubs. Israel was the first practitioner of this approach, negotiating an FTA with the European Community in 1975 and then with the United States in 1985. In the Western Hemisphere, Chile is among the few countries that could adopt this approach.

advantageous trade position increases its attractiveness to investors, who can source and sell freely to a wide range of countries. The competitive position of industries in each spoke country is undercut in the other spoke economies due to the preferential position of industries in the hub country (since they can freely access each spoke as well as the hub), but the discrimination entailed by the addition of another spoke is often minor because intraregional trade among the spokes is generally small.

For example, in North America, both Canada and Mexico trade predominantly with the United States; the US market accounts for about 73 percent and 76 percent of their total exports, respectively. By contrast, Canada-Mexico trade totaled about $2 billion in 1990, just a fraction of their total trade (tables 3.5 and 3.6). Similarly, although not quite as starkly, the predominant share (58 percent) of the exports of the European Free Trade Association (EFTA) spokes in the European hub is with members of the European Union, while only 13 percent of their exports go to other EFTA members.

Nevertheless, while preexisting trade between individual spokes may be small, as more spokes integrate with the hub country, the value of preferences in the hub market accorded to industries in spoke countries is watered down, and the threat of investment diversion to the hub economy is strengthened. Expansion of the preference area thus creates pressures to transform the rimless wheel into an integrated FTA or customs union to safeguard interests in the hub market, to expand competitive opportunities in other spoke markets, and to promote investment throughout the economic area. In effect, Canada did just this by opting for a North American Free Trade Agreement instead of relying on its own FTA with the United States.

The most direct way for a spoke country to integrate with a hub is to join an existing free trade club and undertake its common rules and obligations. This approach usually involves the negotiation of a protocol of accession that establishes how a candidate country will bring its existing laws, regulations, and practices into conformity with the existing pact and sets out a schedule for the liberalization of specific trade and investment barriers. Accession to a common regime avoids the creation of a patchwork quilt of inconsistent and discriminatory trade arrangements that could inhibit trade and investment in the region.

Two variants of this model are currently deployed: the open-ended accession model of the General Agreement on Tariffs and Trade (GATT) and the more selective membership-by-invitation model of the European Union. Both establish eligibility criteria for membership: the GATT standard is based on the market orientation of the candidate countries; the EU criteria involve that test, as well as geographic proximity and democracy tests. More recently, the European Union appears to be realigning its standards to include subjects such as foreign policy that are expected to play a role in the deepening of economic and political integration.

Content of the Negotiations

In many ways, the NAFTA will serve as a blueprint for FTA negotiations between the United States and Latin American countries. Hemispheric negotiations on "traditional" issues, such as tariffs and quotas, and "new" issues, such as intellectual property rights and investment rules, will closely follow the NAFTA model. In addition, "collateral" issues that have recently gained prominence—notably, the environment, workers' rights and labor conditions, human rights, and democratic practices—will inevitably occupy an important place in the WHFTA negotiating agenda.

Traditional Issues

A WHFTA, or the accession of individual countries to NAFTA, will necessarily involve the elimination of tariffs, quotas, and many other nontariff barriers (NTBs) on "substantially all" intraregional trade.[2] Moreover, the existing members of NAFTA are likely to view the willingness of prospective new members to commit to zero tariffs as a threshold indicator of their interest in a larger hemispheric FTA. In addition, quota restrictions will have to be eliminated (with the possible exception of one or two ultrasensitive sectors in each country). At issue is not the ultimate elimination of tariffs and quotas, but rather the schedule for phasing them out—in other words, the length of the transition period and the pace of reforms until full liberalization is achieved.

In 1991, tariff levels in most Latin American countries were relatively high, usually above 20 percent. By 1993, the average may have dropped below 15 percent, owing to extensive unilateral liberalization by many countries, and Uruguay Round reforms will reduce the rates even further over the next 10 years. In several sectors, tariffs are supplemented by quantitative restrictions of unknown severity.

Table 7.1 shows the trade-weighted tariff levels, as of 1991, imposed by 10 Latin American countries. In 1991, these 10 countries absorbed 64 percent of US exports to Latin America (International Monetary Fund, *Direction of Trade Statistics Yearbook*, 1992). The average tariff for these 10 countries was 26 percent at that time; a recent calculation indicates that the average by 1993 had been cut to 12 percent.[3] While the drop is

---

2. Comprehensive liberalization is one of the GATT requirements for free trade areas to qualify for the exemption from the most-favored nation (MFN) obligation of GATT Article I.

3. The 1991 figure is trade-weighted while the 1993 figure is not (see the footnote in table 7.1).

significant, the level is still high compared with US and Canadian average rates of under 5 percent and when calculated in relation to total merchandise imports (dutiable and nondutiable). Moreover, several sectors receive much higher protection in Latin America than the figure indicated by the average tariff. For example, in the foods and feeds sector and in the textiles and apparel sector, both of which are highly protected in seven of the ten countries surveyed, tariff rates often exceed 20 percent. Automotive products in general are amply protected, often above 30 percent. In these sectors, the United States and Canada will push for quick tariff reduction and elimination of nontariff barriers.

While tariff protection in the United States is usually low (textiles and apparel and certain agricultural goods are important exceptions), NTBs are sometimes important. A study by Hufbauer and Elliott (1994) indicates that the tariff equivalents of US barriers (tariffs and NTBs combined) can be quite high, ranging up to 66 percent for sensitive product categories (table 7.2).[4] The most prominent US barriers facing Latin American trade are import quotas on sugar and dairy products, high tariffs on rubber footwear and frozen concentrated orange juice, and voluntary export restraints (VERs) on apparel.

Implementation of the Uruguay Round will erode some long-standing US trade barriers, especially apparel quotas imposed pursuant to the Multi-Fiber Arrangement (MFA). However, many trade barriers will remain intact; for example, the US frozen concentrated orange juice tariff will still exceed 25 percent.

In hemispheric talks, the United States will probably advance both a "Latin American agenda," calling for rapid reduction of barriers to US exports, and a "domestic agenda," trying to ensure both the very slow phaseout of US protection for sensitive products and quick recourse to US trade remedy laws. With these considerations in mind, we now turn to a discussion of sensitive sectors.

Manufactured Goods

Manufactured goods accounted for about 78 percent of total US exports to Latin America in 1991 (GATT, *International Trade 1991–92*, 84). Rapid elimination of barriers to trade in manufactured goods will be a leading US objective in the negotiation of the WHFTA. The main exception to this proposition is the textiles and apparel sector, which will be discussed shortly.

Mexico's NAFTA concessions in the automotive sector offer insight into US objectives for manufactures trade under the WHFTA (see also Hufbauer and Schott 1993a, 37–43). Mexico will eliminate all its automo-

---

4. Indeed, the tariff equivalent for US protection of the maritime industry is 85 percent (Hufbauer and Elliott 1994, 9; Laird and Yeats as cited in Erzan and Yeats 1992, 29).

Table 7.1 Latin America: average tariffs applied on world imports, 1991 and 1993[a] (percentages)

Country	Sector	Tariff 1991	Tariff 1993
Argentina	Average all sectors	27	12
	Foods and feeds	26	
	Agricultural materials	22	
	All manufactures	28	
	Textiles and apparel	37	
	Electrical machinery	42	
	Transport equipment	34	
Bolivia	Average all sectors	20	10
Brazil	Average all sectors	42	14
	Foods and feeds	34	
	Agricultural materials	33	
	All manufactures	46	
	Textiles and apparel	62	
	Electrical machinery	50	
	Transport equipment	47	
Chile	All imports	15	11
Colombia	Average all sectors	22	11
	Foods and feeds	36	
	All manufactures	21	
	Textiles and apparel	37	
	Electrical machinery	11	
	Transport equipment	24	
Ecuador	Average all sectors	23	12
	Foods and feeds	25	
	Agricultural materials	22	
	All manufactures	24	
	Textiles and apparel	31	
	Electrical machinery	24	
	Transport equipment	20	
Paraguay	Average all sectors	10	10
	Agricultural materials	14	
	All manufactures	11	
	Textile and apparel	16	

tive tariffs and almost all nontariff barriers over a transition period lasting 5 to 10 years. Tariffs on autos and light trucks (20 percent in 1993) will be cut in half immediately and then phased out either over 10 years (autos) or 5 years (light trucks). With respect to NTBs in the auto sector, Mexico will phase out its domestic-content requirements over ten years. Mexico's trade balancing requirements, which require auto firms to export a certain amount in order to import components, will be immediately reduced by 60 percent. A further reduction will occur in 2003, and this NTB will be eliminated completely in 2004. Mexico will imme-

Country	Sector	Tariff 1991	Tariff 1993
Peru	Average all sectors	48	18
	Foods and feeds	48	
	Agricultural materials	34	
	All manufactures	52	
	Textiles and apparel	68	
	Electrical machinery	50	
	Transport equipment	37	
Uruguay	Average all sectors	28	22
	Foods and feeds	32	
	Agricultural materials	24	
	Coal and petroleum	29	
	All manufactures	28	
	Textiles and apparel	36	
	Electrical machinery	26	
	Transport equipment	31	
Venezuela	Average all sectors	31	10
	Foods and feeds	42	
	All manufactures	32	
	Textiles and apparel	47	
	Electrical machinery	27	
Average of all	Average all sectors	26	12
above countries	Foods and feeds	28	
	Agricultural materials	22	
	All manufactures	27	
	Textiles and apparel	36	
	Electrical machinery	27	
	Transport equipment	26	

a. The 1991 rates are trade-weighted average tariffs. The 1993 rates for individual countries are unweighted tariff averages imposed on world imports. The 1993 rate for all countries is a trade-weighted average.

Sources: Refik Erzan and Alexander Yeats, *Free Trade Agreements with the United States: What's in It for Latin America?*, World Bank Working Papers, Policy Research, International Trade, January 1992, p. 37; and Sam Laird, "Recent Liberalization of Latin American Trade," 1994, unpublished paper, p. 5.

diately eliminate its quota on new car imports for automobiles produced by companies that also manufacture in Mexico. After a 10-year transition period, all import quotas on new cars will be removed, whether or not they are produced by a company that also has a manufacturing plant in Mexico.

Textiles and Apparel

Textiles and apparel are highly protected by tariffs not only in the United States and Canada, but also in Latin America. Latin American ad val-

Table 7.2 US trade barriers most relevant to Latin America: tariff plus tariff equivalents of quotas, 1990[a]

Product	Barrier	Tariff plus equivalent
Women's footwear, except athletic	High tariffs	10
Canned tuna	High tariffs	11
Women's handbags	High tariffs	14
Meat	Import quotas on beef and veal	15[b]
Wheat	Import quotas	15[b]
Luggage	High tariffs	17
Iron and steel	Average all items	20[b]
Rubber footwear	High tariff	20
Textiles	VER	23
Frozen concentrated orange juice	High tariff, avg. 1988–91	30
Rice	Import quotas	30[b]
Apparel	VER	48
Dairy products	Import quota, avg. 1989–91	50
Peanuts	Import quota, avg. 1986–89	50
Sugar	Import quota	66

VER = voluntary export restraint
a. The tariff plus tariff equivalent rates generally apply to US imports from the whole world, with the exception of Canada, Israel, and the Caribbean Basin Initiative countries, which, in 1990, enjoyed varying preferences for shipments into the US market. With the ratification of the NAFTA, similar preferences will be phased in for Mexico.
b. These figures are taken from Erzan and Yeats (1992). They are estimates of tariff equivalents of nontariff barriers.

Sources: Gary Clyde Hufbauer and Kimberly Ann Elliott, *Measuring the Cost of Protection in the United States*, Washington: Institute for International Economics, 1994, p. 9; and Refik Erzan and Alexander Yeats, *Free Trade Agreements with the United States: What's in It for Latin America?*, World Bank Working Papers, Policy Research, International Trade, January 1992, p. 29.

orem rates range as high as 70 percent. In addition, the textile and apparel sectors have historically benefited from strict quotas throughout the hemisphere.

In the United States, tariff rates are significantly higher for textiles and apparel than for other product categories. On average, thread and yarn are subject to a 9 percent tariff, fabrics 11.5 percent, and apparel 22.5 percent. These figures are much higher than the 6.5 percent average for all manufactures (Cline 1990, 163) and will not be significantly reduced by the Uruguay Round reforms.[5]

In addition to ad valorem tariffs, Latin American exports to the United States are subject to quotas. For example, 36.7 percent of textile and apparel exports from the Dominican Republic are subject to quota restrictions, and more than 12 percent of Brazilian exports are regulated by quotas (Cline 1990, 160). Cline has estimated the ad valorem equiva-

---

5. In the Uruguay Round, US tariff cuts were limited to 12 percent of the base tariff, compared with the average overall US tariff cut of 34 percent for merchandise as a whole.

lent of US NTBs on textiles and apparel at 15 percent and 25 percent, respectively.[6]

Historically, the US textile and apparel industries have fiercely resisted attempts at trade liberalization. Yet in the NAFTA, important segments of the US industry were willing to accept the reduction of US barriers in return for reciprocal concessions in Mexican textile and apparel markets and strict regional rules of origin. The NAFTA provides for a 10-year phaseout of tariffs coupled with immediate removal of quotas for textile and apparel products of North American origin (see also Hufbauer and Schott 1993a, 44–46). By comparison with the GATT achievements, the NAFTA outcome suggests that a WHFTA approach would not only eradicate quotas but might also eliminate tariffs.

But US and Canadian textile and apparel manufacturers will only agree to hemispheric free trade if it is accompanied by readily available safeguard provisions. Moreover, they will insist on strict rules of origin, building on the NAFTA model. In general, to qualify as North American, apparel must pass a "triple transformation test," which requires that essentially all finished products be cut and sewn from fabric spun from North American fibers in order to qualify for NAFTA preferences. A straightforward extension of this rule to encompass the entire hemisphere would substantially dilute its protective effect for existing North American producers; hence, they will likely seek "refinements" that would further limit the zone of liberalization. Almost all plausible outcomes on the rule of origin question in the context of a hemispheric FTA would tend to divide the textile and apparel markets of North and South America from the markets of Asia, including China.

Agriculture

The agricultural sector, represented by foods and feeds in table 7.1, is highly protected in many Latin American countries. As a percentage of total trade, US–Latin American trade in agricultural products is 13 percent, compared with 9 percent for US-Mexican agricultural trade.[7] The United States and Canada will want a relatively quick phaseout of tariffs on field crops, an area of competitive advantage for temperate North America but also an area of competitive advantage for the temperate regions of Brazil and Argentina.

The US negotiating position, however, will be moderated by a desire to protect "speciality" domestic agricultural producers, whose crops are

---

6. The total-protection tariff equivalent (i.e., tariff plus NTBs) is estimated at 28 percent for textiles and 53 percent for apparel (Cline 1990, 191 and 199).

7. These are 1990 figures and represent the sum of exports plus imports (US Department of Agriculture, *Foreign Agricultural Trade of the US, Calendar Year 1991*, supplementary tables, August 1992).

vulnerable to imports from Latin American and Caribbean nations: fruits, vegetables, flowers, and sugar, for example. In the NAFTA debate, these products were the subject of last-minute side letters issued by the Clinton administration promising easier access to safeguard provisions in return for congressional support for the NAFTA. The same products will prove equally sensitive in the WHFTA context.

The NAFTA model points to eventual free agriculture trade between the United States and Mexico, with careful staging provisions along the way.[8] This model could be appropriate for agricultural trade between North and South America as well. The NAFTA contains four schedules for tariff reduction and quota liberalization on agricultural goods traded between the United States and Mexico. Schedule A, which calls for immediate elimination of tariffs, covers 57 percent of all agricultural trade between the United States and Mexico. Schedule B covers commodities that are allowed five years for tariffs to be phased out. This schedule accounts for 6 percent of US-Mexico bilateral farm trade. Schedule C covers 23 percent of US-Mexico agricultural trade; sensitive products in this schedule will be subject to a 10-year transition period. Finally, supersensitive products are put in Schedule C+, constituting 1 percent of trade; tariffs on these are to be phased out in 15 years. In addition, many of the sensitive products in schedules C and C+, accounting for 13.5 percent of bilateral agricultural trade, are protected by tariff-rate quotas (TRQs) during a phaseout period of 10 or 15 years.

The NAFTA results probably anticipate how WHFTA negotiations will progress. The United States may push for NAFTA-type bilateral agricultural agreements rather than for a single hemispherewide agreement. In sensitive product categories where competitive advantage is abundantly clear, such as citrus and sugar, the NAFTA model may also prevail in the sense that a long tariff phaseout, coupled with TRQ safeguards with very light triggers, will be negotiated. For other products, where competitive advantage is not entirely clear (grain and meat, for example), it may be necessary to reach agreement on permitted levels of agricultural subsidization before freer trade is permitted.

NAFTA Precedents on "Unfair" Trade

In addition to specific sector issues, the precedents set by the NAFTA agreement in the realm of "unfair" trade remedy laws deserve mention. Latin American countries are frequently the subject of investigation and retaliation under US trade remedy laws. In 1990, for example, exports of several Latin American countries were subject to one or more counter-

---

8. Separate provisions cover Canada-Mexico agricultural trade. US-Canada agricultural trade continues to be governed by the FTA.

vailing duty (CVD) and antidumping duty (AD) orders. In certain products, notably steel, the CVD and AD proceedings were terminated with voluntary export restraints. Table 7.3 indicates the countries that were subject to these actions. At the same time, many Latin American countries have adopted their own CVD and AD statutes, which are now being used with increasing frequency against US exporters.

The precedent set by the NAFTA indicates that the WHFTA will not alter substantive national rules with respect to unfair trade remedy laws. However, dispute settlement procedures could make a difference in the evolving interpretation of US and Latin American laws over a period of years.

Following the precedent of the Canada-US FTA, the NAFTA provides the option of a trinational panel to review final antidumping and countervailing duty determinations by a member country (Hufbauer and Schott 1993a, 102–04). Panel decisions effectively substitute for judicial review and are binding on the respective governments. When administrative agencies are found to have not followed the procedures or precedents of their own domestic laws, the panel can order the reversal or modification of the final determination.

Moreover, the WHFTA will require an overhaul of foreign administrative procedures to conform with US and Canadian norms, as Mexico is now doing. Based on the Mexican experience, Latin American countries will need to adjust their procedures to ensure "transparency, high standards of due process, and the independence of the administrative bodies from the government" (Grant and Winham 1994, 36).

Importantly, the NAFTA does not exclude Mexico from cumulation in AD and CVD cases for purposes of determining trade injury. If the NAFTA model is followed, Latin American producers will likewise be included in any CVD or AD determination, subject to the new Uruguay Round de minimis rules.[9] In order to ensure full compliance with NAFTA obligations, the United States should not simply rely on cases initiated by private firms. Given the small size of some Latin American markets and the high costs incurred by a firm that brings a dispute, many violations could be overlooked. To deal with this problem, the United States might create an ombudsman's office that would initiate cases in areas where the agreement was not observed or was indirectly undercut by new barriers.

---

9. In the case of an AD or CVD investigation in the United States, generally the volume and effect of imports from more than one country are combined to determine whether the imports injure US business. One exception is the Caribbean Basin Initiative countries. They are excluded from cumulation. However, they are very much smaller than Mexican or Latin American producers (Magill 1992, 921). A similar provision in a trade law amendment by Rep. Frank Guarini (D-NJ) was originally proposed for the Andean Trade Preference Act (ATPA), but it was not included in the final ATPA (Inside U.S. Trade, 4 October 1991, 2).

Table 7.3 US trade barriers specifically imposed on imports from Latin American countries, 1990

Country affected	MFA	VERsᵃ	Quotasᵇ	Seasonal tariffsᶜ	Steel products CVD	Textiles and apparel CVD	Other CVDᵈ	Agriculture AD	Metal products AD	Other ADᵉ
Argentina	X	X	X	X	X	X	X	X	X	
Bolivia			X							
Brazil	X	X	X	X	X	X	X	X	X	
Chile			X	X				X		X
Colombia	X		X	X		X	X	X		
Ecuador			X	X			X	X		
Mexico	X	X	X	X	X	X	X	X	X	
Peru	X		X			X				
Uruguay	X		X			X	X	X		
Venezuela		X	X	X	X		X	X	X	

MFA = Multi-Fiber Arrangement.
VER = voluntary export restraint.
CVD = countervailing duties.
AD = antidumping duties.

a. Mostly steel products.
b. Mostly agricultural and food products.
c. Agricultural products.
d. Mostly chemical and machinery products.
e. Fertilizers.

Source: Refik Erzan and Alexander Yeats, *Free Trade Agreements with the United States: What's in It for Latin America?* World Bank Working Papers, Policy Research, International Trade, January 1992, 59–66.

New Issues

When the Uruguay Round negotiations were launched, new areas for discussion were incorporated: intellectual property rights, trade-related investment measures, and trade in services. These issues now occupy a high place on the US trade policy agenda. They featured prominently in the NAFTA text, they were included in the Uruguay Round package of agreements, and they are sure to be important in WHFTA talks.

Intellectual Property Rights (IPR)

The United States categorizes inadequate IPR protection as an unfair trade practice. The central concern is that US producers lose valuable markets to knock-off or pirate goods. In 1987, a study by the US International Trade Commission (ITC) estimated that inadequate protection and enforcement of intellectual property rights abroad cost US businesses $43 billion to $61 billion annually (statement of US Trade Representative Carla Hills before the US Senate Committee on the Judiciary, Subcommittee on Patents, Copyrights, and Trademarks, 14 May 1991). On the other hand, less-developed countries argued in the Uruguay Round negotiations that strict IPR laws can impede the development of indigenous capacity to use new technologies. In rebuttal, the United States insisted that IPR enforcement is a necessary adjunct of technological innovation within developing countries. Reflecting both a change in view and a tactical compromise, most developing countries accepted the US position in the final Uruguay Round Agreement on Trade-Related Aspects of Intellectual Property Rights (TRIPs).

Despite the successful conclusion of IPR talks in the Uruguay Round, it is likely that the NAFTA provisions on IPRs, not the TRIPs code, will set the standard for the WHFTA. The United States considers the NAFTA accomplishments on IPR issues far superior to TRIPs, which is criticized for allowing developing countries up to 10 years to phase in IPR protection, permitting compulsory licensing in some circumstances, and lacking strong enforcement obligations.

In mid-1991, prior to full-blown NAFTA talks, Mexico enacted comprehensive copyright and patent laws. Subsequently, NAFTA articles were drafted to build on this foundation. The NAFTA ensures copyright protection by including two new areas, computer programs and compilation of individually unprotected material (i.e., data bases); by establishing a minimum 50-year term for the protection of sound recordings and motion pictures; by allowing program owners and producers of sound recordings to prohibit the rental of their products; and by protecting satellite transmissions. The NAFTA text also improves the protection of trademarks and patents by requiring the registration of service marks and trademarks for an initial period of 10 years (renewable for 10-year terms); by prohibiting compulsory licensing and mandatory linking of US and Mexican trademarks; by providing patent protection for a minimum of 20 years; and by extending the new benefits to items already in the pipeline for the grant of patent protection (Hufbauer and Schott 1993a, 87–88).[10]

A similar list of reforms by Latin American countries will have to be enacted in the context of WHFTA negotiations. Some progress has been made in the Andean countries, in Argentina, and in Chile. In August 1992, the Andean countries passed an intellectual property law (Decision 313) that offered 15-year patent protection for goods ranging from pharmaceuticals to beverages and increased the protection of trademarks. In addition, individual Andean countries will be allowed to negotiate stronger regimes with other nations.[11] On October 1993, the term was extended to 20 years (Decision 344). Now the major problem is pipeline protection (*Journal of Commerce*, 3 August 1992, 1A; "Pharmaceuticals: the Patent Controversy," *Business Colombia*, March 1994, 22–23). In September 1991, Chile implemented the Law on Industrial Property, which strengthens its IPR protection, making Chile and Mexico the only countries in Latin America that protect pharmaceutical patents (USITC 1992, 5–17; USTR 1992, 42).

Problems remain. According to the International Intellectual Property Rights Alliance, US companies lost more than $650 million in Latin America in 1991 due to poor intellectual property protection. The worst violators were Paraguay, which accounted for $220 million, and Brazil, for $125 million (*US/Latin Trade*, February 1994, 11).[12]

In Argentina, a patent law bill was introduced to Congress in 1991, but it still has not been approved. As a result, in April 1993, USTR named Argentina to its "priority watch list" (*International Trade Reporter*, 9 March 1994, 380).

Poor IPR protection also remains a thorny issue in US-Brazilian relations. Citing inadequate IPR protection, the United States imposed sanctions in 1988 but lifted them in 1990 after President Collor de Mello

---

10. In two areas, the US intellectual property community did not receive the protection it was seeking: restrictions against "parallel" imports of copyrighted and patented materials and protection for biotechnological inventions. A parallel import is the import of a protected work legitimately produced under license but not authorized for distribution in the importing country. Biotechnology covers microorganisms and plants and animals, including genetic technology.

11. Still to be considered is patenting of biotech products. US government officials criticize the Andean reforms made to date because of the absence of a provision to exclude parallel imports, the lack of transitional protection, the compulsory licensing provisions, and the working requirements (*Journal of Commerce*, 3 August 1992, 1A; US Department of Commerce and USAID 1992, 52; USTR 1992, 55 and 252).

12. Mexico, which is not included in the Latin American total, accounted for $300 million of US companies' IPR losses.

promised to submit an IPR bill. When Brazil failed to address the issue, the United States threatened to invoke Section 301 if Brazil did not pass legislation improving intellectual property protection. On February 1994, Brazil committed to pass legislation by 15 June 1994, and the United States terminated the case (*Inside U.S. Trade*, 4 March 1994, 11).

Investment

Here again the NAFTA will be used as a yardstick, since it accomplished far more than the GATT accord on Trade-Related Investment Measures (TRIMs). The NAFTA liberalizes restrictions on the flow of investment within the North American region by limiting an assortment of performance requirements and by freeing capital movements.[13] In addition, the NAFTA commits the member countries to provide their regional partners the more favorable of national treatment or MFN treatment, to prohibit expropriation without fair compensation, and to permit each country to require that investors adopt environmental technologies (Hufbauer and Schott 1993a, 79).

A few sectors in each of the NAFTA countries still remain off limits to foreign investors. Mexico did not liberalize foreign investment in its energy and rail sectors. The US airlines, US radio and television communications, and Canadian cultural industries are similarly insulated.

Recently, most Latin American countries have reformed their investment regimes, lifting limits on ownership and easing restrictions on profit and capital remittances. Given that they started from extremely restrictive regimes, however, most countries still have a good deal of ground to cover (see chapter 4).

Trade in Services

Trade in services is limited throughout Latin America by various laws and regulations such as restrictions on foreign business presence, restrictions on international movements of professional workers for the purpose of providing high-tech services, and discrimination between foreign and domestic providers. Many of the service issues are close cousins of the investment issues.

Some countries have liberalized trade in services. Chile again is at the forefront. It has lifted all restrictions on foreign activity in a few key service industries, including insurance, telecommunications, and infor-

---

13. While the GATT accord bars domestic content, foreign exchange, and trade balancing requirements, the NAFTA adds to this list of proscribed practices: export performance requirements, domestic sourcing requirements, product mandating, and technology transfer requirements.

mation services.[14] Colombia has made big improvements by liberalizing its financial and maritime sectors (USITC 1992, 6–14).

NAFTA provisions on financial, transportation, and telecommunications services will likely provide a model for hemispheric talks. Under the NAFTA, Mexico will phase out restrictions on participation in its financial services market and on the provision of trucking services. In addition, the NAFTA gives access to public telecommunications connections on a nondiscriminatory basis. These provisions represent major breakthroughs, even though there were no accomplishments in the provision of maritime or radio and television services (Hufbauer and Schott 1993a, 61–77).

Collateral Issues

In recent years, two important collateral issues have gained added prominence on the trade agenda: environment and labor conditions. Prior to the 1990s, these questions were little discussed in the context of trade agreements, but they soon became a big part of the NAFTA debate. Circumstances unique to US-Mexico relations partly explain this outcome: a shared border with visible pollution and huge wage differences between the United States and Mexico. But environmental and labor issues cannot be dismissed as idiosyncratic to US-Mexico relations. They permeate economic relationships between all countries in the hemisphere and seem certain to be part of future negotiations.

Underlying the salience of the issues is the potential impact of freer trade on social conditions in each partner country. Some US labor, environmental, and religious groups worry that expanded commerce will worsen already degraded conditions in Mexico ("Rejecting NAFTA: The North American Free Trade Act," *Catholic Agitator*, January 1993). Important segments of the American public fear that poor environmental and labor conditions in Mexico could drag down standards in the United States as well.

During the NAFTA ratification debate, opponents asserted with considerable political effect that weak Mexican enforcement of environmental and labor standards would encourage US firms to move to Mexico, taking US jobs with them. If the NAFTA is extended to other countries in the hemisphere, similar concerns will almost certainly arise.

The popular fear of runaway plants, attracted by lax environmental and labor standards, is exaggerated. For the vast majority of US and Canadian companies, the cost of moving to Mexico and operating in an unfamiliar setting with higher transport and other costs could not possibly be justified by the savings obtained from weaker environmental and

---

14. A few restrictions remain in banking, advertisement, legal, and accounting services (USITC 1992, 5–21).

labor standards.[15] Moreover, with rising per capita incomes, Mexicans will demand a cleaner environment and better working conditions (World Bank, *World Development Report 1992*, 39 and 41; Grossman and Krueger 1991). As the political system in Mexico becomes more democratic, Mexican leaders will likely respond to these demands by raising standards (see also Hufbauer and Schott 1993a, 96).

The same mechanisms are at work in most other Latin American countries. Higher transport costs and lower productivity levels preclude a stampede of North American firms to Latin America in search of easy environmental or labor standards. Over time, rising incomes and political pressures within each country will prove to be the strongest force for better environmental and labor conditions.

If US real wages improve sharply during the 1990s, the runaway plant issue should lose most of its edge in future free trade debates. On the other hand, if US wage performance continues the dismal record of the 1980s, with very slow increments in the average wage, the NAFTA will accrue far more than its statistical share of blame, and the future negotiation of hemispheric initiatives will face even stronger opposition from US labor groups.

Environment: Lessons from NAFTA

The NAFTA negotiations provoked several studies of the relationship between economic growth, trade, and the environment. Three studies found that pollution levels initially increase as a country industrializes, but after the country has achieved the level of industrialization of a middle-income country, pollution levels start decreasing (Radetzki 1992, 130).[16] The World Bank found that dirty industries account for a growing share of exports from less-developed countries (Low and Yeats 1992, 102).[17] The Bank also found that the share of capital expenditure for pollution abatement (out of total investment in new plant and equipment) is between 1 and 3 percent for most manufacturing sectors. The main exceptions are primary metals, 7 percent; paper, 8 percent; chemi-

---

15. For most US industries, pollution abatement costs represent a small share of total production costs—usually less than 2 percent—and lower wages in most cases reflect lower labor productivity, outdated technology, and poor infrastructure.

16. An inverse-U pattern in a cross-country study of urban air pollution (concentration of sulfur dioxide) was found by Grossman and Krueger (1991) and by Shafik and Bandyopadhyay (1992).

17. Between 1981 and 1989, one-tenth of Mexican export earnings came from pollution-intensive products. In addition, during this period, the export of these products grew faster than total Mexican exports (Low 1992, 108). Developing regions that showed a growing share of ''dirty exports'' were Latin America and the Caribbean, South and Southeast Asia, and West Asia.

cals, 9 percent; and petroleum, 13 percent. The figures indicate that developing countries can introduce new pollution control equipment and technologies without diverting large amounts of investment from other areas. In many instances, 60 to 80 percent of pollution can be eliminated with only small increases in cost (World Bank, *World Development Report 1992*, 128).

Anecdotal evidence from Chile suggests that an open economic system is more friendly to the environment than a closed system (Birdsall and Wheeler 1992). The evidence suggests three reasons why an open economy encourages better environmental practices:

■ Exports must often meet the product and process standards of the importing country (e.g., paper produced with chlorine will have traces of dioxin and thus cannot be exported to Germany).

■ Multinationals face pressure to meet the high standards of the importing country in terms of production and process methods, both because they want to avoid hostile environmental groups back home and because high engineering costs discourage building plants to meet different standards in different countries.

■ The competitive pressures of an open economy will increase investment in the latest technology. To the extent that the newest, most efficient technology embodies cleaner processes, pollution will accordingly be reduced.

While such findings seemingly point to laissez-faire policy conclusions, environmental advocates are generally unwilling to "leave it to the market." Instead, based on the NAFTA experience, they will exert considerable pressure to address environmental concerns in the WHFTA through specific text articles and through new institutions.

The basic NAFTA text included environmental provisions in four chapters on sanitary and phytosanitary measures, standards, investment, and dispute settlement. These are the major environmental features of the agreement (also discussed in Hufbauer and Schott 1993a, 93):

■ Existing federal and subfederal health, safety, and environmental standards are not disturbed. Each partner may ban all nonconforming imports, provided the country's standards do not discriminate between imported and domestic products and provided the standards are "based on data or information derived using scientific methods."

■ The NAFTA parties may enact standards stricter than those included in international agreements.

- Environmental requirements can be imposed on inward foreign investment, so long as those requirements also apply to domestic investment.

- NAFTA members should not encourage investment by relaxing domestic health, safety, or environmental measures.

In addition, the NAFTA side accord on the environment,[18] concluded in August 1993, established a new regional institution—the Commission on Environmental Cooperation, or CEC—to monitor environmental market conditions, to promote compliance with national laws and regulations in each of the three countries, and to administer new dispute settlement procedures. The accord includes dispute settlement procedures that encourage transparency and voluntary compliance. However, as a last resort, they allow fines and trade sanctions in select instances to promote compliance with national laws and regulations.

The environmental agreement falls short in two important areas: review of existing legal systems and the establishment of a procedure to encourage the upward harmonization of environmental standards and enforcement. Submissions may be raised on a wide variety of issues, including process standards, a subject not addressed in the NAFTA provisions. However, as the Sierra Club and Greenpeace have pointed out, natural resource conservation, promotion of clean energy alternatives, and the export of hazardous waste are not among the topics that may be subject to submission (*Orlando Sentinel*, 23 August 1993).

Similar provisions to those in the NAFTA can be expected to emerge from WHFTA talks. In fact, the accession clause in the side accord (Article 49) states that any country or group of countries may accede to the agreement.

Environment Issues in the Latin American Context

Because there is no shared border between the United States and Latin America, environmental talks will be less intense for them than those between the United States and Mexico. However, lower Latin American standards and levels of enforcement will be part of the agenda. Other issues could also attract significant attention, such as deforestation, conservation, and waste trade.

In addition, an agreement to reduce carbon dioxide emissions is likely to be addressed through a global warming treaty at some point in the Clinton administration. Despite the fact that only one Latin American

---

18. Officially, the accord is called the North American Agreement on Environmental Cooperation.

country, Brazil, is among the top 10 carbon-emitting countries,[19] the United States may well push this issue on the hemispheric agenda to complement efforts to conclude a global accord. Latin American countries with poor emissions performance include Brazil, Colombia, Ecuador, Peru, and Venezuela (measured by shares of world emissions). However, if measured by ratios of share of world emissions to share of GNP, the worst offenders are Ecuador, Paraguay, Colombia, Bolivia, and Honduras (table 7.4). Except for Venezuela and Cuba, the major source of emissions is land use change, which encompasses deforestation for logging and for agricultural cultivation.

Deforestation

High tropical deforestation rates have spurred global concern. The world average rates of deforestation increased from 0.6 percent annually during the second half of the 1970s to 0.9 percent annually during the 1980s (World Resources Institute, *World Resources 1992–93*, table 8.2, 119). Deforestation affects global warming, biodiversity and soil quality. It is not a problem exclusive to Latin America: deforestation in Asia and Africa is also severe. However, Latin American deforestation rates, especially in Brazil and Central America, are worrisome for environmental groups.

Starting in the 1960s, Brazil initiated plans to colonize the Amazon Basin. After much internal and external criticism, in 1988 new policies designed to protect the environment were announced, and deforestation was slowed from 1.8 million hectares in 1988–89 to 1.4 million hectares in 1989–90.[20]

Several Central American countries have also tried to slow tropical deforestation. Environmental impact assessments are required for new projects in Costa Rica, El Salvador, and Guatemala. In Nicaragua, an agreement for timber rights along the Atlantic Coast with Taiwan Equipment Enterprise was canceled because the project did not include reforestation plans (*Journal of Commerce*, 12 March 1992, 5A). While commendable, these efforts still fall short of the aspirations of US environmental groups.

It should be noted that only 1 percent of trees felled in less-developed countries are sold in export markets, so an export ban would not curb deforestation. A more efficient and equitable way to address the tropical deforestation problem might involve a commitment by industrial coun-

---

19. The top 10 are the United States, the former Soviet Union, the European Union, China, Brazil, India, Japan, Indonesia, Burma, and Poland, and they account for 70 percent of global carbon dioxide emissions (Cline 1992, 329).

20. The new policies included suspension of subsidies for cattle ranchers, creation of an environmental secretariat, and the banning the export of logs (World Resources Institute, *World Resources 1992–93*, 46 and 119).

Table 7.4   Emissions performance, 1989

Country	Carbon dioxide emissions (millions of tons of carbon equivalent)			Share of world emissions (percent) A	Share of world GNP (percent) B	A/B
	Fossil fuels	Land use change	Total emissions			
World	21,864	6,400	28,264	100.00	100.00	
United States	4,869	22	4,891	17.30	24.18	0.72
Canada	456	n.a.	456	1.61	2.56	0.63
Mexico	320	200	520	1.84	1.68	1.09
Chile	32	n.a.	32	0.11	0.22	0.52
Argentina	118	n.a.	118	0.42	0.61	0.69
Brazil	207	950	1,157	4.09	3.08	1.33
Paraguay	2	67	69	0.24	0.05	5.03
Uruguay	5	n.a.	5	0.02	0.06	0.29
Bolivia	5	37	42	0.15	0.06	2.68
Colombia	54	420	474	1.68	0.40	4.22
Ecuador	15	160	175	0.62	0.11	5.79
Peru	21	140	161	0.57	0.25	2.26
Venezuela	96	59	155	0.55	0.39	1.40
Costa Rica	3	26	29	0.10	0.05	2.26
El Salvador	2	2	4	0.01	0.06	0.24
Guatemala	4	41	45	0.16	0.09	1.77
Honduras	2	42	44	0.16	0.04	4.15
Panama	3	19	22	0.08	0.04	2.05
Trinidad and Tobago	19	0	19	0.07	0.03	2.23
Jamaica	5	1	6	0.02	0.03	0.64
Dominican Republic	7	1	8	0.03	0.07	0.43
Haiti	1	1	2	0.01	0.03	0.20

n.a. = not available

a. ICP estimates of per capita GDP from the equation $\ln(ICP) = 3.085925 + (0.676735 \times [GDP$ per capita])

Sources: William Cline, *The Economics of Global Warming*, Washington: Institute for International Economics, 1992, p. 330. The figures for carbon dioxide emissions were updated using World Resources Institute, *World Resources 1992–93*, table 24–1.

tries to pay a rain forest "services fee" to preserve tracts of virgin land (GATT 1992b). In any event, the issue is likely to spill over into the trade agenda in talks that go beyond forest exports.

Conservation

Conservation issues will probably be brought up in the hemispheric negotiations. One reason is to save unique habitats from destructive development. Another reason is that an improved intellectual property rights framework will have biological implications. Environmental groups are concerned that by granting patents for genetic resources, a market will be created for biological materials but local residents might not participate in the commercial benefits. The hemispheric environmental provisions will probably need to assure that some benefits accrue to the "natural owners" of biological resources, including indigenous and minority populations (Overseas Development Council and World Wildlife Fund 1991; letter to Mickey Kantor from environmental groups, 4 March 1993, 7).

Waste Trade

Waste smuggling could become a growth industry in the early 21st century (*The Economist*, 29 March 1993, 18). The 1989 Basel Convention on the Control of Transboundary Movements of Hazardous Wastes and Their Disposal made an important first attempt to regulate waste exports. The convention calls for detailed notification and consent of the receiving country as a precondition for authorizing international waste shipments. The Basel Convention entered into force in May 1992 and has been adopted by over 100 countries. The United States, which has signed but not ratified the convention, currently regulates hazardous waste exports under the Resource Conservation and Recovery Act (Schoenbaum 1992, 725).

One problem with the convention is the lack of a common definition of hazardous waste; for example, Germany does not regard waste as hazardous if it is intended for recycling. In addition, environmentalists argue that much of the exported waste goes to countries that either do not have the capacity to recycle, have no intention of recycling, or both (*The Economist*, 29 March 1993, 18).

In 1989, another initiative, the Bamako Convention—signed by all African countries except South Africa—banned the importation of hazardous waste into Africa. Environmentalists see this as a more acceptable approach than a fee system for importation of waste. They fear that with a commercial system of waste fees less-developed countries will be too easily tempted to accept industrial countries' wastes as a means of earning foreign exchange, even though they cannot provide effective recycling or disposal services.

Shipments of toxic waste and waste plastic from Europe and the United States are a concern both to Latin American countries and to environmentalists throughout the hemisphere. While this is not a new issue, reliable statistics on toxic waste trade are difficult to find.[21]

A 1990 report by the South American Commission of Peace found that toxic waste exports have increased sharply. The commission found 70 attempts to export toxic waste to Latin America from 1980 and 1988. The deputy director of the Argentine Office of Technology found that an average of 200 tons a week of waste plastics were entering Argentina (*New York Times*, 16 December 1991, A10). Some Latin American countries are implementing laws to halt imports of toxic waste. All countries

---

21. Instead, there are only a few anecdotes. One of the first involved a 1986 ship from Philadelphia with 4,000 tons of toxic incinerator ash. The ship wandered for three years and finally dumped its cargo on a Haitian beach (*Time*, 2 January 1989, 44).

in Central America and Venezuela and Colombia already forbid the import of most toxic wastes (*Journal of Commerce*, 12 March 1992, 5A).

Labor: Lessons from NAFTA

The issue of low wages in Mexico colored the US debate over NAFTA. Ross Perot captured popular fears with his prediction that Americans would hear a "giant sucking sound" as jobs moved from the United States to Mexico (presidential debate, East Lansing, Michigan, 19 October 1992, excerpted in *New York Times*, 20 October 1992, A21; Perot and Choate 1993). Perot, like other commentators, highlighted the dismal living conditions of poorly paid workers in parts of the border region. NAFTA critics frequently cited inadequate and sometimes hazardous labor conditions, especially in maquiladora enterprises in border cities such as Tijuana and Mexicali.

But these critics failed to mention the chief reasons for US-Mexican wage differences. On average, the difference in wages reflects higher US labor productivity. The US worker earns better wages because he produces more output, which in turn reflects his work skills, his complement of sophisticated capital equipment, and the highly articulated infrastructure of the US economy. In the future as in the past, *average* US wages will increase primarily as a result of US success in raising productivity, a task that requires R&D outlays, capital investment, and worker training—not the erection or maintenance of barriers to developing-world exports (Hufbauer and Schott 1993a, 13; Competitiveness Policy Council 1992 and 1993).

Nevertheless, many people in the US work force perceive freer trade as a threat to US jobs, in large part because of adverse wage trends in the 1970s and 1980s. Real hourly compensation in the United States has grown by only 0.7 percent annually since 1973—far less, for example, than the 2.1 percent figure achieved in Japan.[22]

Similar to the environmental pact, the NAFTA side agreement on labor cooperation,[23] also concluded in August 1993, establishes a new regional institution—the Commission on Labor Cooperation, or CLC—to monitor labor market conditions in the region, promote compliance with national laws and regulations in each of the three countries, and administer new dispute settlement procedures. The emphasis is again on promoting compliance by exposure. The agreement falls short in two respects. First, only three labor areas (occupational health and safety,

---

22. Using 1982 as the base year, the index of output per hour of all workers in the nonfarm business sector increased from 96.3 in 1973 to 108.7 in 1991, or by only 0.7 index points per year (*Economic Report of the President*, January 1993, 95–96 and 398). Not surprisingly, over this long period, compensation per hour grew only as fast as output.

23. Officially, the accord is called the North American Agreement on Labor Cooperation.

minimum wages, and child labor) can be subject to fines and trade sanctions. Second, any trade sanction will apparently apply to total trade and not necessarily be directed against the specific firm or industry that is engaged in a pattern of labor abuse.

The agreement covers 11 areas, divided into three groups with procedures for each group. The first group includes the three areas that can ultimately become the subject of fines and trade sanctions: occupational health and safety, child labor, and minimum wages. The second includes five areas that can only be the subject of official consultations and review by independent experts: migrant workers, forced labor, employment discrimination, equal pay for men and women, and compensation in cases of work accidents or occupation-related diseases. The third group includes three areas that can only be the subject of consultations at the ministerial level: the right to strike, the right to bargain collectively, and the right to freely associate and organize.

The agreement is explicitly regarded as a model for a broader regional arrangement. Article 53 states that any country or group of countries may accede to this agreement.

Labor Issues in the Latin American Context

A large wage gap divides the United States from Latin America. Indeed, average weekly wages in manufacturing in Latin American countries are even lower than in Mexico. Compared with the United States, Latin American wages in manufacturing are between 6 and 14 times lower (table 7.5). Using minimum wage figures, Latin American wages are on average 10 times lower than the US wage (Bureau of Labor Statistics, "Minimum Wages Around the World," May 1993). Accordingly, the "pauper labor" thesis will play a conspicuous role each time trade talks are initiated with a Latin American country. The debate will be especially bitter if US wage performance in the 1990s does not show a marked improvement over the 1980s. Since 1986, real hourly earnings in US manufacturing have actually declined year to year (table 7.6); if this performance continues, trade liberalization with developing countries will be very difficult to sell to the US Congress and to the American public.

Despite its appeal to emotions and "common sense," the pauper labor argument is essentially fallacious—a case of *post hoc ergo propter hoc*. Most studies assessing the impact of NAFTA on US jobs conclude that the net impact will be small but positive. Our calculations for the impact of a WHFTA on US jobs likewise suggest that the impact will be small but positive. The argument that enlarged trade with Mexico will drive down US wages cannot be supported with actual data. Likewise, based on the existing composition of trade between the United States and Latin America, the average weekly wage associated with US exports to

Table 7.5   Latin America: average hourly compensation in manufacturing (dollars per hour)

Country	Year	Wage
Argentina	1991	1.34
Brazil	1991	2.55
Colombia	1990	2.27
Costa Rica	1990	1.37
Mexico	1992	2.35
Peru	1991	1.12
United States	1992	16.17

Sources: *Yearbook of Labor Statistics*, 1991, section 17; International Monetary Fund *International Financial Statistics*, Yearbook 1992; US Department of Labor, Bureau of Labor Statistics, *International Comparisons of Hourly Compensation Costs for Production Workers in Manufacturing, 1992*, p. 6; Departamento Administrativo Nacional de Estadistica (DANE), Bogotá.

Latin America is practically identical with the average wage associated with US imports from Latin America: the figures are $442 and $435, respectively, and the difference between these figures is less than 2 percent (table B5).

Moreover, as the earlier discussion indicated, even dramatic expansion of US–Latin American commerce in the context of a WHFTA, biased in favor of low-wage imports, will not put significant downward pressure on US wage levels. The number of jobs affected is just too small to have a measurable effect on US wage levels except for isolated pockets of the work force. There is practically no effect on average US wage levels (table B7).

Assuming that underlying employment and wage conditions permit hemispheric trade talks to go forward, the United States will emphasize that Latin American countries must commit to enforcing their existing labor standards and to raise those standards gradually. As in the NAFTA, occupational health and safety, minimum wages, and child labor will be flagged for attention; compensation for work-related injuries, pay discrimination, and the right to organize will also be on the agenda.

Labor organizations in Chile and the United States are already working together to ensure that any future trade agreement takes workers into consideration. In contrast to Mexico, Chile's unions are independent and previously worked with US labor organizations to defend Chilean workers rights under Pinochet (*Miami Herald*, 23 December 1993).

However, Chile may be the exception in terms of US acceptance of labor laws and working conditions. In October 1993, the AFL-CIO filed a petition asking the US Trade Representative to exclude Costa Rica, El Salvador, Paraguay, and Guatemala from duty-free access under the Generalized System of Preferences (GSP) because of unfair labor practices in those countries (*International Trade Reporter*, 3 November 1993,

Table 7.6 Latin America: real average wages, 1984–92 (1980 = 100)

	1984	1985	1986	1987	1988	1989	1990	1991	1992[a]
Argentina[b]	116.9	106.1	102.0	93.5	92.7	84.6	80.3	76.2	75.6[k]
Brazil									
Rio de Janeiro[c]	105.1	111.8	121.5	105.4	103.2	102.3	87.6	87.8	105.5[k]
São Paulo[d]	96.7	120.4	150.7	143.2	152.1	165.2	142.1	125.4	133.2[k]
Colombia[e]	118.1	114.6	120.1	119.2	117.7	119.4	113.4	115.3	116.7[k]
Costa Rica[f]	84.7	92.2	97.8	89.2	85.2	85.7	87.2	83.1	n.a.
Chile[g]	97.2	93.5	95.1	94.7	101.0	102.9	104.8	109.9	114.9[l]
Mexico[h]	74.8	75.9	71.5	71.3	71.7	75.2	77.9	83.0	85.0[m]
Peru[i]	87.2	77.6	97.5	101.3	76.1	41.5	36.2	41.8	42.5[n]
Uruguay[j]	72.2	67.3	71.9	75.2	76.3	76.1	70.6	73.2	75.1[o]
United States[p]	100.2	100.5	100.7	98.8	97.6	95.8	94.0	93.2	92.7[q]

n.a. = not available.
a. Preliminary figures.
b. Average total wages in manufacturing. Twelve-month average.
c. Average wages in basic industry, deflated by the CPI for Rio de Janeiro. Twelve-month average.
d. Wages in manufacturing in the state of São Paulo, deflated by the cost of living index for the city of São Paulo. Twelve-month average.
e. Wages of manual workers in manufacturing.
f. Average remunerations declared by persons covered by the social security system.
g. Average remunerations of wage earners in nonagricultural sectors. Twelve-month average.
h. Average wages in manufacturing. Twelve-month average.
i. Wages of private-sector manual workers in the Lima metropolitan area.
j. Index of average real wages. Twelve-month average.
k. January–August average.
l. January–October average.
m. January–June average.
n. Average of February, April, and June.
o. January–September average.
p. Index of hourly earnings in manufacturing.
q. January–October average.

Sources: Economic Commission for Latin America and the Caribbean, *Preliminary Overview of the Economy of Latin America and the Caribbean*, 1992, p. 44; International Monetary Fund, *International Financial Statistics Yearbook*, 1992, p. 719.

1860). In late December 1993, GSP reviews on Costa Rica and Paraguay were terminated due to improvements in labor standards in those countries (*International Trade Reporter*, 5 January 1994, 24).

Human Rights

The State Department stressed in May 1993 that human rights and democracy would be a high priority on the Clinton administration's agenda for Latin America.[24] The US Congress will likewise insist that US negotiators address human rights and democracy issues before entering into trade negotiations. In a sense, the administration's insistence on negotiating a side agreement on labor before submitting the NAFTA for ratification also reflected the new link between the trade agenda and human rights issues.

In recent years, Latin American countries have turned toward elected civilian governments. This broad trend has been resisted in Haiti, where the only freely elected government since its independence was overthrown, and to a lesser extent in Peru (with President Fujimori's dissolution of Congress in 1992), in Guatemala (with President Serrano Elias' seizure of authoritarian powers and a subsequent military coup in 1993), and in Venezuela, with repeated coup attempts in 1992. Despite these setbacks, the trend is clearly in favor of elected governments.

Yet elections are not the whole story, since even when free and fair, elections do not guarantee respect for human rights. Widespread violation of human rights by the military forces—political assassination, disappearance, and torture—were common in the 1980s, especially in Colombia, El Salvador, Guatemala, and Peru, and to a lesser extent in Ecuador and Honduras. In Peru, both official and insurgent forces have committed tremendous atrocities against civilians (Human Rights Watch 1991, 129).

Serious assessments of human rights practices will therefore look beyond the electoral process to include politically motivated abuses (disappearances and arbitrary arrests, for example); civil liberties (freedom of speech, press, association, and religion); political rights (the right to change the government and the right to effective political opposition); and workers' rights (US Department of State 1993).

War on Drugs

During the NAFTA negotiations, the drug issue was either ignored or addressed in separate channels.[25] Drug trafficking is a significant US-

---

24. Speech by Deputy Secretary of State Clifton R. Wharton on behalf of Secretary of State Warren Christopher, Council of the Americas conference on Latin America and the United States: The Clinton Administration's Agenda, 3–4 May 1993.

25. The drug issue was mentioned in a few news articles that pointed out that Colombian drug dealers have invested in certain maquiladoras (*New York Times*, 24 May 1993, A1).

Mexico problem, but it was not clear that constructive solutions could be found within the context of NAFTA talks. Solutions are no easier in Latin America, but WHFTA negotiations will not go far if the drug problem is ignored. Peru and Bolivia cultivate most of the world's coca, Colombia is the largest manufacturer of cocaine, and the United States is the largest consumer of illegal drugs in the world (Irving G. Tragen, speech at Drug/Alcohol Education Training Seminar, July 1989 and reprinted in *Congressional Record* 135 E3001–02).

During recent years, the United States has provided assistance to police and military forces to fight drugs in Colombia, Mexico, and Peru. In 1991, for example, Colombia received $93 million in assistance from the United States: $20 million under the International Narcotics Control Program of the US Department of State, $50 million on military assistance, and $24 million under the Economic Support Fund (US State Department 1993, 1194).

However, in Latin America, as in the United States, it is questionable whether even a much larger expansion of police efforts can by itself curtail drug traffic. Because police efforts are not altogether successful, other approaches are also being tried. One shift in US strategy was the passage of the Andean Trade Preference Act (ATPA). Although it is estimated that benefits will initially affect only $300 million worth of goods, the ATPA represents the first attempt to help reduce Andean economic dependency on drugs, which yield the region an estimated export revenue of $5 billion.

Conceivably, the ATPA model could be used in the context of wider hemispheric trade relations. In this context, US trade concessions would be viewed as a carrot for Latin American countries to provide economic alternatives to the cultivation of poppies and coca.

8

The Hemisphere and the World

The launching of the Enterprise for the Americas Initiative in June 1990 elicited a schizophrenic response from the international trading community. Around the globe, countries welcomed the reaffirmation of commitments to trade liberalization by both the United States and its prospective hemispheric partners. They recognized that regional initiatives could establish building blocks for broader multilateral accords. However, countries outside the region also feared that US interest in regional trade initiatives reflected a growing disenchantment with ongoing multilateral negotiations under the auspices of the General Agreement on Tariffs and Trade. Successful conclusion of the GATT talks in December 1993 allayed, but did not totally dispel, those fears.

This chapter examines whether the evolving Western Hemisphere trade arrangements will reinforce or undercut the multilateral trading system as a whole and the obligations of individual countries under the GATT. In addition, we assess the potential diversion of trade and investment from both Europe and South and East Asia as a result of a prospective Western Hemisphere Free Trade Area (WHFTA). Our diversion calculations focus on South and East Asia and Western Europe. Substantial preferences already exist for trade among various countries in the region, owing to recently negotiated integration pacts. Thus, the scope for further trade and investment diversion within the hemisphere due to progressive implementation of a WHFTA is small.

In brief, we can summarize concerns about the evolution of hemispherewide trading arrangements under three broad categories:

- implications of WHFTA for the world trading system;
- trade diversion;
- investment diversion.

This chapter is necessarily speculative because of the variety of integration efforts under way throughout the Western Hemisphere. For the purposes of establishing a baseline for our analysis, we posit a continuation of the incremental approach to hemispheric integration at both the subregional level and between North and South America. We contrast this baseline with a bolder approach—namely, progress toward a hemispheric free trade area, but not toward a customs union or deeper economic community. Under a free trade area, individual countries will retain sovereignty over their *external* trade relations and thus will continue to pursue other bilateral and multilateral arrangements even as they adhere to subregional and hemispheric trade pacts.[1]

Implications of WHFTA for the World Trading System

The first concern focuses on two main questions: Will the United States seek regional solutions and give up on the multilateral approach? Does the WHFTA presage a global movement toward regional trading blocs at the expense of the multilateral trading system? These questions starkly summarize basic concerns about "attention diversion" affecting the world's foremost trading power and the potential erosion of confidence in the world trading system.

The main worry is that the United States will no longer give paramount attention to global economic policy. In turn, smaller nations dependent on the US market may focus their efforts on bilateral deals rather than the multilateral system. Thus, when the Canada-US Free Trade Agreement (FTA) entered into force in 1989, many developing countries expressed interest in negotiating FTAs with the United States. They saw FTAs as part of a defensive strategy to lock in access to the US market in case the United States turned away from the flailing GATT talks, which had just experienced a rancorous mid-term review in Montreal (Schott 1989).

Interestingly, the same reactions surfaced in 1992 in the aftermath of the NAFTA negotiations, and by many of the same countries. While the

---

1. For example, Mexico negotiated a free trade pact with Chile, a framework pact with New Zealand, and numerous preferential arrangements with other Latin American countries in parallel with its negotiation of the NAFTA. It remains to be seen whether developing countries that negotiate agreements among themselves notify the pacts to the GATT under the weak standards of Article XXIV or the completely lax standards of the enabling clause that was designed to permit the Generalized System of Preferences.

successful conclusion of the Uruguay Round has diminished NAFTA's magnetic appeal, some observers of the multilateral trading system are worried that the clamor of smaller countries to enter into FTAs with the United States will drain vitality from the GATT system.

Will the evolving Western Hemisphere trade arrangements erode confidence in the multilateral trading system and in the obligations of individual countries under the new World Trade Organization (WTO)? In our view the answer is a clear "no". We dispute the notion that a WHFTA would promote an insular trading bloc.

Judging by the experience of the NAFTA, which was rapidly followed both by President Clinton's push to launch a summit of Asia Pacific Economic Cooperation (APEC) leaders and to conclude the Uruguay Round, we believe that Western Hemisphere regional initiatives can also be consistent with and complementary to ongoing multilateral trade reforms both in the World Trade Organization and in the Pacific Basin.

A more pointed question is whether the NAFTA and other regional arrangements within the Western Hemisphere will satisfy the letter and the spirit of GATT obligations. In most respects, the NAFTA is consistent with the letter of the GATT obligations of all three countries. In particular, the trade coverage is comprehensive. Unlike most other FTAs, liberalization encompasses agriculture as well as manufacturing industries and also extends to many service sectors. In addition, some barriers to third-country trade will actually be reduced as a result of efforts to harmonize tariffs down toward the lowest level maintained in the region to forestall investment diversion among the NAFTA partners. On that basis, the NAFTA is closer to the explicit obligations of GATT Article XXIV than most other trade pacts that have been notified to the GATT.

However, a "strict constructionalist" reading of GATT obligations is not decisive. While GATT obligations seek to promote the complementarity of regional and multilateral trade objectives, they suffer major defects. GATT standards are incomplete and ignore practices that can have adverse effects on third-country trade.

For example, the lack of a clear definition of "substantially all" has opened a large loophole for sectoral (e.g., agriculture) as well as product exceptions. Equally important, the reviews conducted under Article XXIV skirt the problems caused by gray-area measures such as voluntary export restraints, contingent protection measures (antidumping and countervailing duties), and the selective application of trade rules (e.g., safeguards, dispute settlement provisions, rules of origin)—even though these measures can distort trade and investment flows between the region and third countries. In addition, GATT reviews fail to track regional pacts after they are signed, when transition provisions or rule changes can significantly affect market access for third-country suppliers. As a result, GATT disciplines on regional trading pacts have been ineffective, increasing the risk that such arrangements can contradict the objectives of the GATT.

In brief, we believe that a WHFTA modeled on the NAFTA will be able to meet the lax GATT standards for acceptable FTAs. However, we caution that in many important respects the GATT rules are vague and incomplete, and thus formal compliance with GATT standards is unlikely to satisfy critics in third countries. GATT requirements are not difficult to meet. Moreover, they are open to flexible interpretation. About 100 preferential trading arrangements have been notified to the GATT under Article XXIV (18 in 1992 alone), and none has ever been rejected as inconsistent with GATT obligations. But few have been awarded the GATT seal of approval either.

To ensure consistency with the spirit as well as the letter of the GATT, obligations under Article XXIV and GATT reviews of regional trading pacts need to be strengthened.[2] As a start, the GATT should institute rigorous multilateral monitoring of all preferential trading arrangements both to guard against opaque protectionism hidden within trade rules or transition provisions and to track the implementation of the pacts over time to ensure they do not harm the trade interests of third countries.

The GATT's new trade policy review mechanism (TPRM) is well-suited for those tasks.[3] The GATT could use the TPRM both to examine prospective preferential trade pacts under negotiation and then to monitor the implementation of the final agreement. The TPRM could be used to analyze both the schedule of trade liberalization and the trade rules (e.g., rules of origin, dispute settlement procedures). Regional partners should welcome increased GATT surveillance of trade preferences because GATT reviews can provide external pressure for countries to keep faith with their regional commitments to liberalization. Toward this end, we later outline a plan for GATT surveillance of NAFTA and other regional pacts.

Trade Diversion

Whether or not GATT improves its surveillance, other countries are rightly interested in the probable scope of trade diversion. Accordingly, we assess the potential diversion of trade from both Europe and South and East Asia as a result of a prospective Western Hemisphere Free Trade Area.[4] Broken down by region, we found that the impact on

---

2. Unfortunately, efforts to bolster Article XXIV requirements produced feeble results in the Uruguay Round.

3. Jackson (1993, 121–31) also proposes expanding the scope of TPRM reviews to support GATT Article XXIV reviews.

4. When calculating trade and investment diversion, we consider only Europe and South and East Asia and ignore the relatively small trade and investment ties between the hemisphere and African, Eastern European, and Middle Eastern countries.

exports from East Asia and Western Europe is quite similar and about double the impact on South Asia.

Our methodology, explained in more detail in appendix D, starts by projecting trade under a WHFTA scenario and then estimating (by commodity groups) how much of that increased trade would represent trade diversion. Based on our estimates, East Asia suffers diversion of $7.3 billion of its exports annually by 2002, which amounts to 2.6 percent of projected East Asian exports to the United States in the same year. More than 40 percent of this diversion is concentrated in the textiles and apparel sectors ($3.4 billion).[5] Significant diversion is also experienced in leather products ($908 million), amusement and sporting goods ($448 million), and primary metals ($603 million).

Our model indicates that about $5.7 billion of Western Europe's exports will be diverted annually by 2002, a figure that amounts to 3.5 percent of projected Western European exports. Much of the export loss is concentrated in food products ($1.2 billion) and textiles ($1.3 billion). European exports of primary metals and chemicals will also suffer significant annual diversion ($0.2 billion and $0.5 billion, respectively).

South Asia would experience diversion of about $3.2 billion by 2002, or 2.8 percent of its projected exports to the US market. The sectors experiencing the greatest diversion are food products ($1.0 billion) and textiles and apparel ($1.2 billion).

In calculating the diversion that could reasonably be expected from a WHFTA, we find that, with the exception of agriculture, textiles and apparel, and a few other industrial products, the scope for trade diversion is limited. Our calculations, biased to produce responsibly high estimates, suggest that a WHFTA might cause third countries to lose $27.6 billion of merchandise exports to the US market in the year 2002, or 2.8 percent of their exports to the United States (appendix D, table D1). There would also be some additional, though limited, diversion of third-country exports to Latin America.[6]

In most cases, as these calculations suggest, preferences associated with a WHFTA will not exert a significant impact on foreign suppliers of goods and services to the US market, for several reasons. First, existing barriers to the US market are relatively low. The margin between the

---

5. Using a different methodology, Noland (1993) estimated that trade diversion generated by NAFTA could affect from 1 to 3 percent of total Korean exports by the year 2000 and that similar effects could be felt by exporters in other Asian countries. Almost two-thirds of Noland's calculated impact is in the textile spinning and weaving sector, thus underscoring the importance of GATT reforms of the Multi-Fiber Arrangement to mitigate the adverse trade effects of the regional pact.

6. We do not attempt to calculate the loss of third-country exports to Latin America. The size of the loss will importantly depend on the height of Latin American MFN tariffs when WHFTA preferences are fully implemented. We think that the MFN tariffs will be much lower in 15 years than today.

most-favored nation (MFN) rates that third countries pay and the preferential (zero) rate applied under an FTA is very small in most sectors and will be further reduced by the Uruguay Round tariff cuts. By the year 2000, when the Uruguay Round concessions are essentially implemented, the average US tariff on all imports will be below 3 percent. Most US service sectors are already liberalized on a multilateral basis. Hence preferential treatment under a WHFTA will give Latin American countries only a marginal advantage over third-country exporters in the US market.

Any trade diversion will be partially offset by pressures that arise within each country to reduce its own MFN tariff rates to the level of the low-tariff country in the region. Martin Richardson (1993) provides two explanations for this behavior. First, because of the threat of investment diversion, pressures build in high-tariff countries to reduce their MFN rates so as not to lose production to areas that charge lower duties on imported components.[7] Second, as FTA preferences are phased in, less competitive industries will contract and thus over time lose political influence to lobby for maintenance of high external tariffs. The combined result is continued support for multilateral trade liberalization, despite its eroding effect on regional preferences.

Investment Diversion

Classical trade diversion, however large or small, is not the only third-country worry about a prospective WHFTA. For example, most of the concern voiced by Asian developing countries has focused on possible investment diversion in favor of Latin American nations. In a sense, investment diversion is a major objective of the WHFTA. By forming a common trading area, the region hopes to make Latin America a more attractive location to produce goods and services for the global economy.

A WHFTA could be an integral part of the competitiveness strategy for Latin America. It would reinforce the extensive market-oriented policy reforms in Latin America. US trade concessions would also be welcome, but what is really important from a Latin American standpoint is that a WHFTA would insure against renewed bouts of US protectionism. The double insurance policy would lend confidence to the sustainability of Latin policies—and thereby encourage investment—due both to the lock-in effect on Latin reforms and the guarantee of secure access to the US market.

---

7. This concern was evident in corporate efforts to resist a restrictive NAFTA origin rule for computers and to require a common external tariff after the 10-year transition period. It also led Canada to cut its MFN textile tariffs to aid its apparel makers. However, it should be noted that concerns over investment consequences did not lead industry to seek more relaxed rules of origin in the auto or textile and apparel sectors.

The NAFTA and WHFTA need to be seen as building blocks in national economic reform programs. Compared with other building blocks in the reform programs under way throughout the hemisphere, the trade pacts will play only a supporting role in the investment story. A country's own policies constitute the main link between its economy and the world trading system, not trade pacts. Judging from the development experience of East Asian nations—which achieved astounding rates of growth with extraordinarily high saving and investment rates, later accompanied by homegrown policies of strategic liberalization—the presence or absence of regional trading arrangements was in very few cases a significant element in national economic success (Stephenson 1994).[8]

Still, the WHFTA is designed to make it harder for foreign firms to compete in the regional market—not because of higher barriers against third-country trade, but because of the heightened competitiveness of regional firms. As with the internal market reforms in the European Community pursuant to EC 1992, regional integration in the Western Hemisphere should promote more efficient use of natural and human resources and better exploitation of scale economies, enabling regional firms and workers to compete more effectively against foreign suppliers both at home and in world markets. Faced with investment diversion stemming from a more attractive economic climate in WHFTA, the only remedy available to third countries is to make their own investment climates more enticing.

With that policy prescription in mind, we have made rough estimates of the likely extent of investment diversion resulting from a WHFTA (appendix D, table D2). These estimates start with a rough guess: flows of FDI to Latin America will be higher by an additional $5 billion annually over the 12 years between 1990 and 2002 on account of a WHFTA initiative, or a cumulative additional direct investment in Latin America of $60 billion.

In terms of the impact on stocks of foreign direct investment elsewhere in the world, our calculations are as follows.[9] We assume that half of the additional direct investment in Latin America comes at the expense of home investment in the countries that send the direct investment to Latin America, and half comes at the expense of their direct investment in other regions. The prospective cumulative investment diversion is $6.2 billion from developing Asia, a figure that amounts to

---

8. By contrast, many African, Caribbean, and Pacific countries that have long enjoyed preferential access to the European Community (stemming from prior colonial ties) continued to follow statist economic policies and did not achieve particularly high growth rates.

9. We have tried to be responsibly pessimistic in estimating a high degree of investment diversion. Our model assumes a fixed world level of investment; more investment in Latin America thus implies less investment in other places.

3.1 percent of the global FDI stock that would otherwise be placed in developing Asia by the year 2002. In the case of industrialized Asia and Western Europe, the prospective cumulative diversion figures are $1.8 billion and $10.4 billion, respectively. Both amount to only 0.8 percent of FDI in those regions by the year 2002.

The cumulative diversion from the NAFTA region and the rest of the world is projected at $11.5 billion, which amounts to 1.0 percent of the region's projected stock of FDI by the year 2002. In this connection, it should be noted that investment diverted from North America to Latin America as a result of a WHFTA in large part offsets the FDI gains that North America would have enjoyed at the expense of Latin America due to the NAFTA.

Investment diversion could lead to related merchandise export losses from the same third countries on a much larger scale than the orthodox calculation of trade diversion. On the assumptions spelled out in appendix D, we calculate that third countries might lose an additional $30 billion of potential exports by the year 2002.

GATT Surveillance of Trade Diversion

To answer legitimate concerns about trade diversion and to set a healthy precedent for other regional trading agreements, we propose a new test of trade diversion (this section draws on Hufbauer and Schott 1993b). The new test would be applied reciprocally to the extent that other individual countries and regional groups such as the European Union agree to submit to mirror-image tests of their own trade diversion. This new test would be additional to existing GATT Article XXIV requirements. It is adapted from the suggestions of John McMillan (1993). All the calculations would be carried out by the GATT Secretariat, drawing on submissions from concerned members, using a ''best evidence'' rule. The calculations contemplated by this proposal are illustrated by the example in table 8.1. For the purposes of this example, NAFTA trade is the object of inquiry. However, the same tests should be applied to other WHFTA groups, and indeed to regional trade arrangements elsewhere.

First, the Secretariat would calculate the import shares (relative to global imports) of each NAFTA country from its NAFTA partners on a two-digit Standard International Trade Classification (SITC) basis at 5- and 10-year intervals after the beginning of implementation in January 1994. Any two-digit category for which the NAFTA countries import a *smaller* share from their partners at these intervals in comparison with the base year would be dismissed from further consideration. The rationale for this exclusion is straightforward: if (for example) intra-NAFTA exports of iron and steel decline as a share of total NAFTA imports, the likelihood of net diversion to the disadvantage of third countries seems small.

Table 8.1 Hypothetical calculation of trade compensation to be paid by NAFTA

SITC 78—Road vehicles	1994	1999
Combined imports by all three NAFTA countries		
From NAFTA partners	$50	$80
From all countries	$100	$140
NAFTA import share	0.500	0.571
Change in NAFTA import share		0.071
Trade diversion before trade expansion credit (0.071 × $140)		$9.94
Production by NAFTA countries	$300	$360
NAFTA imports from all countries relative to imports plus production	0.333	0.389
Trade expansion fraction (0.389 − 0.333)		0.056
Trade expansion credit (TEC) ($300 × 0.056 × 0.50)		$8.40
Calculated trade compensation owed to non-NAFTA countries ($9.94 − $8.40)		$1.54
Best estimate of NAFTA import demand elasticity for transport equipment		−2.0
Requisite reduction in NAFTA MFN tariff (Δt × −2.0 × $360 = $1.54)		1.3 percentage points

The choice of a two-digit level of analysis is arbitrary but important. As the tests are set out, any trade diversion against third countries within a given two-digit SITC category will be offset by trade creation in favor of third countries within that same two-digit group. However, there are no offsets between two-digit SITC groups. If the analysis were done at a three-digit SITC level, more diversion would be "detected," without the possibility of compensating offsets. We think analysis at the two-digit level offers a practical compromise between no offsets at all, which would result from analysis at a very fine level of product disaggregation, and total offsets, which would result from looking at total merchandise trade.

Excluding two-digit groups where intra-NAFTA trade shares are smaller than in the base year, it follows that, in the remaining two-digit SITC categories, NAFTA imports from NAFTA partners will account for a *larger* share of total imports than they did in the base year. But the rising share of intraregional trade is not proof of trade diversion. Owing to NAFTA liberalization, the NAFTA countries may be importing a larger share of their own consumption within a given two-digit SITC category. To address this possibility, a comparison would be made between base-year NAFTA ratios of total imports to domestic activity (production plus imports from all sources) and the corresponding ratios at 5- and 10-year intervals. To the extent that the ratios at these intervals are higher than the ratio in the base year, a trade expansion credit (TEC) should be calculated. The TEC would be subtracted from the dollar amount of any rise in the import share from NAFTA partners.

The TEC would be found by multiplying a "TEC fraction" by the dollar value of the rise in the import-to-activity ratio. The TEC fraction would equal the base-year member country imports from other NAFTA partners relative to base-year global imports of all NAFTA partners. This TEC fraction is arbitrary. Scenarios can be devised where the fraction so calculated is too small—for example, *all* the rise in the import-to-activity ratio is attributable to NAFTA trade liberalization. Likewise, scenarios can be devised where the TEC fraction is too large—for instance, *all* the rise in the import-to-activity ratio is attributable to a loss of comparative advantage on a global scale by the NAFTA countries. On balance, we think the TEC fraction represents a conservative estimate of the trade created by regional liberalization that does not come at the expense of third countries.

Third, the calculated trade diversion—that is, the dollar value of the rise in the intra-NAFTA import share less the dollar value, if any, of the TEC—would provide the basis for trade compensation. Compensation would be paid by a reduction in the external tariffs of the NAFTA members for the same two-digit group, provided that a sufficient number of other regional groups acceded to a parallel system of discipline. The compensating cut in external tariffs would be calculated (using standard trade elasticity estimates) so as to produce an equivalent rise in the volume of imports from third countries.[10] The tariff cuts would be implemented on an MFN basis. It would be up to the NAFTA partners to decide which countries would cut their MFN tariffs and which line items would be cut, so as to facilitate the indicated level of trade compensation.

The requirement for reciprocal discipline might be stated in the following way. No compensation would be paid for a given two-digit SITC category unless at least 70 percent of NAFTA partners' imports from third countries come from countries that had agreed to similar compensation for any trade diversion that might be caused by their own existing or future participation in regional groups.

Fourth and finally, there would be a provision for "special circumstances." If the NAFTA members were to establish, by highly persuasive evidence that was not significantly contradicted by third countries, that no trade diversion had occurred in a two-digit group (despite the mechanical tests outlined above), then no trade compensation would be owed. Correspondingly, if other countries were to establish, again by

---

10. However, the tariff cuts would be limited by the requirement that the post-cut MFN tariff not be less than the tariff then applied by each country to its NAFTA partners. This is a transitional requirement, applicable to the period before NAFTA tariffs on intraregional trade go to zero.

highly persuasive evidence not significantly contradicted by the NAFTA members, that trade diversion had occurred to a greater extent than the mechanical tests indicated, then NAFTA would owe additional trade compensation.

Concerns of Asia and Europe

Concerns about the NAFTA and a prospective WHFTA have been most pronounced in South and East Asia. Certain restrictive aspects of the NAFTA seem pointedly directed against East Asian suppliers, especially in the auto and textiles sectors. To date, these countries have voiced only mild political protests. However, they have sought a thorough GATT review of the NAFTA, with a particular focus on the rules of origin.

Contrary to the widespread fear that the NAFTA would provoke development of an exclusive Asian bloc as a counterforce to regionalism in the Western Hemisphere and Europe, one sees little evidence that NAFTA is propelling the world trading system into three competing blocs. In fact, the pace of intra-Asian arrangements has not accelerated to any significant extent, in large measure because of the region's strong trade linkage with the North American market.[11] There is little incentive for Asian countries to create their own trade cocoon: even though the volume of intraregional trade has grown sharply over the past decade, too much of their trade still spans the Pacific for Asian nations to contemplate an inward-looking regional bloc (Frankel 1991). Recent efforts by the ASEAN countries to create a long-awaited ASEAN Free Trade Area (AFTA) are still in the early stages, with meaningful steps not scheduled for a decade or more.

Separate from the AFTA initiative, Malaysian Prime Minister Mahathir has organized an East Asian Economic Caucus (EAEC) to coordinate the positions of member countries in global and regional negotiations. To date, the EAEC has been a platform to voice Malaysia's apprehensions about Western domination in the region, but it is not clear what economic significance the group will attain. Indeed, its political agenda has dominated its economic agenda.

More importantly, continued efforts by North American and Asian countries to cooperate under the umbrella of the APEC initiative are beginning to bear fruit. The APEC forum provides a bridge for Western Hemisphere and East Asian integration efforts. Following the successful APEC ministerial in Seattle in November 1993, the member countries agreed to an extensive work program, including trade facilitation measures (such as common technical standards and testing procedures),

---

11. For example, in 1990, exports to North America represented about 35 percent of total Japanese exports and 21 percent of total exports from members of the Association of Southeast Asian Nations (IMF, *Direction of Trade Statistics Yearbook 1991*).

investment issues, and cooperation on regional infrastructure projects (Bergsten 1994). APEC membership now encompasses 17 countries (18 after Chile joins in November 1994) and represents about 43 percent of world trade. Given its large and diverse membership, the APEC region may become a laboratory for testing ideas for other regional and multilateral accords.

In Europe, the reaction to Western Hemisphere integration efforts has been muted, which is not surprising given the preoccupation with the broadening and deepening of European integration and the direction of the European Union. The EC Commission has expressed only mild concern about potential trade and investment diversion resulting from NAFTA and other initiatives, and it has concluded that the results of the Uruguay Round should allay many of its remaining worries.[12]

Nonetheless, Western Europe has long-standing ties to both North and South America and consults regularly with both the United States and Latin America on bilateral trade and investment relations. Besides its biannual consultations with the United States, the European Community also negotiated a trade cooperation pact with Mexico, which entered into force in October 1991, and may begin discussions with Mexico on a broader trade pact now that the NAFTA is ratified (*Financial Times*, 27 April 1993, 8). In addition, the Community and the Andean Group signed a trade cooperation agreement in April 1993.[13]

Conclusion

Economic integration in the Western Hemisphere has important implications for economic relations between the Americas and the rest of the world. In this chapter, we have examined the concerns of third countries with the movement toward a WHFTA. While not totally assuaging those concerns, we find the following:

- A WHFTA will complement and reinforce the objectives of the GATT system and will not promote the devolution of the world trading system into competing blocs. Each country in the hemisphere greatly

---

12. In an information note released on 12 May 1993 dealing with the NAFTA and the possible extension of comparable provisions throughout the Western Hemisphere, the EC Commission specifically cited concerns about potential diversion of its exports of textiles and dairy products, about potential discrimination if investment and intellectual property reforms are extended only to the NAFTA partners, and about potential conflicts between GATT rulings and those of NAFTA dispute panels.

13. The pact was signed during a meeting of foreign ministers of the EC member states, the Andean Group, Mercosur countries, and Chile and Mexico held in Copenhagen in late April 1993 (*Japan Times*, 25 April 1993, 8). It appears to be mainly a declaration of friendly intentions rather than an agreement of substance.

depends on a strong multilateral trading system and on the successful implementation of the Uruguay Round of GATT negotiations.

■ A WHFTA should qualify under the standards set out in GATT Article XXIV for the exemption for FTAs from the GATT's most-favored nation obligation. However, those requirements do not cover significant trade policy measures that may adversely affect the trading interests of nonmember countries. Accordingly, we propose that GATT should substantially improve its surveillance of regional pacts and introduce easy-to-calculate compensation tests.

■ A WHFTA might divert 2.8 percent of exports from affected third countries to the United States by the year 2002. In addition, a WHFTA might increase foreign direct investment in Latin America by $60 billion, which in turn could cause third countries to lose $30 billion of foreign direct investment stock, and possibly as much as $30 billion annually of associated exports.

■ Like the NAFTA before it, a WHFTA will not prompt the formation of antagonistic trade blocs in Europe, Asia, and the Western Hemisphere. Instead, it will prompt competitive liberalization and integration on a global basis.

9

Toward a WHFTA

In June 1990, the Bush administration proposed the Enterprise for the Americas Initiative (EAI). Latin American countries responded enthusiastically. By providing an umbrella for trade and investment agreements, the EAI was expected eventually to lock in the dramatic economic reforms already under way in Latin America. Many things have changed since 1990. Despite its difficulties in securing congressional ratification of the North American Free Trade Agreement (NAFTA) and notwithstanding its obvious interest in the Asia-Pacific region, the Clinton administration has now reaffirmed the US commitment to free trade negotiations leading toward a Western Hemisphere Free Trade Area, or WHFTA, at some undefined future time.

Our analysis confirms the feasibility and desirability of continued economic integration in the Western Hemisphere. Comprehensive policy reforms in Latin America are adding to the list of countries willing and able to sustain reciprocal free trade obligations, thus improving prospects for a significant expansion of free trade ties in the hemisphere in the coming years.

Both North and South America could benefit from closer trade and investment ties in the hemisphere. In the early 1990s, most countries and subregions in Latin America were severely trade-deficient. A WHFTA could result in substantial trade creation without significantly curbing trade and investment with third countries. In fact, the process of negotiating a WHFTA could stimulate global trade liberalization by inspiring Asia and Europe to push the post–Uruguay Round agenda on financial services, telecommunications, government procurement, and other unfinished business.

Economic Rationale for a WHFTA

The economic case for a WHFTA fundamentally rests on a key observation: regional initiatives can progress faster than unilateral or multilateral liberalization. Recent experience shows that unilateral liberalization has its limits: when tariff barriers are reduced to 10 or 20 percent and when nontariff barriers such as obscure buy-national procurement rules remain in place, the political energy for further unilateral action may be exhausted. Active lobbying by exporters is then needed to make further cuts in import barriers, and exporters can best be energized by promising them, through international negotiations, a larger share of foreign markets.

These negotiations can, of course, take place multilaterally as well as regionally. If the multilateral approach could achieve the same degree of liberalization within the same period, it would clearly be superior to regional initiatives. But the GATT negotiations often suffer from the "convoy problem," in which individual countries (or issues) slow the entire process and talks progress only as fast as the slowest member permits. If properly structured, regional negotiations can move faster and further and even prompt new multilateral initiatives.[1]

Given these important observations, it is worth recapitulating the potential gains from a WHFTA. Based on our calculations, by implementing ambitious trade and investment liberalization measures in the context of a Western Hemisphere Free Trade Area, Latin American countries could greatly expand their trade. Assuming a WHFTA had started in 1990, our calculations indicate that, by 2002, Latin America as a whole could increase its exports by $87 billion and enlarge its imports by $104 billion in comparison with a baseline scenario of continuing reforms by the individual countries (table B2). In conjunction with more open economic systems and greater trade, Latin American GDP might be $273 billion higher (or 18 percent greater) in 2002 with a WHFTA, an increase of about $525 per capita.

Integration throughout the Western Hemisphere thus offers a very attractive option for Latin America. This is true viewed from the stand-

---

1. As evidence of the faster and further progress of regional initiatives, compare the prolonged time required to complete the Uruguay Round (12 years from political start to finish) with the speedy conclusion of the NAFTA (3 years from start to finish), coupled with the much greater liberalization achieved in the NAFTA. As evidence for the boost to multilateral initiatives, recall the positive impact on GATT talks of the services rules established in the Canada-US FTA, the EC disciplines on internal subsidies, and the path-breaking intellectual property rights regime adopted by Mexico in the NAFTA context.

point both of good-customer and strong-neighbor analyses, detailed in chapter 3.[2] For North America, however, regional integration makes economic sense either with Latin America, or with Asia, or with both. Since North America has alternative partners, Latin America must inevitably play the role of *demandeur* in negotiations with the NAFTA countries.

Latin America's commercial diplomacy is not confined to regional ties with North America. Subregional integration in Latin America should continue, driven by the logic of neighborhood trade links. After a certain point, however, good-customer considerations will prompt each of the Latin American subregions to seek closer ties with North America. The same good-customer logic will likewise prompt the United States, Brazil, Chile, and many other hemispheric countries to avoid policies that would damage their trade links with Europe and Asia.

Investment analysis points to similar conclusions. It makes economic sense for Latin America to improve investment ties both with the United States and with Japan. In addition, strong-neighbor considerations make a persuasive argument for the United States to expand its investment ties with Latin America.

Stronger hemispheric trade and investment ties should not undercut—and in most instances should reinforce—the multilateral trading system. Nonetheless, concerns arise as to the potential trade and investment diversion that could result from a WHFTA. Our calculations indicate that the scope of trade and investment diversion from Asia and Europe as a result of a WHFTA is modest. Substantial preferences already exist for trade among countries in the region, owing to recently negotiated and newly energized pacts. At most, a WHFTA would add manageable sums to the trade diversion already inherent in the NAFTA, Mercosur, Andean Group, and other subregional arrangements.

We calculate that by 2002 and with a WHFTA in place, South Asia would suffer classic trade diversion amounting to about $3.2 billion of exports annually (2.8 percent of its projected exports to the US market), East Asia would suffer diversion of $7.3 billion of exports annually (2.6 percent of its projected exports to the US market), and Europe would lose about $5.7 billion exports annually (3.5 percent of projected Western European exports). All told, on a global basis, classic trade diversion from a WHFTA could amount to $28 billion (table D1).[3] This figure is

---

2. The good-customer index is calculated as the share of the destination country (or region) in the total exports of the origin country (or region). The strong-neighbor index is calculated as the ratio between the share of the origin area's exports sold in a particular destination and the share of world GDP accounted for by that destination.

3. In calculating "classic trade diversion," we do not include export losses that third countries may experience because the WHFTA nations improve their standing in the global investment beauty contest. While this figure could be large (see chapter 8), it is not a

about a quarter of the additional imports projected for Latin America in a WHFTA scenario.[4]

We also calculate that, with a WHFTA, cumulative new foreign direct investment (FDI) in Latin America over a 12-year period could reach $60 billion. Out of this total, perhaps $30 billion represents investment diversion from other regions. The prospective cumulative investment diversion from developing Asia is $6.2 billion, a figure that amounts to 3.1 percent of the global FDI stock that would otherwise be placed in developing Asia by 2002. In the case of industrialized Asia and Europe, the prospective cumulative diversion figures are $1.8 billion and $10.4 billion, respectively. Both figures amount to only 0.8 percent of FDI projected for those regions by 2002 (table D2).

The Widening Process

The United States has signaled its interest in free trade negotiations with countries in the Western Hemisphere. President Clinton reaffirmed a previous US commitment to negotiate a free trade pact with Chile, and the Congress has asked the administration to devise a plan for trade talks with other Latin American countries. To that end, Clinton called a Summit of the Americas meeting to be held in Miami in December 1994.

What is the most likely course for Western Hemisphere economic integration? Given sharp differences in economic development within Latin America, the "big bang" approach to a Western Hemisphere Free Trade Area seems highly unlikely. A more pragmatic avenue would entail subregional integration, followed by hub-and-spoke agreements, with the NAFTA as the hub and individual countries or whole subregions as the spokes.

The United States dominates economic activity in the hemisphere. The US economy accounts for about three-fourths of the GDP of the entire hemisphere and almost a quarter of global output; the United States, standing alone, could be the prototypical hub, not only for the Western Hemisphere, but also for wide reaches of the Pacific Basin.

US policy has so far been agnostic as to whether free trade talks should proceed bilaterally, with the United States as a common hub, or

---

component of trade diversion as customarily understood. As a result of internal and external reforms, Latin American countries may attract more investment and increase their share of world exports. But these gains are part and parcel of a competitive world economy, just as the spectacular rise of Southeast Asia over the past two decades has been.

4. Our calculations for the NAFTA likewise concluded that trade created vastly exceeded trade diverted, mainly because the United States is already Mexico's dominant trading partner. We calculated that as much as $33 billion of additional trade would be created by NAFTA and about $4 billion of trade would be diverted from third countries (Hufbauer and Schott 1992, 53–55; Hufbauer and Schott 1993b, 299).

via accession to the NAFTA. Some NAFTA adversaries, particularly the AFL-CIO, are pushing the Clinton administration toward bilateral talks with Chile. The AFL-CIO apparently hopes to negotiate stiffer labor provisions in bilateral negotiations than the provisions agreed in the NAFTA.

For political and economic reasons, however, we take a highly negative attitude toward a "go-it-alone" approach, with the United States becoming the hub for spokes in Latin America or the Pacific. Instead, we strongly recommend that the United States conduct enlargement talks through the NAFTA. In political terms, stand-alone bilateral negotiations would surely divide the hemisphere: existing NAFTA members would feel they were being played off against potential new partners. In economic terms, if the United States negotiates separate arrangements with individual countries, the spokes will be shortchanged in their trading relations with one another. In addition, disparate rules on everything from performance requirements to patent protection to product standards will create enormous confusion in the world trading system.

For those reasons, US talks with Chile and other Latin American countries should be conducted within the NAFTA framework rather than through a series of bilateral negotiations. The NAFTA approach has several advantages: it provides a good model for the type of accord the United States would like to conclude throughout the hemisphere, it would foster a common regime, and it already contains an accession clause, modeled after the GATT text.[5]

Several countries in Latin America have already approached the United States, Canada, and Mexico about accession to the NAFTA. However, expansion of the NAFTA will be constrained by factors at work both within NAFTA and in the hemisphere at large:

- Membership criteria remain to be worked out by the existing NAFTA partners. In practice, the criteria will probably be announced on a case-by-case basis, but the readiness indicators set out in chapter 5 should serve as an eligibility guide for candidate countries.

- The United States will seek to expand the agenda of future trade talks to cover an ever-broadening array of nontrade issues: environment, labor standards, democratic rule, and human rights. These issues promise to complicate and prolong accession negotiations (see chapter 7).

---

5. In the NAFTA, unlike the GATT, prospective new members must be accepted by all three current members; in other words, there is a one-country veto of any new member. In the GATT, new members are admitted by a consensus process; any existing member can invoke its own nonapplication to the new member, but it cannot simply veto admission of the new member.

- Extensive negotiations will be required both to adapt the national practices of candidate countries to the NAFTA norms and to accommodate the concerns of existing partners. Such concerns are particularly relevant for the NAFTA rules of origin and safeguard clauses, since broader country coverage will dilute the effect of existing regional-content requirements and could lead to trade disruption in some sectors.

- US fast-track authority to conduct new free trade negotiations has expired and will need to be reinstated. Congressional extension of fast-track negotiating authority will prove contentious. Broad new authority is a poor candidate for action in 1994, a mid-term election year already burdened by health care legislation. However, since free trade talks with Chile command bipartisan support, Congress might provide authority in 1994 exclusively for Chilean negotiations.

Given these qualifications, the NAFTA hub might be prepared to open free trade talks with its hemispheric neighbors in the next three years. But the situation in the Latin American spokes is more complicated. The readiness indicators in table 6.1 demonstrate that members of various subregional groups are progressing at different speeds. As a general proposition, subregional integration should precede wider Western Hemisphere talks, but in some instances countries might decide to seek free trade negotiations with NAFTA ahead of talks with their own subregional partners. This option is particularly apt for Argentina, which has reformed and liberalized faster than its major Mercosur partner, Brazil. Owing to internal Brazilian difficulties, the Mercosur timetable is now beset by the ''convoy problem.''

Since the circumstances of each country and each subregional group widely differ, the formation of a WHFTA will reflect variable geometry rather than linear progression. Each country must decide for itself whether its interests are best promoted by working within its own subregional group, by reaching out to the NAFTA, or by seeking some combination of the two.[6] Several considerations will influence these decisions:

- For many Latin American countries, the disciplines imposed by subregional pacts are a useful and politically acceptable way station to the more severe disciplines that would accompany NAFTA membership.

- Countries will have to judge whether they are in a better negotiating position by proceeding independently or as part of a group. For the

---

6. To minimize the ensuing tangle over rules of origin, subregional groups could adopt the general Harmonized Tariff System transformation requirements agreed in the NAFTA, but not the industry-specific rules (Hufbauer and Schott 1993a).

microstates of the Caribbean and for the Central American countries, size alone virtually dictates joint action. But joint action does not necessarily require the participation of all members of a subregional group. A subset of members could move at a faster pace if policies were established to integrate other countries at a later date. For example, the Caribbean Community (Caricom) could proceed without Guyana, the Central American Common Market (CACM) could exempt Nicaragua, and the Andean Group could move ahead without Peru and Ecuador (as it already has for its own obligations).[7]

- Strategists will have to consider whether individual-country negotiations might unnecessarily spotlight difficult national problems—for example, environmental abuses, drug trade, and labor practices. Judging from the NAFTA debate, nontrade issues could well dominate future US talks with certain individual partners in Latin America. For example, concerns about the drug trade could easily bog down bilateral US talks with Colombia. However, the focus might shift toward broader commercial issues if US talks with Colombia were part of broader NAFTA negotiations with other Andean countries (either the whole Andean Group or just Colombia, Venezuela, and Bolivia).

In sum, there are many paths available for Latin American and Caribbean countries to integrate with North America. Governments should maintain the flexibility to proceed at different speeds and in different ways. But an important constraint should limit this flexibility: integration should proceed on a country-by-country basis, or on a subregional basis, in a context where all issues are addressed: agriculture, manufactured goods including sensitive sectors such as textiles and apparel, services, investment, intellectual property, customs rules, and dispute settlement. At the end of the day, a new spoke should join an ever-enlarging NAFTA hub.

An all-or-nothing approach will create the greatest scope for cross-sectoral concessions, will help ensure a rapid pace of liberalization, and will prompt the acceptance of new obligations. Such an approach will also yield the greatest amount of trade created among the member countries relative to the trade diverted from outside suppliers. Importantly, an all-or-nothing approach between North America and Latin America is feasible because differences on labor, environmental, and human

---

7. The fact that Colombia, Venezuela, and Mexico have already negotiated the so-called G-3 Pact indicates that the Andeans can accommodate a multispeed approach. However, if a subregional group forms a customs union, as the Mercosur plans to do, each country in the group will surrender some control over its external tariff to the subregional pact. In turn, this makes individual-country negotiations with outside regions—for example, with the NAFTA—substantially more difficult, legally and politically.

rights questions have become bridgeable with greater Latin American acceptance of internationally agreed social norms.

Not everyone subscribes to our all-or-nothing strategy. US Trade Representative Mickey Kantor has proposed negotiating topic-by-topic or sector-by-sector with those Latin American countries that are not yet ready for full-blown free trade negotiations.[8] On the surface, limited deals might seem to keep the bicycle of trade reform moving forward. On closer inspection, Kantor's strategy is fundamentally flawed.

Limited sectoral negotiations seldom yield significant results because they do not let countries trade concessions in one issue area for concessions in another. The failure of similar efforts in US-Canada talks in the early 1980s clearly illustrated this weakness—a weakness that prompted both countries to engage in broader FTA negotiations in 1986. Within the context of sectoral negotiations, the United States would find it hard to persuade Latin American countries to adopt investment and intellectual property reforms and to accept environmental and labor obligations. Latin American countries would be reluctant to trade away their negotiating chips without US commitments to far-reaching reciprocal concessions of the sort spelled out in NAFTA. In brief, the United States should recognize that it will have to give concessions to get concessions. Moreover, sectoral negotiations carry a strong risk: negotiators may find political "glue" in the diversion of exports from outside countries, to the great detriment of the world trading system.

A reason sometimes advanced for sectoral talks is to enable poorer members to keep weak or politically sensitive sectors outside the free trade arrangement. Instead of sector-by-sector negotiations, however, differing levels of development can be addressed by granting poorer Latin countries longer phasein periods—a device already used in some subregional agreements. Use of phasein periods rather than sectoral exclusions will ensure the coverage of all issues, even if implementation for some sectors is delayed.

Finally, integration between NAFTA and Latin America should be legally open-ended; potentially the WHFTA should include countries outside the hemisphere. It is critical that WHFTA not acquire even the appearance of an exclusive Western Hemisphere bloc.

Our summary table of readiness indicators (table 6.1) illustrates which hemispheric countries are best-positioned to negotiate and sustain the free trade and investment obligations spelled out in the NAFTA and to accept minimum environmental and labor standards. Based on those indicators, only a few countries now seem well-prepared. At the top of the list are Chile, Trinidad and Tobago, and Barbados, which respectively scored 4.4, 4.4, and 4.1 on our readiness scale. Venezuela rated as

---

8. Kantor's proposals were vetted at a symposium at the Georgetown University Law Center on 21 January 1994 (*Inside U.S. Trade*, 28 January 1994, 7–8).

high (3.9) as Mexico did right before the NAFTA was negotiated, and Colombia and Bolivia also have good scores (3.7).[9] Other countries can earn sharply higher scores if their policy reforms are sustained and reinforced over the next few years. For example, Argentina has made tremendous progress in arresting inflation, but its score on price stability still reflects its dismal experience during the late 1980s and into the early 1990s.

From a readiness standpoint, our analysis confirms the economic logic of the current initiative to link the NAFTA with Chile and to explore prospects for talks with other countries. Individual-country readiness is not, however, the sole criterion on which to judge the likelihood of prospective trade talks. Individual countries and subregions have their own particular problems that need to be overcome before they can integrate successfully within the neighborhood, much less with other hemispheric groups.

In the Mercosur, price and currency stability are the main problem areas, and Brazil is the major roadblock. Slow progress toward the regional common market could increase pressures for individual members to pursue other initiatives. In that event, we think the next candidate to join the NAFTA, after Chile, would logically be Argentina.[10]

In the Andean Group, price and currency stability also pose problems, and Peru presents the major drag on subregional integration. In contrast, the CACM countries suffer because of an overreliance on trade taxes and a nascent but untested commitment to market-oriented policies.

Caricom countries (with the exception of Guyana) do much better, and individual members receive relatively high readiness scores. Because of the threat of trade and investment diversion, particularly in the textile and apparel sector, the issue of NAFTA accession is more urgent. Specific proposals already have been vetted to provide a halfway house to NAFTA via the so-called Caribbean Basin Initiative (CBI) parity legislation.[11] The purpose is to grant CBI countries the same benefits as Mexico in those sectors where NAFTA provides superior access to Mexico (especially textiles and apparel). As explained earlier, we prefer an all-or-nothing approach to CBI parity. To be sure, accession to NAFTA by the Caricom countries would require that they accept zero tariffs after a phasein period. Since most Caribbean countries depend

9. We would characterize a good score as 3.6 or higher.

10. Uruguay and Paraguay have relatively high readiness indicators. However, US trade with these two countries is about a fourth of US trade with either Argentina or Chile. If diplomatic difficulties with Brazil could be sidestepped, it might make more sense for NAFTA to negotiate simultaneously with Argentina, Uruguay, and Paraguay.

11. CBI parity legislation (S 1155 and HR 1404) was introduced in both the Senate and the House in the 1993 congressional session.

heavily on tariffs for their budget revenue, this is a difficult commitment. However, a relatively long phasein period could make the transition to new tax systems politically acceptable.

Links between the Western Hemisphere and Asia

Economic logic suggests that the expansion of NAFTA in an Asian direction is just as desirable as its expansion in a Latin American direction. The Asia-Pacific region buys 24 percent of North America's exports while Latin America buys 6 percent (table 3.2). Moreover, Asian countries also buy a healthy share of Latin American exports. In 1992, Japan, Taiwan, Korea, and China combined purchased 26 percent of total Chilean exports, 22 percent of total Peruvian exports, and 11 percent of total Brazilian exports.

Despite the strong and growing commercial ties across the Pacific, we think that over the next decade formal links between the NAFTA and Asia will be limited by several considerations. First, regional pacts tend to grow out of political or economic necessity. Asia is booming without the benefit of an institutional superstructure. Second, the inclusion of environment and labor issues as essential components—from the US standpoint—for NAFTA enlargement has already caused some Asian countries to question direct links with the NAFTA.

Finally, trans-Pacific differences over the balance between individual rights and social order will be hard to bridge. The high-level US political attention given to Singapore's flogging of teenager Michael Fay illustrates these differences.

Nevertheless, both North America and Latin America want the benefits of closer ties with huge, fast-growing Asian markets. A clear indication was the prominence President Clinton accorded the Asia Pacific Economic Cooperation (APEC) summit held in Seattle on 17–19 November 1993. Latin American countries, especially Chile, are also working to strengthen their ties with Asia. Chile has been accepted for membership in APEC and will be admitted in November 1994.[12]

Asian countries also desire closer ties with the Western Hemisphere. Japan has long-standing cultural and economic ties to Brazil; Japan has also extended a warm welcome and financial assistance to President Albert Fujimori of Peru. In addition, Singapore has expressed an interest in joining the NAFTA, the Korean foreign minister has called for an association between Korea and the NAFTA, and Thailand and Singapore have publicly raised the possibility of AFTA-NAFTA linkages

---

12. Other Latin American countries around the Pacific Rim will not be able to follow suit for at least three years because of the freeze on new APEC members after the Chilean accession.

(*Asahi Evening News*, 6 November 1993; *International Trade Reporter*, 9 March 1994, 378; speech by Korean Minister of Foreign Affairs Han Sung-Joo, Twenty-First Century Council meeting, 18 February 1994, Washington; *Business Times*, 28 December 1993).

In our view, NAFTA negotiations with Asia should differ sharply from NAFTA negotiations with Latin America.[13] In large measure, this conclusion reflects the economic, political, and cultural diversity of the Asia-Pacific region. In addition, it recognizes the complex trade and investment relationships that have already evolved among these countries because of the market-driven opportunities in their dynamic, high-growth economies.

The greater institutional and social differences between North America and Asia commend a topic-by-topic approach to a subset of negotiable questions. For the time being, disparities on environment, labor, human rights, and democracy issues may be too large to be bridged within the NAFTA context. However, a great deal can be accomplished if negotiations between NAFTA and Asia focus on framework rules both for specific functional areas such as investment and product standards and for specific commercial sectors such as financial services, telecommunications, and civil aviation. A rule-making agenda may not, in the first instance, achieve dramatic liberalization. However, it will set the stage for liberalization when underlying conditions are propitious.

The Clinton administration has demonstrated great interest in the Asia-Pacific region, but this interest has not distracted its attention from Latin America. President Clinton coupled his APEC initiatives with new initiatives in the Western Hemisphere, notably the convocation of the Summit of the Americas to be held in December 1994, and the reaffirmation of his desire to open free trade talks with Chile as soon as possible.

Clinton's strategy reflects the fact that the United States has much to gain from closer trade and investment ties with its hemispheric neighbors. A WHFTA has the potential to significantly increase trade between Latin America and the United States, to improve social conditions, and to boost living standards from Anchorage to Tierra del Fuego. Properly structured, hemispheric integration can act not only as a catalyst for deeper commercial relations among the APEC nations but also as a beacon for the entire world trading system.

---

13. One possible exception: NAFTA might be enlarged in the next decade to include Korea. US-Korean commercial disputes are modest, not major; Korea is rapidly establishing an array of democratic institutions; and Korea is not now a member of another regional group. According to our calculations, the readiness indicator for Korea is 4.3 compared to a score of 3.9 for Mexico at the time NAFTA was signed.

Appendix A:
Trade Deficiency in Latin America

The purpose of our calculations is to size up the shortfall in Latin American merchandise imports and exports in 1990 that was due to import barriers and debt problems in the region. The method we have adopted is to compare actual 1990 Latin American imports and exports with the levels that would have been achieved if Latin American trade had reached the amounts predicted by two regression equations. The regression equations were estimated from the experience of 58 market-oriented countries.

Based on the model developed by Collins and Rodrik (1991), the ratio of merchandise exports to GDP (X/GDP) and the ratio of merchandise imports to GDP (M/GDP) were treated as dependent variables and regressed in two separate equations against several independent variables: the logarithm of GDP, the logarithm squared of GDP, the logarithm of population, and a special "entrepôt country" variable.[1]

The two regression equations are estimated based on the cross-section data in table A1:

---

1. There are several differences between our approach and the Collins-Rodrik approach. Our formulations were chosen to minimize the difference between predicted and actual trade ratios for large countries—the United States, Japan, Germany, France, and Italy. Unlike Collins and Rodrik, we do not include area dummy terms in the regression equation because we are trying to discover trade intensity differences between countries. Further, while the Collins-Rodrik equation was estimated on the basis of data from 91 countries, our equation is estimated on the basis of 58 countries. We have deliberately excluded Africa, the Middle East, Eastern Europe, and the former Soviet Union from our equation on the argument that these countries have been so isolated from international commerce, or are so dependent on oil exports, that their presence would distort the estimates of parameters that might reasonably describe the trade potential of most Latin countries after a period of market-oriented economic policies.

Table A1   Actual and predicted trade-to-GDP ratios and values, 1990

Region/country	Actual exports (billions of dollars)	Actual imports (billions of dollars)	GDP (billions of dollars)	Population (millions)	Actual vs. predicted exports (percent)	Actual vs. predicted imports (percent)	Actual vs. predicted exports (billions of dollars)	Actual vs. predicted imports (billions of dollars)
North America	566.4	683.0	6,200.1	362.7	-2.6	-1.6	-163.8	-98.7
Canada	131.7	124.4	570.2	26.5	-2.1	-2.5	-11.8	-14.2
United States	393.6	517.0	5,392.2	250.0	-2.7	-1.4	-145.1	-77.2
Mexico[a]	41.1	41.6	237.8	86.2	-2.9	-3.1	-7.0	-7.3
Western Europe	1,595.1	1,662.2	6,945.8	415.3	-0.2	1.3	-11.1	90.9
European Union	1,359.0	1,412.7	5,995.8	327.0	0.7	2.1	43.3	126.4
Belgium-Luxembourg	117.7	119.7	192.4	10.0	31.3	33.0	60.3	63.6
Denmark	35.1	31.8	131.0	5.1	-5.9	-7.8	-7.7	-10.2
France	216.6	234.4	1,190.8	56.4	-2.6	-0.5	-30.6	-6.5
Germany[b]	398.4	342.6	1,488.2	62.5	6.9	3.6	102.7	53.6
Greece	8.1	19.8	57.9	10.1	-14.5	4.7	-8.4	2.7
Ireland	23.7	20.7	42.5	3.5	23.2	15.1	9.9	6.4
Italy	170.3	182.0	1,090.8	57.7	-5.2	-3.6	-56.7	-39.4
Netherlands	131.8	126.1	279.2	14.9	19.1	17.8	53.4	49.8
Portugal	16.4	25.3	56.8	10.4	0.6	15.2	0.3	8.6
Spain	55.6	87.7	491.2	39.0	-12.2	-5.1	-60.1	-25.2
United Kingdom	185.2	222.8	975.2	57.4	-2.0	2.3	-19.8	22.9
European Free Trade Association	223.2	227.1	853.4	32.2	-5.5	-4.2	-46.6	-35.9
Austria	41.3	49.1	157.4	7.7	-4.7	0.9	-7.4	1.4
Finland	26.6	27.0	137.3	5.0	-13.4	-12.4	-18.4	-17.0
Norway	34.0	26.9	105.8	4.2	-1.1	-7.5	-1.2	-7.9
Sweden	57.6	54.4	228.1	8.6	-5.3	-5.8	-12.1	-13.2
Switzerland	63.8	69.7	224.9	6.7	-3.3	0.3	-7.4	0.8
Other								
Turkey	13.0	22.3	96.5	56.1	-8.1	0.4	-7.9	0.4

	778.6	742.4	4,698.3	2,767.2	-2.1	-3.7	-97.0	-172.4
Asia	778.6	742.4	4,698.3	2,767.2	-2.1	-3.7	-97.0	-172.4
Australia–New Zealand Closer Economic Relations	49.3	51.5	339.1	20.5	-13.6	-12.4	-46.1	-42.1
Australia	39.8	42.0	296.3	17.1	-14.0	-12.6	-41.6	-37.2
New Zealand	9.5	9.5	42.8	3.4	-10.6	-11.4	-4.5	-4.9
Japan	287.6	235.4	2,942.9	123.5	-5.3	-7.3	-157.4	-215.2
ASEAN	139.0	158.3	308.3	316.4	12.5	15.0	38.6	46.3
Indonesia	25.7	21.8	107.3	178.2	7.4	2.2	8.0	2.3
Malaysia	29.4	29.3	42.4	17.9	44.0	41.9	18.7	17.8
Philippines	8.1	13.0	43.9	61.5	-1.5	7.5	-0.6	3.3
Singapore[c]	52.8	60.9	34.6	3.0	19.1	22.3	6.6	7.7
Thailand	23.1	33.4	80.2	55.8	7.4	18.9	5.9	15.2
Other East Asia	275.2	259.1	785.0	1,202.3	9.8	5.6	77.3	43.9
Korea	65.0	69.6	236.4	42.8	4.1	6.1	9.7	14.5
Taiwan	67.2	54.7	124.0	20.0	27.7	17.5	34.4	21.7
China	60.9	52.3	364.9	1,133.7	8.1	4.3	29.5	15.5
Hong Kong[c]	82.2	82.5	59.7	5.8	6.2	-13.0	3.7	-7.8
West Asia	27.4	38.0	323.1	1,104.5	-2.9	-1.7	-9.4	-5.4
Bangladesh	1.7	3.7	22.9	106.7	-8.4	-3.8	-1.9	-0.9
India	18.0	23.6	254.5	849.5	-2.9	-2.2	-7.4	-5.7
Nepal	0.2	0.7	2.9	18.9	-7.7	0.1	-0.2	0.0
Pakistan	5.6	7.4	35.5	112.4	-0.9	1.0	-0.3	0.4
Sri Lanka	2.0	2.7	7.3	17.0	7.5	11.3	0.5	0.8

(Table continues next page)

187

Table A1 Actual and predicted trade-to-GDP ratios and values, 1990 (Continued)

Region/country	Actual exports (billions of dollars)	Actual imports (billions of dollars)	GDP (billions of dollars)	Population (millions)	Actual vs. predicted exports (percent)	Actual vs. predicted imports (percent)	Actual vs. predicted exports (billions of dollars)	Actual vs. predicted imports (billions of dollars)
Latin America	96.4	69.8	730.7	330.2	-7.7	-12.6	-56.3	-92.4
Chile	8.6	7.0	27.8	13.2	5.2	-2.8	1.4	-0.8
Mercosur	45.4	27.9	515.5	185.8	-10.1	-14.0	-52.2	-72.0
Argentina	12.4	4.1	93.3	32.3	-10.8	-20.5	-10.0	-19.1
Brazil	31.4	22.5	414.1	150.4	-10.0	-12.5	-41.5	-51.6
Uruguay	1.7	1.3	8.2	3.1	-7.4	-16.5	-0.6	-1.4
Andean Group	31.2	18.8	142.1	91.2	-2.0	-13.0	-2.8	-18.5
Bolivia	0.9	0.7	5.3	7.2	-4.9	-15.1	-0.3	-0.8
Colombia	6.8	5.6	41.1	32.3	-6.2	-11.2	-2.5	-4.6
Ecuador	2.7	1.9	10.9	10.3	1.2	-11.1	0.1	-1.2
Peru	3.3	3.2	36.6	21.7	-15.2	-17.5	-5.5	-6.4
Venezuela	17.5	7.4	48.3	19.7	11.1	-11.5	5.4	-5.5
CACM	3.6	5.7	20.7	21.1	-6.7	-2.3	-1.4	-0.5
Costa Rica	1.5	2.0	5.7	2.8	-1.3	3.1	-0.1	0.2
El Salvador	0.6	1.3	5.4	5.2	-13.3	-6.6	-0.7	-0.4
Guatemala	1.2	1.6	7.6	9.2	-7.0	-6.9	-0.5	-0.5
Nicaragua	0.3	0.8	2.0	3.9	-3.0	11.5	-0.1	0.2
CARICOMd	6.4	7.7	13.1	4.9	0.6	0.4	0.1	0.1
Bahamasc	2.7	3.8	2.5	0.3	-25.3	-9.3	-0.6	-0.2
Barbados	0.2	0.7	1.5	0.3	-16.3	8.2	-0.2	0.1
Guyana	0.2	0.2	0.4	0.8	42.8	22.6	0.2	0.1
Jamaica	1.1	1.7	4.0	2.4	2.7	11.0	0.1	0.4
Trinidad and Tobago	2.1	1.3	4.8	1.2	13.9	-7.7	0.7	-0.4
Other Latin America	1.3	2.7	11.4	14.0	-12.2	-6.0	-1.4	-0.7
Dominican Republic	0.8	2.2	7.3	7.1	-12.8	0.5	-0.9	0.0
Haiti	0.1	0.3	2.8	6.5	-14.7	-18.0	-0.4	-0.5
Surinam	0.3	0.3	1.3	0.4	-4.0	-16.7	-0.1	-0.2

a. Includes trade to and from the maquiladoras.
b. Germany refers to Federal Republic.
c. Entrepôt country. For Singapore and Hong Kong, data includes reexports and imports for reexports.
d. Also part of CARICOM: Antigua and Barbuda, Belize, Dominica, Grenada, Monserrat, St. Kitts, St. Lucia, and St. Vincent.

$X/GDP = 21.78 +$ (A1)

$15.26(\log GDP) - 3.16(\log^2 GDP) - 10.33(\log P) + 100.50(E)$
   (± 7.33) (± 1.93) (± 3.66) (± 8.95)

$R^2 = 0.77$

Standard error of regression estimate of $X/GDP = 14.3$ percent

$M/GDP = 32.71 +$ (A2)

$6.22(\log GDP) - 1.67(\log^2 GDP) - 9.05(\log P) + 119.65(E)$
   (± 6.84) (± 1.80) (± 3.41) (± 8.35)

$R^2 = 0.84$

Standard error of regression estimate of $M/GDP = 13.3$ percent

Where:

X/GDP	= ratio of merchandise exports to GDP, expressed as a percentage figure (e.g., 10.7 percent).
M/GDP	= ratio of merchandise imports to GDP, expressed as a percentage figure (e.g., 11.2 percent).
$\log GDP$	= logarithm to the base 10 of 1990 GDP (expressed in billions of dollars).
$\log^2 GDP$	= squared value of logarithm to the base 10 of GDP (expressed in billions of dollars).
$\log P$	= logarithm to the base 10 of population (expressed in millions of persons).
E	= dummy variable for entrepôt trading countries (E = 1 for Hong Kong, Singapore, and the Bahamas; E = 0 for all other countries).

The figures in parentheses are standard errors of the estimated coefficients.

In an alternative formulation, the member countries of the European Union were treated as a single country, and intra-EU trade was netted out (box A1).

Comparisons between predicted and actual trade levels for 1990 appear in table A1. The results of the model for Latin American countries are discussed in the text. Here we summarize the findings for other regions. Canada and the United States are both trade-deficient, according to these equations. Canada exhibits a shortfall of $11.8 billion in exports and $14.2 billion in imports. The United States shows an export deficiency of $145.1 billion and an import deficiency of $77.2 billion. The US results, however, partly reflect the choice of independent variables in regression equations A1 and A2. The United States is an extreme outlier in terms of GDP and population size; moreover, the terms in the regression equations were

Box A1   Regression equations with EU countries treated as a unit

Using the alternative formulation, there were 48 country observations, and the regression equations become:

$$X/GDP = 22.31 + \qquad\qquad\qquad\qquad\qquad\qquad\qquad\text{(A1*)}$$

$$10.75(\log GDP) - 2.43(\log^2 GDP) - 7.59(\log P) + 103.52(E)$$
$$(\pm 7.26)\qquad\quad (\pm 1.81)\qquad\qquad (\pm 3.83)\qquad\quad (\pm 8.87)$$

$R^2 = 0.81$

Standard error of regression estimate of X/GDP = 13.89 percent

$$M/GDP = 33.67 + \qquad\qquad\qquad\qquad\qquad\qquad\qquad\text{(A2*)}$$

$$-0.34(\log GDP) - 0.58(\log^2 GDP) - 5.65(\log P) + 123.94(E)$$
$$(\pm 6.70)\qquad\quad (\pm 1.67)\qquad\qquad (\pm 3.54)\qquad\quad (\pm 8.18)$$

$R^2 = 0.88$

Standard error of regression estimate of M/GDP = 12.82 percent

The figures in parentheses are standard errors of the estimated coefficients.
    Using equations (A1*) and (A2*), the export deficiency of Latin America in 1990 may be calculated as $51 billion (versus $56 billion in the basic model), while the import deficiency may be calculated as $80 billion (versus $92 billion).

chosen to minimize the residuals for outlier countries. Plausible alternative formulations of the regression equations would make the United States seem even more trade-deficient, or perhaps even trade-intensive.[2] Within Western Europe, the European Union seems trade-intensive, while the European Free Trade Association appears somewhat trade-deficient. Asia and Oceania give a mixed picture. Australia and New Zealand taken together, long protected by high tariffs and quotas, are export-deficient by $46.1 billion and import deficient by $42.1 billion. Japan shows up as export-deficient by $157.4 billion, and import-deficient by $215.2 billion. These are high numbers for Japan, and they may be statistical artifacts, but equally well they could reflect an array of semiofficial and private trade barriers protecting the Japanese market.[3] For ASEAN, the estimated dollar amount of above-average export intensity is $38.6 billion, and above-average import intensity is calculated at $46.3 billion. For other East Asian nations, the above-average intensities are $77.3 billion and $43.9 billion, respectively. However, West Asia, an area that includes protected countries such as India and Pakistan, shows up as trade-deficient.

---

2. Alternative formulations of the regression equations have far less impact on the characterization of mid-sized and mid-GDP-level countries, either as trade-intensive or trade-deficient.

3. Japan appeared trade-deficient in all our alternative formulations of the regression equations.

Appendix B:
Impact on Latin America
and the United States

Latin America Trade Expansion and GDP Growth

As discussed in the text, a two-way process connects trade expansion and GDP growth. Higher trade levels spur GDP growth through the stimulus to economic efficiency; higher GDP growth promotes trade expansion through a supply-side boost to exports and through a demand-side pull for imports.

Our regression equations are designed to assess the strength of causation in both directions. In the first relationship (equation B1 below), compound annual real growth in GDP is the dependent variable; in the other two relationships (equations B2 and B3 below), compound annual real growth in exports and imports are the dependent variables. The regression equations are estimated based on the cross-section data in table B1:

$$\Delta GDP/GDP = 2.61 + 0.25(\Delta X/X) + 0.20(\Delta M/M) \qquad (B1)$$
$$(\pm 0.08) \qquad (\pm 0.08)$$

$R^2 = 0.61$

Standard error of regression estimate of $\Delta GDP/GDP$ = 1.8 percentage points

$$\Delta X/X = -3.11 + 1.41(\Delta GDP/GDP) \qquad (B2)$$
$$(\pm 0.16)$$

$R^2 = 0,57$

Standard error of regression estimate of $\Delta X/X$ = 3.5 percentage points

$$\Delta M/M = -3.79 + 1.29(\Delta GDP/GDP) \qquad \text{(B3)}$$
$$(\pm 0.16)$$

$R^2 = 0.54$

Standard error of regression estimate of $\Delta M/M = 3.5$ percentage points

$\Delta GDP/GDP$ = percent increase in GDP, expressed as the compound annual real GDP growth over 1980–1990 (e.g., 2.8 percent).

$\Delta X/X$ = percent increase in merchandise exports, expressed as the compound annual growth in the constant dollar value of exports over 1980–1990 (e.g., 2.4 percent).

$\Delta M/M$ = percent increase in merchandise imports, expressed as the compound annual growth in the constant dollar value of imports over 1980–1990 (e.g., 0.7 percent).

The figures in parentheses are standard errors of the estimated coefficients.

In these equations, export and import real growth rates were calculated by first multiplying nominal 1980 trade values by a factor of 1.536 (table B1). This factor reflects the average increase in US export and import unit value indexes over the decade. It is intended as a rough-and-ready adjustment for global inflation in dollar prices.

Regression equations B1, B2, and B3 can be regarded as a three-equation system for finding three unknowns. Looked at in this way, the equations can be solved for the three unknowns. The solution gives predicted values for 1980–90 for the "typical" country (where "typical" refers only to the panel of 58 nations listed in table B1), for real annual GDP growth, real annual export growth, and real annual import growth. The predicted values for the "typical" country were real GDP growth, 2.7 percent; real export growth, 0.7 percent; and real import growth, −0.3 percent.

The predicted values for "typical" country trade performance in the 1980s were negatively affected by declines in real Latin American export and import levels during the decade. Most Latin American countries experienced a very hard decade because of the debt crisis, because of falling terms of trade, and because of a resurgence of restrictive trade policies.

The equation system represented by B1, B2, and B3 can be used to make a rough forecast of Latin American trade and GDP growth prospects in the 1990s. This rough forecast assumes that the relevant coefficients in the regression equations remain the same for 1990–2000 as for 1980–90. It also requires a number of ad hoc assumptions regarding the constant terms in the three equations.

Table B1 Export and import performance, 1980–90

Region/Country	Compound real annual growth rates, 1980–90 (percentages)			Exports (billions of dollars)			Imports (billions of dollars)		
	GDP	Exports	Imports	1980	Adjusted 1980[a]	1990	1980	Adjusted 1980[a]	1990
North America				311.4	478.3	566.4	340.7	523.4	683.0
Canada	3.4	2.4	2.6	67.7	104.0	131.7	62.5	96.1	124.4
United States	3.4	1.3	2.7	225.6	346.5	393.6	257.0	394.7	517.0
Mexico	1.0	4.0	2.5	18.1	27.8	41.1	21.2	32.6	41.6
Western Europe									
European Union				691.3	1,061.8	1,359.0	773.5	1,188.0	1,412.7
Belgium-Luxembourg	2.0	1.7	0.8	64.5	99.1	117.7	71.9	110.4	119.7
Denmark	2.4	3.1	0.7	16.7	25.7	35.1	19.3	29.7	31.8
France	2.2	2.0	1.2	116.0	178.2	216.6	134.9	207.2	234.4
Germany[b]	2.1	3.0	1.7	192.9	296.2	398.4	188.0	288.8	342.6
Greece	1.8	0.2	2.0	5.2	7.9	8.1	10.5	16.2	19.8
Ireland	3.1	6.3	1.9	8.4	12.9	23.7	11.2	17.1	20.7
Italy	2.4	3.6	1.6	78.1	120.0	170.3	100.7	154.7	182.0
Netherlands	1.9	1.5	0.5	74.0	113.6	131.8	78.0	119.9	126.1
Portugal	2.7	8.7	5.9	4.6	7.1	16.4	9.3	14.3	25.3
Spain	3.1	5.7	5.3	20.7	31.8	55.6	34.1	52.3	87.7
United Kingdom	3.1	0.9	2.3	110.1	169.2	185.2	115.5	177.5	222.8
European Free Trade Association				110.7	170.1	223.2	126.8	194.7	227.1
Austria	2.1	4.4	2.7	17.5	26.9	41.3	24.4	37.5	49.1
Finland	3.4	2.0	1.2	14.2	21.7	26.6	15.6	24.0	27.0
Norway	2.9	1.8	0.3	18.6	28.5	34.0	16.9	26.0	26.9
Sweden	2.2	1.9	0.6	30.9	47.5	57.6	33.4	51.4	54.4
Switzerland	2.2	3.4	2.2	29.6	45.5	63.8	36.3	55.8	69.7
Other									
Turkey	5.1	11.2	6.4	2.9	4.5	13.0	7.8	12.0	22.3

(Table continues next page)

Table B1 Export and import performance, 1980–90 (Continued)

Region/Country	Compound real annual growth rates, 1980–90 (percentages)			Exports (billions of dollars)			Imports (billions of dollars)		
	GDP	Exports	Imports	1980	Adjusted 1980ᵃ	1990	1980	Adjusted 1980ᵃ	1990
Asia									
Australia–New Zealand Closer Economic Relations				27.4	42.0	49.3	27.9	42.8	51.5
Australia	3.4	1.7	2.0	21.9	33.7	39.8	22.4	34.4	42.0
New Zealand	1.9	1.3	1.2	5.4	8.3	9.5	5.5	8.4	9.5
Japan	4.1	3.7	0.8	130.4	200.4	287.6	141.3	217.0	235.4
ASEAN				66.5	102.1	139.0	63.2	97.0	158.3
Indonesia	5.5	−2.7	2.7	21.9	33.7	25.7	10.8	16.6	21.8
Malaysia	5.2	4.0	5.8	13.0	19.9	29.4	10.8	16.6	29.3
Philippines	0.9	−0.9	0.2	5.7	8.8	8.1	8.3	12.7	13.0
Singapore	6.4	5.9	5.1	19.4	29.8	52.8	24.0	36.9	60.9
Thailand	7.6	8.7	9.0	6.5	10.0	23.1	9.2	14.2	33.4
Other East Asia				75.1	115.4	275.2	84.4	129.7	259.1
Korea	9.7	9.2	7.4	17.5	26.9	65.0	22.3	34.2	69.6
Taiwan	11.0	8.3	6.1	19.8	30.4	67.2	19.8	30.4	54.7
China	9.5	8.2	5.5	18.1	27.8	60.9	19.9	30.6	52.3
Hong Kong	7.1	10.5	9.1	19.8	30.3	82.2	22.4	34.5	82.5
West Asia				13.1	20.2	27.4	25.2	38.7	38.0
Bangladesh	4.3	3.2	−0.9	0.8	1.2	1.7	2.6	4.0	3.7
India	5.3	3.1	0.3	8.6	13.2	18.0	14.9	22.8	23.6
Nepal	4.6	5.5	2.7	0.1	0.1	0.2	0.3	0.5	0.7
Pakistan	6.3	3.3	−1.1	2.6	4.0	5.6	5.4	8.2	7.4
Sri Lanka	4.0	1.9	−1.5	1.1	1.6	2.0	2.0	3.1	2.7
Latin America				80.7	123.9	96.4	84.4	129.7	69.7
Chile	3.2	1.8	−1.1	4.7	7.2	8.6	5.1	7.9	7.0
Mercosur				29.2	44.9	45.4	37.2	57.1	27.9
Argentina	−0.4	0.0	−12.9	8.0	12.3	12.4	10.5	16.2	4.1
Brazil	2.7	0.2	−5.2	20.1	30.9	31.4	25.0	38.3	22.5
Uruguay	0.3	0.4	−6.5	1.1	1.6	1.7	1.7	2.6	1.3

Andean Group				30.5	46.8	31.2	21.9	33.7	18.8
Bolivia	−0.1	−4.4	−3.7	0.9	1.4	0.9	0.7	1.0	0.7
Colombia	3.7	1.1	−2.4	3.9	6.1	6.8	4.7	7.2	5.6
Ecuador	2.0	−3.3	−6.0	2.5	3.8	2.7	2.3	3.5	1.9
Peru	−0.3	−5.8	−1.7	3.9	6.0	3.3	2.5	3.8	3.2
Venezuela	1.0	−5.1	−8.6	19.2	29.5	17.5	11.8	18.2	7.4
CACM				3.9	6.1	3.6	5.0	7.7	5.7
Costa Rica	3.0	−0.5	−1.5	1.0	1.5	1.5	1.5	2.4	2.0
El Salvador	0.9	−9.1	−1.6	1.0	1.5	0.6	1.0	1.5	1.3
Guatemala	0.8	−6.4	−4.0	1.5	2.3	1.2	1.6	2.5	1.6
Nicaragua	−2.2	−7.2	−5.3	0.5	0.7	0.3	0.9	1.4	0.8
CARICOM[d]				10.7	16.4	6.4	12.7	19.5	7.7
Bahamas[c]	2.8	−9.9	−10.7	5.0	7.7	2.7	7.5	11.6	3.8
Barbados	0.3	−4.9	−1.4	0.2	0.3	0.2	0.5	0.8	0.7
Guyana	−3.3	−8.5	−8.7	0.4	0.6	0.2	0.4	0.6	0.2
Jamaica	1.6	−2.6	0.2	1.0	1.5	1.1	1.1	1.7	1.7
Trinidad and Tobago	−4.7	−10.4	−12.7	4.1	6.3	2.1	3.2	4.9	1.3
Other Latin America				1.7	2.6	1.3	2.5	3.9	2.7
Dominican Republic	2.1	−5.9	−1.5	1.0	1.5	0.8	1.6	2.5	2.2
Haiti	−0.6	−7.9	−7.3	0.2	0.3	0.1	0.4	0.6	0.3
Surinam	−0.9	−8.6	−9.8	0.5	0.8	0.3	0.5	0.8	0.3

a. Nominal trade values for the year 1980 are increased by a factor of 1.536 to reflect inflation over 1980–90. The factor of 1.536 represents the average of the increase in the US export unit value and the US unit import value indexes, as reported in *International Financial Statistics*.

b. Germany refers to the Federal Republic.

c. GDP data for Bahamas comes from the Inter-American Development Bank and covers 1981–90.

d. Also part of CARICOM: Antigua and Barbuda, Belize, Dominica, Grenada, Monserrat, St. Kitts, St. Lucia, and St. Vincent.

Sources: General Agreement on Tariffs and Trade, *International Trade 90–91*; World Bank, *World Development Report 1992*; Inter-American Development Bank, *Economic and Social Progress in Latin America, 1991 Report*; Council for Economics Planning and Development, Republic of China, *Taiwan Statistical Data Book, 1991*; International Monetary Fund, *International Financial Statistics, Yearbook 1991*.

For purposes of equation B3, we assume that, for the 1990s, Latin American real annual import growth will be adjusted upward by a constant term equal to the standard error of the estimating equation (i.e., by 3.5 percentage points). The rationale for adding this new constant term is that the depressing effects of the debt crisis and falling terms of trade on Latin America's ability to purchase imports will not recur in the 1990s. With this adjustment, the assumed version of equation B3 that applies to 1990–2000 becomes:

$$\Delta M/M = (3.50 - 3.79) + 1.29(\Delta GDP/GDP) \tag{B3*}$$

Using adjusted equation B3*, together with original equations B1 and B2, the three-equation system can be solved to yield the following outlook:

No New Reforms[a]

	Amount in 1990 (dollars in billions)	Projected growth rate 1990–2002	Amount in 2002 (dollars in billions)
Predicted GDP	$731	4.5	$1,239
Predicted exports	$96	3.2	$141
Predicted imports	$70	5.5	$132

a. Real growth and real dollar levels (1990 prices).

These results would mean that Latin American nations as a group will not significantly improve their domestic economic or trade policies, beyond the changes made up to 1990. This is not a realistic scenario, given the recent strong trend in favor of policy reform.

Our forecasts are intended to capture two scenarios, the base scenario, or continuing-reform scenario, and the WHFTA scenario. A qualitative description of the scenarios appears in chapter 4.

The WHFTA scenario assumes a policy-induced expansion of $19 billion in real exports and $31 billion in real imports. Spread over a 10-year period, these trade-expansion values imply a policy-induced boost in the real export growth rate of 1.8 percent per year and a policy-induced boost in real import growth of 3.7 percent per year. These additions to trade growth, resulting from policy reform, can be added as special terms to the export and import growth equations. This adjustment leads to two new trade growth equations for the WHFTA scenario:

$$\Delta X/X = (1.80 - 3.11) + 1.41(\Delta GDP/GDP) \tag{B2**}$$

$$\Delta M/M = (3.70 + 3.50 - 3.79) + 1.29(\Delta GDP/GDP) \tag{B3**}$$

Table B2   GDP and trade growth projected under two scenarios

Scenarios	Projected growth rate 1990–2002 (percentages)	Amount in 2002 (dollars in billions)
WHFTA scenario[a] (real growth and real dollar levels)		
Predicted GDP	7.6	1,760
Predicted exports	9.7	292
Predicted imports	13.2	309
Continuing-reform scenario[b] (real growth and real dollar levels)		
Predicted GDP	6.1	1,487
Predicted exports	6.5	205
Predicted imports	9.4	205
WHFTA scenario vs. continuing-reform scenario[c] (real growth and real dollar levels)		
Increment in GDP	1.5	273
Increment in exports	3.2	87
Increment in imports	3.8	104

a. Equations B2** and B3**, together with equation B1, can be solved to yield the following outlook under the WHFTA scenario.
b. The continuing-reform scenario is assumed to be midway between the no-new-reform scenario and the WHFTA scenario shown above.
c. The difference between the continuing-reform and WHFTA scenarios can be interpreted as a very rough calculation of the potential economic gains from extensive trade liberalization and associated domestic policy reforms.

Equations B2** and B3**, together with equation B1, can be solved to yield the outlook under the WHFTA scenario shown in table B2.

Impact on the United States

We are now in a position to calculate the impact of a WHFTA on US imports and exports under the continuing-reform scenario and the WHFTA scenario, and the related impact on jobs and wages in 1997 and 2002.

US Export Gains

Table B3 shows base-year US exports to Latin America (excluding Mexico) for 86 major commodity groups sorted by the US median weekly wage level associated with each commodity group (the derivation of the median wage is discussed later). The base-year figures are determined by averaging the level of US exports for 1989, 1990, and 1991 for each commodity group. The residual group, "commodity groups not shown," is itself treated as a separate commodity.[1]

---

1. The commodity groups included in the industrial classifications are those with exports of more than $5 million for the base year. Those commodity groups with exports of less than $5 million are excluded from the list of identified industrial classifications and instead grouped under the heading "unlisted commodities."

Table B3 US exports to Latin America,[a] by commodity group, annual average 1989–91, and projected for 1997 and 2002

Commodity group[b]	Exports to Latin America 1989–91 average (millions of dollars)[c]	US median weekly wages (dollars)	Projected 1997 (millions of dollars)		Projected 2002 (millions of dollars)	
			Continuing reform scenario[d]	WHFTA scenario[d]	Continuing reform scenario[d]	WHFTA scenario[d]
All commodities	23,907.8	442	44,839.5	56,946.2	70,266.4	105,851.5
1 27–MINERAL FUEL, OIL ETC.; BITUMIN SUBST; MINERAL WAX	1,393.9	493	2,614.3	3,320.2	4,096.8	6,171.6
2 85–ELECTRIC MACHINERY ETC; SOUND EQUIP; TV EQUIP; PTS	1,978.2	492	3,710.1	4,711.9	5,814.0	8,758.4
3 30–PHARMACEUTICAL PRODUCTS	155.2	479	291.1	369.7	456.2	687.3
4 88–AIRCRAFT, SPACECRAFT, AND PARTS THEREOF	1,409.9	479	2,644.3	3,358.2	4,143.7	6,242.3
5 29–ORGANIC CHEMICALS	1,086.3	474	2,037.5	2,587.6	3,192.8	4,809.8
6 28–INORG CHEM; PREC & RARE-EARTH MET & RADIOACT COMPD	512.2	474	960.6	1,220.0	1,505.4	2,267.7
7 26–ORES, SLAG AND ASH	62.1	465	116.4	147.8	182.4	274.8
8 38–MISCELLANEOUS CHEMICAL PRODUCTS	526.1	463	986.7	1,253.1	1,546.2	2,329.2
9 36–EXPLOSIVES; PYROTECHNICS; MATCHES; PYRO ALLOYS ETC	15.7	463	29.4	37.3	46.1	69.4
10 32–TANNING & DYE EXT ETC; DYE, PAINT, PUTTY ETC; INKS	129.2	463	242.3	307.8	379.7	572.1
11 34–SOAP ETC; WAXES, POLISH ETC; CANDLES; DENTAL PREPS	74.5	463	139.7	177.4	218.9	329.8
12 37–PHOTOGRAPHIC OR CINEMATOGRAPHIC GOODS	93.6	463	175.6	223.0	275.2	414.6
13 35–ALBUMINOIDAL SUBST; MODIFIED STARCH; GLUE; ENZYMES	26.5	463	49.8	63.2	78.0	117.5

14	33–ESSENTIAL OILS ETC; PERFUMERY, COSMETIC ETC PREPS	166.1	463	311.5	395.5	488.1	735.2
15	91–CLOCKS AND WATCHES AND PARTS THEREOF	9.8	453	18.3	23.3	28.7	43.3
16	49–PRINTED BOOKS, NEWSPAPERS ETC; MANUSCRIPTS ETC	116.2	450	217.9	276.7	341.4	514.3
17	31–FERTILIZERS	338.3	450	634.4	805.7	994.1	1,497.6
18	89–SHIPS, BOATS AND FLOATING STRUCTURES	89.2	450	167.4	212.6	262.3	395.1
19	25–SALT; SULFUR; EARTH & STONE; LIME & CEMENT PLASTER	70.3	448	131.9	167.5	206.7	311.4
20	84–NUCLEAR REACTORS, BOILERS, MACHINERY ETC.; PARTS	4,835.8	448	9,069.7	11,518.5	14,212.8	21,410.7
21	90–OPTIC, PHOTO ETC, MEDIC OR SURGICAL INSTRMENTS ETC	842.7	444	1,580.5	2,007.3	2,476.8	3,731.1
22	24–TOBACCO AND MANUFACTURED TOBACCO SUBSTITUTES	158.4	438	297.2	377.4	465.7	701.5
23	22–BEVERAGES, SPIRITS AND VINEGAR	103.8	436	194.6	247.1	304.9	459.4
24	80–TIN AND ARTICLES THEREOF	9.9	429	18.7	23.7	29.2	44.0
25	74–COPPER AND ARTICLES THEREOF	56.0	429	105.1	133.5	164.7	248.1
26	75–NICKEL AND ARTICLES THEREOF	7.1	429	13.3	16.9	20.9	31.5
27	76–ALUMINUM AND ARTICLES	140.1	429	262.8	333.8	411.9	620.5
28	97–WORKS OF ART, COLLECTORS' PIECES AND ANTIQUES	8.7	429	16.4	20.8	25.7	38.7
29	96–MISCELLANEOUS MANUFACTURED ARTICLES	46.2	429	86.6	110.0	135.7	204.4
30	98–SPECIAL CLASSIFICATION PROVISIONS, NESOI	1,046.4	429	1,962.6	2,492.4	3,075.4	4,632.9
31	73–ARTICLES OF IRON OR STEEL	263.4	428	493.9	627.3	774.0	1,166.0
32	72–IRON AND STEEL	154.3	428	289.3	367.4	453.4	683.0
33	86–RAILWAY OR TRAMWAY STOCK ETC; TRAFFIC SIGNAL EQUIP	35.5	427	66.5	84.5	104.3	157.1
34	19–PREP CEREAL, FLOUR, STARCH OR MILK; BAKERS WARES	37.1	425	69.6	88.4	109.1	164.4

(Table continues next page)

Table B3   US exports to Latin America,[a] by commodity group, annual average 1989–91, and projected for 1997 and 2002 (Continued)

Commodity group[b]	Exports to Latin America 1989–91 average (millions of dollars)[c]	US median weekly wages (dollars)	Projected 1997 (millions of dollars)		Projected 2002 (millions of dollars)	
			Continuing reform scenario[d]	WHFTA scenario[d]	Continuing reform scenario[d]	WHFTA scenario[d]
35 11–MILLING PRODUCTS; MALT; STARCH; INULIN; WHT GLUTEN	72.1	425	135.3	171.8	212.0	319.4
36 10–CEREALS	956.9	425	1,794.7	2,279.3	2,812.4	4,236.7
37 68–ART OF STONE, PLASTER, CEMENT, ASBESTOS, MICA ETC.	42.1	424	78.9	100.2	123.6	186.2
38 69–CERAMIC PRODUCTS	51.1	424	95.8	121.7	150.1	226.2
39 71–NAT ETC PEARLS, PREC ETC STONES, PR MET ETC; COIN	90.7	424	170.1	216.0	266.6	401.6
40 87–VEHICLES, EXCEPT RAILWAY OR TRAMWAY, AND PARTS ETC	1,079.9	422	2,025.3	2,572.2	3,173.8	4,781.1
41 92–MUSICAL INSTRUMENTS; PARTS AND ACCESSORIES THEREOF	17.0	421	31.9	40.5	50.0	75.3
42 93–ARMS AND AMMUNITION; PARTS AND ACCESSORIES THEREOF	42.9	421	80.5	102.2	126.2	190.1
43 95–TOYS, GAMES & SPORT EQUIPMENT; PARTS & ACCESSORIES	105.4	421	197.6	251.0	309.7	466.5
44 82–TOOLS, CUTLERY ETC. OF BASE METAL & PARTS THEREOF	77.5	421	145.3	184.5	227.7	343.0
45 81–BASE METALS NESOI; CERMETS; ARTICLES THEREOF	18.7	421	35.2	44.6	55.1	83.0
46 83–MISCELLANEOUS ARTICLES OF BASE METAL	64.5	421	121.0	153.7	189.7	285.7
47 47–PULP OF WOOD ETC; WASTE ETC OF PAPER & PAPERBOARD	131.0	415	245.8	312.1	385.1	580.2

No.	Description						
48	PAPER & PAPERBOARD & ARTICLES (INC PAPR PULP ARTL)	581.3	415	1,090.2	1,384.5	1,708.3	2,573.5
49	GLASS AND GLASSWARE	85.5	413	160.3	203.6	251.2	378.4
50	PLASTICS AND ARTICLES THEREOF	946.7	411	1,775.6	2,255.0	2,782.5	4,191.6
51	RUBBER AND ARTICLES THEREOF	265.8	411	498.4	633.0	781.1	1,176.6
52	DAIRY PRODS; BIRDS EGGS; HONEY; ED ANIMAL PR NESOI	45.6	406	85.5	108.6	134.0	201.9
53	FURNITURE; BEDDING ETC; LAMPS NESOI ETC; PREFAB BD	116.5	405	218.5	277.5	342.4	515.9
54	ANIMAL OR VEGETABLE FATS, OILS ETC. & WAXES	223.6	405	419.4	532.7	657.3	990.2
55	COCOA AND COCOA PREPARATIONS	10.3	405	19.3	24.5	30.3	45.6
56	MISCELLANEOUS EDIBLE PREPARATIONS	108.6	405	203.7	258.8	319.3	481.0
57	FOOD INDUSTRY RESIDUES & WASTE; PREP ANIMAL FEED	195.4	405	366.5	465.4	574.3	865.1
58	LAC; GUMS, RESINS & OTHER VEGETABLE SAP & EXTRACT	20.0	405	37.5	47.6	58.7	88.4
59	PRODUCTS OF ANIMAL ORIGIN, NESOI	14.2	405	26.7	33.9	41.9	63.0
60	FISH, CRUSTACEANS & AQUATIC INVERTEBRATES	7.5	404	14.1	17.9	22.1	33.3
61	MEAT AND EDIBLE MEAT OFFAL	68.5	404	128.5	163.1	201.3	303.2
62	EDIBLE PREPARATIONS OF MEAT, FISH, CRUSTACEANS ETC	10.9	404	20.4	26.0	32.0	48.3
63	PREP VEGETABLES, FRUIT, NUTS OR OTHER PLANT PARTS	51.2	400	96.1	122.0	150.6	226.8
64	RAW HIDES AND SKINS (NO FURSKINS) AND LEATHER	79.9	397	149.8	190.3	234.8	353.7
65	FURSKINS AND ARTIFICIAL FUR; MANUFACTURES THEREOF	20.6	397	38.7	49.1	60.6	91.3
66	LEATHER ART; SADDLERY ETC; HANDBAGS ETC; GUT ART	20.0	397	37.5	47.6	58.7	88.5
67	SUGARS AND SUGAR CONFECTIONARY	61.5	396	115.3	146.4	180.6	272.1

(Table continues next page)

Table B3 US exports to Latin America,[a] by commodity group, annual average 1989–91, and projected for 1997 and 2002 (Continued)

Commodity group[b]	Exports to Latin America 1989–91 average (millions of dollars)[c]	US median weekly wages (dollars)	Projected 1997 (millions of dollars)		Projected 2002 (millions of dollars)	
			Continuing reform scenario[d]	WHFTA scenario[d]	Continuing reform scenario[d]	WHFTA scenario[d]
68 54–MANMADE FILAMENTS, INCLUDING YARNS & WOVEN FABRICS	159.2	394	298.6	379.2	467.9	704.8
69 53–VEG TEXT FIB NESOI; VEG FIB & PAPER YNS & WOV FAB	12.1	394	22.8	28.9	35.7	53.7
70 56–WADDING, FELT ETC; SP YARN; TWINE, ROPES ETC.	34.6	394	64.9	82.4	101.7	153.2
71 58–SPEC WOV FABRICS; TUFTED FAB; LACE; TAPESTRIES ETC	48.5	394	91.0	115.6	142.6	214.8
72 51–WOOL & ANIMAL HAIR, INCLUDING YARN & WOVEN FABRIC	5.1	394	9.5	12.0	14.9	22.4
73 52–COTTON, INCLUDING YARN AND WOVEN FABRIC THEREOF	125.4	394	235.2	298.6	368.5	555.1
74 59–IMPREGNATED ETC TEXT FABRICS; TEX ART FOR INDUSTRY	83.8	394	157.2	199.6	246.3	371.1
75 55–MANMADE STAPLE FIBERS, INCL YARNS & WOVEN FABRICS	111.1	394	208.4	264.7	326.6	492.0
76 60–KNITTED OR CROCHETED FABRICS	43.5	394	81.5	103.6	127.8	192.5
77 57–CARPETS AND OTHER TEXTILE FLOOR COVERINGS	16.6	394	31.2	39.6	48.8	73.6
78 44–WOOD AND ARTICLES OF WOOD; WOOD CHARCOAL	124.7	392	233.8	296.9	366.4	551.9
79 64–FOOTWEAR, GAITERS ETC. AND PARTS THEREOF	74.8	381	140.3	178.2	219.9	331.2
80 62–APPAREL ARTICLES AND ACCESSORIES, NOT KNIT ETC.	689.6	381	1,293.3	1,642.5	2,026.7	3,053.0

81	63–TEXTILE ART NESOI; NEEDLECRAFT SETS; WORN TEXT ART	56.0	381	105.0	133.3	164.5	247.8
82	61–APPAREL ARTICLES AND ACCESSORIES, KNIT OR CROCHET	287.2	381	538.7	684.1	844.1	1,271.6
83	07–EDIBLE VEGETABLES & CERTAIN ROOTS & TUBERS	63.0	280	118.2	150.1	185.2	279.0
84	12–OIL SEEDS ETC.; MISC GRAIN, SEED, FRUIT, PLANT ETC	166.6	280	312.4	396.8	489.6	737.5
85	08–EDIBLE FRUIT & NUTS; CITRUS FRUIT OR MELON PEEL	46.2	280	86.7	110.1	135.8	204.6
86	01–LIVE ANIMALS	46.5	271	87.1	110.7	136.5	205.7
87	Commodity groups not shown	31.2	442	58.4	74.2	91.6	137.9

a. Argentina, Bahamas, Barbados, Belize, Bolivia, Brazil, Chile, Columbia, Costa Rica, Dominican Republic, Ecuador, El Salvador, Guatemala, Guyana, Haiti, Honduras, Jamaica, Nicaragua, Panama, Paraguay, Peru, Surinam, Trinidad and Tobago, Uruguay, and Venezuela.

b. Ranked by US median weekly wage in industry that produces commodity group.

c. US Department of Commerce, Bureau of the Census, National Trade Data Bank, "US Merchandise Exports–Commodity by Country."

d. Exports to Latin America are expected to grow by 9.4 percent per annum in the continuing reform scenario and by 13.2 percent per year in the WHFTA scenario.

In both scenarios, US trade with Latin America is projected to grow at the same rate as Latin American trade with the world. Hemispheric trade arrangements should prompt intrahemisphere trade to grow marginally faster, but we have not factored that possibility into the calculations that follow.

Under the continuing-reform and the WHFTA scenarios, annual real growth rates for US exports to Latin America are put at 6.5 and 9.7 percent, respectively (table B2). Under both scenarios, the projected growth in US exports is distributed proportionally to US base-year exports by commodity group. We do not expect that each commodity group exported by the United States to Latin America will grow at exactly the same rate. However, we do assume that US export growth to Latin America will not be significantly biased toward higher-wage or lower-wage commodity groups over the next decade. The rationale for this assumption is that there is hardly any difference in the median wage associated with the composition of US exports to rich Canada ($437) by comparison with the median wage associated with the composition of US exports to poorer Mexico ($440) or to Latin America ($442) (Hufbauer and Schott 1994, table 11).

US Import Gains

Table B4 gives projections as to the level of US imports from Latin America (excluding Mexico) in 1997 and 2002, again under both scenarios. Base-year imports for 85 commodity groups are shown sorted by the US median weekly wage level associated with the commodities. As before, the residual group is treated as a separate commodity. The annual real growth rates used for the continuing-reform and WHFTA scenarios are 6.5 percent and 9.7 percent, respectively (table B2). In other words, both scenarios envisage a slower growth of Latin American exports (and hence US imports) than the growth of Latin American imports. The difference between projected export and import growth rates is based on the cross-section analysis explained in appendix A; slower export growth ultimately implies merchandise trade deficits for Latin America. The deficits in turn would be financed by inflows of foreign capital. The greater the extent of Latin American reforms, the larger the expected inflows of foreign private capital, and hence the larger the projected merchandise trade deficits.

In table B4, the projected increase in total US imports from Latin America is not distributed proportionally among the commodity groups. Instead, the commodity group associated with the *highest* US median weekly wage is assumed to be responsible for the *smallest* percentage share of the projected increase in total US imports. The commodity associated with the *lowest* wage is responsible for the *biggest* percentage share of the projected increase in US imports. Under the continuing-reform scenario, the biggest percentage share of the projected increase in US imports is assumed to be three times larger than the smallest percentage share. With a WHFTA scenario, this ratio is put at 10 to 1. The size of the Latin American export-growth pie assigned to intermediate commodity groups is proportional to each group's ranking in order of increasing US median weekly wage rates. The basic premise underlying these assumptions is that Latin American reforms will cause a disproportionate increase in US imports of commodities associated with lower US median weekly wages. The resulting calculations are deliberately designed to exaggerate the adverse impact of a WHFTA on lower-skilled US workers.

The assumption that trade expansion with Latin America is likely to usher in disproportionate growth of US imports of low-wage products finds little or no support in the composition of existing US imports from other parts of the world. The US median weekly wages associated with US imports from select countries representing various regions and wage levels do not differ dramatically one from the other (Hufbauer and Schott 1994, table 10). For Canada, the average wage associated with US imports of all commodity groups is $435; for Mexico the figure is $444; for South Korea, $428; for Taiwan, $429; for France, $444; for Germany, $439; and for the United Kingdom, $449. For all of Latin America, the figure is $435. These wage figures associated with US imports are all within 5 percent of one another. Taking the biggest difference, average wages associated with US imports from Korea and Taiwan are just 4.2 percent lower than average wages associated with US imports from France and the United Kingdom.

Despite this overwhelming and contrary empirical evidence, in order to trace out the consequences of a more pessimistic scenario, we have assumed that the growth of US imports from Latin America will be concentrated in lower-wage products.

The consequences of this imposed low-wage bias for US import growth may be illustrated by the calculations for two commodity groups. US imports of petroleum from Latin America, a high-wage product, are projected to rise from the base-year level of $10.5 billion to $10.72 billion in the continuing-reform scenario and to $10.65 billion in the WHFTA scenario by the year 2002 (table B4). By contrast, US imports of footwear, a low-wage product, are projected to increase from a base-year level of $1.3 billion to $1.8 billion in the continuing-reform scenario and $2.4 billion in the WHFTA scenario.

US Job Effects

In order to translate the trade scenarios into their job and wage impacts in the United States, we need coefficients that link jobs and wage rates to trade flows. This section discusses jobs; the next section discusses

Table B4 US imports from Latin America,[a] by commodity group, annual average 1989–91, and projected for 1997 and 2002

Commodity group[b]	Imports from Latin America 1989–91 average (millions of dollars)[c]	US median weekly wages (dollars)
All commodities	30,433.7	435
1 27—MINERAL FUEL, OIL ETC.; BITUMIN SUBST; MINERAL WAX	10,523.5	493
2 85—ELECTRIC MACHINERY ETC; SOUND EQUIP; TV EQUIP; PTS	570.6	492
3 30—PHARMACEUTICAL PRODUCTS	10.3	479
4 88—AIRCRAFT, SPACECRAFT, AND PARTS THEREOF	248.2	479
5 29—ORGANIC CHEMICALS	571.1	474
6 28—INORG CHEM; PREC & RARE-EARTH MET & RADIOACT COMPD	374.0	474
7 26—ORES, SLAG AND ASH	419.9	465
8 37—PHOTOGRAPHIC OR CINEMATOGRAPHIC GOODS	21.6	463
9 33—ESSENTIAL OILS ETC; PERFUMERY, COSMETIC ETC PREPS	52.0	463
10 35—ALBUMINOIDAL SUBST; MODIFIED STARCH; GLUE; ENZYMES	17.9	463
11 38—MISCELLANEOUS CHEMICAL PRODUCTS	31.3	463
12 34—SOAP ETC; WAXES, POLISH ETC; CANDLES; DENTAL PREPS	12.8	463
13 32—TANNING & DYE EXT ETC; DYE, PAINT, PUTTY ETC; INKS	19.9	463
14 49—PRINTED BOOKS, NEWSPAPERS ETC; MANUSCRIPTS ETC	23.3	450
15 31—FERTILIZERS	48.7	450
16 89—SHIPS, BOATS AND FLOATING STRUCTURES	5.6	450
17 25—SALT; SULFUR; EARTH & STONE; LIME & CEMENT PLASTER	105.9	448
18 84—NUCLEAR REACTORS, BOILERS, MACHINERY ETC.; PARTS	917.5	448
19 90—OPTIC, PHOTO ETC, MEDIC OR SURGICAL INSTRMENTS ETC	179.3	444
20 24—TOBACCO AND MANUFACTURED TOBACCO SUBSTITUTES	215.7	438
21 22—BEVERAGES, SPIRITS AND VINEGAR	82.1	436
22 74—COPPER AND ARTICLES THEREOF	406.8	429
23 79—ZINC AND ARTICLES THEREOF	65.4	429
24 75—NICKEL AND ARTICLES THEREOF	16.1	429
25 76—ALUMINUM AND ARTICLES THEREOF	279.4	429
26 80—TIN AND ARTICLES THEREOF	115.8	429
27 96—MISCELLANEOUS MANUFACTURED ARTICLES	26.5	429
28 97—WORKS OF ART, COLLECTORS' PIECES AND ANTIQUES	45.7	429
29 99—SPECIAL IMPORT PROVISIONS, NESOI	114.1	429
30 98—SPECIAL CLASSIFICATION PROVISIONS, NESOI	336.9	429

Share projected increase in total imports (percent)		Projected 1997 (millions of dollars)		Projected 2002 (millions of dollars)	
Continuing reform scenario	WHFTA scenario	Continuing reform scenario	WHFTA scenario	Continuing reform scenario	WHFTA scenario
		47,293.5	58,183.6	64,796.2	92,434.5
0.58	0.21	10,621.6	10,582.2	10,723.3	10,654.6
0.60	0.23	670.9	635.5	775.1	715.6
0.61	0.26	112.9	81.4	219.5	169.1
0.62	0.28	353.2	325.5	462.1	420.9
0.64	0.30	678.4	654.7	789.7	757.7
0.65	0.32	483.5	463.7	597.2	574.4
0.66	0.35	531.8	515.9	647.9	634.3
0.68	0.37	135.8	123.7	254.3	249.8
0.69	0.39	168.4	160.3	289.3	294.1
0.70	0.41	136.6	132.4	259.9	273.9
0.72	0.44	152.4	152.1	278.1	301.2
0.73	0.46	136.2	139.8	264.3	296.6
0.75	0.48	145.6	153.1	276.1	317.5
0.76	0.50	151.3	162.7	284.2	334.8
0.77	0.52	179.1	194.4	314.3	374.1
0.79	0.55	138.3	157.5	275.9	344.9
0.80	0.57	240.8	264.0	380.9	459.1
0.81	0.59	1,054.7	1,081.8	1,197.2	1,284.5
0.83	0.61	318.9	349.8	463.7	560.2
0.84	0.64	357.5	392.4	504.8	610.5
0.85	0.66	226.3	265.0	375.9	490.8
0.87	0.68	553.3	596.0	705.3	829.4
0.88	0.70	214.2	260.8	368.6	501.8
0.90	0.73	167.2	217.7	324.0	466.4
0.91	0.75	432.8	487.2	592.0	743.6
0.92	0.77	271.5	329.8	433.1	593.9
0.94	0.79	184.5	246.7	348.5	518.5
0.95	0.82	206.0	272.1	372.4	551.5
0.96	0.84	276.7	346.7	445.5	633.8
0.98	0.86	501.8	575.7	673.0	870.5

(Table continues next page)

Table B4 US imports from Latin America,[a] by commodity group, annual average 1989–91, and projected for 1997 and 2002 (Continued)

	Commodity group[b]	Imports from Latin America 1989–91 average (millions of dollars)[c]	US median weekly wages (dollars)
31	73—ARTICLES OF IRON OR STEEL	229.2	428
32	72—IRON AND STEEL	794.3	428
33	10—CEREALS	19.1	425
34	19—PREP CEREAL, FLOUR, STARCH OR MILK; BAKERS WARES	14.0	425
35	11—MILLING PRODUCTS; MALT; STARCH; INULIN; WHT GLUTEN	7.3	425
36	68—ART OF STONE, PLASTER, CEMENT, ASBESTOS, MICA ETC.	25.0	424
37	69—CERAMIC PRODUCTS	95.0	424
38	71—NAT ETC PEARLS, PREC ETC STONES, PR MET ETC; COIN	901.0	424
39	87—VEHICLES, EXCEPT RAILWAY OR TRAMWAY, AND PARTS ETC	638.9	422
40	93—ARMS AND AMMUNITION; PARTS AND ACCESSORIES THEREOF	34.7	421
41	95—TOYS, GAMES & SPORT EQUIPMENT; PARTS & ACCESSORIES	65.3	421
42	82—TOOLS, CUTLERY ETC. OF BASE METAL & PARTS THEREOF	33.6	421
43	83—MISCELLANEOUS ARTICLES OF BASE METAL	18.2	421
44	81—BASE METALS NESOI; CERMETS; ARTICLES THEREOF	11.2	421
45	48—PAPER & PAPERBOARD & ARTICLES (INC PAPR PULP ARTL)	66.8	415
46	47—PULP OF WOOD ETC; WASTE ETC OF PAPER & PAPERBOARD	213.4	415
47	70—GLASS AND GLASSWARE	20.6	413
48	39—PLASTICS AND ARTICLES THEREOF	157.1	411
49	40—RUBBER AND ARTICLES THEREOF	123.4	411
50	04—DAIRY PRODS; BIRDS EGGS; HONEY; ED ANIMAL PR NESOI	23.7	406
51	94—FURNITURE; BEDDING ETC; LAMPS NESOI ETC; PREFAB BD	88.6	405
52	23—FOOD INDUSTRY RESIDUES & WASTE; PREP ANIMAL FEED	31.9	405
53	21—MISCELLANEOUS EDIBLE PREPARATIONS	76.0	405
54	15—ANIMAL OR VEGETABLE FATS, OILS ETC. & WAXES	53.7	405
55	18—COCOA AND COCOA PREPARATIONS	326.8	405
56	09—COFFEE, TEA, MATE & SPICES	1,310.9	405
57	13—LAC; GUMS, RESINS & OTHER VEGETABLE SAP & EXTRACT	12.4	405
58	05—PRODUCTS OF ANIMAL ORIGIN, NESOI	14.5	405
59	02—MEAT AND EDIBLE MEAT OFFAL	155.9	404
60	16—EDIBLE PREPARATIONS OF MEAT, FISH, CRUSTACEANS ETC	251.5	404

Share projected increase in total imports (percent)		Projected 1997 (millions of dollars)		Projected 2002 (millions of dollars)	
Continuing reform scenario	WHFTA scenario	Continuing reform scenario	WHFTA scenario	Continuing reform scenario	WHFTA scenario
0.99	0.88	396.4	474.2	570.0	776.7
1.01	0.91	963.8	1,045.5	1,139.8	1,355.6
1.02	0.93	190.9	276.5	369.3	594.3
1.03	0.95	188.2	277.7	369.0	603.1
1.05	0.97	183.8	277.2	367.0	610.3
1.06	0.99	203.7	301.1	389.3	641.8
1.07	1.02	276.1	377.3	464.0	725.8
1.09	1.04	1,084.4	1,189.5	1,274.7	1,545.6
1.10	1.06	824.6	933.7	1,017.4	1,297.4
1.11	1.08	222.7	335.7	417.8	707.1
1.13	1.11	255.6	372.4	453.1	751.5
1.14	1.13	226.2	347.0	426.2	733.8
1.16	1.15	213.1	337.7	415.4	732.2
1.17	1.17	208.4	337.0	413.1	739.1
1.18	1.20	266.3	398.7	473.4	808.5
1.20	1.22	415.2	551.6	624.7	969.0
1.21	1.24	224.8	365.1	436.7	790.2
1.22	1.26	363.5	507.7	577.8	940.5
1.24	1.29	332.1	480.2	548.8	920.7
1.25	1.31	234.8	386.8	453.9	834.9
1.27	1.33	301.9	457.9	523.4	913.6
1.28	1.35	247.5	407.4	471.4	870.8
1.29	1.38	293.9	457.6	520.2	928.8
1.31	1.40	274.0	441.6	502.6	920.4
1.32	1.42	549.3	720.9	780.4	1,207.3
1.33	1.44	1,535.8	1,711.2	1,769.2	2,205.3
1.35	1.46	239.6	418.9	475.4	920.7
1.36	1.49	244.0	427.2	482.2	936.7
1.37	1.51	387.7	574.9	628.4	1,092.0
1.39	1.53	485.6	676.7	728.6	1,201.4

(Table continues next page)

Table B4   US Imports from Latin America,[a] by commodity group, annual average 1989–91, and projected for 1997 and 2002 (Continued)

Commodity group[b]	Imports from Latin America 1989–91 average (millions of dollars)[c]	US median weekly wages (dollars)
61 03—FISH, CRUSTACEANS & AQUATIC INVERTEBRATES	1,034.1	404
62 20—PREP VEGETABLES, FRUIT, NUTS OR OTHER PLANT PARTS	617.2	400
63 42—LEATHER ART; SADDLERY ETC; HANDBAGS ETC; GUT ART	145.8	397
64 43—FURSKINS AND ARTIFICIAL FUR; MANUFACTURES THEREOF	31.7	397
65 41—RAW HIDES AND SKINS (NO FURSKINS) AND LEATHER	244.2	397
66 17—SUGARS AND SUGAR CONFECTIONARY	496.3	396
67 51—WOOL & ANIMAL HAIR, INCLUDING YARN & WOVEN FABRIC	37.2	394
68 52—COTTON, INCLUDING YARN AND WOVEN FABRIC THEREOF	116.5	394
69 55—MANMADE STAPLE FIBERS, INCL YARNS & WOVEN FABRICS	20.7	394
70 60—KNITTED OR CROCHETED FABRICS	10.1	394
71 54—MANMADE FILAMENTS, INCLUDING YARNS & WOVEN FABRICS	22.1	394
72 58—SPEC WOV FABRICS; TUFTED FAB; LACE; TAPESTRIES ETC	9.3	394
73 53—VEG TEXT FIB NESOI; VEG FIB & PAPER YNS & WOV FAB	5.1	394
74 56—WADDING, FELT ETC; SP YARN; TWINE, ROPES ETC.	53.0	394
75 44—WOOD AND ARTICLES OF WOOD; WOOD CHARCOAL	235.4	392
76 64—FOOTWEAR, GAITERS ETC. AND PARTS THEREOF	1,252.0	381
77 61—APPAREL ARTICLES AND ACCESSORIES, KNIT OR CROCHET	791.4	381
78 65—HEADGEAR AND PARTS THEREOF	25.7	381
79 63—TEXTILE ART NESOI; NEEDLECRAFT SETS; WORN TEXT ART	83.4	381
80 62—APPAREL ARTICLES AND ACCESSORIES, NOT KNIT ETC.	1,703.0	381
81 07—EDIBLE VEGETABLES & CERTAIN ROOTS & TUBERS	95.9	280
82 12—OIL SEEDS ETC.; MISC GRAIN, SEED, FRUIT, PLANT ETC	41.4	280
83 08—EDIBLE FRUIT & NUTS; CITRUS FRUIT OR MELON PEEL	1,415.7	280
84 01—LIVE ANIMALS	8.1	271
85 06—LIVE TREES, PLANTS, BULBS ETC.; CUT FLOWERS ETC.	241.1	271
86 Commodity groups not shown	24.7	435

a. Argentina, Bahamas, Barbados, Belize, Bolivia, Brazil, Chile, Colombia, Costa Rica, Dominican Republic, Ecuador, El Salvador, Guatemala, Guyana, Haiti, Honduras, Jamaica, Nicaragua, Panama, Paraguay, Peru, Surinam, Trinidad, Uruguay, Venezuela.
b. Ranked by US median weekly wage in industry that produces commodity group.
c. US Department of Commerce, Bureau of the Census, National Trade Data Bank, "US Merchandise Imports–Commodity by Country."

Share projected increase in total imports (percent)		Projected 1997 (millions of dollars)		Projected 2002 (millions of dollars)	
Continuing reform scenario	WHFTA scenario	Continuing reform scenario	WHFTA scenario	Continuing reform scenario	WHFTA scenario
1.40	1.55	1,270.5	1,465.5	1,515.9	1,997.9
1.42	1.58	855.9	1,054.7	1,103.7	1,594.9
1.43	1.60	386.8	589.6	637.1	1,137.4
1.44	1.62	275.0	481.7	527.6	1,037.2
1.46	1.64	489.9	700.5	744.9	1,263.6
1.47	1.67	744.3	958.8	1,001.7	1,529.5
1.48	1.69	287.5	505.9	547.2	1,084.3
1.50	1.71	369.1	591.4	631.2	1,177.5
1.51	1.73	275.6	501.8	540.2	1,095.6
1.53	1.76	267.3	497.4	534.2	1,098.8
1.54	1.78	281.5	515.6	550.9	1,124.7
1.55	1.80	271.1	509.0	542.8	1,125.8
1.57	1.82	269.2	511.1	543.4	1,135.5
1.58	1.85	319.4	565.1	595.9	1,197.2
1.59	1.87	504.1	753.7	783.0	1,393.5
1.61	1.89	1,523.0	1,776.6	1,804.3	2,424.0
1.62	1.91	1,064.7	1,322.2	1,348.5	1,977.3
1.63	1.94	301.3	562.7	587.5	1,225.5
1.65	1.96	361.4	626.6	649.9	1,297.1
1.66	1.98	1,983.3	2,252.4	2,274.2	2,930.6
1.68	2.00	378.5	651.6	671.8	1,337.3
1.69	2.02	326.2	603.2	621.9	1,296.6
1.70	2.05	1,702.8	1,983.7	2,000.9	2,684.9
1.72	2.07	297.6	582.4	598.1	1,291.2
1.73	2.09	532.9	821.6	835.8	1,538.0
1.74	2.11	318.8	611.4	624.1	1,335.5

associated wage levels. Table B5 gives calculations of the impact of the projected trade changes on US jobs, sorted by average wage levels under both scenarios. Recall that US import growth is disproportionally assigned to low-wage product groups (contrary to past experience). On the other hand, US export growth is proportionally assigned to base-level exports. Hence, the assumptions introduce a deliberate bias against lower-skilled US workers.

The number of US jobs supported by each $1 billion of total US exports is distributed over four groups of US workers, first identified by industry and then sorted by their industry-average weekly wages.[2] To arrive at the number of US jobs dislocated by imports, it is assumed that as many jobs as are created by a billion dollars of exports in a given commodity category are dislocated by a billion dollars of imports in the same commodity category. The number of jobs supported by exports and dislocated by imports is first calculated for the base year. As table B5 shows, US exports to Latin America supported over 470,000 jobs in the base year, while US imports from Latin America dislocated almost 616,000 jobs. The difference between jobs supported by exports and jobs dislocated by imports largely reflects US trade deficits with Latin America during 1989–91.

For the future trade scenarios, the calculated impact on US jobs resulting from the changes in trade levels is adjusted for projected improvements in productivity in the traded goods industries. It is assumed that average productivity will increase by 14.8 percent for the 1990–97 period and by 28.8 percent for the entire 1990–2002 period. These figures are based on the average annual increase in productivity in US export industries between 1983 and 1990—namely, 2.4 percent per year (US Department of Commerce, Economics and Statistics Administration, *US Jobs Supported by Merchandise Exports*, April 1992, table 5, 25).

For the base year, actual US imports and exports for each commodity group are distributed between four wage groups according to the US median weekly wage level associated with each commodity group. The total number of US jobs supported by US exports, or dislocated by US imports, can then be derived for each US median weekly wage group in the base year and in the future trade scenarios.

The US median weekly wages associated with different groups of traded goods are derived as follows. The employees in each of the 47

---

2. The figure for all US export-related jobs (19,146 US jobs per $1 billion of US exports in 1990) is taken from US Department of Commerce (Economics and Statistics Administration, *US Jobs Supported by Merchandise Exports*, April 1992). For different groups of the wage distribution, this figure is adjusted by the ratio of median wages for industries in that group to median wages for all exports ($442). For example, for the first group (median wages ranging from $451 to $493, with an average of $472), the number of US jobs supported by each $1 billion of US exports is calculated as ($442/$472) x 19,146 = 17,929. This calculation assumes that nonwage value added is proportional to wage levels for different industries.

major industries were divided into 11 occupational categories. For each occupational category, there is a median weekly wage for all workers in the US economy. The number of employees in each occupational category was used as a weight to calculate the median weekly wage of all workers in each of the 47 industries. Each group of traded goods is then assigned a median weekly wage level equivalent to the median weekly wage in the industry most closely identified with production of the goods traded in that commodity group.

From the US perspective, the two reform scenarios show an improvement in the US–Latin American trade balance. The scenarios reflect an assumption that capital inflows from the world will enable Latin America overall to run merchandise trade deficits in the late 1990s and into the next century.

Starting with a base-year trade deficit of $6.5 billion, table B5 shows that the United States is projected to run a trade deficit with Latin America in 1997 of $2.5 billion under the continuing-reform scenario and $1.2 billion under the WHFTA scenario. In the year 2002, the United States would run trade surpluses of $5.5 billion in the continuing-reform scenario and $13.4 billion in the WHFTA scenario.

Because the US trade balance with Latin America improves in the reform scenarios, the calculated net impact on US jobs will be positive. The WHFTA scenario shows a net increase of 60,800 US jobs in the year 2002 by comparison with the continuing-reform scenario.

The reason that still-larger net job increases do not emerge in the WHFTA scenario, despite a favorable swing of an additional $8 billion in the US trade balance,[3] has to do with the assumed composition of trade. Under our assumptions, US import growth from Latin America is concentrated in low-wage products. Hence, as table B5 shows, in the year 2002, the total number of US jobs created by higher US exports to Latin America under the WHFTA scenario (1.25 million) is largely offset by the number of US jobs dislocated by expanded US imports (1.06 million).

In net terms, a WHFTA could cause a modest rotation of the US job market in favor of high-wage industries and against low-wage industries. Over the long run, the United States should welcome the implied upgrading in the skill characteristics of the labor market. In the short run, however, the potential dislocation of lower-skilled workers would need to be addressed in the larger context of training and relocation programs.

Associated US Wage Levels

To start the analysis, note that the base-year average wage level of US imports from Latin America was $435 while the base-year average wage

---

3. The additional US trade surplus is calculated as the WHFTA scenario of a $13.4 US trade surplus minus the continuing-reform scenario's $5.5 billion US trade surplus.

Table B5 US jobs supported by US exports and dislocated by imports associated with worker groups sorted by median weekly wage levels, under two scenarios

| | | | | Projected, 1997 | | | | Projected, 2002 | | | |
| | | | | Continuing reform | | WHFTA scenario | | Continuing reform | | WHFTA scenario | |
US median weekly wage group	US jobs supported (dislocated) per billion dollars of trade, 1990[a]	Trade with Latin America (1989–91 average, millions of dollars)[b]	Associated US jobs 1990	Trade with Latin America (millions of dollars)[c]	Net impact on US jobs[d]	Trade with Latin America (millions of dollars)[c]	Net impact on US jobs[d]	Trade with Latin America (millions of dollars)[c]	Net impact on US jobs[d]	Trade with Latin America (millions of dollars)[c]	Net impact on US jobs[d]
US exports											
$493–$451	17,929	7,639	136,966	14,328	102,668	18,196	162,050	22,452	206,199	33,823	364,479
$450–$422	19,409	10,683	207,359	20,037	155,434	25,447	245,335	31,399	312,175	47,301	551,802
$421–$396	20,716	3,391	70,242	6,359	52,652	8,076	83,106	9,965	105,747	15,012	186,919
$395–$271	25,413	2,194	55,767	4,116	41,802	5,227	65,980	6,450	83,956	9,716	148,400
Total	19,146	23,908	470,334	44,840	352,556	56,946	556,471	70,266	708,077	105,852	1,251,601
Average wage (dollars)			442		442		442		442		442
US imports											
$493–$451	(17,929)	(12,873)	(230,804)	(14,327)	(22,322)	(14,120)	(19,145)	(15,837)	(41,257)	(15,660)	(38,790)
$450–$422	(19,409)	(5,734)	(111,290)	(10,106)	(72,649)	(11,964)	(103,537)	(14,644)	(134,273)	(19,654)	(209,777)
$421–$396	(20,716)	(5,660)	(117,243)	(11,544)	(104,375)	(15,965)	(182,783)	(17,653)	(192,911)	(28,685)	(370,338)
$395–$271	(25,413)	(6,167)	(156,728)	(11,316)	(112,032)	(16,134)	(216,852)	(16,662)	(207,062)	(28,435)	(439,364)
Total	(19,146)	(30,434)	(616,064)	(47,294)	(311,378)	(58,184)	(522,317)	(64,796)	(575,502)	(92,434)	(1,058,269)
Average wage (dollars)			435		424		417		419		410

US net trade										
$493–$451	(5,234)	(93,838)	0	80,346	4,076	142,905	6,615	164,942	18,163	325,689
$450–$422	4,950	96,070	9,931	82,785	13,483	141,798	16,755	177,902	27,646	342,025
$421–$396	(2,269)	(47,001)	(5,185)	(51,723)	(7,889)	(99,678)	(7,688)	(87,163)	(13,673)	(183,419)
$395–$271	(3,973)	(100,961)	(7,201)	(70,230)	(10,907)	(150,872)	(10,212)	(123,106)	(18,720)	(290,964)
Total	(6,526)	(145,731)	(2,454)	41,178	(1,237)	34,154	5,470	132,575	13,417	193,332

a. US Department of Commerce, Economics and Statistics Administration, "US Jobs Supported by Merchandise Exports," April 1992.

b. US Department of Commerce, Bureau of the Census, National Trade Data Bank, "US Merchandise Exports (Imports)—Commodity by Country."

c. Projections of trade with Latin America for 1997 and 2002 under the two scenarios are from tables B3 and B4.

d. The net job impact figures show the change by comparison with associated jobs in 1990. The job impact figures in 1997 and 2002 are based on US jobs supported (dislocated) per billion dollars of trade in 1990, but adjusted for projected productivity improvement of 2.4 percent per year (this figure represents the average yearly increase in productivity for 1985 through 1990).

Table B6   US exports and imports by product group, sorted by US median weekly wage levels, under two scenarios[a]

Product groups sorted by US median weekly wage levels	Base-year average wage (dollars)	Projected, 1997		Projected, 2002	
		Continuing reform	WHFTA scenario	Continuing reform	WHFTA scenario
US exports					
$493–$451	481	481	481	481	481
$450–$422	439	439	439	439	439
$421–$396	410	410	410	410	410
$395–$271	371	371	371	371	371
Average wage all products	442	442	442	442	442
US imports					
$493–$451	490	488	489	486	486
$450–$422	432	432	432	432	431
$421–$396	404	406	406	406	406
$395–$271	352	355	355	356	356
Average wage all products	435	424	417	419	410

a. The median wage levels per product group are derived from the trade projections in tables B3 and B4. The average wage figures for all products are taken from table B5.

level for US exports to Latin America was $442 (table B5). In other words, the difference between the wage level associated with US exports to Latin America and the wage level associated with US imports from Latin America in the base year was just $7 per week, a difference of less than 2 percent. Bluntly, the "pauper labor" argument receives virtually no support from the base-year composition of trade. Judging from wage levels embodied in trade, the skill composition of US imports from and exports to Latin America was practically identical.

As a consequence of our pessimistic (and counterfactual) assumptions concerning the skill composition of expanded trade, the average median wage rate of US imports drops under the continuing-reform and WHFTA scenarios, as disproportionally more low-wage products are imported from Latin America in 1997 and 2002 under the two scenarios. Table B6 shows that under the reform scenarios the average wage level embodied in US imports drops from $435 to $419 by 2002 under the continuing-reform scenario and to $410 under the WHFTA scenario.[4] The drop in the average wage level embodied in all imports from Latin America is also mirrored in individual product groups. For example, by the year 2002, imports in the highest-wage product group are projected to change composition (by virtue of our assumption as to the low-wage bias in import growth) so that the average wage associated with this

---

4. To keep the analysis simple and to focus on the composition of employment by wage group, we do not allow for real growth in wages over time.

Table B7 Impact on total US jobs and median weekly wage levels, per worker group, under two scenarios, 2002

Job Impact	Base-year US jobs, trading industries (thousands)[a]	Continuing reform		WHFTA scenario	
		Net impact on US jobs (thousands)[b]	Percent change	Net impact on US jobs (thousands)[b]	Percent change
$493–$451	3,693	165	0.26	326	0.51
$450–$422	5,480	178	1.79	342	3.45
$421–$396	4,863	–87	–0.29	–183	–0.62
$395–$271	4,698	–123	–1.84	–291	–4.36
Total	18,734	133	0.12	193	0.18

Wage Impact	Base-year US wages for all industries[a]	Continuing reform		WHFTA scenario	
		US wages for all industries	Percent change[c]	US wages for all industries	Percent change[c]
$493–$451	472	474	0.52	477	1.03
$450–$422	435	450	3.59	465	6.89
$421–$396	404	402	–0.59	399	–1.23
$395–$271	328	316	–3.69	299	–8.71
Total	441	442	0.24	443	0.35

a. US Department of Labor, Bureau of Labor Statistics figures.
b. From table B5.
c. Calculated by applying a demand elasticity of 0.5 to the percent change in total US jobs associated with changing trade levels with Latin America. No allowance has been made for the normal real wage growth that would accompany the projected annual productivity gain of 2.4 percent per year.

group drops from $490 in the base year to $486 in the year 2002 under the WHFTA scenario.[5]

The impact on US wages resulting from different scenarios of trade expansion with Latin America can be estimated using a very simple model of the US labor market. In our simple model, the net job change calculated for each worker group is treated as an exogenous shift in the supply curve for labor. For example, if the net effect of expanded trade with Latin America is to employ more US workers in a given wage group, then that job change is treated as a subtraction, or inward shift, in the supply of labor available to produce goods and services for the US domestic market. Conversely, if the net effect of expanded trade is to dislocate US workers in a given wage group, then that job change is treated as an addition, or outward shift, in the supply of labor available to produce goods and services for the US domestic market.

Using this framework, we make the further assumption that supply curves for labor in each wage group are vertical. In other words, we assume that there is no response of labor supply to changing real wage rates.[6] The impact on US average wages resulting from different trade scenarios with Latin America can then be estimated if we know only the elasticity of demand for labor. The literature suggests that demand elasticities for labor, particularly low-wage workers and manufacturing employees, are rather low (Freeman 1987, vol. 3, 74). For the sake of a responsibly pessimistic assumption, we assume that the demand elasticity for each employee group within the US work force is only 0.50. This means that a 1 percent increase in the quantity of labor supplied in a given group would cause wages for that group to fall by 2 percent. Conversely, a 1 percent decrease in the labor supplied would cause wages for that group to rise by 2 percent.

Based on this simple model, table B7 gives the calculated impact of different trade scenarios on US wage rates by worker groups. The results are summarized in chapter 4.

---

5. However, imports in the lowest-wage product group are projected to change composition so that the associated average weekly wage rate actually increases from $352 to $356. This result reflects the complexities involved in base-year weighing.

6. Stiglitz (1988, 465) states that "if labor economists had to vote on the best elasticity [of labor supply], the average might be 0.11." If the true elasticity value is only 0.11, our exercise will not go far wrong by assuming a value of zero.

Appendix C:
Chronologies of Regional Agreements

North American Free Trade Agreement

Goods and Services

1934   The United States enacts the Reciprocal Trade Agreements Act of 1934, setting the foundation for US trade policy in the postwar era: reciprocal reduction of tariffs and other trade barriers bilaterally, and later multilaterally. Two bilateral agreements with Canada pursuant to the 1934 act are signed in 1935 and 1938 (Winham 1988, 39).

1942   The United States and Mexico sign a bilateral trade agreement, but it has little effect and is later repudiated (Hufbauer and Rosen 1986, 10).

1948   At the initiative of the US government, officials from both the United States and Canada enter secret negotiations on a free trade area. The talks falter when Canada becomes concerned about the potential loss of sovereignty and the uncertainties of the approval process in the United States (Winham 1988, 39–40).

1958   The United States and Canada sign the Defense Production Sharing Agreement, which gives Canada preferred status compared to other NATO allies in bidding on US military procurement contracts (Diebold, 144).

1965   The United States and Canada sign the Automotive Products Trade Agreement (Auto Pact), which substantially eliminates tariffs on bilateral trade in automobiles, trucks, and auto parts. The pact resulted from complaints by US industry about Canadian subsidization of its auto parts industry. Spurred by the Auto Pact, US-Canada trade in the automotive sector (parts and vehicles) increased 24 times between 1965 and 1988 (Gilbert 1988, 6).

1965   Mexico establishes a maquiladora ("twin plant") program as part of its Border Industrialization Program. Maquiladoras are production facilities involved in secondary assembly of duty-free, imported materials for eventual reexport (mostly to the United States). The program is used by Mexico both to enhance exports and to attract foreign direct investment. By 1991, there are more than 1,900 maquiladora plants in Mexico, employing 470,000 workers (Hufbauer and Schott 1992, 91–94).

1971   Faced with balance of payments problems, the United States refuses to exempt Canada from the imposition of a temporary import surcharge (Leyton-Brown 1985, 4).

1983   The Trade Policy Review (Canada) recognizes the economic imperative of assured access to the US market both to guarantee export markets and to make Canada an attractive investment site. To avoid the negative sovereignty implications of a broad free trade agreement, the review advocates freer trade on a sectoral basis, modeled after the Auto Pact. A joint US-Canada examination proved the sectoral approach to be unworkable (Lea 1987, 26–27).

1985   (March) President Ronald Reagan and Prime Minister Brian Mulroney meet at the Shamrock Summit and sign the Declaration on Trade in Goods and Services, pledging to improve trade relations between the two countries and pointing toward a broad free trade agreement (Wonnacott 1987, 1).

1985   The Royal Commission on the Economic Union and Development Prospects for Canada (the Macdonald Commission) recommends negotiating a comprehensive free trade agreement with the United States (Winham 1988, 16–17).

1985   Mexico and the United States sign the Understanding on Subsidies and Countervailing Duties. It is the first major trade accord between the two countries since the 1942 agreement, it presages Mexican accession to the GATT, and it provides an impetus for future NAFTA negotiations (Hufbauer and Schott 1992, 3).

1986   (May) The United States and Canada initiate negotiations for a free trade agreement.

1986   The United States and Canada resolve a long-running dispute concerning the softwood lumber industry. US lumber producers argue they are harmed by low Canadian stumpage fees and other subsidy practices. The US Department of Commerce, reversing a 1983 ruling, finds the Canadian lumber exports to be countervailable (Wonnacott 1987, 91–100).

1986   Mexico joins GATT; the United States represents GATT in negotiating a protocol of accession.

1987   Mexico and the United States sign the Framework of Principles and Procedures for Consultation Regarding Trade and Investment Relations. The agreement initiates talks on sectoral liberalization in steel and textiles and establishes a dispute resolution mechanism Hufbauer and Schott 1992, 4).

1988   The Canada-US Free Trade Agreement (FTA) is signed in January 1988. The US Congress passes implementing legislation under fast-track procedures in July 1988. The Canadian election of November 1988 becomes a virtual referendum on the accord, which is ratified after the Conservative Party is returned to power. The FTA enters into force in January 1989. The FTA calls for the phaseout of tariffs within 10 years and the elimination of most nontariff barriers. Investment controls are relaxed between the two countries. Differences are not resolved in five important areas: subsidies, government procurement, investment in the energy sector, transportation services, and intellectual property rights (Schott 1988, 1–4).

1989   Mexico and the United States sign the Understanding Regarding Trade and Investment Facilitation Talks, initiating broad-ranging bilateral trade talks (Hufbauer and Schott 1992, 4).

1990   (March) Mexico and Canada sign 10 accords on trade and nontrade issues, including a trade and investment framework agreement similar to the 1987 US-Mexico accord (Hufbauer and Schott 1992, 4).

1990   (June) Mexican President Carlos Salinas de Gortari proposes the initiation of FTA negotiations between the United States and Mexico.

1991   (February) Presidents George Bush, Carlos Salinas, and Prime Minister Brian Mulroney announce that Canada will participate in negotiations on a North American Free Trade Agreement (NAFTA), with talks to begin in June (after the Congress extends US fast-track authority).

1991   (June) Trilateral negotiations on NAFTA begin in Toronto.

1992   (August) The United States, Canada, and Mexico announce the successful conclusion of the NAFTA negotiations.

1992   (September) President Bush notifies the NAFTA to Congress under provisions of US trade law, starting the 90 calendar-day clock, the period the President must wait before he can sign the Agreement.

1992   (September) The US House of Representatives approves the Torricelli bill (Cuban Democracy Act). The act prohibits foreign subsidiaries of US companies from trading with Cuba and bars vessels that have been in a Cuban port from entering US ports for trading purposes (*Inside U.S. Trade*, 9 October 1992, 8). Mexico and Canada state they will not apply similar restrictions.

1992   (December) The United States, Canada, and Mexico sign the NAFTA. The agreement has far-reaching implications for trade and investment of goods and services between the three countries. It remains to be approved by the legislative bodies of the three countries. These are the main NAFTA provisions:

- The NAFTA makes modest progress in opening Mexico's energy market. Most notably, the agreement gradually opens Pemex and CFE (the State Electricity Commission) contracts to foreign participation; these are worth about $8.5 billion a year. The NAFTA also increases US and Canadian access to Mexican electricity, petrochemical, and gas and energy services. However, the NAFTA does not break the Pemex monopoly on Mexico's energy sector; does not ensure foreign investment in oil exploration, production, or refining; does not provide for risk-sharing contracts; and does not permit US and Canadian firms to enter Mexico's retail gasoline market.

- The United States and Canada gain access to Mexico's highly protected automotive market, the fastest-growing major auto market in the world. The NAFTA will eliminate all of Mexico's automotive tariffs and most of its nontariff barriers over a transition period lasting five to ten years. However, the agreement embraces a semirestrictive rule of origin for autos: the ultimate figure will be 62.5 percent, compared with the current FTA figure of 50 percent.

- For the first time, the United States and Canada open their heavily protected textile and apparel sectors to significant trade competition with a large developing country. The NAFTA textiles and apparel chapter eliminates virtually all quotas on North American trade in textiles and apparel and phases out tariffs in a short period. The benefits of liberalization are limited by the NAFTA's ultrastrict rule of origin, which could divert textile and apparel trade from other suppliers.

- Trade barriers on bilateral US-Mexico farm trade will be eliminated within 15 years—a notable achievement compared with the snail's pace of GATT negotiations. Tariffs will be eliminated immediately on $3.1 billion of US-Mexico agricultural trade. However, US-Canada farm trade will continue to face important constraints.

- The right to establish a business presence in the Mexican financial services market is phased in at a measured pace, with interim caps placed on the market share that can be controlled by foreign financial firms. Nonetheless, by 1 January 2000, all Mexican restrictions on entry into the financial services market and individual firm size will be eliminated.

- In the transportation sector, the NAFTA permits US, Mexican, and Canadian trucking companies to carry international cargo to and from the contiguous US and Mexican states by the end of 1995 and to have cross-border access to all the United States and Mexico by the end of 1999. In addition, the NAFTA allows US and Canadian investment in Mexico's bus and trucking firms and harmonizes many of the technical and safety standards for truck and rail operations.

- The NAFTA makes rapid progress in opening access for North American firms to Mexico's telecommunications market for enhanced or value-added services, and this should accelerate both cross-border trade and investment in telecommunications goods and enhanced services. Mexico will immediately eliminate the majority of tariffs and nontariff barriers to its telecommunications equipment market.

Supraregional Institutions and Dispute Settlement

1988   The Canada-US FTA contains skeletal administrative provisions and innovative dispute settlement procedures. The agreement creates a two-track dispute resolution process. Disputes concerning the interpretation of the FTA are covered by chapter 18, which requires disputes to be heard by a panel of experts. Similar to GATT procedures, the rulings of the panel may be reviewed by a governing body (the Canada–United States Trade Commission). Disputes concerning antidumping and countervailing duty actions are heard under Chapter 19 by a panel of experts. Chapter 19 requires that the parties submit to binding panel rulings (a significant departure from GATT) (Hufbauer and Schott 1992, 37).

1992   (December) These are the main NAFTA accomplishments:

- The NAFTA creates a Free Trade Commission to supervise the implementation of the agreement, to oversee its further elaboration, to resolve disputes that may arise regarding its interpretation or application, and to supervise the work of all committees and working groups established by the NAFTA. In addition, the NAFTA creates eight committees (trade in goods, trade in worn clothing, agricultural trade, sanitary and phytosanitary measures, standards-related measures, small business, financial services, and private commercial disputes) and six working groups on (US and Canada-Mexico bilateral working groups, rules of origin, agricultural subsidies, trade and competition, and temporary entry).

- The dispute settlement provisions are noteworthy: in return for significant reform of its judicial and administrative practices in the application of its trade laws, Mexico gains full rights under the innovative dispute mechanism for reviewing antidumping and countervailing duty cases. In addition, the NAFTA fine-tunes the Canada-US FTA by adopting compliance provisions to insure that the panel procedures are not impeded and by strengthening the extraordinary challenge process.

1993   (August) The United States, Canada, and Mexico reach an agreement on three NAFTA side accords dealing with environmental issues, labor issues, and import surges. The accords establish new North American institutions (the Commission on Environmental Cooperation and the Commission on Labor Cooperation) to monitor environmental and labor market conditions in the region, promote compliance with national laws and regulation in each of the three countries, and administer new dispute settlement procedures (Hufbauer and Schott 1993, 157).

Monetary and Fiscal Policies

1962   Canada and the United States become charter members of the Group of Ten (G-10) (Dobson 1991, 12).

1986   At the Tokyo Summit, Canada and the United States become members of the newly formed G-7, seeking increased policy coordination (Dobson 1991, 40).

Summary: The United States and Canada reform their corporate tax system in the 1980s, reducing the rates and broadening the base. The Bank of Canada and the US Federal Reserve follow dedicated anti-inflation policies. However, at a formal level, there is no explicit coordination of fiscal and monetary policies.

Labor Mobility

1942   Because of labor shortages, the United States institutes the Bracero Program, which recruits Mexican agricultural workers. The program runs until 1964 (Weintraub 1990, 179–81).

1986   The US Congress passes the US Immigration Reform and Control Act of 1986 (IRCA, or the Simpson-Rodino Act), seeking (among other goals) to curtail undocumented migration from Mexico to the United States. The ICRA grants legal status to illegal immigrants residing in the United States before 1 January 1982. It also contains employer penalty provision for the hiring of undocumented aliens. By 1987, Census Bureau estimates show 2 million to 3 million undocumented aliens who are Mexican citizens (Weintraub 1990, 179 and 183–86).

1988   Chapter 15 of the US-Canada Free Trade Agreement includes provisions for the temporary entry of professional labor. Mobility for blue collar workers is not liberalized (Schott and Smith, 141).

1992   The NAFTA addresses the entry of business and professional personnel: intra-company transferees will be allowed to enter if they have been with the company for at least one year out of the previous three years. Also, 5,500 Mexican professionals will be allowed to enter the United States annually in addition to those admitted under global immigration limits.

Investment

1967   Canada revises its Bank Act, prohibiting all foreign residents combined from holding more than a 25 percent share in the equity of a financial institution (Parizeau 1987, 146).

1973   Canada establishes the Foreign Investment Review Agency (FIRA) to screen incoming direct investment. The creation of the agency underscores Canadian fears about US control over key segments of the Canadian economy (Lea 1987, 26).

1980   Amid growing concerns about the influence of foreign investment in the energy sector in Canada and the changing international oil market, the Trudeau administration institutes a National Energy Program (1980–82) with three broad goals in mind: energy security (self-sufficiency by 1990), fairness in energy pricing for consumers, and an increase in Canadian participation in the oil and gas industry (Leyton-Brown 1985, 5 and 26–27).

1985   Prime Minister Mulroney underscores Canada's new policy of welcoming foreign investment by creating Investment Canada as a successor to FIRA (Smith, 46–47).

1986   The US-Canada FTA liberalizes foreign investment between the two countries. Existing regulations, notably in the energy sector, are grandfathered. Future regulations concerning foreign direct investment must respect the national treatment provisions of the FTA. Transportation services, basic telecommunications, and cultural industries are excluded from the agreement (Schott and Smith 19, 148).

1989   Mexico reforms its foreign direct investment policy, significantly liberalizing investment in the country. Sectors of the economy are divided into two areas: classified activities, which are subject to foreign investment restrictions, and unclassified activities, which are broadly deregulated. After the reform, capital investments of under $100 million receive semiautomatic approval from the Comisión Nacional de Inversión Extranjera, or CNIE (Hufbauer and Schott 1992, 76–77).

1992   (December) The NAFTA commits all three countries to provide national treatment to investors from NAFTA partners, and contains a most-favored nation (MFN) obligation ensuring that NAFTA investors are treated as well as any other foreign investor. As in the Canada-US FTA, the primary energy sector is a notable exception to these provisions. Private investors may seek binding arbitral rulings in an international forum, directly against the host government. In parallel negotiations, the United States and Mexico agreed to a tax treaty that reduces the high statutory withholding rates charged on interest, dividends, and royalties flowing in both directions.

Chile

1969   Chile signs the Cartagena Declaration, creating the Andean Group in 1969. However, in 1976 Chile leaves the group to pursue market-oriented trade and investment policies.

1970   Salvador Allende is elected president and embarks on a program of industry nationalization and import substitution; the average tariff is increased to 105 percent with a maximum rate of 750 percent (Butelman and Frohmann 1992, 8). During the first year, the Allende program increases real wages and economic growth and improves income distribution. The following year, growth stagnates and inflation rapidly escalates (Kline 1992, 13).

1973   (September) General Augusto Pinochet seizes control of the government in a coup supported by the US government; Allende is assassinated. To consolidate power, the Pinochet regime represses political rights and murders hundreds of opposition leaders.

1974   Chile institutes an economic liberalization program. Price controls are lifted, and interest rates freed. Most NTBs are removed (import licensing is phased out, and import quotas are removed on most foreign products), and tariffs are reduced to a maximum of 35 percent in 1977 and 10 percent by 1980 (Kline 1992, 14). The government starts a privatization campaign. (By 1992 over 460 companies had been privatized.) On foreign investment, Chile approves a statute known as Decree Law 600, which requires the government and the foreign investor to sign a written contract that regulates taxation and repatriation (US GAO 1992, 9).

1982   A financial collapse prompts Pinochet to temporarily reverse the regime's privatization campaign (Kline 1992, 17). In addition, maximum tariffs are increased to 35 percent but are later progressively cut to 15 percent by 1988 (Butelman et al. 1992, 8).

1985   Together with its macroeconomic stabilization program, Chile establishes Latin America's first sustained and arguably most successful debt conversion program (Kline 1992, 17). The Chilean Central Bank creates a process to swap debt denominated in Chilean pesos and held by foreign institutions for equity in Chilean companies (US GAO 1992, 10).

1990   (January) Chile passes a law on pharmaceutical patents that provides patent protection for 15 years (retroactive to products introduced starting in 1985) (*Financial Times*, 1 February 1990, 6).

1990   (March) Patricio Aylwin is elected president; General Pinochet remains as head of the army.

1990   (October) Chile signs a bilateral framework agreement with the United States.

1990   (October) Chile and Venezuela sign the (Acta de Decisión para Establecer un Espacio Ecónomico Ampliado), which reaffirms their commitment to work towards a free trade agreement similar to the one later signed with Mexico (in September 1991).[1]

---

1. One problem that needs to be solved is Venezuela's membership in the Andean Group (Butelman and Frohmann 1992, 12).

1991   (June) The first "investment sector loan," a $150 million loan for Chile was approved by the Inter-American Development Bank (IDB) (White House, "Fact Sheet: Advancing the Enterprise for the Americas Initiative," 27 June 1991). Chile also becomes the first country to receive debt forgiveness under the EAI. However, only about $16 million is written off (PL-480 loans) (US GAO 1992, 22).

1991   (June) In response to an incoming tide of foreign investment, Chile imposes a capital reserve requirement (*encaje*) on foreign borrowed capital entering the country. All investors are required to post a cash reserve of 20 percent of the total capital obtained from foreign-source loans brought into Chile.[2]

1991   (July) Chile and Colombia establish a bilateral council to consider the total liberalization of tariffs and other restrictions with the exception of a short list of products (Butelman et al. 1992, 13).

1991   (August) Chile signs an agreement (Acuerdo de Complementación Económica) with Argentina to facilitate trade and promote investment.[3] The agreement covers mutual access to mining, energy, ports, and highways, and transportation; and a double-taxation agreement (*Latin American Weekly Reports*, 8 April 1993, 160). Chile also explores possible ties with the Mercosur group. The Asunción Treaty (under which Mercosur was created) invites applications for membership under criteria that only Chile can meet (Butelman et al. 1992, 14).

1991   (September) Chile signs a free trade agreement with Mexico. Starting 1 January 1992, 94 percent of the products (5,862 out of 6,237) will have a maximum tariff of 10 percent; these tariffs will then decrease by 2.5 percent per year for the next four years (*El Nacional*, 23 September 1991, 1). The remaining products will maintain their 10 percent tariffs until 1994, at which time tariffs will be reduced by 2 percent per year until completely eliminated, unless the products are subject to special provisions (*El Nacional*, 18 September 1991, 23; 22 September 1991, 10). An exceptions list of 101 products is excluded from the liberalization program (e.g., agricultural products such as wheat, flour, vegetable oil, sugar, milk; and petroleum and derivatives) (*Financial Times*, 19 September 1991, 5). The agreement covers services such as air and maritime transportation as well as merchandise trade (*El Nacional*, 23 September 1991, 1; *Financial Times*, 19 September 1991, 5).

1991   (September) Chile implements a new patent, trademark, industrial design, and utility law. It provides protection for pharmaceuticals but not for plant and animal varieties. It does not provide "pipeline" protection. The term of protection is 15 years (USTR 1993, 45).

1992   Chile revised its copyright law. The term of protection is the author's life plus 50 years (USTR 1993, 45).

1992   (January) The Chilean Central Bank revalues the Chilean peso 5 percent against the US dollar and relaxes exchange controls. By March, the peso appreciates about 8 percent against the dollar, inflation falls, and so do money market interest rates (*Journal of Commerce*, 24 January 1992, 2A).

1992   (February) Chile signs an agreement with the United States to establish an EAI Environmental Fund (US GAO 1992, 23).

1992   (May) The Chilean government passes a law allowing the state-owned copper company, CODELCO, to enter into joint ventures with foreign investors.[4]

---

2. Chile's high interest rates stimulated an inflow of short-term foreign capital in late 1990. These inflows were overheating the Chilean economy and putting an upward pressure on the value of the peso (US GAO 1992, 13).

3. This type of agreement covers alternative levels of economic integration, ranging from sectoral liberalization, to a free trade area, to a common market (Butelman *et al.* 1992, 12).

4. CODELCO had financial and production problems that could be solved with money and technology from foreign investors. Chile has 23 percent of the world's copper reserves. In 1990, CODELCO produced 75 percent of Chile's copper (US GAO 1992, 15).

1992 (May) Argentina and Chile undertake a program to integrate their mining industries. The program seeks to promote the exchange of information, to update mining legislation, and to expedite transit between the two countries of people, goods, and services in the mineral sector.[5]

1992 (May) Chilean President Patricio Aylwin visits the United States. Prospective negotiations for a US-Chile free trade agreement are announced, but the start of negotiations is delayed until after the conclusion of the NAFTA negotiations (*Wall Street Journal*, 14 May 1992, A2).

1992 The Chilean government considers reforms on foreign investment, such as allowing capital repatriation after one year instead of three, establishing a specific time for approving foreign investment applications, and lowering the corporate tax rate (US GAO 1992, 12).

1992 (November) Japan announces that it will offer Chile $193 million in loans (*Journal of Commerce*, 17 November 1992, 2A).

1992 (November) Chile signs bilateral agreements with Malaysia covering bilateral investment guarantees, cultural exchanges, and Chile's admission into two data banks covering technology and investment. Duties on trade between the two will be limited to 11 percent with all tariffs removed after five years (*Journal of Commerce*, 17 November 1992, 5A).

1993 (April) Chile signs an agreement with Venezuela that will phase out tariffs on 300 products by 1999 (*Latin American Weekly Report*, 8 April 1993, 160).

1993 (December) Chile signs a trade agreement with Colombia. The agreement will eliminate tariffs between the two countries by January 1999.

1994 (January) Heraldo Muñoz, Chilean ambassador to the Organization of American States (OAS), says Chile is ready to join the NAFTA, including provisions on environmental commitments (*International Trade Reporter*, 26 January 1994, 148).

1994 (May) Richard Gephardt (D-MO) announces that he will introduce legislation for the negotiation of a US-Chile free trade agreement under fast-track procedures, but the agreement must include environmental and labor provisions (*International Trade Reporter*, 11 May 1994, 751).

1994 (May) Chile and Brazil sign an investment agreement. The agreement guarantees national treatment and includes intellectual property rights provisions (*US/Latin Trade*, May 1994, 16).

Mercado Común del Sur (Mercosur)

1977 The Financial Fund for the Development of the River Plate Basin starts operations. The fund was created in 1974 to promote development and integration in the subregion, with the following members: Argentina, Bolivia, Brazil, Paraguay, and Uruguay. Total assets in 1988 were $135 million (IMF, *Directory of Regional Economic Organizations*, July 1990, 168; *Directorio Latinoamericano de Instituciones Financieras de Desarrollo 1988–1989*, Asociación Latinoamericana de Instituciones Financieras de Desarrollo: Lima, Peru, 575).

1979 Argentina, Brazil, and Paraguay sign a trilateral agreement concerning the use of the Paraná River; this agreement resolves a major conflict in regional relations and enables plans for the construction of the Itaipu e Corpus hydroelectric dam to go forward (CEPAL 1992d).

---

5. As an outgrowth of Argentine-Chilean border disputes in the 1970s, both countries prohibit foreign investment within 31 miles of the border (*Journal of Commerce*, 13 May 1992, 4A).

1985   Brazil and Argentina sign the Iguazu Memorandum of Agreement, Ata de Iguaçu, creating a bilateral commission for cooperation in the economic integration of the two countries (CFC 1992, 24).

1986   Brazil and Argentina sign an agreement creating the Program for Economic Integration and Cooperation (PEIC). No specific timetables are set. Twelve bilateral protocols are signed creating the following working groups: capital goods, wheat, food supply reciprocity, expansion of trade, binational enterprises, financial affairs, investment funds, energy, biotechnology, economic research, assistance in the event of nuclear accidents and radiological emergencies, and cooperation in aeronautics.
At this stage, Brazil and Argentina seek to promote commercial and industrial harmonization. Tariff reductions are to be negotiated on case by case. However, no deadlines are set for the implementation of tariff reductions because of the unstable economic situation in both countries (Tavares 1991, 10).

1986   Argentina and Brazil conclude trade pacts with Uruguay, the Convênio Argentino-Uruguaio de Cooperação Econômica (Cauce, or Argentine-Uruguayan Convention for Economic Cooperation) and the Programa de Expansão Comercial (PEC, or Commercial Expansion Program between Brazil and Uruguay), which exempt most of Uruguay's exports to the two countries from import taxes and other barriers (Tavares 1991, 7).

1987   Brazil and Argentina sign protocols under the Program for Economic Integration and Cooperation (PEIC) that establish working groups on steel, land transport, nuclear cooperation, cultural matters, public administration, and currency exchange (Perelli and Rial 19, 27).

1988   (April) Two new protocols are added under PEIC dealing with the automotive and food industries (Perelli and Rial 19, 28).

1988   (November) Argentina and Brazil sign the Treaty for Integration, Cooperation, and Development, which pledges to create within 10 years a common economic area through the elimination of tariffs and nontariff trade barriers for goods and services and the harmonization of macroeconomic policies. Article 10 of the treaty provides for the accession of other ALADI members five years after the treaty takes effect. The treaty is ratified by the Argentine and Brazilian congresses in August 1989 (Tavares 1991, 11; Perelli and Rial 19, 29).

1989   (February) General Alfredo Stroessner, Paraguay's dictator for more than three decades, is deposed by a coup led by General Andrés Rodríguez ("Latin American Regional Reports–Southern Cone," Latin American Newsletters, 9 March 1989, 6).

1990   (July) Brazilian President Fernando Collor de Mello and Argentine President Carlos Menem sign the Buenos Aires Act, which accelerates the timetable for the establishment of a common market between Argentina and Brazil to 31 December 1994. In addition, the two nations agree to institute scheduled, automatic tariff reductions on all products, replacing the old product-by-product negotiations. A Treaty on Binational Enterprises, granting national treatment to firms whose majority stock lies in Argentine or Brazilian hands, is also signed (Tavares 1991, 12).

1990   (August) Paraguay and Uruguay join in integration negotiations, reflecting their strong economic and social ties with Argentina and Brazil (Perelli and Rial 19, 32).

1991   (April) Argentina introduces a tariff reform package replacing changes made in 1988 and 1989. Tariffs on autos and some electronics are increased to 35 percent. Finished goods are subject to a 22 percent tariff, intermediate goods to an 11 percent tariff, and primary products and capital goods not produced in the country are not subject to tariffs. The average tariff is 9.5 percent (GATT 1992c, 94).

1991   (November) Argentina again reforms its tariffs. A 35 percent tariff still applies to electronic goods. However, the tariffs on autos and auto parts are reduced to 22 percent. Finished goods continue with a 22 percent tariff. Tariffs for intermediate goods are raised to 13 percent, and duty-free items are now subject to a 5 percent tariff. The average tariff is 12.2 percent (GATT 1992c, 94).

1991   (March) Presidents Collor of Brazil, Menem of Argentina, Luis Lacalle of Uruguay, and Andrés Rodríguez of Paraguay sign the Treaty of Asunción, forming the Mercado Común del Sur (Mercosur). The treaty provides for free circulation of goods and services within the region by 1995. Tariffs are to be reduced according to a progressive, automatic schedule. A common external tariff will be instituted at the start of 1995. The agreement also aims at harmonizing laws and regulations concerning rules of origin, dispute settlement, and safeguard measures (CEPAL 1991, 15; Tavares 1991, 13; Coes 1992).

   The treaty establishes two administrative bodies: the Common Market Council and the Common Market Group. The Common Market Council, formed by the ministers of foreign affairs and the ministers of economy, is the executive body and is responsible for ensuring the timely, scheduled formation and operation of the common market. The Common Market Group, composed of representatives from the economic and foreign affairs ministries, and the central banks, is responsible for managing the affairs of 10 subgroups: trade matters, customs matters, technical regulations, monetary and fiscal measures that affect trade, overland transport, maritime transport, industrial and technological policy, agriculture energy policy, and coordination of macroeconomic policies. The Common Market Group has an administrative secretariat, temporarily located in Montevideo (Perelli and Rial 19, 40–42).

1991   (April) Uruguay and Chile sign several agreements to promote bilateral cooperation and increased trade between the two countries (in 1990, trade between Chile and Uruguay was only $37 million) (Banco Nacional de Comercio Exterior 1992, 499).

1991   (April) Argentina and Chile sign an accord to facilitate direct investment between the two countries (Banco Nacional de Comercio Exterior 1992, 499).

1991   Argentina approves the Convertibility Law.

1991   (June) President Carlos Salinas of Mexico proposes negotiations for a free trade agreement with the nations of Mercosur (*El Nacional*, 13 June 1992, 4).

1991   (June) The United States and the Mercosur group sign a framework agreement on trade and investment under the Enterprise for the Americas Initiative *Washington Post*, 19 June 1991, B2).

1991   (September) As intraregional trade increases, Brazilian exporters voice concerns about trademark infringement in Argentina, Uruguay, and Paraguay (*Journal of Commerce*, 13 September 1991, 5A).

1991   (December) The first ministerial meeting of Mercosur occurs in Brasilia. Representatives sign the Protocol on Dispute Settlement, patterned after chapters 18 and 19 on the US-Canada FTA of 1988. The process stresses the quick resolution of disputes by an arbitration panel. Working rules for the Common Market Group are also agreed upon (Antonio Barbusa 1992, 2–3).

1991   (December) Brazil vows to enforce tougher trademark protection under Article 6–B of the Paris Convention (the international agreement on trademarks)(*Journal of Commerce*, 6 December 1991, 1A).

1992   (February) Brazil enacts a plan to accelerate its already-scheduled reductions of import tariffs in order to bring Brazilian duties in line with its Mercosur partners. Tariff cuts previously planned for 1 January 1993 are set to be instituted on 1 October 1992. Reductions scheduled for 1 January 1994 are moved up to 1 January 1993 (*Journal of Commerce*, 19 February 1991, 3A).

1992   (June) At the Las Leñas summit in Argentina, the four countries adopt 10 decisions for facilitating the transition period toward a common market. The main decision is a timetable for identifying all the barriers not already addressed in the automatic mechanisms. Secondly, the ommon Market Group is asked to present another plan of action for the measures that need to be taken after 1995 (once the common market is established). A third decision is agreement on a dispute settlement procedure (for the transition period only). Under this mechanism, "any industry or domestic production located in any member country can initiate a complaint procedure when it finds itself threatened by imports by Mercosur countries that are being dumped or subsidized." Other decisions include agreements on education (such as the instruction of Spanish and Portuguese) and cooperation on international highway construction.[6]

1992   (July) The United States calls for the GATT to review the Mercosur integration plans to ensure consistency with GATT principles. The United States insists that, given the size of the economies involved and the long-term goal of a common market, Mercosur's integration must be reviewed according to Article XXIV (i.e., must be subject to the rigorous review by the GATT Council). Instead, Mercosur representatives invoke the GATT's enabling clause, which allows the extension of trade preferences among developing countries (the integration would be reviewed by the less rigorous Trade and Development Committee). The European Community suggests reviewing Mercosur by establishing a separate working party (as required under Article XXIV) but under the terms of the enabling clause and under the control of the committee (*Inside U.S. Trade*, 13 November 1992, 4).

1992   (July) Brazil announces that import duties on computer components will fall 50 percent immediately and continue to decrease (*Journal of Commerce*, 14 July 1992, 5A).

1992   (July) Brazilian and Peruvian investors announce the formation of a consortium to close the gaps in a highway-railroad link that could pave the way for agriculture exports in northwestern Brazil to be shipped from a Peruvian port by 1994 (*Journal of Commerce*, 21 July 1992, 2B).

1992   (July) Argentina sells 51 percent of the state-owned electric utility Servicios Eléctricos Del Gran Buenos Aires, which had recently been divided between two companies: Edenor and Edesur. Edenor was sold to a joint venture consisting of an Argentine oil company, a French electric company, and a Spanish electric company for $428 million plus an assumption of debt of $95 million. Edesur was sold to an Argentine energy company and a group of Chilean utilities for $511 million and an assumption of the $135 million debt (*Wall Street Journal*, 1 September 1992, A11).

1992   (August) Brazil and Bolivia sign an accord to build a gas pipeline. Brazil will import 282 million cubic feet of Bolivian gas a day starting in late 1995; by 2000 the volume will double to 564 million cubic feet (*Journal of Commerce*, 19 August 1992, 7B).

1992   (September) Impeachment proceedings begin against Brazilian President Fernando Collor de Mello, who is accused of corruption. Vice President Itamar Franco becomes the acting president (*Financial Times*, 2 September 1992, 4).

1992   (September) Mercosur announces a plan to transform the Paraná and Paraguay Rivers into the "Hydrovia" (a 2,000-mile long, year-round commercial waterway), cutting transportation costs by up to a third. The estimated cost ranges from $1 billion to $2 billion (*The Economist*, 5 September 1992, 50).

1992   (September) Brazil proposes a broad bilateral trade liberalization accord to Mexico (including tariff cuts, dispute settlement mechanism, investment rules, and intellectual property rights) (*Journal of Commerce*, 25 September 1992, 5A).

---

6. The countries also agreed to complete work on an investment proposal by June 1993 (*El Nacional*, 28 June 1992, 11).

1992	(October) Argentina revises its foreign trade policies, including a temporary increase from 3 to 10 percent in the flat-rate tax charged on all imports, reductions in maximum tariffs from 35 to 20 percent (imposed on such consumer goods as clothing, home appliances, and cars), and elimination of the 1.5 percent flat-rate tax on farm imports (*Financial Times*, 29 October 1992, 6).
1992	(October) Argentina sells 80 percent of state-owned steel mill Aceros Paraná, to an Argentine industry conglomerate for $409 million (*Financial Times*, 30 October 1992, 23).
1992	(October) Brazil removes internal barriers to sales of foreign computers but maintains stiff import duties (*Journal of Commerce*, 30 October 1992, 4A).
1992	(October) Vice President Itamar Franco becomes Brazil's president.
1992	(November) Argentina implements a "statistical tax" on imports of from 3 to 10 percent ad valorem (USTR 1993, 21).
1992	(November) Argentina, Uruguay, and Brazil begin plans for a highway, 2,500 kilometers long, from Buenos Aires to São Paulo. The estimated cost is $2.5 billion (*Financial Times*, 4 November 1992, 8).
1992	(December) Argentina privatizes the state-owned gas company, Gas del Estado, receiving more than $2 billion.
1992	(December) The third Mercosur summit meeting takes place in Uruguay, with two notable results:

- The maximum common external tariff for import products is set at 20 percent. (Some items will be charged 35 percent until 2001, when the top rate for all goods will be 20 percent.)
- Brazil and Argentina will eliminate tariffs within the group by 1995; Uruguay and Paraguay will do so by 1996 (*Journal of Commerce*, 8 January 1993, 4A).

1993	(January) Brazil and Colombia agree on coffee export quotas. Brazil's share will be 27 percent of the market, Colombia's 18 percent (*Journal of Commerce*, 21 January 1993, 9A).
1993	(January) Brazil ends the labor union monopoly in its ports by opening them to private investment and administration (*Journal of Commerce*, 21 January 1993, 1B).
1993	(July) Brazil lowers its average tariff to 14.2 percent. Autos and other sectors keep a 35 percent tariff (First Boston 1993). Paraguay joins the GATT.
1993	(September) Argentina adopts reforms to encourage foreign investment.
1993	(November) Argentina signs a bilateral investment treaty with the United States guaranteeing US investors the best of national or MFN treatment, free transfer of profits, and access to international arbitration (*International Trade Reporter*, 10 and 24 November 1993, 1909 and 1990).
1993	(November) Brazil abolishes the 40 percent ceiling on foreign investor stockholdings in privatized companies. Foreign investors may now bid for as much as 100 percent.
1993	(December) President Franco announces a program that lists 36 companies for privatization during 1994. He also proposes to negotiate trade agreements with its Amazon neighbors: Peru, Bolivia, Guyana, Surinam, Colombia, Ecuador, and Venezuela (*International Trade Reporter*, 8 December 1993, 2072). An agreement with Peru had already been completed in November 1993 and was expected to be signed soon.
1993	(December) The IDB approves $450 million in loans for Argentina—$300 million to create a funding source for the country's banking system and $150 million for environmental cleanup (*International Trade Reporter*, 12 January 1994, 69).
1994	(December) Brazil plans to liberalize trade on a bilateral basis with countries in the Amazon region. Toward this end, President Franco proposes the Amazon Initiative and signs two framework agreements, one with Peru and one with Bolivia.

1994 (January) At a Mercosur meeting in Colonia, Uruguay, Bolivia is officially admitted as a permanent official observer. A common external tariff of 12 to 14 percent is established for 85 percent of products. However, a decision on the rate for capital goods, computers, telecommunications, and petrochemical technology is postponed until June 1994 (*International Trade Reporter*, 26 January 1994, 64).

1994 (January 11) Paraguay becomes a GATT member.

1994 (February) In Argentina, a deregulation decree goes into effect, under which foreign banks can open branches in Argentina under the same conditions as local banks. The reciprocity principle—that the Argentine bank sector be open only to banks from countries that are open to Argentine banks—is eliminated (*International Trade Reporter*, 23 March 1994, 471).

1994 (February) Brazil announces an economic plan. The national currency is to be changed. The new *real* will be loosely tied to the dollar and automatically indexed (*International Trade Reporter*, 2 March 1994, 345; *Journal of Commerce*, 10 May 1994, 2A).

1994 (March 2) Brazil approves a decree that further closes market access to foreign telecommunications companies. The decree requires the Brazilian government to give preference to Brazilian-owned or -controlled companies in bids for computers and telecommunication equipment (*International Trade Reporter*, 16 March 1994, 428).

1994 (March 11) Brazil announces reductions on import duties for 135 items whose prices have increased faster than the rate of inflation. Tariffs were reduced from 10 and 20 percent to 2 percent. Some of the products are steel wool, light bulbs, paper bags, bricks, toothpaste, palm oil, soap, and margarine (*International Trade Reporter*, 16 March 1994, 428).

1994 (April 19) Brazil lowers tariffs on 19 products that were subject to a 20 percent tariff. The new rate will be 2 percent. Reduced-tariff products include trucks and tractors, auto generators and alternators, and auto tires and inner tubes (*International Trade Reporter*, 27 April 1994, 659).

Andean Group

1969 The Cartagena Declaration, signed by Bolivia, Chile, Colombia, Ecuador, and Peru, establishes the Andean Group (also known as the Andean Pact). The declaration seeks to promote economic development through sectoral planning (especially for heavy industries),[7] through multilateral control of foreign investment, and through regional trade liberalization (while maintaining import substitution policies). The agreement establishes two main institutions: the Andean Commission, which makes decisions, and the Andean Junta, which evaluates achievements and makes recommendations to the commission (US Department of Commerce 1992).

1970 The Andean Development Corporation (ADC) or Corporación Andina de Fomento, was created in 1968, but it entered into force only in 1970. The ADC provides technical assistance and financing for prefeasibility studies as well as financial assistance for various investment projects. Its purpose is to help the integration process. The ADC starts with capital of $100 million, but in 1989, through the Galápagos Declaration, its authorized capital is raised to $2 billion (CEPAL 1992b, 18; IMF, *Directory of Regional Economic Organizations*, July 1990, 141; *Directorio Latinoamericano de Instituciones Financieras de Desarrollo 1988–1989*, Asociación Latinoamericana de Instituciones Financieras de Desarrollo: Lima, Peru, 571).

---

7. Agreements were reached only in metalworking and petrochemicals (Fontaine 1977; Wengel 1980).

1971	Multilateral control of foreign investment is to be achieved by adopting a common investment code for the community (Decision 24). In practice, this code is designed to restrict and regulate foreign investment (Fontaine 1977).
1973	Venezuela joins the Andean Group.
1976	Chile decides to leave the Andean Group mainly because it favors a more liberal approach to foreign capital than permitted by Decision 24.
1978	The agreement establishing the Andean Reserve Fund enters in force in mid-1978. It is a regional financial institution created to assist the member countries to coordinate their monetary, exchange, and financial policies and to promote the liberalization of trade and payments in the Andean region (IMF, *Directory of Regional Economic Organizations*, July 1990, 143).
1979	Three organizations are created under the Andean Group: the Justice Tribunal of the Cartagena Agreement, the Andean Parliament (to supervise political aspects of the Cartagena agreement), and the Andean Council (to provide guidance toward achieving economic integration and political cooperation). These organizations experience difficulty performing their assigned functions (CEPAL 1992b).
1980	Venezuela and Mexico sign the San José Pact, which offers oil on concessionary terms to Barbados, Jamaica, and the Dominican Republic, as well as to six Central American countries. The recipients will pay 70 percent of the cost of their oil imports; the rest will be covered by a five-year loan at 4 percent interest ("Latin American Regional Reports–Caribbean," Latin American Newsletters, 22 August 1980, 2).
1985	Up to 1985, progress is achieved only on political cooperation. Action in reducing trade barriers is delayed until the late 1980s, when the Andean Group members start implementing market-oriented programs substantially different from the development strategies of the past. In 1985, Bolivia launches an orthodox stabilization program to stop hyperinflation (in September 1985, the annualized inflation rate reached 24,000 percent). The program includes tax reform, reduced government spending, devaluation of the currency, and a uniform tariff. The fiscal deficit was slashed from 26.7 percent of GNP in 1984 to 3.2 percent in 1986, and inflation dropped from 8,171 percent in 1985 to 22 percent in 1988 (Cariaga 1990, 42).
	Following Bolivia, Venezuela implements reforms in early 1989 designed to correct macroeconomic imbalances and to make structural changes. In 1990, Colombia adopts the Program for the Modernization of the Colombian Economy, and later in the same year Peru also implements stabilization measures and structural reforms (Pascó-Font 1992).
1987	Throughout the 1980s, the Andean Group loses influence. As a consequence, the Quito Protocol is signed with the intention of making significant reforms to the Cartagena agreement. The protocol attempts to make Andean tariff reduction schemes more certain and investment procedures and regional industrial programming more flexible.[8] It also makes progress on lifting nontariff barriers.[9]
1989	The Galápagos Declaration (also called the Andean Commitment to Peace, Security, and Cooperation) emphasizes cooperation on noneconomic topics (joint decisions on international negotiations, fighting terrorism, and strengthening democracy) and establishes the goal of a customs union by 1995 for the three largest economies (Venezuela, Colombia, and Bolivia), and by 1999 for the other two (CEPAL 1991, 23).

8. For example, the regulations on repatriation and reinvestment for foreign companies were practically abolished. Also, public industrial programs were replaced by private-sector programs.

9. While the purpose of the Quito Protocol was to revive regional trade, it contained safeguard measures that were used to avoid the abolition of nearly all trade restrictions (CEPAL 1991, 21).

1990   (February) At the Cartagena Drug Summit, the United States commits to provide balance of payments support to the Andean countries (except Venezuela) to replace the funds generated by drug trafficking; no specific figures of US aid are mentioned. The Cartagena accord also notes the importance of US trade concessions, but it does not include any specific promises from the United States ("Latin American Regional Reports–Andean Group," Latin American Newsletters, 8 March 1990, 2).

1990   (May) Andean leaders meet in Peru and agree to hold presidential meetings every six months and eventually to form an integrated economic group like the European Community (CEPAL 1991, 24).

1990   (May–July) The United States signs bilateral framework agreements with Bolivia on 8 May, with Colombia on 17 July, and with Ecuador on 23 July.

1990   (October) The European Community grants Colombia, Bolivia, Peru, and Ecuador trade concessions on an exceptional basis to support their efforts to combat drug production and trafficking. The concessions include zero duties on ECU 1.1 billion of goods for four years (expiring 29 October 1994) under the Community's GSP. The preferences cover all industrial products and most agricultural products.[10]

1990   (November) Andean leaders promulgate the Acta de la Paz, in which:

- the deadline for achieving a free trade zone and for defining a common external tariff is advanced to 1 January 1992;

- each country's list of exceptions (products subject to higher tariffs) is to be phased out by 31 December 1991;

- the adoption of a customs union is to be achieved by 1995.

1991   (April) Mexico, Venezuela, and Colombia (the Group of Three), plan to establish a free trade zone by July 1994 (*Financial Times*, 4 April 1991, 3).

1991   (April) Decision 24, which regulated and restricted foreign investment in the Andean region, is repealed ("Latin American Regional Reports–Andean Group," Latin American Newsletters, May 1991, 5). In May, the group adopts Decision 291, reforming previously restrictive foreign investment rules and providing national treatment for foreign investors.[11]

1991   (May) The United States signs bilateral framework agreements with Venezuela and Peru.

1991   (May) The five Andean countries sign the Caracas Declaration, which reaffirms decisions taken in the Acta de la Paz:

- The Andean Common Market should be created, and each country's list of exceptions should be eliminated by 31 December 1995.

- Andean integration should contribute to the creation of a Latin American Common Market before the year 2000.

- A free trade zone should be created by 31 December 1991. However, Ecuador is allowed to reduce its intraregional tariffs by 50 percent by 31 December 1991 and the other 50 percent by 1 July 1992.

- The common external tariff should give a margin of preference to other Latin American countries.

---

10. Exceptions include bananas, strawberries, lemons, processed meat, dairy products, and others (US Department of Commerce and Agency for International Development 1992, 53).

11. These include equal application of tax and fiscal incentives, elimination on restrictions on capital gains and net profit remittances, and elimination of the requirement that foreign companies establish joint ventures in order to operate or sell their products within the region (US Department of Commerce and Agency for International Development 1992, 51).

1991 (July) In accordance with the Caracas Declaration, Venezuela proposes to establish a free trade area with the Central American Common Market (CACM) and offers to drop its tariffs on Central American products to zero. Products on the exceptions list will retain a 20 percent tariff, but these tariffs will also be reduced to zero at the end of five years. (Venezuela offers Caribbean countries a similar proposal.) (*Journal of Commerce*, 1 July 1991; 16 July 1991, 7A).

1991 (July) In conjunction with Mexico, the amount of concessional oil made available to CACM nations under the San José Pact is increased from 130,000 to 160,000 barrels per day. Venezuela also proposes joint petroleum exploration and development efforts with Guatemala, Honduras and Nicaragua (*Journal of Commerce*, 15 July 1991, 5A).

1991 (August) Colombia proposes to form a coffee axis together with Brazil and Guatemala to fill the void left by the collapse of the quota system in the International Coffee Organization (ICO) (*Journal of Commerce*, 7 August 1991, 6A).

1991 (September) The Andean countries sign the Compromiso de Guayaquil, which declares that:

- the common external tariff should be as transparent as possible;

- a single safeguard clause should be established for all intraregional trade (in place of the several safeguards that now exist).

1991 (December) The Barahona Declaration is signed. Peru is accorded the same preferences given to Ecuador (delayed implementation of the free trade zone). Mexico, Chile, and other Latin countries are invited to negotiate with the Andean Group as a bloc. This clause was designed to preclude an FTA between Venezuela, Colombia, and Mexico. The Barahona Declaration also includes the elimination of subsidy programs for intra-Andean trade (even if legal under GATT).[12]

- Each country is allowed a list of exceptions with duties to be phased out by 1 January 1993 (Ecuador is allowed to phase out 30 percent of its tariffs by 1 January 1993, another 30 percent by 1 January 1994, and the final 40 percent by 30 June 1994). Venezuela, Colombia, and Peru have lists of exceptions with 50 items, while Bolivia and Ecuador have 100 items on their lists. Exceptions are concentrated in petrochemicals, iron and steel, leather, and textile products.

- A common external tariff (CET) is established with four tariff levels of 5, 10, 15, and 20 percent and zero duties for products not produced in the region. However, Bolivia is allowed to maintain indefinitely its 5 and 10 percent tariff levels and is not required to adopt the 15 and 20 percent tariffs; Colombia, Ecuador, and Venezuela are allowed to adopt temporarily a 40 percent tariff on autos. By 1 January 1994, the CET will come into effect, with levels of 5, 10, and 15 percent and an auto tariff of 25 percent. Finally, a CET for the agricultural sector is deferred pending the adoption of a common agricultural policy (US Department of Commerce, telegram from Embassy of Bogota).

1991 (December) The US Congress approves the Andean Trade Preference Act of 1991 (ATPA). The ATPA, which is authorized for 10 years, is designed to help overcome coca dependence, which is estimated to provide export revenue of $5 billion for the Andean Group. It is estimated that immediate trade benefits will affect $300 million worth of goods. Key excluded products are canned tuna, rum, most textiles and apparel, footwear, and petroleum. In addition, sugar remains subject to US tariff rate quotas (*Journal of Commerce*, 16 January 1992,

---

12. The countries agreed to eliminate various exchange rate, financial, and fiscal subsidies by 31 December 1992. Also a high-level commission will be created with the purpose of "identifying the products or sectors whose production or intraregional trade could be viewed as injured by practices which distort competition." The idea is not only to take action expost but also to prevent violations.

1A). In addition, products from Andean countries will be treated separately in any antidumping or countervailing duty case.[13] ATPA requires that each country be reviewed by the administration to determine its eligibility based on criteria set forth in the act. In July 1992, Bolivia and Colombia are formally designated as beneficiaries of the ATPA.

1992   (January) As agreed in the Barahona Declaration, Colombia and Venezuela eliminate tariffs on specified products, adopt a 20 percent common external tariff (to be reduced to 15 percent within two years), and agree to eliminate the list of exceptions within one year. Bolivia is revising its tariff schedule (*The International Economy*, March/April 1992, 32). Ecuador and Peru commit to adopt the CET by mid-1992 (Janice Bruce, 11 March 1992, speech before Washington Policy Dialogue Council of the Americas).

1992   (February) At the trade ministers meeting in Quito, Ecuador refuses to accept the CET schedule proposed by the other countries. Ecuador argues for special treatment—defined as the right to assess tariffs differing from CET rates on about 1,000 products. Ecuador seeks lower-than-CET tariffs so that it can continue to import from cheaper sources rather than relying upon Andean Group producers.[14]

1992   (February) GATT approves the US request to waive its MFN GATT obligations for 10 years under Article XXV:5, thereby allowing the United States to extend preferential treatment to Andean nations. The special duty-free treatment covers imports of over $290 million a year. It will be applied to products that do not already receive duty-free treatment under the ATPA. However, it still excludes sensitive US imports such as textiles and apparel, footwear, leather products, petroleum, canned tuna, and rum (*Journal of Commerce*, 19 February 1992, 3A; *Inside U.S. Trade*, 21 February 1992, 7).

1992   (February) A drug summit is held in San Antonio, Texas, where issues related to the ATPA are discussed. One issue is whether Venezuela should be included in the ATPA, since it is not a drug-producing country and has a higher per capita income. Another issue is the possible investment of Section 936 funds in the Andean Group. These funds (which arise from tax-preference operations in Puerto Rico) may currently be invested only in Puerto Rico and the Caribbean Basin Initiative countries.[15]

1992   (March) Colombian officials announce they are willing to reduce coffee exports, if necessary, to convince other producer nations to accept a return to the ICO quota system. In 1990–91 Colombia's share of the world market was 21.2 percent (up from 16.8 percent when the quota system was eliminated) (*Journal of Commerce*, 16 March 1992, 7A).

1992   (April) Peruvian President Alberto Fujimori dissolves Congress and assumes dictatorial powers. His stated goals are to wipe out the corruption, inefficiency, and inequality that pervade the country and to eliminate the Shining Path guerrilla movement by 1995. He promises to restore democracy soon, and to hold elections for a new congress within 18 months. Venezuela severs diplomatic ties with Peru (*Washington Post*, 12 April 1992, A31).

---

13. "This exemption from the cumulation rule means that the US would be less likely to find injury caused by imports of products from Andean countries when the US industry brings a case against several countries" (*Inside U.S. Trade*, 4 October 1991, 2).

14. Vegetable oil has been assigned a "finished product" rate of 20 percent. Ecuador claims that it is not a finished product (Janice Bruce, 11 March 1992, speech before the Washington Policy Dialogue Council of the Americas).

15. Companies that invest in CBI countries get a tax preference if they reinvest their profits in that country or in a CBI country that has a tax information exchange agreement with the United States (*Inside U.S. Trade*, 6 March 1992, 10).

1992 (June) Mexico, Venezuela, and Colombia sign an agreement fixing December 1992 as the deadline for an agreement on a free trade zone (*Wall Street Journal*, 12 June 1992, A11).

1992 (July) Ecuador fails to join the Andean free trade area as planned, though it does reduce import tariffs down to a range of 2 to 17 percent, with a higher level for vehicles, compared with the pact range of 5 to 20 percent) (*Financial Times* 7 July 1992, 5).

1992 (July) Peruvian and Brazilian investors form a consortium to close the gaps in a highway-railroad link that could pave the way for agriculture exports in north-western Brazil to be shipped from a Peruvian port by 1994 (*Journal of Commerce*, 21 July 1992, 2B).

1992 (August) The Andean countries pass a new intellectual property law (Decision 313) that offers 15-year patent protection for a variety of goods ranging from pharmaceuticals to beverages. The new law will also increase the protection of trademarks. Individual countries will be allowed to negotiate stronger regimes with other nations. Still to be considered is patenting of biotech products. US government officials criticize the reform because of the absence of a provision to exclude "parallel imports," the lack of transitional protection, the compulsory licensing provisions, and the working requirements (*Journal of Commerce*, 3 August 1992, 1A; US Department of Commerce and Agency for International Development 1992, 52).

1992 (August) Peru withdraws from the Andean Group and assumes observer status until the end of 1993 (*Financial Times*, 28 August 1992, 4).

1992 (September) Abimael Guzmán, leader of the "Shining Path" guerrilla movement, is captured in Peru.

1992 (September) Ecuador withdraws from OPEC and instead adopts associate status (*Wall Street Journal*, 18 September 1992, A2).

1992 (October) Bolivia officially joins the Andean FTA, lifting barriers to Colombia, Venezuela, and Ecuador ("Latin American Regional Reports–Andean Group," Latin American Newsletters, 2 November 1992). Imports from Andean Countries (except Peru) are scheduled to enter Bolivia duty-free as of 1 January 1993. There are 11 exceptions (a few are industrial goods). Bolivia also signs a bilateral agreement with Peru eliminating all tariffs for Peruvian exports as of January 1993 (GATT 1993, 83).

1992 (October) Ecuador privatizes its state-owned oil company, Petroecuador (*Financial Times*, 31 October 1992, 3).

1992 (October) Andean transport ministers sign an agreement for a "multimodal" transport project expected to decrease freight charges by up to 40 percent ("Latin American Regional Reports–Andean Group," Latin American Newsletters, 2 November 1992, 1).

1992 (October) Venezuela and Caricom sign a "one-way" free trade pact. By 1993, 15 percent of Caricom products will enter Venezuela duty-free; by 1994, 50 percent; by 1995, 75 percent; and by 1996, all 1,300 products will enter Venezuela duty-free. After the initial five-year "one-way" period, a reciprocal arrangement will give Venezuelan products duty-free access to the Caricom market ("Latin American Regional Reports–Andean Group," Latin American Newsletters, 12 November 1992).

1992 (November) Colombia announces that it will cut coffee exports by 9 percent (*Journal of Commerce*, 5 November 1992).

1992 (November) Coup by army officers fails to overthrow Alberto Fujimori and return to the 1979 constitution (*The Economist*, 28 November 1992, 43).

1992 (November) In Peru, elections for the new Democratic Constituent Congress are held. Alberto Fujumori's party alliance wins an absolute majority of the seats (*The Economist*, 28 November 1992, 43).

1992 (November) Another coup attempt fails to oust President Carlos Andrés Pérez in Venezuela.

1993 (December) Ecuador officially joins the Andean FTA.

1993 (January) Colombia and Brazil agree on coffee export quotas. Colombia's quotas will be 18 percent of the market, Brazil's 27 percent (*Journal of Commerce*, 21 January 1993, 9A).

1993 (February) Colombia and Venezuela sign a free trade agreement with CACM countries. On 1 July 1993, 500 CACM products will have duty-free access to the Colombia and Venezuela markets. A maximum tariff of 20 percent will apply to all other products (but a 40 percent tariff will apply to Nicaragua). All trade barriers will be lifted within 10 years, except on very sensitive products, which will be exempted ("Latin American Regional Reports–Caribbean and Central America," Latin American Newsletters, 25 February 1993, 1). Negotiations have also been initiated for a G-3 free-trade agreement (Mexico, Colombia, and Venezuela). Under the agreement, 70 percent of the products would be eligible for immediate tariff elimination, tariffs for another 25 percent of the products would be phased out in four years, and tariffs for the remaining 5 percent would be phased out in eight years ("Latin American Regional Reports–Mexico & NAFTA Report," Latin American Newsletters, 14 January 1993, 4).

1993 (March) The Peruvian privatization agency reports that in the previous year privatization revenues reached $265 million and they have been entirely devoted to public works (*Latin American Weekly Report*, 25 March 1993, 135).

1993 (March) The Ecuadorian president, Sixto Durán Ballén, presents to Congress a privatization bill that includes the airline, telecommunications, and ports. The privatization program is expected to yield $13 billion in revenues in the next three years (*Latin American Weekly Report*, 18 March 1993, 129).

1993 (August) Colombia and Venezuela sign a trade agreement covering agricultural produce, oil, electrical power cooperation, and the auto industry. The CET for autos is set at 35 percent, and measures are taken to limit the massive influx of Venezuelan rice into Colombia and Colombian potatoes into Venezuela (*International Trade Reporter*, 25 August 1993, 1420).

1993 (November) Peru and Brazil sign an agreement to reduce tariffs on bilateral trade by 50 percent (*International Trade Reporter*, 8 December 1993, 2072).

1993 (December) Colombia, Venezuela, and Mexico (the G-3) conclude negotiations for a free trade agreement that covers six areas: access to markets, rules of origin, investment rules, government purchases, trade in services, and intellectual property (*Financial Times*, 7 December 1993. However, the agreement has not been signed yet.

1994 (March) In Bolivia, a new capitalization law is approved. The law authorizes the government to sell 50 percent of state-owned companies, including the telephone company, oil and gas monopolies, the national railroad, the national airline, and the electricity monopoly (*International Trade Reporter*, 13 April 1994, 581). The remaining 50 percent will become private pension funds for Bolivians (*US/Latin Trade*, April 1994, 12).

1994 (April) The Andean Group maximum CET of 15 percent goes into effect. Bolivia is allowed to keep 10 percent.

1994 (April) Andean Pact Decision 353 lays out the stages for the gradual reincorporation of Peru into the Andean Group. Peru will eliminate tariffs on products it imports from the region in three stages. In May 1994, tariffs on 569 products are eliminated. By 1 January 1995, tariffs on another 1,564 products are to be eliminated. All products will be duty-free by 31 June 1995 (*International Trade Reporter*, 13 April 1994, 581).

1994 (May 12) Mexico, Colombia, and Venezuela (the G-3 countries) finish negotiations on a free trade agreement. The agreement goes into effect in 1995. No decision on rules of origin for polyester is included in the agreement (*Journal of Commerce*, 17 May 1994, 5A).

Central American Common Market (CACM)

1960   Costa Rica, El Salvador, Guatemala, Honduras, and Nicaragua sign the Managua Declaration and form the Central American Common Market (CACM). Its goals are to establish a common market with internal free trade and a common external tariff by 1966. During its first 10 years, the CACM helped spur intraregional trade. Measured by imports, intraregional CACM trade increased from 7 percent of total imports in 1960 to 24 percent in 1969 (CEPAL 1991, 27; Caribbean Community 1992, 7–8).

1960   The Central American Bank for Economic Integration is established by Costa Rica, El Salvador, Guatemala, Honduras, and Nicaragua. Its main objective is to "implement the economic integration and the balanced economic growth of the member countries" (IMF, *Directory of Regional Economic Organizations*, July 1990, 156).

1961   The Central American Compensation Chamber is created; its functions include a multilateral payments system (CEPAL 1991, 27).

1964   The Central American Monetary Union is established by the central banks of the five Central American countries. Its goal is to promote the coordination of monetary, credit, and exchange policies (IMF, *Directory of Regional Economic Organizations*, July 1990, 159).

1969   The Central American Stabilization Fund is created to give financial support to the balance of payments of Central American countries (CEPAL 1991, 27).

1969   Honduras leaves CACM when war breaks out with El Salvador after a soccer match riot between the two countries. The war is brief, but CACM is effectively disbanded (*The Economist*, 4 January 1992, 63).

1979   Civil war breaks out in El Salvador, putting economic issues on the back burner. Leftist guerrillas fight for 12 years against a military junta, the government of Christian Democrat Napoleon Duarte, and Arena Party chief Alfredo Cristiani. Government-backed death squads kill an estimated 75,000 civilians during the war (*The Economist*, 6 June 1992, 18; *Wall Street Journal*, 13 February 1992, A1).

1979   President Anastasio Somoza of Nicaragua is overthrown; the Sandinistas take power and remain in office until 1990. One consequence is extreme antagonism between Nicaragua and the United States; another consequence is disinterest in Central American economic integration.

1980   During the first half of the decade, intraregional trade decreases sharply, reaching 10 percent of total trade in 1986. By 1989 the intraregional trade share recoveres to 15 percent but is still below the 1970s' level (CEPAL 1991, 30). Three countries—El Salvador, Guatemala, and Costa Rica—provide the bulk of total CACM trade, accounting for 92 percent of all exports within the area and 84 percent of all imports from other member states.

1988   (February) The Plan de Acción Immediata sets Central American priorities, including an emergency fund to reactivate the region (CEPAL 1991, 32).

1990   (January) Panama's new civilian president, Guillermo Endara, asks the United States for emergency economic aid to help rebuild the damage caused by the invasion that toppled General Manuel Noriega in December 1989. Between the invasion and June 1992, the United States provides $1.28 billion in grants, credits, and trade guarantees to Panama. However, the US General Accounting Office criticizes the inept administration of $420 million of "dire emergency" funding voted by Congress in May 1990 (*New York Times*, 18 January 1990, A16; *Washington Post*, 13 June 1992, A1).

1990   (April) The Sandinista regime loses elections in Nicaragua. As the Sandinistas leave office, there is 1,700 percent inflation, 40 percent unemployment, and exports under $300 million. Nicaragua's trade will be distorted because of US sanctions (Ramírez 1991).

1990 (April) Delegates from Central America, the Contadora Group (Colombia, Mexico, and Venezuela), and the European Community, meet in Dublin. The Community contributes $165 million as part of a three-year program to spur intraregional trade in Central America (CEPAL 1991, 32).

1990 (June) Central American presidents meet in Guatemala to focus on economic issues. At the meeting, the Plan de Acción Económica de Centro América (PAECA) is approved, providing for the free movement of people and goods (CEPAL 1991, 33; Sistema Económico Latinamericano 1991, 6).

1990 (November) US signs bilateral framework agreements with Honduras and Costa Rica. These framework agreements are regarded as the first step toward full-fledged trade agreements with the United States.

1990 (December) Through the Puntarenas Declaration, the Central American presidents announce that the goal of the CACM is the establishment of a common Central American customs and tariff policy (*Washington Report*, Council of the Americas, Winter 1992, 40).

1991 (January) The Central American presidents meet in Tuxtla, Mexico, and sign a framework agreement to create a free trade zone among Mexico and the six Central American countries by 1997. Within the framework agreement, bilateral and trilateral agreements are envisaged. In addition, the amount of oil available under the San José Pact (by which Mexico and Venezuela offer oil on favorable terms to the Central American and Caribbean nations) is increased from 130,000 barrels per day to 160,000 (CEPAL 1991, 34).

1991 (February) Mexico and Costa Rica sign a bilateral trade agreement (*Times of the Americas*, 12 June 1991, 10).

1991 (March) Central America asks the European Community for an aid package similar to that given to Andean Countries. In 1990, the Andean countries received special EC assistance to aid their fight against drugs; Central American countries point to their own struggle to emerge from a decade of civil wars (*Journal of Commerce*, 29 October 1991, 5A).

1991 (March) El Salvador and Guatemala sign the Guatemala Accord, promising to eliminate obstacles to bilateral trade. The agreement also proposes the creation of ambitious infrastructure links between the two countries covering ports, railroads, and highways (Banco Nacional de Comercio Exterior 1992, 499).

1991 (April) Costa Rica and Venezuela sign a free trade agreement promising future efforts to reduce trade barriers and to cooperate in housing and urban development (Caribbean Community 1992, 35).

1991 (April) Honduras and Guatemala sign a free trade agreement, promising to lower barriers to trade (Banco Nacional de Comercio Exterior 1992, 500).

1991 (May–June) US signs bilateral framework agreements with El Salvador, Nicaragua, and Panama (*Journal of Commerce*, 14 May 1991, 3A; *Washington Post*, 28 June 1991, A15).

1991 (July) The Central American and Panama Federation of Private Entities hold a meeting in Tegucigalpa. Some of the recommendations include reduced internal barriers, streamlined customs regulations, lower tariffs and export duties, and improved infrastructure (*Journal of Commerce*, 25 June 1991, 4A).

1991 (July) The CACM meets in San Salvador (its tenth meeting since 1986). At this meeting, Panama formally joins as an active member, but it does not fully adhere to the CACM agenda. (Panama has important economic differences with its neighbors: a strong services sector, a weak agricultural sector, and low import duties on consumer durables.) (*Journal of Commerce*, 16 July 1991, 7A) Some of the decisions taken at the meeting include:

- tariff barriers to trade in basic grains are to be eliminated by the end of 1991;
- duties on all agricultural produce are to be eliminated by June 1992 (agricultural output accounts for about 25 percent of the regional GDP) (*Financial Times*, 18 July 1991, 7);

- a uniform 20 percent ceiling and 5 percent floor on all import tariffs is to be achieved by 1995 (*Journal of Commerce*, 12 September 1991, 3A).

1991   (September) US and Central American officials meet to discuss fraud in the transshipment of textiles and apparel. Central America pledges tighter monitoring of textiles from Asian countries, such as China and Pakistan (*Journal of Commerce*, 16 September 1991, 1A).

1991   (October) The United States and Guatemala sign a bilateral trade agreement (*Journal of Commerce*, 4 October 1991, 4A).

1991   (November) The CACM meets with the European Community to negotiate for greater access to the European market. Central American immigration departments seek to create a single passport for all residents, similar to the visa-free system used by the European Community (*Journal of Commerce*, 27 November 1991, 10A).

1991   (November) Throughout Central America, labor tensions increase due to privatization and budget reduction programs (*Journal of Commerce*, 22 November 1991).

1991   (December) The CACM holds its 11th meeting since 1986 and issues the Protocol of Tegucigalpa. This protocol reactivates the Organization of Central American States in order to accelerate the integration process, promote democracy and stability, and preserve the environment (Caribbean Community 1992, 13).

1992   (January) A cease-fire in El Salvador is signed in Mexico City. The peace agreement is engineered by UN Secretary General Pérez de Cuellar, the United States, and Mexico, and it brings together Salvadoran President Cristiani and the rebel alliance. The guerrilla leadership agrees to lay down its arms by October 1992 in exchange for guarantees that rebel political leaders will be incorporated into existing, democratic institutions. General elections are scheduled for March 1994.

1992   (March) US textile and clothing lobbies offer to support an extension of NAFTA benefits to Central America and the Caribbean in exchange for their support in Uruguay Round talks for a phaseout of the Multi-Fiber Agreement in 15 years instead of 10 years (*Journal of Commerce*, 3 March 1992, 5A; *Inside U.S. Trade*, 20 March 1992, 1).

1992   (March) Labor tensions rise in Nicaragua over privatization plans for the government-owned airline, Aeronica, that threaten the jobs of half the labor force. Workers strike and demand severance pay and shares in the company if they are fired. Such tension illustrates the problems Central American governments confront when they sell state-owned companies (*Journal of Commerce*, 6 March 1992, 2B).

1992   (May) Honduras, Guatemala, and El Salvador sign a trilateral free trade agreement, establishing new import tariffs to take effect on 1 January 1993. In addition, Honduras and El Salvador sign an agreement covering free trade, investment, and economic integration, also to take effect on 1 January 1993 (*Journal of Commerce*, 14 May 1992, 4A).

1992   (June) Delegates from the Caribbean and Central America discuss the need for united action to fight the economic threat posed by NAFTA. They fear Mexico will attract investment and technology that otherwise would have come to the Caribbean/Central American region (*Journal of Commerce*, 8 June 1992, 5A).

1992   (July) The Banco Centro Americano de Integración Económica builds up a surplus after collecting some of its accumulated arrears and incorporating Venezuela as a member with a $122 million capital contribution (*Latin American Weekly Report*, 16 July 1992, 9).

1992   (July) Honduras liberalizes foreign exchange transactions ("Latin American Regional Reports–Mexico and Central America," Latin American Newsletters, 16 July 1992, 3).

1992	(July) Seven Central American nations (all CACM countries and Belize) and the governors of 13 southern US states sign a declaration to intensify trade and investment between the two areas (*Washington Post*, 29 July 1992, A14).
1992	(August) The San José Pact is renewed. Under the pact, Mexico and Venezuela agree to sell up to 160,000 barrels of oil to 11 Caribbean and Central American nations under preferential conditions (*El Nacional*, 6 August 1992, 22).
1992	(August) Mexico and the Central American countries (except Panama) sign a framework agreement that paves the way for a Mexico–Central American free trade area by 1997. In addition, bilateral negotiations on a trade accord between Costa Rica and Mexico are advanced ("Latin American Regional Reports–Mexico and Central America," Latin American Newsletters, 24 September 1992, 6).
1992	(August) El Salvador announces a major tax reform to begin in September that aims to increase government revenue by 35 percent; a 10 percent value-added tax will replace the stamp tax (*Journal of Commerce*, 24 August 1992, 5A).
1992	(October) Central American treasury officials work out a customs agreement that will eliminate bureaucratic obstacles to trade in the region; it is expected to be implemented in early 1993 (*Journal of Commerce*, 1 October 1992, 4A).
1992	(October) US assistance programs for Central America are criticized for using US funds to attract US businesses to Central America and for neither enforcing or encouraging intellectual property rights and worker rights (*Journal of Commerce*, 5 October 1992, 12A).
1992	(December) A group of Central American businessmen plan a regional integrated rail and road system that would link Mexico and Colombia (*Journal of Commerce*, 4 December 1992, 1A; *The Miami Herald*, 5 December 1992, 15A).
1993	(April) The Central American free trade zone comes into effect. Tariffs on intraregional trade for 5,000 product lines are reduced to a range of 5 to 20 percent. Nicaragua is given special treatment. Costa Rica does not sign the treaty (*Latin American Weekly Report*, 15 April 1993, 171; and 6 May 1993, 200). The group now becomes the Grupo América Central 4.
1994	(April 6) Mexico and Costa Rica sign a free trade agreement. The agreement removes tariffs on more than 8,300 products, establishes a dispute settlement mechanism, and protects intellectual property rights.

Trade Summary

In the decade of the 1980s, the United States solidified its position as the main trading partner for Central America. From 1980 to 1990 the share of the region's exports absorbed by the United States increased from 36 to 43 percent. The share of imports supplied by the United States rose from 33 to 42 percent. The ratio of merchandise trade (imports and exports) to GDP for the region is about 60 percent (as of 1990). Due to large fuel imports, trade with the rest of Latin America, including Mexico, is asymmetrical. Latin America absorbs 6 percent of Central America's exports and supplies 19 percent of the region's imports (Saborio 1992, 2).

The Caribbean Community (Caricom) and Other Caribbean Countries

1968	The Caribbean Free Trade Association (CARIFTA) is formed to liberalize trade among its 13 members (CEPAL 1991, 36).
1969	The Caribbean Development Bank is established by 16 regional and 2 nonregional countries. By the 1990s the members had increased to 20 regional and 5 nonregional countries (Canada, France, Germany, Italy, and the United Kingdom). The objective of the bank is to contribute to economic cooperation and integration among the Caribbean countries. In 1988 total assets amounted to

$628 million (IMF, *Directory of Regional Economic Organizations*, July 1990, 149; *Directorio Latinoamericano de Instituciones Financieras de Desarrollo, 1988–1989*, Asociación Latinoamericana de Instituciones Financieras de Desarrollo: Lima, Peru, 568).

1972   Eight of the less-developed CARIFTA countries (Antigua, Belize, Dominica, Grenada, Monserrat, St. Kitts and Nevis, St. Lucia, and San Vincent and the Grenadines) agree to establish a common external tariff (CET).

1973   Through the Treaty of Chaguaramas, the Caribbean Community (Caricom) replaces CARIFTA. Its purpose is not only to liberalize trade but also to establish a CET and to reach agreements in other areas such as agriculture, energy, and transportation. It is formed with 13 members: Jamaica, Trinidad and Tobago, Barbados, Guyana, St. Lucia, Dominica, St. Vincent and the Grenadines, Grenada, Antigua, the Bahamas, Belize, Montserrat, and St. Kitts (IMF, *Directory of Regional Economic Organizations*, July 1990, 147). The four major countries—Barbados, Guyana, Jamaica, and Trinidad and Tobago—immediately adopt a CET (higher than that of the relatively less-developed countries) (CEPAL 1991, 36).

1974   The Agreement on Fiscal Incentives for Industry (Acuerdo de Incentivos Fiscales a la Industria) is approved, with the purpose of harmonizing income taxes and import tariffs (CEPAL 1991, 40).

1980   Venezuela and Mexico sign an agreement (known as the San José Pact) offering oil on concessionary terms to Barbados, Jamaica, and the Dominican Republic, as well as to six Central American countries. The recipients will pay 70 percent of the cost of their oil imports; the rest will be covered by a five-year loan at 4 percent interest ("Latin America Regional Reports–Caribbean," Latin American Newsletters, 22 August 1880, 2).

1981   The relatively less-developed countries, still part of Caricom, form the Organization of Eastern Caribbean States (Antigua and Barbuda, Dominica, Grenada, Montserrat, St. Kitts and Nevis, St Lucia, St. Vincent). Three years later, the British Virgin Islands is admitted as an associate member.

1983   The original seven members of the Organization of Eastern Caribbean States establish the Eastern Caribbean Central Bank (four years later Anguilla becomes a member). They adopt a common currency, the Eastern Caribbean dollar (CEPAL 1991, 36; IMF, *Directory of Regional Economic Organizations*, July 1990, 166 and 183).

1983   The United States enacts the Caribbean Basin Initiative (CBI), allowing 23 Caribbean and Central American countries preferential access to the US market for 12 years, for a broad range of products. However, the CBI legislation notably excludes important goods such as textiles, apparel, footwear, and watches ("Special Report: Caribbean," *Journal of Commerce*, 5 June 1990, 6B).

1985   The Industrial Program Framework (Esquema de Programación Industrial) is approved; it is similar to the Andean Group program. Its goal is to assign a series of regional industrial projects to the Caricom members. By 1989, the program is still not implemented, and intellectual support for the philosophy of assigned investment has become weaker (CEPAL 1991, 36).

1986   Trade among Caribbean states drops by half from 1981 to 1986. Intraregional trade recovers to $481 million by 1990 but still remains below its 1980 value (*Journal of Commerce*, 3 December 1991, 4A).

1986   The United States establishes a Special Access Program for apparel exports from CBI countries arriving under HTS 9802.00.80. The program is designed both to increase production in the Caribbean and to expand exports of US garment and fabric parts (Hufbauer and Schott 1992, 273).

1986   Canada's Caribcan program began. It provides unilateral, duty-free access for an unlimited term for most commonwealth Caribbean products.

1988   (October) The System of Rules for Enterprises (Régimen de Empresas) is approved, with the goal of promoting investment in designated priority sectors (CEPAL 1991, 36).

1989 (July) The Grand Anse Declaration is signed, stating that the Caricom goal is to work toward economic integration. Among the measures adopted:

- By 1 January 1991, the CET, the rules of origin, and fiscal incentives should be revised.

- The Industrial Program Framework (Esquema de Programación Industrial) and the System of Rules for Enterprises (Régimes de Empresas) are to be implemented.

- No passport will be necessary for citizens of Caricom traveling within the region. The ultimate goal is free movement of people, including working permits and mutual recognition of social security rights.

- With the objective of monetary union by 1995, the members agree to work toward the adoption of a common currency (CEPAL 1991, 41).

- A regional stock exchange is proposed by Jamaica (only Trinidad and Tobago, Jamaica, and Barbados have stock exchanges).

1989 Venezuela extends preferential tariff rates to Trinidad & Tobago for specified products ("Latin American Regional Reports—Andean Group," Latin American Newsletters, 31 August 1989, 1).

1990 (August) A Caricom Summit held in Jamaica adopts decisions:

- The CET, rules of origin, and harmonization of fiscal incentives, must be implemented by April 1991 (moved up from January 1991). The CET is to be implemented first by the largest countries; other countries have until the end of 1991 to implement it (the Bahamas, which is not a signatory of the trading agreements and which has very low tariffs, is exempted; Monserrat has until 1 January 1994 for implementation) ("Special Report: Caribbean," Journal of Commerce, 4 December 1990, 11A; 26 September 1991, 3A).

- All quantitative restrictions to trade are to be eliminated by mid-1991.

- Members resolve to establish free travel within the region without passports by 1991. In addition, no work permits for Caricom nationals will be required within the region. By 1993, a uniform Caricom passport will be issued for travel ("Latin American Regional Reports—Caribbean Report," Latin American Newsletters, 4 October 1990, 1).

- A Caribbean stock exchange is planned for 1 January 1991.

1990 (August) The US Caribbean Basin Initiative is extended by President Bush (CBI II), and the original CBI tariff concessions granted to the 23 countries are made permanent.[16] Exports to the United States are facilitated by offering free entry to products with 35 percent local content that have been "substantially transformed" from components imported from outside the region. Key industries (clothing and sugar among others) continue to be excluded from the agreement, however (Financial Times, 16 August 1990, 5). CBI II includes nontariff measures such as the permitted investment of Section 936 funds in the CBI area as well as Puerto Rico (Section 936 funds are generated by tax-preferred investments in Puerto Rico), Guaranteed Access Levels (GALS) for textile products, and separate cumulation for antidumping and countervailing duty investigations (US Department of Commerce, Latin America/Caribbean Business Development Center).[17]

---

16. Regional exports to the United States in 1989 were $6.6 billion, still below the pre-CBI total of $8.5 billion reached in 1983. (In 1983, however, oil shipments from Trinidad and the Bahamas accounted for a large portion of the value of the region's exports.)

17. By 1992, 28 countries were elegible for CBI benefits: Antigua and Barbuda, Aruba, Bahamas, Barbados, Belize, British Virgin Islands, Costa Rica, Dominica, Dominican Republic, El Salvador, Grenada, Guatemala, Guyana, Honduras, Jamaica, Montserrat,

1991   (April) Trading on the Caribbean stock market begins, four months after initially scheduled. The market is capitalized at US$1.5 billion and lists 92 companies (*Journal of Commerce*, 9 April 1991, 3A).

1991   (April) The deadline for implementing the CET passes. Government officials remain confident it will be in place by the end of 1991. The CET tariff schedule ranges from 5 to 45 percent, replacing an older structure of 5 to 70 percent. Caricom still hopes to establish a common market by 1993 and monetary union by 1994 (*Financial Times*, 25 April 1991, 3).

1991   (July) Venezuela offers preferential access to its markets for exports from Caricom. At the end of five years, Caricom member states will be expected to lower their duties on Venezuelan exports progressively over the succeeding five years, eventually culminating in free trade at the end of ten years. Venezuela currently exports much more to Caricom countries (mostly oil) than it imports from Caricom countries (*Financial Times*, 2 July 1991, 4).

1991   (July) The United States and Caricom sign a framework agreement on trade and investment under the Enterprise for the Americas Initiative (EAI). The agreement establishes the US-Caricom Trade and Investment Council and begins to address debt relief and investment issues (Worrell, 1990; *Washington Post*, 23 July 1991, D3).

1991   (July) Caricom's single-market goal is pushed back to 1994. Only seven members have implemented the common external tariff, and October 1991 is set as the new deadline (*Financial Times*, 1 July 1991, 4).

1991   (August) US government forgives $217 million of Jamaican foreign debt under the EAI. This amount represents 80 percent of what Jamaica owes for food imports under PL-480 (*Journal of Commerce*, 26 August 1991, 3A).

1991   (September) The United States extends duty-free access to US markets for imports of shoes and sneakers from Caricom (*Journal of Commerce*, 13 September 1991, 1).

1991   (October) Venezuela applies for membership in Caricom (*Journal of Commerce*, 16 October 1991, 5A).

1991   (December) Implementation of the common external tariff is again postponed until 1 February 1992. Belize, St. Kitts, St. Lucia, Antigua, and Montserrat have yet to implement the CET (*Journal of Commerce*, 3 December 1991, 4A).

1991   (December) The United States and the Dominican Republic sign a framework agreement on trade and investment under the EAI (*International Trade Reporter*, 1 January 1992, 19).

1992   (April) The United States tells Caricom that it will not get preferential treatment under EAI, citing a conflict with the goal of hemispheric free trade. Caricom argues that its small economies will face problems meeting competition (*Journal of Commerce*, 30 April 1992, 4A).

1992   (April) The Caribbean Development Bank, in reviewing the regional economy in 1991, cites the 35 percent reduction in the region's US sugar import quota as an important factor in the low growth rate (*Journal of Commerce*, 1 April 1992, 4A).

1992   (May) Caricom lobbies against a proposed cutback in the labor program by which US farmers annually employ 14,000 Caricom farm workers who in turn remit about $70 million in earnings to the region (*Journal of Commerce*, 23 March 1992, 4A).

1992   (May) The US Treasury allows investors in the Caribbean to borrow at below-market rates from the Overseas Private Investment Corporation. The move is designed to boost private investment in the region (*Wall Street Journal*, 5 May 1992, A2).

Netherlands Antilles, Nicaragua, Panama, St. Kitts-Nevis, St. Lucia, St. Vincent/ Grenadines, Trinidad and Tobago, Haiti (temporarily suspended as of November 1991) and Anguilla, Cayman Islands, Surinam, and Turks and Caicos Islands, which are eligible but not yet included.

1992   (May) Four Caribbean islands (St. Lucia, Dominica, St. Vincent, and Grenada) agree on a plan to create a political union. Officials expect to hold a referendum in each island by early 1993. Apprehensive about the impending creation of a North American Free Trade Area, they hope political union will improve their economic prospects (*Journal of Commerce*, 20 May 1992, 5A).

1992   (August) Cuba asks Caricom to be granted observer status; a decision is not expected before mid-1993 (*Financial Times*, 19 August 1992, P5).

1992   (August) The San José Pact is renewed. Under the pact, Mexico and Venezuela agree to sell up to 160,000 barrels of oil to 11 Caribbean and Central American nations under preferential conditions (*El Nacional*, 6 August 1992, 22).

1992   (October) Venezuela and Caricom sign a "one-way" free trade pact. By 1993, 15 percent of Caricom products will enter Venezuela duty-free; by 1994, 50 percent; by 1995, 75 percent; and by 1996, all 1,300 products will enter Venezuela duty-free. After the initial five-year "one-way" period, Caricom will start lowering its tariffs for imports from Venezuela ("Latin American Regional Reports–Andean Group," Latin American Newsletters, 12 November 1992, 5).

1992   (October) Caricom meets to discuss its common external tariff, and makes these agreements:

- It will reduce the CET from 45 percent to 35 percent in 1993; 30 to 25 percent in 1995; and 20 percent in 1998. The common external tariffs in some agricultural products, including citrus fruits, will only be reduced to 40 percent while the CET for rice will be reduced from 30 to 25 percent beginning 1994. Belize delays its first reduction to 30 June 1993 (*Inside U.S. Trade*, 6 November 1992, 16).

- It will enlarge the integration process by creating the Association of Caribbean States, open to all the countries of the Caribbean Basin (including the islands and states around it).

- It will consider the creation of a Caricom Commission to see that Caricom decisions are put into place ("Latin American Regional Reports–Caribbean," Latin American Newsletters, 10 December 1992, 2).

1992   (December) Caribbean and US private-sector groups join forces to seek legislation that would give CBI countries increased preferential access to the US market, comparable to that extended to Mexico in the NAFTA, in return for improvements in labor and environmental standards, investment rules, and intellectual property rights (*Inside U.S. Trade*, 11 December 1992, 12).

1992   (December) The European Community reached an agreement with respect to banana imports from the African, Caribbean, and Pacific (ACP) group, to be implemented by July 1993. The Community agrees to reduce the duty on bananas for countries outside the ACP to ECU 100 ($117), for a fixed annual import quota of 2 million tons and an ECU 850 per ton duty (i.e., $995, about 170 percent ad valorem tariff equivalent) on imports above that level. Total EC banana imports in 1991 were 3.6 tons (of which 0.6 million came from ACP) ("Latin American Regional Reports–Caribbean and Central America," Latin American Newsletters, 21 January 1993, 1; Office of Official Publications of the European Community, *Eurostat: External Trade*, 1991). Belgium, the Netherlands, and Germany, which consumes about 35 percent of all bananas sold in Europe and imports them with no tariff, favored the elimination of ACP preferences and are taking the European Commission to the European Court of Justice over the decision reached. Moreover, the agreement can be blocked in the European Council if Luxembourg and Denmark back Germany, Belgium, and the Netherlands (*Journal of Commerce*, 11 February 1993, 3A). Some European countries (e.g., United Kingdom, France, and Spain) favored a common EC policy that would maintain preferences for banana imports from their former colonies (preferences were first established under the Lomé Convention). Eastern Caribbean nations including Dominica, St. Lucia, St. Vincent, and the Grenadines and Grenada charge that a change in the conditions of sale of their bananas would destroy their economies, since bananas make up as much as 96 percent of their exports to the European Community (*Inside U.S. Trade*, 9 October 1992, 22).

1993   Guyana's new government suspends the privatization program (*Journal of Commerce*, 8 January 1993, 3A).

1993   (December) Caricom countries sign an agreement with Cuba establishing a commission aimed at increasing trade between them. The agreement will encourage joint efforts in key sectors such as sugar and cooperation in developing livestock and fisheries (*Journal of Commerce*, 15 December 1993).

1993   (October) President Fidel Castro announced the creation of five free-trade zones in eastern Cuba (*Journal of Commerce*, 29 November 1993).

1994   (February) The United States and Jamaica sign a bilateral investment treaty (BIT). The agreement guarantees national treatment, free transfer of capital, profits, royalties, and access to international arbitration. It also prohibits performance requirements (*International Trade Reporter*, 9 February 1994, 223).

1994   (March) Caricom and nine other countries (Mexico, Colombia, Cuba, Haiti, Martinique, Guadeloupe, Costa Rica, Nicaragua, and Venezuela) reach an agreement to create the Association of Caribbean States. The organization will not be a trading bloc but rather a forum for discussions of economic and security issues. The agreement was to be signed on July 1994.

1994   (March) St. Kitts and Nevis becomes a GATT member.

Established Hemispheric Institutions and the Enterprise for the Americas Initiative

1948   The Charter of the Organization of American States (OAS) was approved at the Bogotá conference in April 1948. Originally, there were 21 members; today there are 33. The role of the OAS is political, its main purpose being to resolve conflicts between members. Some of its basic principles include the obligation to settle disputes by peaceful means, mutual assistance in case of external aggression, the importance of "representative democracy" to the "solidarity of the American States," the need for economic cooperation, and the recognition of basic human rights (Kryzanek 1990; Molineu 1990; IMF, *Directory of Regional Economic Organizations* 1990, 185).

1960   Inter-American Development Bank (IDB) begins operations in October 1960 with an initial budget of $813 million in ordinary capital and $146 million in the Fund for Special Operations. The initial members are 20 Latin American countries. In 1976, nonregional members are also accepted, and by 1992 the IDB has 43 members (IDB Annual Report 1984, 5).

1960   Seven Latin American countries (Argentina, Brazil, Chile, Mexico, Paraguay, Peru, and Uruguay) sign the Montevideo Treaty establishing the Latin American Free Trade Agreement (LAFTA). They are joined later by Colombia and Ecuador. LAFTA embodies provisions for gradual trade liberalization within the area and establishes the basic structure of a regional economic integration program (Wionczek 1966).

1975   The Latin American Economic System is established as an organization for regional cooperation, coordination, and joint development. By 1994 it has 26 member countries (IMF, *Directory of Regional Economic Organizations*, July 1990, 177).

1977   The Latin American Export Bank is organized as a specialized multinational bank to promote and finance Latin American and Caribbean exports. The bank comprises 22 members (IMF, *Directory of Regional Economic Organizations*, July 1990, 179).

1980	A new Montevideo Treaty replaces LAFTA with the Latin American Integration Association (LAIA). The main difference between LAFTA and LAIA is that, while LAFTA intended to reach economic integration in 12 years, LAIA does not establish any deadline but maintains as an ultimate goal the formation of a Latin American Common Market. In addition, LAIA allows partial agreements among two or more countries. The member countries increase to 11, with four observer organizations: IDB, ECLAC, OAS, and the European Community.
1983	By the end of 1982, Central America is close to total war. Colombia, Mexico, Panama, and Venezuela form the Contadora group to try to encourage negotiations in the Central American conflict. Contadora's Support Group (Grupo de Apoyo) later becomes the Rio Group, also known as Permanent Mechanism for Latin American Political Consultation and Cooperation (Rosenthal 1992; Ulloa et al. 1985).
1990	(June) President Bush launches the Enterprise for the Americas Initiative (EAI) to strengthen Latin American and Caribbean economies through trade (using framework agreements on trade and investment and free trade areas), investment (using an Investment Sector Loan Program and the Multilateral Investment Fund) and debt reductions. The debt component of the initiative contemplates the forgiveness of part of the $7 billion concessional debt ($5.1 billion of AID loans and $1.9 billion of PL-480 loans) and part of the $5.5 billion of nonconcessional debt ($4.0 billion owed to the US Export-Import Bank and $1.5 billion to the Commodity Credit Corporation) (US Department of Commerce, "Enterprise for the American Initiative: Fact Sheet," 15 January 1993, 17–18).
1990	Before the EAI was announced, the United States signed framework agreements on trade and investment with Mexico and Bolivia. From July 1990 through December 1991, the United States signed several additional framework agreements: with Colombia and Ecuador in July 1990, with Chile in October 1990, with Honduras and Costa Rica in November 1990, with Venezuela in April 1991, with El Salvador and Peru in May 1991, with Mercosur, Nicaragua, and Panama on June 1991, with the Caricom group in July 1991, with Guatemala in October 1991, and with the Dominican Republic in December 1991. These framework agreements are the most visible part of US diplomacy in furthering the EAI; they are widely regarded in Latin America as the first stepping stone toward closer economic relations with the United States.
1990	(October) The 1990 US farm bill authorizes the reduction of PL-480 loans ($1.9 billion). In August 1992, Congress appropriated an additional $40 million to carry out "debt restructuring" of PL-480 debt in fiscal 1993 (US Department of Commerce, "Enterprise for the American Initiative: Fact Sheet", 15 January 1993, 5).
1990	(October) The Rio Group, or the Permanent Mechanism for Latin American Political Consultation and Cooperation, meets in Caracas. Members are Argentina, Brazil, Colombia, Chile, Ecuador, Mexico, Peru, Uruguay, and Venezuela. They accept as new members Bolivia and Paraguay. They meet again in December 1990 and April 1991 with EC ministers. The issues discussed include support for the EAI, a call for restructuring the OAS and LAIA, and commission studies on the feasibility of setting up a strategic investment fund (*Financial Times*, 16 October 1990, 6).
1991	(June) The first investment sector loan under the EAI, a $150 million loan for Chile, is approved by the Inter-American Development Bank (IDB) (White House, "Fact Sheet: Advancing the Enterprise for the Americas Initiative," 27 June 1991). Also, under the EAI debt initiative, a debt reduction agreement between the United States and Chile is signed on June reducing Chilean debt by about $16 million (US GAO 1992, 22).
1991	(August) Two investment sector loans are approved: one for Bolivia ($140 million) and another for Jamaica ($75 million). Both countries also sign debt reduction agreements. Bolivia reduces its PL-480 debt by $30 million; Jamaica reduces its PL-480 debt by $217 million (US Department of Commerce, Office for Latin America, "Fact Sheet: Enterprise for the Americas," 17 January 1992; *Journal of Commerce*, 18 February 1992, 2A).

1991 (October) An investment sector loan of $200 million for Colombia is approved (US Department of Commerce, Office of Latin America, "Fact Sheet: Enterprise for the Americas," 17 January 1992).

1992 (February) As part of the Investment Initiative, a Multilateral Investment Fund (MIF) is established in the IDB. The target size of the fund is $1.5 billion over five years (1992–96) to support export promotion in Latin America. Twenty countries sign the agreement, including Japan, Spain, Germany, Italy, France, Portugal, and Canada. As of February, $1.3 billion had been pledged to the fund, including $500 million each from the United States and Japan.[18] The Enterprise for the Americas Initiative Act of 1991 accordingly seeks an appropriation of $500 million for 1992–96, to be transferred to the IDB in five installments of $100 million, beginning in fiscal 1992.

1992 (May) The US Congress fails to approve the initial $100 million for the MIF. It also denies the request for $210 million for the debt reduction package (*Inside U.S. Trade*, 1 May 1992, 8).

1992 (June) A panel of the US House of Representatives turns down a proposal to provide $202 million in debt relief, but it does agree to contribute $75 million toward the proposed $1.3 billion for the MIF (*Journal of Commerce*, 15 June 1992).

1992 (October) EAI legislation authorizes reduction of AID loans ($5.1 billion face amount). Congress also authorizes debt swaps using part of the credits owed to the US Export-Import Bank and the Commodity Credit Corporation (US Department of Commerce, "Enterprise for the American Initiative: Fact Sheet," 15 January 1993, 4).

1992 (December) Several investment sector loans are approved: $90 million for El Salvador, $350 million for Argentina, $70 million for Paraguay, and $65 million for Uruguay. In addition, Congress authorizes $40 million in PL-480 debt reduction for El Salvador and Uruguay, and the National Advisory Council approves 10 percent AID debt reductions for Chile, Colombia, Uruguay, and Argentina and 70 percent for El Salvador (US Department of Commerce, Office of Latin America, "Fact Sheet: Enterprise for the Americas," 15 January 1993).

1992 (December) The Rio Group meets in Buenos Aires for talks about the future of democracy. President-elect Bill Clinton speaks by telephone to the leaders at this meeting and expresses his support for the EAI. He also calls Caribbean leaders at the Annual Conference on Trade, Investment, and Development in the Caribbean Basin and expresses his intention of including Caribbean countries in US efforts to expand regional trade and investment initiatives (*Inside U.S. Trade*, 4 December 1992, 3).

1993 The Clinton administration proposes a reduction of the debt forgiveness under the EAI. Between 1994 and 1997, PL-480 debt forgiveness will be reduced by $79 million, and AID debt forgiveness will be reduced by $107 million (White House, "A Vision for Change," 17 February 1993, 123–24).

1993 (April) The Rio Group meets in Bolivia. Panama and Peru are invited to rejoin the organization. Panama rejects the offer; Peru accepts it ("Latin American Weekly Report," Latin American Newsletters, 29 April 1993, 192).

1993 (December) During Vice President Al Gore's visit to Mexico, he reaffirms the Clinton administration's commitment to hemispheric integration. He also proposes a meeting of all the Western Hemisphere leaders (*New York Times*, 2 December 1993).

1994 (February) The Clinton administration confirms that it intends to create a Western Hemisphere Free Trade Zone in 10 to 15 years and to start by negotiating Chile's accession to NAFTA by late 1995 (*New York Times*, 4 February 1994, D1).

---

18. Other contributions include $50 million from Spain, $30 million each from Germany and Italy, $32 million from Canada, and $20 million each from Mexico, Venezuela, Brazil, and Argentina (US Department of Commerce, "Enterprise for the Americas Fact Sheet," July 1992; *Inside U.S. Trade*, 6 March 1992, 10).

| 1994 | (March) The OAS approves an accord establishing a framework for settling trade contract disputes (*International Trade Reporter*, 30 March 1994, 506). |

1994 (March) The OAS approves an accord establishing a framework for settling trade contract disputes (*International Trade Reporter*, 30 March 1994, 506).

1994 (March) Cesar Gaviria, the Colombian president, is elected secretary general of the OAS and says one of his main goals will be regional integration. He takes office in August 1994.

1994 (March) Brazil proposes the creation of a South American Free Trade Area to accelerate liberalization and regional integration. It would open the door for Mercosur countries to negotiate individual FTAs with other South American countries (*International Trade Reporter*, 23 March 1994, 471).

1994 (May 3) USTR releases a report required under the Danforth amendment to the NAFTA implementing legislation. The report is intended to list countries that "provide fair and equitable market access to US exports . . . or have made significant progress in opening their markets . . . and the further opening of those markets has the greatest potential to increase US exports. . . ." Based on this report, the president is to determine prospective partners for free trade area negotiations by July 1994.[19]

1994 (March 11) President Clinton formally announces the Summit of the Americas for 9–10 December 1994 in Miami.

---

19. This language is contained in the NAFTA implementing legislation (HR 3450), Section 108, on "congressional intent regarding future accessions."

Appendix D:
Trade and Investment Diversion

In order to assess the possible trade diversion resulting from a WHFTA, we have constructed a simple model designed to produce *responsibly high* estimates of the adverse trade impact on South Asia, East Asia, and Western Europe.[1] Because access to the US market will remain of primary interest to those regions, we concentrate on the potential diversion generated by a WHFTA on third-country trade flows to the United States. We assume that additional Latin American imports from the United States are the product of greater economic activity and do not come at the expense of imports from third countries. In other words, trade diversion is caused only by additional US imports from Latin America, not by additional Latin American imports from the United States.

As a result, our model may underestimate to a small extent trade diversion from third countries by ignoring the diversion of their exports to Latin American markets. While we assume that, in the aggregate, diversion of third-country trade flows to Latin America will be more than offset by the positive income effect of regional integration, this generalization will not apply to all sectors and regions. Some regions will likely suffer some export diversion in Latin American markets. One such region is Western Europe, which accounts for about 20 percent of

---

1. In our model, the following countries are included in each group: South Asia (Australia, New Zealand, Association of Southeast Asian Nations, Bangladesh, India, Nepal, Pakistan, and Sri Lanka); East Asia (Japan, South Korea, Taiwan, China, and Hong Kong); Western Europe (European Union, European Free Trade Association, and Turkey).

total Latin American imports and whose commodity export mix to Latin America is similar to the US commodity export mix.

Trade Diversion Calculations

In calculating the diversion of trade flows to the United States, we employ a "top-down" approach that is, we estimate the total amount of trade that would likely be adversely affected by the regional initiative and then allocate that total among industrial sectors. By contrast, other studies take a "bottom-up" approach that cumulates the calculated trade effect for individual industrial sectors. It should be noted, however, that many of those studies overstate the potential trade diversion effects because they calculate the size of the preferences using the GATT-bound most-favored nation (MFN) tariffs rather than the current applied rates, which are often lower. For example, estimates of the potential trade diversion of the North American Free Trade Agreement (NAFTA) are often inflated because the bulk of the calculated diversion occurs in the textile and apparel sector (this sector accounts for about half of South Asian exports to the United States). In these calculations, Mexican textile and apparel exports without the NAFTA are ascribed the US MFN tariff rate, but in fact Mexico already receives generous US tariff preferences.[2]

The starting point for our calculations is an estimation of additional US imports (by commodity) from Latin America under the scenarios described in appendix B. Projections under the continuing-reform and the WHFTA scenarios for 1997 and 2002 are taken from table B4. For purposes of our trade diversion analysis, we group the commodities listed in table B4 into 21 industrial classifications (table D1).[3]

Next we calculate how much of this US import growth from Latin America might come at the expense of imports from third countries. Basically, we assume that the difference in US import growth between the continuing-reform scenario and the WHFTA scenario corresponds to trade diversion from third countries. The rationale for this assumption can be briefly explained.

The continuing-reform scenario envisages continuing progress in subregional arrangements but no umbrella hemispheric accord that would give Latin American countries preferential access to the US market.

---

2. This calculation error occurs, for example, in Safadi and Yeats (1993) and in Kreinin and Plummer (1992, 1345–66).

3. Note that US import growth under a "no new reforms" scenario is distributed among commodity groupings pro rata to 1990 US trade levels. By contrast, additional US imports under the continuing-reform and WHFTA scenarios are distributed disproportionately in favor of commodity groups associated with lower median US weekly wages.

Table D1 Projected merchandise trade diversion from South Asia, East Asia, and Western Europe by WHFTA, 1997 and 2002 (millions of dollars except where noted)

		Latin American exports to the United States					
		Projected 1997			Projected 2002		
			WHFTA scenario			WHFTA scenario	
	Base level (1989–91 average)	Continuing reform scenario[a]	Level[a]	Change vs. continuing reform scenario	Continuing reform scenario[a]	Level[a]	Change vs. continuing reform scenario
Nonmanufactures	12,274	14,801	16,618	1,817	17,426	21,980	4,554
Agriculture	1,645	3,939	5,772	1,833	6,322	10,866	4,544
Mining	10,629	10,862	10,846	−16	11,104	11,114	10
Durable manufactures	7,038	12,462	14,870	2,408	18,091	24,534	6,443
Lumber and wood products	235	504	754	250	783	1,394	611
Furniture and fixtures	89	302	458	156	523	914	390
Stone, clay, and glass products	1,042	1,789	2,233	444	2,565	3,703	1,138
Primary metal industries	2,390	4,179	4,949	770	6,035	8,107	2,072
Machinery, excl. electrical	917	1,055	1,082	27	1,197	1,285	87
Electrical machinery	571	671	636	−35	775	716	−60
Transportation equipment	893	1,316	1,417	101	1,755	2,063	308
Professional equipment	179	319	350	31	464	560	97
Amusement and sporting goods	100	478	708	230	871	1,459	588
Miscellaneous industries	622	1,849	2,284	435	3,123	4,335	1,212
Nondurable manufactures	11,097	19,713	26,085	6,372	28,655	44,583	15,928
Food and kindred products	4,691	7,348	9,383	2,035	10,106	15,174	5,068
Tobacco manufactures	216	358	392	35	505	611	106
Textile mill products	274	2,341	4,197	1,856	4,486	9,039	4,553
Apparel and textile products	3,856	5,234	6,541	1,307	6,664	9,854	3,190
Paper and allied products	280	681	950	269	1,098	1,778	680
Printing and allied products	23	151	163	11	284	335	51
Chemicals and products	1,055	1,752	1,699	−53	2,475	2,494	19
Rubber and plastics products	281	696	988	292	1,127	1,861	734
Leather and products	422	1,152	1,772	620	1,910	3,438	1,528
Total, listed commodities	30,409	46,975	57,573	10,598	64,172	91,098	26,925
Total, unlisted commodities	25	319	611	375	624	1,336	971
Total	30,434	47,294	58,184	10,890	64,797	92,433	27,637

a. These figures are taken from table B4.

(Table continues next page)

Table D1 Projected merchandise trade diversion from South Asia, East Asia, and Western Europe by WHFTA, 1997 and 2002 (millions of dollars except where noted) (Continued)

	World exports to US, 1990	Base level (average 1989–91)	South Asian exports to United States[b]				
			Percent of world exports to US (avg. 1989–91)	Projected exports[c]		Calculated exports diverted by WHFTA	
				1997	2002	1997	2002
Nonmanufactures	64,951	2,517		4,905	7,899	108	269
Agriculture	5,436	321	6	625	1,007	108	268
Mining	59,515	2,196	4	4,279	6,892	–1	0
Durable manufactures	298,801	19,790		38,565	62,109	147	387
Lumber and wood products	5,211	563	11	1,098	1,768	27	66
Furniture and fixtures	6,315	502	8	978	1,575	12	31
Stone, clay, and glass products	16,850	1,840	11	3,585	5,774	48	124
Primary metal industries	27,046	897	3	1,749	2,817	26	69
Machinery, excl. electrical	64,030	5,864	9	11,428	18,405	2	8
Electrical machinery	57,618	7,916	14	15,426	24,844	–5	–8
Transportation equipment	82,126	473	1	922	1,486	1	2
Professional equipment	13,203	377	3	735	1,184	1	3
Amusement and sporting goods	8,638	449	5	876	1,411	12	31
Miscellaneous industries	17,764	907	5	1,767	2,846	22	62
Nondurable manufactures	111,275	14,149		27,572	44,405	985	2,446
Food and kindred products	21,635	4,314	20	8,407	13,539	406	1,011
Tobacco manufactures	750	27	4	53	85	1	4
Textile mill products	4,416	658	15	1,282	2,065	277	678
Apparel and textile products	33,581	5,587	17	10,888	17,535	217	531
Paper and allied products	11,110	45	0	87	140	1	3
Printing and allied products	1,610	87	5	169	273	1	3
Chemicals and products	21,321	1,759	8	3,428	5,521	–4	2
Rubber and plastics products	11,734	1,203	10	2,344	3,776	30	75
Leather and products	5,117	469	9	913	1,471	57	140
Total, listed commodities	475,027	36,456		71,041	114,413	1,239	3,101
Total, unlisted commodities	5,505	516	9	1,006	1,620	35	91
Total	480,531	36,972		72,047	116,033	1,274	3,192

b. South Asia includes Australia, New Zealand, Association of Southeast Asian Nations, Bangladesh, India, Nepal, Pakistan, and Sri Lanka.
c. Projection figures assume an annual growth rate of 10 percent.

Table D1 (Continued)

	Base level (average 1989–91)	Percent of world exports to US (avg. 1989–91)	East Asian exports to the United States[d] Projected exports[e] 1997	2002	Calculated exports diverted by WHFTA 1997	2002
Nonmanufactures	1,052		1,481	1,890	57	141
Agriculture	168	3	237	302	57	141
Mining	884	1	1,244	1,587	0	0
Durable manufactures	120,136		169,043	215,747	663	1,791
Lumber and wood products	392	8	551	703	19	46
Furniture and fixtures	2,330	37	3,279	4,185	58	144
Stone, clay, and glass products	2,444	15	3,439	4,389	64	165
Primary metal industries	7,877	29	11,083	14,146	224	603
Machinery, excl. electrical	26,760	42	37,655	48,058	11	36
Electrical machinery	31,127	54	43,799	55,900	–19	–32
Transportation equipment	33,143	40	46,636	59,520	41	124
Professional equipment	6,411	49	9,021	11,513	15	47
Amusement and sporting goods	6,583	76	9,263	11,822	175	448
Miscellaneous industries	3,069	17	4,318	5,511	75	209
Nondurable manufactures	32,716		46,035	58,754	2,003	4,951
Food and kindred products	1,495	7	2,103	2,685	141	350
Tobacco manufactures	7	1	10	12	0	1
Textile mill products	1,612	37	2,269	2,896	678	1,662
Apparel and textile products	18,063	54	25,416	32,438	703	1,716
Paper and allied products	446	4	628	802	11	27
Printing and allied products	428	27	603	769	3	13
Chemicals and products	3,308	16	4,655	5,941	–8	3
Rubber and plastics products	4,315	37	6,072	7,749	107	270
Leather and products	3,041	59	4,279	5,462	369	908
Total, listed commodities	153,905		216,559	276,391	2,723	6,883
Total, unlisted commodities	2,669	48	3,755	4,793	91	471
Total	156,573		220,314	281,183	2,814	7,354

d. East Asia includes Japan, South Korea, Taiwan, China, and Hong Kong.
e. Projection figures assume an annual growth rate of 5 percent.

(Table continues next page)

Table D1 Projected merchandise trade diversion from South Asia, East Asia, and Western Europe by WHFTA, 1997 and 2002 (millions of dollars except where noted) (Continued)

	Base level (average 1989–91)	Percent of world exports to US (avg. 1989–91)	Western European exports United States[f] Projected exports[g] 1997	2002	Calculated exports diverted by WHFTA 1997	2002
Nonmanufactures	5,523		7,268	8,843	142	356
Agriculture	425	8	560	681	143	356
Mining	5,098	9	6,708	8,162	–1	1
Durable manufactures	68,675		90,372	109,951	623	1,681
Lumber and wood products	188	4	248	302	9	22
Furniture and fixtures	1,320	21	1,738	2,114	33	82
Stone, clay, and glass products	5,950	35	7,830	9,527	157	402
Primary metal industries	6,931	26	9,121	11,097	197	531
Machinery, excl. electrical	20,318	32	26,737	32,530	9	28
Electrical machinery	5,944	10	7,822	9,516	–4	–6
Transportation equipment	15,564	19	20,482	24,919	19	58
Professional equipment	4,688	36	6,170	7,506	11	34
Amusement and sporting goods	844	10	1,111	1,351	22	57
Miscellaneous industries	6,926	39	9,114	11,089	170	473
Nondurable manufactures	26,483		34,850	42,400	1,351	3,430
Food and kindred products	5,174	24	6,809	8,284	487	1,212
Tobacco manufactures	326	43	429	522	15	46
Textile mill products	1,275	29	1,677	2,041	536	1,314
Apparel and textile products	3,434	10	4,518	5,497	134	326
Paper and allied products	1,430	13	1,882	2,290	35	88
Printing and allied products	683	42	898	1,093	5	21
Chemicals and products	10,542	49	13,873	16,879	–26	9
Rubber and plastics products	2,826	24	3,719	4,525	70	177
Leather and products	793	16	1,044	1,270	96	237
Total, listed commodities	100,681	24	132,489	161,194	2,116	5,467
Total, unlisted commodities	1,327		1,746	2,124	90	234
Total	102,008		134,235	163,318	2,206	5,702

f. Western Europe includes European Union, European Free Trade Association, and Turkey.
g. Projection figures assume an annual growth rate of 4 percent.

Hence, under the continuing-reform scenario, we assume that there is no policy-induced trade diversion on account of Latin American export growth abetted by preferences in the US market. By contrast, the WHFTA scenario entails Latin America preferences in the US market. Hence we assume that Latin American export growth in the WHFTA scenario, beyond the export growth portrayed in the continuing-reform scenario, represents policy-induced displacement of exports from third countries to the United States.

The amount of diversion in each industrial classification from each region outside Latin America is assumed to be proportional to that region's average share of the US market for imports of products in the industrial classification in 1989–91. For example, on average between 1989 and 1991, South Asian exports of food products to the US market ($4.3 billion) account for 19.94 percent of world exports of food products to the United States ($21.6 billion). The amount of South Asian food exports diverted by 1997 is calculated by multiplying this 20 percent market share figure by the difference in the growth of food product exports in the WHFTA scenario and the continuing-reform scenario in 1997 ($0.1994 \times [\$9,383 - \$7,348 = 406]$). The result is an estimated diversion of $406 million in South Asian exports (table D1).[4]

The diversion calculated at the industry classification level is aggregated to derive subtotals for diversion of exports of nonmanufactures, durable manufactures, and nondurable manufactures, as well as the totals for listed and unlisted commodities and for all commodities. The results of this exercise are presented in table D1.

Investment Diversion Calculations

Our methodology is as follows. First, the world aside from Latin America is divided into four regions: developing Asia (Asia not including Japan, New Zealand, and Australia); industrialized Asia (Japan, New Zealand, and Australia); Western Europe (the EU and EFTA); and NAFTA plus the rest of the world.

To calculate investment diversion, we explore the same two scenarios: the continuing-reform scenario and the WHFTA scenario. During 1985–90, the stock of foreign direct investment (FDI) in Latin America grew by

---

4. In some cases, exports of goods in an industrial classification, such as mining, grow more under the continuing-reform scenario than under the WHFTA scenario. The reason for this is that the calculated rate of growth in Latin American exports for high-wage commodities is actually higher under the continuing-reform scenario than under the WHFTA scenario because of the underlying assumptions of additional WHFTA export growth biased toward low-wage products (see appendix B). The result is that, in these sectors, the difference in Latin American exports to the US market between the WHFTA and continuing-reform scenarios is negative, and producers outside Latin America actually experience additional growth in exports due to a WHFTA.

27.6 percent in nominal terms, from a level of $78.4 billion to about $100 billion (Rutter 1991). In the continuing-reform scenario, we assume that investment inflows continue to grow at about the same rateabout $5 billion per year in real terms for the 12 years up to 2002. Hence, in 2002 the Latin American FDI stock would reach $160 billion (expressed in 1990 dollars).

In the WHFTA scenario, we assume that a hemispheric arrangement will help level the playing field between NAFTA members and Latin America with respect to competition for investment funds. As a result, between 1990 and 2002 we expect the ratio between Latin American and Mexican inward flows of FDI to maintain the 1985–90 ratio of 2-to-1. With NAFTA, FDI in Mexico is projected to grow at an average rate of $5 billion annually over the next decade; correspondingly, with WHFTA, we expect FDI flows to Latin America to increase to an average rate of $10 billion annually over the 12 years between 1990 and 2002. The stock of FDI in Latin America, which stood at about $100 billion in 1990, is thus expected to reach $220 billion by 2002 under a WHFTA scenario, or $60 billion more than the $160 billion level projected in the continuing-reform scenario (table D2).

In our calculations of investment diversion, we assume that approximately half of this extra investment comes at the expense of foreign investment elsewhere in the world, and the other half comes at the expense of investment within the domestic economies of the countries that provide the foreign investment destined for Latin America. We also assume that foreign direct investments in developing Asia are three times as likely to be diverted to Latin America as investments in developed nations. The reason for this assumption is that, because of process and product characteristics, the rate of investment substitution between Brazil and Indonesia, for example, is likely to be much higher than the rate between Brazil and Germany.

Half of the $60 billion additional FDI secured by Latin America under a WHFTA scenario is drawn from the four regions in proportion to each region's share of the world's stock of total investment inflows, multiplied by a factor reflecting the assumed rate of investment substitution between that region and Latin America.[5] Developing Asia, which accounts for about 7 percent of total worldwide FDI inflows, incurs a cumulative loss of nearly 21 percent (3 times 7 percent), or $6.2 billion of the $30 billion diverted by 2002. Industrialized Asia accounts for about 6 percent, or $1.8 billion, of the total $30 billion diverted. Western Europe accounts for $10.4 billion of the investment diverted. North America and

---

5. The calculations embody an adjustment such that the rate of substitution between larger FDI in Latin America and smaller FDI in regions outside developing Asia is reduced to accommodate the high rate of substitution assumed between FDI in Latin America and developing Asia.

Table D2 Investment diversion from third countries resulting from WHFTA (billions of dollars except where noted)

Destination region	In 1990 Investment	In 1990 Percent of world stock	Projected annual growth in FDI	Projected annual growth in FDI (percent)	Total investment in 2002	WHFTA scenario In 2002 Total investment	WHFTA scenario In 2002 Change vs. continuing reform	WHFTA scenario In 2002 Percent of projected 2002 levels	WHFTA scenario In 2002 Percent of diversion to Latin America	FDI-related export gains and losses
Latin America	100.0	8.2	5.0	5.0	160.0	220.0	60.0	37.5		30.0
Developing Asia[a]	90.0	7.4	9.0	10.0	198.0	191.8	−6.2	−3.1	10.4	−6.2
Japan, Australia, New Zealand	80.0	6.6	12.0	15.0	224.0	222.2	−1.8	−0.8	3.1	−1.8
Western Europe	450.0	36.9	65.0	14.4	1230.0	1219.6	−10.4	−0.8	17.3	−10.4
NAFTA and the rest of world	500.0	41.0	50.0	10.0	1100.0	1088.5	−11.5	−1.0	19.2	−11.5
World	1220.0	100.0	141.0	11.6	2912.0	2942.0	30.0	1.0	50.0	0.0

FDI = foreign direct investment
a. Includes all Asia and Pacific except Japan, Australia, and New Zealand.

the rest of the world account for the remaining $11.5 billion of the investment diverted (table D2).

To put these diversion figures in perspective, we construct a scenario of foreign investment trends over the period to 2002, in order to shed light on the damage estimates due to investment diversion on account of a WHFTA. In this scenario, we predict that investment flows to all regions will grow by 10 percent annually. (This is a lower FDI growth rate than experienced between 1985 and 1989; it reflects a less buoyant world economic outlook in the 1990s than the 1980s.) The WHFTA investment diversion calculations are then expressed as a percentage of projected investment levels in the year 2002. As table D2 shows, these percentages are all small.

The final column in table D2 attempts to calculate third-country exports diverted as a consequence of lost investment. If the investment diversion is as large as these crude estimates suggest, the related trade consequences could be greater than our earlier estimates of trade diversion would indicate. This can be illustrated as follows. In 1990, the stock of US nonbank FDI, at historic cost, was $404 billion, and merchandise exports from the host countries generated by these facilities amounted to $363 billion (*Survey of Current Business*, August 1992, 68).[6] These figures suggest an export-to-FDI ratio of about 90 percent.

As a conservative estimate, we assume that the export-to-FDI ratio for diverted investment is just 50 percent.[7] More speculatively, we also assume that the corresponding gain to Latin American exports on account of larger FDI ($30 billion) is entirely absorbed by lower exports suffered on the part of those that experience reduced FDI inflows.

These assumptions lead to FDI-related export losses by the year 2002 of $6.2 billion for developing Asia, $1.8 billion for industrialized Asia, $10.4 billion for Western Europe, and $11.5 billion for the NAFTA region and the rest of the world. In a worst-case scenario, these figures are additional to the trade diversion calculated in the previous section.

These estimates of investment diversion and FDI-related export gains and losses are subject to large errors. The flows of FDI to Latin America may not increase by $5.0 billion annually owing to a WHFTA initiative. If FDI flows to Latin America do surge, the extra amounts may be funded by new financial sources rather than drawing down plant and equipment investment that would otherwise have occurred within capital-exporting countries, or FDI that would otherwise have been placed else-

---

6. The figures refer only to majority-owned foreign affiliates of US parent firms. Of these exports, about 29 percent were shipped to the United States, and about 71 percent were shipped to other countries outside the host nations.

7. The reason we assume a figure lower than 90 percent is our supposition that WHFTA would attract a large amount of new investment intended to produce goods and services for the local market.

where in the global economy. Any FDI-related export losses in Western Europe and South and East Asia may be replaced by larger exports shipped by national suppliers. Nevertheless, these investment diversion estimates and their trade implications underscore the key reason that developing countries worry about NAFTA. The worries are all the more acute because competitive investment diversion does not violate existing or prospective international norms.

References

Antonio Barbosa, Rubens. 1992. "The Brazilian Perception on the Southern Common Market." Paper presented at the Workshop on the Mercosur Trade Agreement, Council on Foreign Relations, Washington (March).

Baer, M. Delal. 1991. *The 1991 Mexican Midterm Elections*. CSIS Latin American Election Study Series.

Balassa, Bela, Gerardo M. Bueno, Pedro-Pablo Kuczynski, and Mario Henrique Simonsen. 1986. *Toward Renewed Economic Growth in Latin America*. Washington: Institute for International Economics.

Bergsten, C. Fred. 1994. "Sunrise in Seattle." *International Economic Insights* (January/February): 18–20.

Birdsall, Nancy, and David Wheeler. 1992. "Trade Policy and Industrial Pollution in Latin America." In Patrick Low, *International Trade and the Environment*. World Bank Discussion Papers 159. Washington: World Bank.

Borjas, George J., Richard Freeman, and Lawrence F. Katz. 1991. "On the Labor Market Effects of Immigration & Trade." Harvard Institute of Economic Research, Discussion Paper No. 1556. Cambridge, MA: Harvard University (June).

Brown, Drusilla K., Alan V. Deardorff, David L. Hummels, and Robert M. Stern. 1993. *An Assessment of Extending NAFTA to Other Major Trading Countries in South America*. Ann Arbor, MI: Institute of Public Policy Studies, University of Michigan (December).

Butelman, Andrea, and Alicia Frohmann. 1992. *Hacia un Acuerdo de Libre Comercio entre Chile y Estados Unidos*, no. 3, February. Santiago: FLASCO and CIEPLAN.

Cariaga, Juan. 1990. "Bolivia." In John Williamson, *Latin American Adjustment: How Much Has Happened?* Washington: Institute for International Economics.

Caribbean Community. 1992. "Recent Political, Economic and Social Developments in Central America." Paper presented at the CARICOM/Central America Conference, 29–31 January.

Caribbean Policy Development Centre. 1992. *Latin American Regional Reports—Caribbean* (10 December).

Cline, William R. 1990. *The Future of World Trade in Textiles and Apparel*. Washington: Institute for International Economics.

Cline, William R. 1992. *The Economics of Global Warming*. Washington: Institute for International Economics.

Cline, William R. 1994. *International Debt Reexamined*. Washington: Institute for International Economics. Forthcoming.

Coes, Donald. 1991. "Brazilian Trade Policy and Regional Trade Initiatives." Paper presented to the International Center for Econmic Growth Conference, Panama (March).

Collins, Susan M., and Dani Rodrik. 1991. *Eastern Europe and the Soviet Union in the World Economy*. POLICY ANALYSES IN INTERNATIONAL ECONOMICS 32. Washington: Institute for International Economics.

Comisión Económica para América Latina y el Caribe (CEPAL). 1991. "La Evolución Reciente de los Procesos de Integración en América Latina y el Caribe" (April).

Comisión Económica para América Latina y el Caribe (CEPAL) 1992a. "Los Nuevos Projectos de Integración en América Latina y el Caribe y la Dinámica de la Inversión" (May).

Comisión Económica para América Latina y el Caribe (CEPAL). 1992b. "La Institucionalidad en el Grupo Andino" (June).

Comisión Económica para América Latina y el Caribe (CEPAL). 1992c. *Panorama Reciente de los Procesos de Integración en América Latina y el Caribe*. (September).

Competitiveness Policy Council. 1992. *First Annual Report to the President and the Congress: Building a Competitive America*. Washington: CPC (March).

Competitiveness Policy Council. 1993. *Second Annual Report to the President and the Congress: A Competitiveness Strategy for America*. Washington: CPC (March).

Diebold, Jr. William, 1988. "The New Bilateralism." In William Diebold, Jr., *Bilateralism, Multilateralism, and Canada in US Trade Policy*. Boston: Council on Foreign Relations.

Dobson, Wendy. 1991. *Economic Policy Coordination: Requiem or Prologue?* POLICY ANALYSES IN INTERNATIONAL ECONOMICS 30. Washington: Institute for International Economics.

Edwards, Alejandra Cox, and Sebastian Edwards. 1992. "Markets and Democracy: Lessons from Chile." *World Economy* 15, no. 2 (March): 205–06.

Erzan, Refik, and Alexander Yeats. 1992. "Free Trade Agreements with the United States: What's in It for Latin America?" World Bank Working Paper, Policy Research, International Trade, January.

First Boston. 1993. "Latin America Research—Latin America's Reforms: A Report Card." (30 August).

Fontaine, Roger. 1977. *The Andean Pact: A Political Analysis*. Washington: Center for Strategic and International Studies.

Frankel, Jeffrey A. 1991. "Is a Yen Bloc Forming in Pacific Asia?" In Richard O'Brien, *Finance and the International Economy: 5*. London: Oxford University Press for the Amex Bank Review.

Freedom House. 1990. *Freedom in the World: The Annual Survey of Political Rights and Civil Liberties 1989–1990*. New York: Freedom House.

Freedom House. 1992. *Freedom in the World: The Annual Survey of Political Rights and Civil Liberties 1991–92*. New York: Freedom House.

Freeman, R. B. 1987. "Labor Economics." In John Eatwell et al. *The New Palgrave Dictionary of Economics*, vol 3. New York: Stockton Press.

General Agreement on Tariffs and Trade (GATT). 1992a. *Argentina* vol. 1. Trade Policy Review. Geneva.

General Agreement on Tariffs and Trade (GATT). 1992b. "Trade and the Environment" (February).

General Agreement on Tariffs and Trade (GATT). 1992c. *Uruguay*, vol. 1. Trade Policy Review. Geneva.

General Agreement on Tariffs and Trade (GATT). 1993. *Bolivia*, vol. 1. Trade Policy Review. Geneva.

Gitli, Eduardo, and Gunilla Ryd. 1991. "Latin American Integration and the Enterprise for the Americas Initiative." UNCTAD, December.

Grant, Heather, and Gilbert Winham. 1994. "Antidumping and Countervailing Duties in Regional Trade Agreements: Canada-US FTA, NAFTA, and beyond." *Minnesota Journal of Global Trade* 3 (Spring): 1–34.

Grossman, Gene, and Alan Krueger. 1991. *Environmental Impacts of a North American Free Trade Agreement*." National Bureau of Economic Research Paper 3914, November; Also published in Peter Garber, editor, *The US-Mexico Free Trade Agreement*. Cambridge, MA: MIT Press 1993.

Haggard, Stephan. 1992. "Democracy and Economic Development: A Comparative Perspective." *Democratic Institutions* 1, 50. New York: Carnegie Council on Ethics and International Affairs.

Henning, C. Randall, Eduard Hochreiter, and Gary Clyde Hufbauer. 1994. *Reviving the European Union*. Washington: Institute for International Economics.

Hufbauer, Gary Clyde. 1990. *Europe 1992: An American Perspective*. Washington: Brookings Institution.

Hufbauer, Gary Clyde, and Howard F. Rosen. 1986. *Trade Policy for Troubled Industries*. POLICY ANALYSES IN INTERNATIONAL ECONOMICS 15. Washington: Institute for International Economics.

Hufbauer, Gary Clyde, and Jeffrey J. Schott. 1992. *North American Free Trade: Issues and Recommendations*. Washington: Institute for International Economics.

Hufbauer, Gary Clyde, and Jeffrey J. Schott. 1993a. *NAFTA: An Assessment, Revised edition*. Washington: Institute for International Economics.

Hufbauer, Gary Clyde, and Jeffrey J. Schott. 1993b. "Regionalism in North America." In Koichi Ohno, *Regional Integration and its Impact on Developing Countries*. Tokyo: Institute of Developing Economies.

Hufbauer, Gary Clyde, and Kimberly Ann Elliott. 1994. *Measuring the Costs of Protection in the United States*. Washington: Institute for International Economics.

Hufbauer, Gary Clyde, and Jeffrey J. Schott. 1994. "Western Hemisphere Economic Integration: Starting Point, Long-Term Goals, Readiness Indicators, Paths to Integration." Inter-American Development Bank. Forthcoming.

Human Rights Watch. 1991. *Human Rights Watch Report 1992*. New York: Human Rights Watch.

Iglesias, Enrique V. 1990. "From Policy Consensus to Renewed Economic Growth." In John Williamson, *Latin American Adjustment: How Much Has happened?* Washington: Institute for International Economics.

Iglesias, Enrique V. 1992. *Reflections on Economic Development: Toward a New Latin American Consensus*. Washington: Inter-American Development Bank.

Iglesias, Enrique V. 1994. "Economic Reform: A View from Latin America." In John Williamson, *The Political Economy of Policy Reform*. Washington: Institute for International Economics.

Industry Functional Advisory Committee for Trade in Intellectual Property Rights. 1992. "Report of the Industry Functional Advisory Committee for Trade in Intellectual Property Rights (IFAC-3) on the North American Free Trade Agreement." (September).

The Institute of International Finance. 1990. "Fostering Foreign Direct Investment in Latin America." Institute Report (July).

Inter-American Development Bank. 1984. *Annual Report*. Washington.

Inter-American Development Bank. 1992. *Economic and Social Progress in Latin America 1992 Report*. Washington.

Jackson, John. 1993. "Regional Blocs and the GATT." *World Economy* 16, no. 2 (March): 121–31.

Joint Economic Committee, US Congress. 1993. *The Caribbean Basin: Economic and Security Issues*. Washington: Congress of the United States (January).

Jovanović, Miroslav N. 1992. *International Economic Integration*. London: Routledge.

Karatnycky, Adrian, and Joseph E. Ryan. 1994. "Freedom in Retreat." *Freedom Review* 25, no. 1 (January/February): 4–21. New York: Freedom House.

Kissinger, Henry. 1992. "The Bush Initiative That Could Create a New World Order—If He Would Push It." *Los Angeles Times*, 10 May 1992, p. M2.

Kline, John. 1992. *Foreign Investment Strategies in Restructuring Economies: Learning from Corporate Experiences in Chile*. New York: Quorum Books.

Kreinin, Max, and Michael Plummer. 1992. "Effects of Economic Integration on ASEAN and the Asian NIEs." *World Development* 20(9): 1345–1366.

Kryzanek, Michael. 1990. *US-Latin American Relations*. 2nd ed. New York: Praeger.

Laird, Sam. 1994. "Recent Liberalization of Latin American Trade." Unpublished paper. Trade Policy Review Division, GATT Secretariat.

Lea, Sperry. 1987. "A Historical Perspective." In Robert M. Stern, Philip H. Trezise, and John Whalley, *Perspectives on a US-Canadian Free Trade Agreement*. Washington: The Brookings Institution.

Leyton-Brown, David. 1985. *Weathering the Storm: Canadian-U.S. Relations, 1980–83*. Toronto: Canadian-American Committee.

Low, Patrick, and Alexander Yeats. 1992. "Do 'Dirty' Industries Migrate?" In Patrick Low, *International Trade and the Environment*. World Bank Discussion Papers 159. Washington: World Bank.

Magill, Robert T. 1992. "Andean Trade Preference Act: A Step in the Right Direction?" *Law and Policy in International Business* 23, no. 4 (summer): 987–1007.

Martin, Philip. 1993. *Trade and Migration: NAFTA and Agriculture*. POLICY ANALYSES IN INTERNATIONAL ECONOMICS 38. Washington: Institute for International Economics.

McMillan, John. 1993. "Does Regional Integration Foster Open Trade? Economic Theory and GATT's Article XXIV." In Kym Anderson and Richard Blackhurst, *Regional Integration and the Global Trading System*. New York: St. Martin Press.

Michaely, Michael, Demetris Papageorgiou, and Armeane M. Choksi. 1991. *Liberalizing Foreign Trade: Lessons of Experience in the Developing World*. Oxford: Basil Blackwell.

Molineu, Harold. 1990. *US-Policy Towards Latin America: from Regionalism to Globalism*. 2nd ed. Boulder, CO: Westview Press.

Noland, Marcus. 1993. "Asia and the NAFTA." Paper presented at the Asia Society's conference on Korea and East Asia: Trade Relations and Investment in the Pacific Rim, held in Hong Kong, 22–24 February.

North-South Center, Universty of Miami. 1992. "North—South Focus: El Salvador." Miami: University of Miami, North—South Center (March).

Organization for Economic Cooperation and Development. OECD, *Financing and External Debt of Developing Countries*, 1992.

Overseas Development Council and World Wildlife Fund, *Environmental Challenges to International Trade Policy*, Conference Report, February 1991.

Parizeau, Jacques. 1987. "Specific Objectives and Practical Solutions." In Edward R. Fired, Frank Stone, and Phillip Trezise, *Building a Canadian—American Free Trade Area*. Washington: The Brookings Institution.

Park, Yung Chul, and Jung Ho Yoo. 1989. "More Free Trade Areas: A Korean Perspective." In Jeffrey J. Schott, *Free Trade Areas and U.S. Trade Policy*. Washington: Institute for International Economics.

Pascó-Font, Alberto 1992. "US-Andean Pact Free Trade." In Sylvia Saborio, *The Premise and the Promise: Free Trade in the Americas*. Washington: Overseas Development Council.

Perelli, Carina, and Juan Rial. 1992. "MERCOSUR: Regional Integration's Dilemmas and Alternatives." Washington: Council on Foreign Relations (March).

Perot, Ross, and Pat Choate. 1993. *Save Your Job Save Your Country: Why NAFTA Must Be Stopped Now!* New York: Hyperion.

Preeg, Ernest H. 1993. *Cuba and the New Caribbean Economic Order*, Washington: Center for Strategic and International Studies.

Price, Margaret. 1994. *Emerging Stock Markets*. New York: McGraw-Hill.

Radetzki, Marian 1992. "Economic Growth and Environment." In Patrick Low, *International Trade and the Environment*. World Bank Discussion Papers 159. Washington: World Bank.

Rainford, Roderick. 1991. "Review of the Achievements and Shortcomings of CARICOM." Paper presented for the West Indian Commission, November.

Ramírez, Noel. 1991. "Nicaragua: una década de política económica revolucionaria." In Noel Ramírez, *Economía y Populismo: Ilusión y Realidad en América Latina*. Quito: Instituto Centroamerico de Administración de Empresas.

Reynolds, Clark, Francisco Thoumi, and Reinhart Wettmann. 1993. *A Case for Open Regionalism in the Andes*. Report prepared for the US Agency for International Development (October).

Richardson, Martin. 1993. "Endogenous Protection and Trade Diversion." *Journal of International Economics* 34 (May): 309–24.

Rodrik, Dani. 1992. *The Rush to Free Trade in the Developing World: Why So Late? Why Now? Will It Last?* National Bureau for Economic Research Working Paper no. 3947, Cambridge, MA: NBER (January).

Rosenthal, Gert. 1992. "Mercados Communes, Zonas de Libre Comercio, y Competitividad en las Américas." Paper presented at a seminar at the Argentine Council on Foreign Relations, July 1992.

Rutter, John. 1991. "Trends in International Direct Investment." TIA staff paper no. 91-5, US Department of Commerce (July).

Rutter, John. 1993. "Recent Trends in International Direct Investment: the Boom Years Fade." US Department of Commerce, International Trade Administration, Office of Trade and Economic Analysis (August).

Saborio, Sylvia. 1992. "Central America and the EAI." Paper presented at the ODC conference "US/Central America Free Trade." In Saborio, *The Premise and the Promise: Free Trade in the Americas*. New Brunswick and Oxford (UK): Transaction Publishers.

Safadi, Raed, and Alexander Yeats. 1993. *The North American Free Trade Agreement: Its Effect on South Asia*. World Bank Working Paper 1119, March.

Salomon Brothers. 1992. "Privatization: A Latin American Success Story." Sovereign Assessment Group: Emerging Markets report (1 April).

Schoenbaum, Thomas. 1992. "Agora: Trade and Environment." *The American Journal of International Law* 86: 700–28.

Schott, Jeffrey J. 1988. "The Free Trade Agreement: A US Assessment." In Jeffrey J. Schott and Murray G. Smith, *The Canada-United States Free Trade Agreement: The Global Impact*. Washington: Institute for International Economics.

Schott, Jeffrey J. 1989. *More Free Trade Areas?* POLICY ANALYSES IN INTERNATIONAL ECONOMICS 27. Washington: Institute for International Economics (May).

Schott, Jeffrey J., and Murray G. Smith. 1988. "Services and Investment." In Jeffrey J. Schott and Murray G. Smith, *The Canada-United States Free Trade Agreement: The Global Impact*. Washington: Institute for International Economics.

Schumpeter, Joseph A. 1942. *Capitalism, Socialism and Democracy*. New York: Harper.

Sewell, John, Peter M. Storm, and contributors. 1992. *Challenges and Priorities in the 1990s: An Alternative U.S. International Affairs Budget*. ODC Paper Series. Washington: Overseas Development Council.

Shafik, Nemat, and Sushenjit Bandyopadhyay. 1992. "Economic Growth and Environmental Quality: Time Series and Cross-country Evidence." In World Bank, *World Development Report 1992*.

Smith, Murray, G. 1987. "A Canadian Perspective." In Robert M. Stern, Philip H. Trezise, and John Whalley, *Perspectives on a US-Canadian Free Trade Agreement*. Washington: The Brookings Institution.

Stephenson, Sherry M. 1994. "ASEAN and the Multilateral Trading System." *Law and Policy in International Business*.

Stiglitz, Joseph. 1988. *Economics of the Public Sector*. 2nd ed. New York: W. W. Norton.

Summers, Robert, and Alan Heston. 1991. "The Penn World Table (Mark 5): An Expanded Set of International Comparisons, 1950–1988." *Quarterly Journal of Economics* (May).

Tavares de Araujo, Jr., José. 1991. "MERCOSUR, The Bush Initiative, and the International Competitiveness of Brazilian Industry." Rio de Janeiro: Universidade Federal do Rio de Janeiro, Instituto de Economía (October).

Ulloa, Fernando Cepeda, Gerhard Drekonja-Kornat, Mario Ojeda, Nina Maria Serafino, and Rodrigo Pardo Garcia-Peña. 1985. *Contadora: Desafío a la Diplomacia Tradicional*. Bogotá: Editorial Oveja Negra.

Urrutia, Miguel. 1994. "Colombia." In John Williamson, *The Political Economy of Policy Reform*. Washington: Institute for International Economics.

US Department of Commerce. 1992. *Guidebook to the Andean Trade Preference Act* (July).

US Department of Commerce. 1993. "Enterprise for the Americas Fact Sheet." 15 January 1993.

US Department of Labor 1993. "Minimum Wages Around the World." Bureau of Labor Statistics (May).

US Department of State. 1993. *Country Reports on Human Rights Practices* (February).

US General Accounting Office (GAO) 1992. "Chilean Trade: Factors Affecting US Trade and Investment." Washington: GAO (June).

US International Trade Commission (USITC) 1992. *U.S. Market Access in Latin America: Recent Liberalization Measures and Remaining Barriers*. Washington: USITC (June).

US Trade Representative (USTR). 1992. *1992 National Trade Estimate Report on Foreign Trade Barriers*. Washington: Government Printing Office.

US Trade Representative (USTR). 1993. *National Trade Estimate Report on Foreign Trade Barriers*. Washington: Government Printing Office.

Vernon, Raymond. 1963. *The Dilemma of Mexico's Development*. Cambridge, MA: Harvard University Press.

Vernon, Raymond. 1971. *Sovereignty at Bay*. New York: Basic Books.

Weintraub, Sidney. 1990. *A Marriage of Convenience: Relations between Mexico and the United States*. Oxford University Press.

Wengel, Jan ter. 1980. *Allocation of Industry in the Andean Common Market*. Boston: M. Nijhoff Pub.

White House. 1991. "Fact Sheet: Advancing the Enterprise for the Americas Initiative," 27 June.

Williamson, John, ed. 1990. *Latin American Adjustment: How Much Has Happened?* Washington: Institute for International Economics.

Williamson, John, ed. 1994. *The Political Economy of Policy Reform*. Washington: Institute for International Economics.

Winham, Gilbert. 1988a. *Trading with Canada: The Canada-US Free Trade Agreement*. New York: Priority Press Publications—Twentieth Century Fund.

Winham, Gilbert. 1988b. "Why Canada Acted." In William Diebold, Jr., *Bilateralism, Multilateralism and Canada in US Trade Policy*. Boston: Council on Foreign Relations.

Wonnacott, Paul. 1987. *The United States and Canada: The Quest for Free Trade*, POLICY ANALYSES IN INTERNATIONAL ECONOMICS 15. Washington: Institute for International Economics.

Wonnacott, Ronald J. 1991. *The Economics of Overlapping Free Trade Areas and the Mexican Challenge*. Toronto and Washington: C.D. Howe Institute and the National Planning Association.

World Resources Institute, 1992. *World Resources 1992–93*.

Worrell, DeLisle. 1990. "The Caribbean." In John Williamson, *Latin American Adjustment: How Much Has Happened?* Washington: Institute for International Economics.

Index

Act of Caracas, 9
Act of La Paz, 9, 113
Africa
    foreign direct investment in, 43–47, 44t
    merchandise trade, 28–31, 29t, 31t
    strong-neighbor indexes, 30, 32t, 43, 46t
AFTA. *See* ASEAN Free Trade Area
Agriculture, 139–40
Andean Commission, 7
Andean Council, 8
Andean Development Corporation, 7
Andean Group, 4n, 9, 10, 65, 113–20. *See also*
        specific countries
    domestic investment, 54–55, 55t
    economic integration achievement scores, 6n
    foreign direct investment, 43–47, 44t, 58
    good-customer indexes, 34–35, 38t–39t
    income diversity index, 48–49, 49t
    readiness assessment, 181
    readiness scores, 102t, 115, 118
    regional agreements, 231–37
    strong-neighbor indexes, 34–35, 40t–41t, 43,
        46t
    supraregional institutions, 7–8
    trade deficiency, 26, 186–90, 188t
    trade expansion, 191–97, 195t
    trade values, 34–35, 36t–37t
Andean Junta, 7
Andean Parliament, 7–8
Andean Trade Preference Act (ATPA), 119,
        119n, 141n, 158
APEC. *See* Asia Pacific Economic Cooperation
Argentina, 107–08
    budget deficits, 74, 75, 83t
    consumer prices, 73, 80t
    domestic investment, 54–55, 55t
    emissions performances, 150, 151t
    exchange rates, 75–76, 92t, 93t
    external debt, 16, 19, 75, 88t
    foreign direct investment, 55–57, 56t, 58, 58n

good-customer indexes, 34–35, 38t–39t
interest payments, 75, 91t
readiness assessment, 181
readiness scores, 102t, 107–08
stock exchange cooperation agreements, 59
strong-neighbor indexes, 34–35, 40t–41t
tariffs, 134–35, 136t
trade deficiency, 186–90, 188t
trade expansion, 191–97, 194t
trade taxes, 77, 95t
trade values, 34–35, 36t–37t
US trade barriers, 140–41, 142t
wages, 154–57, 155t, 156t
ASEAN. *See* Association of Southeast Asian
        Nations
ASEAN Free Trade Area (AFTA), 169
Asia. *See also specific regions*
    links with Western Hemisphere, 182–83
    trade deficiency, 186–90, 187t
    trade expansion, 191–97, 194t
    WHFTA concerns, 169–70
Asia Pacific Economic Cooperation (APEC), 22,
        22n, 169–70, 182, 182n
Association of Southeast Asian Nations
        (ASEAN)
    income diversity index, 48–49, 49t
    trade deficiency, 186–90, 187t
    trade expansion, 191–97, 194t
ATPA. *See* Andean Trade Preference Act
Australia. *See also* Australia, New Zealand, and
        South Africa; Japan, Australia, New
        Zealand
    trade deficiency, 186–90, 187t
    trade expansion, 191–97, 194t
Australia, New Zealand, and South Africa
    foreign direct investment in, 43–47, 44t, 45t
    strong-neighbor indexes, 43, 46t
Australia-New Zealand Closer Economic
        Relations, 4n
    income diversity index, 48–49, 49t

trade deficiency, 186–90, 187*t*
trade expansion, 191–97, 194*t*

Bahamas, 126
  budget deficits, 74, 75, 84*t*
  consumer prices, 73, 81*t*
  exchange rates, 75–76, 92*t*, 94*t*
  good-customer indexes, 34–35, 38*t*–39*t*
  readiness scores, 102*t*, 126
  strong-neighbor indexes, 34–35, 40*t*–41*t*
  trade deficiency, 186–90, 188*t*
  trade expansion, 191–97, 195*t*
  trade taxes, 77, 96*t*
  trade values, 34–35, 36*t*–37*t*
Balassa, Bela, 64
Bamako Convention, 152
Bandyopadhyay, Sushenjit, 147*n*
Bank Act, 98
Bank of Canada, 10
Barbados, 126
  budget deficits, 74, 75, 84*t*
  consumer prices, 73, 81*t*
  domestic investment, 54–55, 55*t*
  exchange rates, 75–76, 92*t*
  external debt, 75, 89*t*
  good-customer indexes, 34–35, 38*t*–39*t*
  readiness assessment, 180
  readiness scores, 102*t*, 126
  strong-neighbor indexes, 34–35, 40*t*–41*t*
  trade deficiency, 186–90, 188*t*
  trade expansion, 191–97, 195*t*
  trade taxes, 77, 96*t*
  trade values, 34–35, 36*t*–37*t*
Basel Convention on the Control of
  Transboundary Movements of Hazardous
  Wastes and Their Disposal, 152
Benelux Union, 11
Bergsten, C. Fred, 170
Big bang model, 131–32
Birdsall, Nancy, 148
Bolivia, 115*n*, 116–17
  budget deficits, 74, 75, 83*t*
  consumer prices, 73, 80*t*
  current account balances, 74, 85*t*–87*t*
  domestic investment, 54–55, 55*t*
  emissions performances, 150, 151*t*
  exchange rates, 75–76, 92*t*, 93*t*
  external debt, 19, 75, 88*t*
  foreign direct investment, 58
  good-customer indexes, 34–35, 38*t*–39*t*
  interest payments, 75, 91*t*
  readiness assessment, 181
  readiness scores, 102*t*, 115
  secondary loan prices, 75, 90*t*
  strong-neighbor indexes, 34–35, 40*t*–41*t*
  tariffs, 134–35, 136*t*
  trade deficiency, 186–90, 188*t*
  trade expansion, 191–97, 195*t*
  trade taxes, 77, 95*t*
  trade values, 34–35, 36*t*–37*t*

US trade barriers, 140–41, 142*t*
Bracero Program, 100
Brady Plan, 16, 16*n*
Brazil, 108–11, 115*n*
  budget deficits, 74, 75, 83*t*
  consumer prices, 73, 80*t*
  current account balances, 74, 85*t*–87*t*
  domestic investment, 54–55, 55*t*
  emissions performances, 150, 151*t*
  exchange rates, 75–76, 92*t*, 93*t*
  external debt, 75, 88*t*
  foreign direct investment, 55–57, 56*t*, 59
  good-customer indexes, 34–35, 38*t*–39*t*
  interest payments, 75, 91*t*
  portfolio investment, 55–57, 56*t*
  readiness scores, 102*t*, 108–9, 111
  secondary loan prices, 75, 90*t*
  strong-neighbor indexes, 34–35, 40*t*–41*t*
  tariffs, 20, 134–35, 136*t*
  trade deficiency, 186–90, 188*t*
  trade expansion, 191–97, 194*t*
  trade taxes, 77, 95*t*
  trade values, 34–35, 36*t*–37*t*
  US trade barriers, 140–41, 142*t*
  wages, 154–57, 155*t*, 156*t*
Brown, Drusilla K., 52*n*
Budget discipline, 73–75
  readiness scores, 83*t*–84*t*, 102*t*
Bush, George, 1

CACC. *See* Central American Compensation
  Chamber
CACM. *See* Central American Common Market
Canada, 100–01
  budget deficits, 74, 83*t*
  consumer prices, 73, 80*t*
  domestic investment, 54–55, 55*t*
  emissions performances, 150, 151*t*
  external debt, 75, 88*t*
  foreign direct investment, 43–47, 44*t*, 45*t*
  good-customer indexes, 34–35, 38*t*–39*t*
  readiness scores, 101, 102*t*
  strong-neighbor indexes, 34–35, 40*t*–41*t*, 43,
    46*t*
  trade deficiency, 186*t*, 186–90
  trade expansion, 191–97, 193*t*
  trade taxes, 77, 95*t*
  trade values, 34–35, 36*t*–37*t*
Canada-US FTA, 4*n*, 7, 99, 100
Canada-US Trade Commission, 99
CAP. *See* Common Agricultural Policy
Cariaga, Joan, 58
Caribbean Basin Initiative (CBI), 127–28, 181
Caribbean Community (Caricom), 4*n*, 9, 10–11,
  124–27
  consumer prices, 73, 81*t*
  domestic investment, 54–55, 55*t*
  economic integration achievement scores, 6*n*
  good-customer indexes, 34–35, 38*t*–39*t*
  income diversity index, 48–49, 49*t*

readiness assessment, 181–82
readiness scores, 102t, 127
regional agreements, 241–46
strong-neighbor indexes, 34–35, 40t–41t
supraregional institutions, 8
trade deficiency, 186–90, 188t
trade expansion, 27, 191–97, 195t
trade taxes, 77, 96t
trade values, 34–35, 36t–37t
Caribbean Development Bank, 8
Caribbean Environmental Health Institute, 8
Caribbean Examinations Council (CXC), 9
Caribbean Meteorological Organization, 8
Caribbean Policy Development Centre, 8n
Caribbean Regional Drug Testing Laboratory, 8
Caricom. *See* Caribbean Community
Caricom Commission, 8, 8n
CBI. *See* Caribbean Basin Initiative
Central America, public and private financing,
 67n, 67–69, 68t
Central American Bank for Economic
 Integration, 8
Central American Common Market (CACM),
 4n, 9, 10, 63, 120–24. *See also specific*
 countries
 domestic investment, 54–55, 55t
 economic integration achievement scores, 6n
 good-customer indexes, 34–35, 38t–39t
 income diversity index, 48–49, 49t
 readiness scores, 102t, 121, 124
 regional agreements, 238–41
 strong-neighbor indexes, 34–35, 40t–41t
 supraregional institutions, 8
 trade deficiency, 26, 186–90, 188t
 trade expansion, 191–97, 195t
 trade taxes, 77, 96t
 trade values, 34–35, 36t–37t
Central American Compensation Chamber
 (CACC), 8, 10
Central American Monetary Union, 8
Central American Stabilization Fund, 8
CEPAL. *See* Comisión Económica para América
 Latina y el Caribe
CET. *See* Common external tariff
Chile, 4n, 78, 103–06, 115n
 budget deficits, 74, 75, 83t
 consumer prices, 73, 80t
 current account balances, 74, 85t–87t
 domestic investment, 54–55, 55t
 emissions performances, 150, 151t
 exchange rates, 75–76, 92t, 93b
 external debt, 19, 75, 88t
 foreign direct investment, 55–57, 56t, 58
 good-customer indexes, 34–35, 38t–39t
 interest payments, 75, 91t
 portfolio investment, 55–57, 56t
 readiness assessment, 180
 readiness scores, 102t, 105–6
 regional agreements, 224–26
 secondary loan prices, 75, 90t

strong-neighbor indexes, 34–35, 40t–41t
tariffs, 20, 134–35, 136t
trade deficiency, 186–90, 188t
trade expansion, 27, 191–97, 194t
trade taxes, 77, 95t
trade values, 34–35, 36t–37t
US trade barriers, 140–41, 142t
wages, 154–57, 156t
China. *See* China and centrally planned Asia;
 East Asia
China and centrally planned Asia
 foreign direct investment in, 43–47, 44t, 45t
 strong-neighbor indexes, 43, 46t
Choate, Pat, 153
Choksi, Armeane M., 11, 12, 57, 72n, 78
Christopher, Warren, 22
CLC. *See* Commission on Labor Cooperation
Cline, William, 15n, 75, 116, 118n, 138
Clinton, Bill, 2–3, 22, 176, 182
Clinton administration, 22, 105, 157, 173
Collins, Susan M., 185
Colombia, 4n, 19, 78, 115n, 116
 budget deficits, 74, 75, 83t
 consumer prices, 73, 80t
 current account balances, 74, 85t–87t
 debt cooperativeness rating, 116n
 domestic investment, 54–55, 55t
 emissions performances, 150, 151t
 exchange rates, 75–76, 92t, 93t
 foreign direct investment, 55–57, 56t, 58, 59
 good-customer indexes, 34–35, 38t–39t
 interest payments, 75, 91t
 portfolio investment, 55–57, 56t
 readiness assessment, 181
 readiness scores, 102t, 115, 116
 strong-neighbor indexes, 34–35, 40t–41t
 tariffs, 20, 134–35, 136t
 trade deficiency, 186–90, 188t
 trade expansion, 191–97, 195t
 trade taxes, 77, 95t
 trade values, 34–35, 36t–37t
 US trade barriers, 140–41, 142t
 wages, 154–57, 155t, 156t
Comisión Económica para América Latina y el
 Caribe (CEPAL), 8, 10, 71n
Commission on Environmental Cooperation,
 149
Commission on Labor Cooperation (CLC),
 153–54
Common Agricultural Policy (CAP), 67n
Common external tariff (CET), 106–07, 120
Common Market Council, 106
Common Market Group, 10, 106
Competitiveness Policy Council, 153
Conservation, 151–52
Consumer prices, 73, 80t–81t
Costa Rica, 4n, 122–23
 budget deficits, 74, 75, 83t
 consumer prices, 73, 80t
 current account balances, 74, 85t–87t

domestic investment, 54–55, 55t
emissions performances, 150, 151t
exchange rates, 75–76, 92t, 94t
external debt, 75, 89t
foreign direct investment, 60
good-customer indexes, 34–35, 38t–39t
interest payments, 75, 91t
readiness scores, 102t, 122
secondary loan prices, 75, 90t
strong-neighbor indexes, 34–35, 40t–41t
trade deficiency, 186–90, 188t
trade expansion, 191–97, 195t
trade taxes, 77, 96t
trade values, 34–35, 36t–37t
wages, 154–57, 155t, 156t
Cuba, 4n, 128–29
Cuban Democracy Act, 129
Currency stability, 75–76
readiness scores, 93t–94t, 102t
CXC. See Caribbean Examinations Council

Debt
external, 75, 88t–89t, 102, 102t
Latin American, 16–17
Debt cooperativeness, 101n, 116n, 118n
Defense Production Sharing Agreement, 98
Deforestation, 150–51
Democracy, functioning, 77–79, 102t
Developing Asia, 28n
good-customer indexes, 30–34, 33t
merchandise trade, 28–31, 29t, 31t
strong-neighbor indexes, 30–34, 32t, 33t
Direct investment. See Foreign direct
investment
Dominican Republic
budget deficits, 74, 75, 84t
consumer prices, 73, 81t
current account balances, 74, 85t–87t
emissions performances, 150, 151t
exchange rates, 75–76, 92t, 94t
external debt, 75, 89t
trade deficiency, 186–90, 188t
trade expansion, 191–97, 195t
trade taxes, 77, 96t
Drugs, 119, 119n, 157–58

EAI. See Enterprise for the Americas Initiative
East Asia
income diversity index, 48–49, 49t
trade deficiency, 186–90, 187t
trade expansion, 191–97, 194t
East Asian Economic Caucus (EAEC), 169
Eastern Caribbean dollar, 10
Economic Charter of the Americas, 99
Economic integration. See also readiness
assessment; specific free trade agreements
achievement scores, 5, 6t
big bang model, 131–32
elements of, 3–11
hub-and-spoke model, 132–34

issues, 134–42, 143–46, 146–58
Mexico-Canada, 100–101
paths to, 131–34
readiness for, 12–13
regional, 27–47
sequencing, 11–13
subregional, 97–129
US-Canada, 99
US-Latin American, 15–23
US-Mexico, 100
Economic neighborliness, 27–28
Ecuador
budget deficits, 74, 75, 83t
consumer prices, 73, 80t
current account balances, 74, 85t–87t
domestic investment, 54–55, 55t
emissions performances, 150, 151t
exchange rates, 75–76, 92t, 93t
external debt, 75, 88t
foreign direct investment, 58, 58n
good-customer indexes, 34–35, 38t–39t
interest payments, 75, 91t
readiness scores, 115, 117
secondary loan prices, 75, 90t
strong-neighbor indexes, 34–35, 40t–41t
tariffs, 134–35, 136t
trade deficiency, 186–90, 188t
trade expansion, 191–97, 195t
trade taxes, 77, 95t
trade values, 34–35, 36t–37t
US trade barriers, 140–41, 142t
Edwards, Alejandra Cos, 104
Edwards, Sebastian, 104
EEC. See European Economic Community
EFTA. See European Free Trade Association
Elliott, Kimberly Ann, 135n
El Salvador, 4n, 121–22
budget deficits, 74, 75, 83t
consumer prices, 73, 80t
current account balances, 74, 85t–87t
domestic investment, 54–55, 55t
emissions performances, 150, 151t
exchange rates, 75–76, 92t, 94t
external debt, 19, 75, 89t
good-customer indexes, 34–35, 38t–39t
readiness scores, 102t, 121
strong-neighbor indexes, 34–35, 40t–41t
trade deficiency, 186–90, 188t
trade expansion, 191–97, 195t
trade taxes, 77, 96t
trade values, 34–35, 36t–37t
Emissions, 150, 151t
Enterprise for the Americas Initiative (EAI), 1,
2–3, 173
chronology, 246–49
concerns, 15
debt reduction, 19
Environmental Fund, 105
Environment
Latin American issues, 149–53

NAFTA lessons, 147–49
standards, 22
Erzan, Refik, 20*n*
EU. *See* European Union
Europe. *See also* Western Europe
  WHFTA concerns, 169–70
European Coal and Steel Community, 11
European Community (EC), 12, 67*n*
European Economic Community (EEC), 2, 11–12
European Free Trade Association (EFTA), 2, 133
  foreign direct investment in, 43–47, 44*t*, 45*t*
  income diversity index, 48–49, 49*t*
  strong-neighbor indexes, 43, 46*t*
  trade deficiency, 186*t*, 186–90
  trade expansion, 191–97, 193*t*
European Monetary System, 12
European Payments Union, 11
European Union (EU), 12
  economic integration achievement scores,
    5–6, 6*t*
  foreign direct investment in, 43–47, 44*t*, 45*t*
  income diversity index, 48–49, 49*t*
  strong-neighbor indexes, 43, 46*t*
  trade deficiency, 186*t*, 186–90
Exchange Rate Mechanism and Economic and
    Monetary Union, 2
Exchange rates, 75–76, 92*t*, 93*t*–94*t*
Exchange rate stability, 75–76
  readiness scores, 93*t*–94*t*, 102*t*
Exports, US, 60, 197–204, 198*t*–203*t*
External debt, 75, 102
  readiness scores, 88*t*–89*t*, 102*t*

Financing
  interest payments, 75, 91*t*
  public and private, 67*n*, 67–69, 68*t*
  secondary loan prices, 75, 90*t*
FIRA. *See* Foreign Investment Review Agency
First Boston, 76
Fiscal coordination, 10–11
Fontaine, Roger, 65
Foreign direct investment, 42, 43–47. *See also*
    Investment diversion
  bilateral treaties, 58, 58*n*
  historical cost basis, 43, 44*t*
  inflows for Latin American countries, 55–57,
    56*t*
  Latin American regulations, 57–60
  regional ties, 42–47
  stock exchange cooperation agreements, 59
  stock shares, 43, 45*t*
  strong-neighbor indexes, 43, 46*t*
Foreign Investment Review Agency (FIRA), 98
Framework of Principles and Procedures for
    Consultation Regarding Trade and
    Investment Relations, 100
Frankel, Jeffrey A., 169
Freeman, R. B., 218
Free trade agreements (FTAs), 3, 4, 4*n*, 159–60.
    See also specific agreements

Free Trade Commission, 7
FTAs. *See* free trade agreements
Functioning democracy, 77–79
  readiness scores, 102*t*

General Agreement on Tariffs and Trade
    (GATT), 99, 99*n*, 113*n*, 133–34, 134*n*, 151
  assessment of, 161–62
  trade diversion surveillance, 166–69
  trade policy review mechanism (TPRM), 162
General Agreement on Trade in Services
    (GATS), 99*n*
Gitli, Eduardo, 113
Good-customer indexes, 30, 175*n*
  for foreign direct investment, 43
  for trade, 30–34, 33*t*, 34–35, 38*t*–39*t*
Good customers, 21, 30, 31*t*, 175
Gore, Al, 22*n*
Grant, Heather, 141
Grossman, Gene, 147, 147*n*
Group of Ten, 10
Guarini, Frank, 141*n*
Guatemala, 4*n*, 123
  budget deficits, 74, 75, 83*t*
  consumer prices, 73, 80*t*
  current account balances, 74, 85*t*–87*t*
  domestic investment, 54–55, 55*t*
  emissions performances, 150, 151*t*
  exchange rates, 75–76, 92*t*, 94*t*
  external debt, 75, 89*t*
  good-customer indexes, 34–35, 38*t*–39*t*
  readiness scores, 102*t*, 123
  strong-neighbor indexes, 34–35, 40*t*–41*t*
  trade deficiency, 186–90, 188*t*
  trade expansion, 191–97, 195*t*
  trade taxes, 77, 96*t*
  trade values, 34–35, 36*t*–37*t*
Guyana, 126–27
  budget deficits, 74, 75, 84*t*
  consumer prices, 73, 81*t*
  domestic investment, 54–55, 55*t*
  exchange rates, 75–76, 92*t*, 94*t*
  external debt, 75, 89*t*
  good-customer indexes, 34–35, 38*t*–39*t*
  readiness assessment, 181
  readiness scores, 102*t*, 126
  strong-neighbor indexes, 34–35, 40*t*–41*t*
  trade deficiency, 186–90, 188*t*
  trade expansion, 191–97, 195*t*
  trade taxes, 77, 96*t*
  trade values, 34–35, 36*t*–37*t*

Haggard, Stephan, 79
Haiti
  budget deficits, 74, 75, 84*t*
  consumer prices, 73, 81*t*
  current account balances, 74, 85*t*–87*t*
  emissions performances, 150, 151*t*
  exchange rates, 75–76, 92*t*, 94*t*
  external debt, 75, 89*t*

trade deficiency, 186–90, 188*t*
trade expansion, 191–97, 195*t*
trade taxes, 77, 96*t*
Han Sung-Joo, 183
Henning, C. Randall, 2
Hills, Carla, 143
Hochreiter, Eduard, 2
Honduras, 4*n*, 123
  budget deficits, 74, 75, 83*t*
  consumer prices, 73, 80*t*
  current account balances, 74, 85*t*–87*t*
  domestic investment, 54–55, 55*t*
  emissions performances, 150, 151*t*
  exchange rates, 75–76, 92*t*, 94*t*
  external debt, 75, 89*t*
  good-customer indexes, 34–35, 38*t*–39*t*
  readiness scores, 102*t*, 123
  secondary loan prices, 75, 90*t*
  strong-neighbor indexes, 34–35, 40*t*–41*t*
  trade taxes, 77, 96*t*
  trade values, 34–35, 36*t*–37*t*
Hub-and-spoke model, 132–34
Hufbauer, Gary Clyde, 2, 73*n*, 74*n*, 100, 101,
  135*n*, 139, 141, 145, 146, 148, 153, 166,
  176*n*, 178*n*, 204, 205
Human rights, 22, 157
Human Rights Watch, 157

IDB. *See* Inter-American Development Bank
Iglesias, Enrique, 65, 66
Immigration Reform and Control Act, 100
Imports, US, 60, 204–5, 206*t*–211*t*
Import tariffs, 20, 134–35, 136*t*–137*t*
Income diversity indexes, 48–49, 49*t*
Industry Functional Advisory Committee for
  Trade in Intellectual Property Rights, 105*n*
Institute of International Finance, 58
Intellectual property rights (IPRs), 143–45
Inter-American Development Bank (IDB), 4*n*,
  67, 71*n*
Interest Equalization Tax, 10
Interest payments, 75, 91*t*
International Intellectual Property Rights
  Alliance, 110, 144
International Monetary Fund, 169*n*
International trade taxes, 77, 95*t*–96*t*
Investment, 145. *See also* Foreign direct
  investment; Portfolio investment
  Latin American prospects, 53–54
Investment Canada, 99
Investment diversion, 164–66, 175, 176
  calculations, 257–61, 259*t*
  model, 251–61
IPRs. *See* Intellectual property rights
IRCA. *See* Immigration Reform and Control Act

Jackson, John, 162*n*
Jamaica, 19, 58*n*, 126
  budget deficits, 74, 75, 84*t*
  consumer prices, 73, 81*t*

domestic investment, 54–55, 55*t*
emissions performances, 150, 151*t*
exchange rates, 75–76, 92*t*, 94*t*
external debt, 75, 89*t*
good-customer indexes, 34–35, 38*t*–39*t*
interest payments, 75, 91*t*
readiness scores, 102*t*, 126
secondary loan prices, 75, 90*t*
strong-neighbor indexes, 34–35, 40*t*–41*t*
trade deficiency, 186–90, 188*t*
trade expansion, 191–97, 195*t*
trade taxes, 77, 96*t*
trade values, 34–35, 36*t*–37*t*
Japan. *See also* Japan, Australia, New Zealand
  foreign direct investment, 43–47, 44*t*, 45*t*
  strong-neighbor indexes, 43, 46*t*
  trade deficiency, 186–90, 188*t*
  trade expansion, 191–97, 194*t*
Japan, Australia, New Zealand
  good-customer indexes, 30–34, 33*t*
  merchandise trade, 28–31, 29*t*, 31*t*
  strong-neighbor indexes, 30–34, 32*t*, 33*t*
Jobs, WHFTA effects on, 60–62, 205–13, 214*t*–
  215*t*, 217*t*
Joint Commission on Technical Cooperation,
  125, 129
Joint Economic Committee, 122, 128*n*
Justice Tribunal of the Cartagena Agreement, 7

Kantor, Mickey, 152, 180
Karatnycky, Adrian, 72
Kissinger, Henry, 1*n*
Krueger, Alan, 147, 147*n*

Labor
  free movement of, 8–9
  Latin American issues, 154–57
  lessons from NAFTA, 153–54
  standards, 22
LAIA. *See* Latin American Integration
  Association
Laird, Sam, 115*n*, 135*n*
Latin America. *See also specific countries; specific
  regional agreements*
  budget deficits, 74, 82*t*
  current account balances, 74, 85*t*–87*t*
  economic history, 63–66
  economic indicators, 17, 18*t*
  economic ties, 27–47
  environmental issues, 149–53
  exchange rates, 75–76, 92*t*
  external debt, 16–17, 18–19
  foreign direct investment, 17, 20–21, 43–47,
  44*t*, 45*t*
  GDP growth, 51–53, 196*t*, 196–97, 197*t*
  good-customer indexes, 30–34, 33*t*
  growth prospects, 53–54
  income diversity index, 48–49, 49*t*
  interest payments, 75, 91*t*
  investment prospects, 54–60

investment regulations, 57–60
labor issues, 154–57
merchandise trade, 28–31, 29t, 31t
readiness assessment, 12–13
readiness indicators, 66–79
reforms, 63–96
secondary loan prices, 75, 90t
strong-neighbor indexes, 30–34, 32t, 33t, 43, 46t
tariffs, 134–35, 136t–137t
trade deficiency, 26–27, 185–90, 186–90, 188t
trade expansion, 191–97, 194t–195t
trade prospects, 53–54
US economic relations, 15–23
US trade, 17, 19–20, 135, 138t, 140–41, 142t
wages, 154–57, 155t, 156t
WHFTA implications for, 51–54
Latin America (term), 1n
Latin American Free Trade Area (LAFTA), 63
Latin American Integration Association (LAIA), 3, 4n
Law on Industrial Property, 144
Loans, secondary loan prices, 75, 90t
Low, Patrick, 147, 147n

Maastricht Treaty, 6, 12, 67n
Macdonald Commission, 98
Macroeconomic stability, 72
Magill, Robert T., 141n
Manufactured goods, 135–37
Maquiladora program, 4, 100
Market exchange rates, 75–76, 92t
Market-oriented policies, 76–77
    readiness scores, 102t
Martin, Philip, 9
McMillan, John, 166
Mercado Común del Sur (Mercosur), 9, 10, 106–13. See also specific countries
    domestic investment, 54–55, 55t
    economic integration achievement scores, 6n
    foreign direct investment in, 43–47, 44t, 45t
    good-customer indexes, 34–35, 38t–39t
    income diversity index, 48–49, 49t
    readiness assessment, 181
    readiness scores, 102t, 107, 112–13
    regional agreements, 226–31
    strong-neighbor indexes, 34–35, 40t–41t, 43, 46t
    supraregional institutions, 7
    trade deficiency, 26, 186–90, 188t
    trade expansion, 191–97, 194t
    trade taxes, 77, 95t
    trade values, 34–35, 36t–37t
Merchandise trade, 28–31, 29t, 31t, 135–37. See also Trade
Mercosur. See Mercado Común del Sur
Mexico, 4, 4n, 78–79, 100–01, 101–02, 115n
    budget deficits, 74, 75, 83t
    consumer prices, 73, 80t
    current account balances, 74, 85t–87t

domestic investment, 54–55, 55t
emissions performances, 150, 151t
exchange rates, 75–76, 92t, 93t
external debt, 75, 88t
foreign direct investment in, 43–47, 44t, 45t
good-customer indexes, 34–35, 38t–39t
interest payments, 75, 91t
readiness scores, 101, 102t
secondary loan prices, 75, 90t
strong-neighbor indexes, 34–35, 40t–41t, 43, 46t
trade deficiency, 186t, 186–90
trade expansion, 191–97, 193t
trade taxes, 77, 95t
trade values, 34–35, 36t–37t
US trade, 100, 140–41, 142t
wages, 154–57, 155t, 156t
Michaely, Michael, 11, 12, 57, 72n, 78
Middle East
    foreign direct investment in, 43–47, 44t, 45t
    merchandise trade, 28–31, 29t, 31t
    strong-neighbor indexes, 30, 32t, 43, 46t
MNEs. See multinational enterprises
Monetary coordination, 10–11
Most-favored nation (MFN) status, 134n
Mulford, David C., 16n
Multilateral trade liberalization, 27
Multinational enterprises (MNEs), 42–43

NAEC. See North American Commission for Environmental Cooperation
NAFTA. See North American Free Trade Agreement
NALC. See North American Commission on Labor Cooperation
National Energy Program, 98
Natural trading partner (term), 27n
Negotiations, hemispheric, 131–58
Neighborliness, economic, 27–28. See also Strong neighbors
New Zealand. See also Australia, New Zealand, and South Africa; Australia-New Zealand Closer Economic Relations; Japan, Australia, New Zealand
    trade deficiency, 186–90, 187t
    trade expansion, 191–97, 194t
Nicaragua, 124
    budget deficits, 74, 75, 83t
    consumer prices, 73, 80t
    current account balances, 74, 85t–87t
    domestic investment, 54–55, 55t
    exchange rates, 75–76, 92t, 94t
    external debt, 75, 89t
    good-customer indexes, 34–35, 38t–39t
    readiness scores, 102t, 124
    secondary loan prices, 75, 90t
    strong-neighbor indexes, 34–35, 40t–41t
    trade deficiency, 186–90, 188t
    trade expansion, 191–97, 195t
    trade taxes, 77, 96t

trade values, 34–35, 36t–37t
North America. *See also* Canada; Mexico;
    United States
    domestic investment, 54–55, 55t
    foreign direct investment, 43–47, 44t, 45t
    good-customer indexes, 30–34, 33t, 34–35,
        38t–39t
    income diversity index, 48–49, 49t
    merchandise trade, 28–31, 29t, 31t
    readiness scores, 101, 102t
    strong-neighbor indexes, 30–34, 32t, 33t, 34–
        35, 40t–41t, 43, 46t
    trade deficiency, 186t, 186–90
    trade expansion, 191–97, 193t
    trade values, 34–35, 36t–37t
North American Agreement on Environmental
    Cooperation, 149, 149n
North American Agreement on Labor
    Cooperation, 153n, 153–54
North American Commission for
    Environmental Cooperation (NAEC), 7
North American Commission on Labor
    Cooperation (NALC), 7
North American Free Trade Agreement
    (NAFTA), 2, 4n, 10, 52n, 97–103, 143, 161
    chronology, 219–24
    Danforth amendment, 22n, 97
    economic integration achievement scores, 6n
    environmental lessons, 147–49
    expansion of, 177n, 177–78
    investment, 145, 145n
    labor lessons, 8–9, 153–54
    supraregional institutions, 7
    trade compensation by, 166–69, 167t
    trade diversion, 176n
    trade model, 133, 146
    unfair trade precedents, 140–42

ODECA. *See* Organization of Central American
    States
OECD. *See* Organization for Economic
    Cooperation and Development
OECS. *See* Organization of Eastern Caribbean
    States
Open economy, environmental benefits, 148
Organization for Economic Cooperation and
    Development (OECD), 67n
Organization of Central American States
    (ODECA), 120
Organization of Eastern Caribbean States
    (OECS), 9, 10
Overseas Development Council, 152

Panama
    budget deficits, 74, 75, 83t
    consumer prices, 73, 80t
    current account balances, 74, 85t–87t
    exchange rates, 75–76, 92t
    external debt, 75, 89t
    foreign direct investment, 58n

secondary loan prices, 75, 90t
    trade taxes, 77, 96t
Papageorgiou, Demetris, 11, 12, 57, 72n, 78
Paraguay, 111–12
    budget deficits, 74, 75, 83t
    consumer prices, 73, 80t
    current account balances, 74, 85t–87t
    domestic investment, 54–55, 55t
    emissions performances, 150, 151t
    exchange rates, 75–76, 92t, 93t
    external debt, 75, 88t
    good-customer indexes, 34–35, 38t–39t
    readiness assessment, 181n
    readiness scores, 102t, 112
    stock exchange cooperation agreements, 59
    strong-neighbor indexes, 34–35, 40t–41t
    tariffs, 137t
    trade taxes, 77, 95t
    trade values, 34–35, 36t–37t
Park, Yung Chul, 132
Pascó-Font, Alberto, 113
Permanent Secretariat of the General Treaty for
    Central American Economic Integration
    (SIECA), 8
Perot, Ross, 153
Peru, 115n, 117–18
    budget deficits, 74, 75, 83t
    consumer prices, 73, 80t
    current account balances, 74, 85t–87t
    domestic investment, 54–55, 55t
    emissions performances, 150, 151t
    exchange rates, 75–76, 92t, 93t
    external debt, 75, 88t
    foreign direct investment, 58
    good-customer indexes, 34–35, 38t–39t
    interest payments, 75, 91t
    readiness scores, 102t, 115, 117
    secondary loan prices, 75, 90t
    strong-neighbor indexes, 34–35, 40t–41t
    trade deficiency, 186–90, 188t
    trade expansion, 191–97, 195t
    trade taxes, 77, 95t
    trade values, 34–35, 36t–37t
    US trade barriers, 140–41, 142t
    wages, 154–57, 155t, 156t
Pipeline protection, 105, 105n, 144
Political reform, 77–79, 101–02
Portfolio investment, 55–57, 56t
Prebisch's center-periphery thesis of trade, 64
Preeg, Ernest, 128, 129
Price, Margaret, 58
Price stability, 72–73
    readiness scores, 80t–81t, 102t
Public and private financing, 67n, 67–69, 68t
Puntarenas Declaration, 120

Quito Protocol, 113n

Radetzki, Marian, 147
Rainford, Roderick, 8n, 9

Readiness assessment, 12–13. *See also specific countries*
subregional, 97–129
Readiness indicators, 66–79. *See also specific indicators*
performance scores, 101, 102*t*
scales, 70–72
Reagan, Ronald, 98
Reciprocal Trade Agreements Act, 98
Reforms, 63–96. *See also* Political reform
Resource Conservation and Recovery Act, 152
Reynolds, Clark, 115*n*, 117, 117*n*, 118
Rodrik, Dani, 72*n*, 185
Rutter, John, 54*n*
Ryan, Joseph F., 72
Ryd, Gunilla, 113

Salinas, Carlos, 100
Schoenbaum, Thomas, 152
Schott, Jeffrey J., 73*n*, 74*n*, 100, 101, 139, 141, 145, 148, 153, 160, 166, 176*n*, 178*n*, 204, 205
Schumpeter, Joseph A., 69
Secondary loan prices, 75, 90*t*
Services trade, 145–46. *See also* Trade
Shafik, Nemat, 147*n*
Shining Path, 119–20
SIECA. *See* Permanent Secretariat of the General Treaty for Central American Economic Integration
South Africa. *See* Australia, New Zealand, and South Africa
South America, public and private financing, 67*n*, 67–69, 68*t*
South American Commission of Peace, 152
South American Free Trade Area, 111
South and East Asia
foreign direct investment in, 43–47, 44*t*, 45*t*
strong-neighbor indexes, 43, 46*t*
Stiglitz, Joseph, 218*n*
Stock exchange cooperation agreements, 59
Strong-neighbor indexes
calculation of, 175*n*
for foreign direct investment, 43, 46*t*
for trade, 30–34, 32*t*, 33*t*, 34–35, 40*t*–41*t*
Strong neighbors, 21, 27*n*, 27–28, 30
Subregional integration, 97–129
Summit of Western Hemisphere democracies, 2–3, 22, 176, 183
Supraregional institutions, 7–8, 224
Surinam
budget deficits, 74, 75, 84*t*
consumer prices, 73, 81*t*
exchange rates, 75–76, 92*t*
trade deficiency, 186–90, 188*t*
trade expansion, 191–97, 195*t*

Tariffs, 20, 134–35, 136*t*–137*t*, 137–39
Taxes, trade, 77, 95*t*–96*t*, 102*t*
Textiles and apparel tariffs, 137–39
Thoumi, Francisco, 115*n*, 117, 117*n*, 118

Tokyo Round, 27
Torricelli bill. *See* Cuban Democracy Act
Trade
good-customer indexes, 30–34, 33*t*, 34–35, 38*t*–39*t*
Latin American prospects, 53–54
merchandise, 28–31, 29*t*, 31*t*, 135–37
NAFTA precedents, 140–42
natural partners, 27*n*
Prebisch's center-periphery thesis, 64
regional ties, 28–42
in services, 145–46
strong-neighbor indexes, 30–34, 33*t*, 34–35, 40*t*–41*t*
summary, 241
US-Latin American relations, 17
waste, 152–53
WHFTA effects, 60, 160–62
Trade Act of 1974, 98
Trade Agreements Act of 1979, 98
Trade barriers, US, 135, 138*t*, 140–41, 142*t*
Trade compensation, by NAFTA, 166–69, 167*t*
Trade creation
NAFTA, 176*n*
WHFTA, 174
Trade deficiency, 185–90, 186*t*–188*t*
Trade diversion
calculation, 175*n*, 252–57, 253*t*–256*t*
GATT surveillance of, 166–69
model, 251–61
NAFTA, 176*n*
WHFTA, 25–27, 163–64, 174–76
Trade expansion, WHFTA, 51–53, 191–97, 193*t*–195*t*
Trade expansion credits (TECs), 168
Trade liberalization, 78. *See also specific free trade agreements*
multilateral, 27
unilateral, 27, 27*n*, 174
Trade Policy Review, 98
Trade-Related Aspects of Intellectual Property Rights (TRIPs), 143
Trade-Related Investment Measures (TRIMs), 145
Trade taxes, 77, 95*t*–96*t*
Trade tax reliance, 77
readiness scores, 95*t*–96*t*, 102*t*
Trade values, 34–35, 36*t*–37*t*
Tragen, Irving G., 158
Treaty of Asunción, 107
Treaty of Chaguaramas, 10–11
Treaty of Rome, 2, 11–12
TRIMs. *See* Trade-Related Investment Measures
Trinidad and Tobago, 126
budget deficits, 74, 75, 84*t*
consumer prices, 73, 81*t*
domestic investment, 54–55, 55*t*
emissions performances, 150, 151*t*
exchange rates, 75–76, 92*t*
external debt, 75, 89*t*

good-customer indexes, 34–35, 38*t*–39*t*
readiness assessment, 180
readiness scores, 102*t*, 126
strong-neighbor indexes, 34–35, 40*t*–41*t*
trade deficiency, 186–90, 188*t*
trade expansion, 191–97, 195*t*
trade taxes, 77, 96*t*
trade values, 34–35, 36*t*–37*t*
Triple transformation test, 139
Twin plant program. *See* Maquiladora program

Understanding on Subsidies and
    Countervailing Duties, 4, 100
Understanding Regarding Trade and
    Investment Facilitation Talks, 100
Unfair trade, NAFTA precedents on, 140–42
Unilateral trade liberalization, 27, 27*n*, 174
United States, 99, 100. *See also* US Trade
    Representative
    budget deficits, 74, 83*t*
    Clinton administration, 22, 105, 157, 173
    consumer prices, 73, 80*t*
    foreign direct investment, 17, 20–21, 43–47,
        44*t*, 45*t*, 54*n*
    foreign direct investment treaties, 58, 58*n*
    domestic investment, 54–55, 55*t*
    emissions performances, 150, 151*t*
    exchange rates, 75–76, 93*t*
    exports, 60, 197–204, 198*t*–203*t*
    external debt, 75, 88*t*
    good-customer indexes, 34–35, 38*t*–39*t*
    imports, 60, 204–5, 206*t*–211*t*
    international trade taxes, 77, 95*t*
    jobs, 205–13, 214*t*–215*t*, 217*t*
    Latin American debt and, 16–17, 18–19
    Latin American economic relations and,
        15–23
    Latin American trade and, 17, 19–20
    readiness scores, 101, 102*t*
    strong-neighbor indexes, 34–35, 40*t*–41*t*, 43,
        46*t*
    trade agenda, 21–22, 157
    trade barriers, 135, 138*t*, 140–41, 142*t*
    trade deficiency, 186*t*, 186–90
    trade expansion, 191–97, 193*t*
    trade values, 34–35, 36*t*–37*t*
    wage levels, 154–57, 155*t*, 156*t*, 213–18, 216*t*,
        217*t*
    WHFTA effects, 60–62, 197–281
University of the West Indies. *See* Caribbean
    Examinations Council
Urrutia, Miguel, 116
Uruguay, 78, 112
    budget deficits, 74, 75, 83*t*
    consumer prices, 73, 80*t*
    current account balances, 74, 85*t*–87*t*
    domestic investment, 54–55, 55*t*
    emissions performances, 150, 151*t*
    exchange rates, 75–76, 92*t*, 93*t*
    external debt, 19, 75, 88*t*

good-customer indexes, 34–35, 38*t*–39*t*
interest payments, 75, 91*t*
readiness assessment, 181*n*
readiness scores, 102*t*, 112
secondary loan prices, 75, 90*t*
strong-neighbor indexes, 34–35, 40*t*–41*t*
tariffs, 134–35, 137*t*
trade deficiency, 186–90, 188*t*
trade expansion, 191–97, 194*t*
trade taxes, 77, 95*t*
trade values, 34–35, 36*t*–37*t*
US trade barriers, 140–41, 142*t*
wages, 154–57, 156*t*
Uruguay Round, 27
US-Canada Auto Pact, 4, 11, 98
US-Caricom Trade and Investment Council, 125
US Congress Joint Economic Committee, 9
US Department of Commerce, 4*n*, 212, 212*n*
US Department of Labor, 61*n*
US Department of State, 157, 158
US International Trade Commission (USITC),
    59, 60, 71*n*, 117*n*, 143, 144, 146*n*
USITC. *See* US International Trade Commission
USTR. *See* US Trade Representative
US Trade Representative (USTR), 22, 59, 71*n*,
    122, 123, 123*n*, 144

Venezuela, 4*n*, 115, 115*n*
    budget deficits, 74, 75, 83*t*
    consumer prices, 73, 80*t*
    current account balances, 74, 85*t*–87*t*
    debt cooperativeness rating, 118*n*
    domestic investment, 54–55, 55*t*
    emissions performances, 150, 151*t*
    exchange rates, 75–76, 92*t*, 93*t*
    external debt, 75, 88*t*
    foreign direct investment, 55–57, 56*t*, 58, 59
    good-customer indexes, 34–35, 38*t*–39*t*
    interest payments, 75, 91*t*
    portfolio investment, 55–57, 56*t*
    readiness assessment, 180–81
    readiness scores, 102*t*, 115
    secondary loan prices, 75, 90*t*
    strong-neighbor indexes, 34–35, 40*t*–41*t*
    tariffs, 20, 134–35, 137*t*
    trade deficiency, 186–90, 188*t*
    trade expansion, 191–97, 195*t*
    trade taxes, 77, 95*t*
    trade values, 34–35, 36*t*–37*t*
    US trade barriers, 140–41, 142*t*
Vernon, Raymond, 42

Wage levels, 60–62, 154–57, 155*t*, 156*t*, 213–18,
    216*t*, 217*t*
War on drugs, 157–58
Waste trade, 152–53. *See also* Trade
Weintraub, Sidney, 100
Werner Plan, 12
West Asia
    income diversity index, 48–49, 49*t*

trade deficiency, 186–90, 187*t*
trade expansion, 191–97, 194*t*
Western Europe
  good-customer indexes, 30–34, 33*t*
  merchandise trade, 28–31, 29*t*, 31*t*
  strong-neighbor indexes, 30–34, 32*t*, 33*t*
  trade deficiency, 186*t*, 186–90
  trade expansion, 191–97, 193*t*
Western Hemisphere. *See also* Economic
    integration, Western Hemisphere Free
    Trade Area
  Asia links, 182–83
  institutions, 246–49
  negotiations, 131–58
  regional agreements, 219–49
  regional diversity, 48–49
  regional ties, 28–42, 42–47
  summit, 2–3, 22, 176, 183
  world relations, 159–71
Western Hemisphere Free Trade Area
    (WHFTA)
  concerns about, 159–60, 169–70
  effects on Latin America, 191–97
  effects on US, 60–62, 197–218
  effects on world trading system, 160–62
  formation of, 173–83

investment diversion, 164–66, 175, 176,
    257–61, 259*t*
job effects, 60–62
negotiations, 131–58
rationale for, 25–27, 174–76
regional effects, 51–62
trade creation, 174
trade diversion, 25–27, 163–64, 174–76
trade effects, 51–53, 60
trade and income expansion, 51–53, 191–97,
    193*t*–195*t*
wage effects, 60–62
Wettmann, Reinhart, 115*n*, 117, 117*n*, 118
Wharton, Clifton R., 22*n*, 157*n*
Wheeler, David, 148
WHFTA. *See* Western Hemisphere Free Trade
    Area (WHFTA)
Williamson, John, 71*n*, 113
Winham, Gilbert, 141
Wonnacott, Paul, 132
World Bank, 11, 12, 67, 67*n*
World Trade Organization (WTO), 99*n*
World Wildlife Fund, 152

Yeats, Alexander, 20*n*, 135*n*, 147
Yoo, Jung Ho, 132

Other Publications from the
Institute for International Economics

POLICY ANALYSES IN INTERNATIONAL ECONOMICS Series

1   The Lending Policies of the International Monetary Fund
John Williamson/*August 1982*
ISBN paper 0-88132-000-5   72 pp.

2   "Reciprocity": A New Approach to World Trade Policy?
William R. Cline/*September 1982*
ISBN paper 0-88132-001-3   41 pp.

3   Trade Policy in the 1980s
C. Fred Bergsten and William R. Cline/*November 1982*
(out of print)   ISBN paper 0-88132-002-1   84 pp.
Partially reproduced in the book *Trade Policy in the 1980s.*

4   International Debt and the Stability of the World Economy
William R. Cline/*September 1983*
ISBN paper 0-88132-010-2   134 pp.

5   The Exchange Rate System, Second Edition
John Williamson/*September 1983, rev. June 1985*
(out of print)   ISBN paper 0-88132-034-X   61 pp.

6   Economic Sanctions in Support of Foreign Policy Goals
Gary Clyde Hufbauer and Jeffrey J. Schott/*October 1983*
ISBN paper 0-88132-014-5   109 pp.

7   A New SDR Allocation?
John Williamson/*March 1984*
ISBN paper 0-88132-028-5   61 pp.

8   An International Standard for Monetary Stabilization
Ronald I. McKinnon/*March 1984*
ISBN paper 0-88132-018-8   108 pp.

9   The Yen/Dollar Agreement: Liberalizing Japanese Capital Markets
Jeffrey A. Frankel/*December 1984*
ISBN paper 0-88132-035-8   86 pp.

10 Bank Lending to Developing Countries: The Policy Alternatives
C. Fred Bergsten, William R. Cline, and John Williamson/*April 1985*
ISBN paper 0-88132-032-3   221 pp.

11 Trading for Growth: The Next Round of Trade Negotiations
Gary Clyde Hufbauer and Jeffrey J. Schott/*September 1985*
ISBN paper 0-88132-033-1   109 pp.

12 Financial Intermediation Beyond the Debt Crisis
Donald R. Lessard and John Williamson/*September 1985*
ISBN paper 0-88132-021-8   130 pp.

13 The United States-Japan Economic Problem
C. Fred Bergsten and William R. Cline/*October 1985, 2d ed. January 1987*
(out of print)   ISBN paper 0-88132-060-9   180 pp.

14 Deficits and the Dollar: The World Economy at Risk
    Stephen Marris/*December 1985, 2d ed. November 1987*
                    ISBN paper 0-88132-067-6   415 pp.

15 Trade Policy for Troubled Industries
    Gary Clyde Hufbauer and Howard F. Rosen/*March 1986*
                    ISBN paper 0-88132-020-X   111 pp.

16 The United States and Canada: The Quest for Free Trade
    Paul Wonnacott, with an Appendix by John Williamson/*March 1987*
                    ISBN paper 0-88132-056-0   188 pp.

17 Adjusting to Success: Balance of Payments Policy
    in the East Asian NICs
    Bela Balassa and John Williamson/*June 1987, rev. April 1990*
                    ISBN paper 0-88132-101-X   160 pp.

18 Mobilizing Bank Lending to Debtor Countries
    William R. Cline/*June 1987*
                    ISBN paper 0-88132-062-5   100 pp.

19 Auction Quotas and United States Trade Policy
    C. Fred Bergsten, Kimberly Ann Elliott, Jeffrey J. Schott,
    and Wendy E. Takacs/*September 1987*
                    ISBN paper 0-88132-050-1   254 pp.

20 Agriculture and the GATT: Rewriting the Rules
    Dale E. Hathaway/*September 1987*
                    ISBN paper 0-88132-052-8   169 pp.

21 Anti-Protection: Changing Forces in United States Trade Politics
    I. M. Destler and John S. Odell/*September 1987*
                    ISBN paper 0-88132-043-9   220 pp.

22 Targets and Indicators: A Blueprint for the International
    Coordination of Economic Policy
    John Williamson and Marcus H. Miller/*September 1987*
                    ISBN paper 0-88132-051-X   118 pp.

23 Capital Flight: The Problem and Policy Responses
    Donald R. Lessard and John Williamson/*December 1987*
                    ISBN paper 0-88132-059-5   80 pp.

24 United States-Canada Free Trade: An Evaluation of the Agreement
    Jeffrey J. Schott/*April 1988*
                    ISBN paper 0-88132-072-2   48 pp.

25 Voluntary Approaches to Debt Relief
    John Williamson/*September 1988, rev. May 1989*
                    ISBN paper 0-88132-098-6   80 pp.

26 American Trade Adjustment: The Global Impact
    William R. Cline/*March 1989*
                    ISBN paper 0-88132-095-1   98 pp.

27 More Free Trade Areas?
    Jeffrey J. Schott/*May 1989*
                    ISBN paper 0-88132-085-4   88 pp.

28 The Progress of Policy Reform in Latin America
    John Williamson/*January 1990*
                    ISBN paper 0-88132-100-1   106 pp.

29 The Global Trade Negotiations: What Can Be Achieved?
Jeffrey J. Schott/*September 1990*
ISBN paper 0-88132-137-0   72 pp.

30 Economic Policy Coordination: Requiem or Prologue?
Wendy Dobson/*April 1991*
ISBN paper 0-88132-102-8   162 pp.

31 The Economic Opening of Eastern Europe
John Williamson/*May 1991*
ISBN paper 0-88132-186-9   92 pp.

32 Eastern Europe and the Soviet Union in the World Economy
Susan M. Collins and Dani Rodrik/*May 1991*
ISBN paper 0-88132-157-5   152 pp.

33 African Economic Reform: The External Dimension
Carol Lancaster/*June 1991*
ISBN paper 0-88132-096-X   82 pp.

34 Has the Adjustment Process Worked?
Paul R. Krugman/*October 1991*
ISBN paper 0-88132-116-8   80 pp.

35 From Soviet disUnion to Eastern Economic Community?
Oleh Havrylyshyn and John Williamson/*October 1991*
ISBN paper 0-88132-192-3   84 pp.

36 Global Warming: The Economic Stakes
William R. Cline/*May 1992*
ISBN paper 0-88132-172-9   128 pp.

37 Trade and Payments After Soviet Disintegration
John Williamson/*June 1992*
ISBN paper 0-88132-173-7   96 pp.

38 Trade and Migration: NAFTA and Agriculture
Philip L. Martin/*October 1993*
ISBN paper 0-88132-201-6   160 pp.

BOOKS

IMF Conditionality
John Williamson, editor/*1983*
ISBN cloth 0-88132-006-4   695 pp.

Trade Policy in the 1980s
William R. Cline, editor/*1983*
ISBN cloth 0-88132-008-1   810 pp.
ISBN paper 0-88132-031-5   810 pp.

Subsidies in International Trade
Gary Clyde Hufbauer and Joanna Shelton Erb/*1984*
ISBN cloth 0-88132-004-8   299 pp.

International Debt: Systemic Risk and Policy Response
William R. Cline/*1984*
ISBN cloth 0-88132-015-3   336 pp.

Trade Protection in the United States: 31 Case Studies
Gary Clyde Hufbauer, Diane E. Berliner, and Kimberly Ann Elliott/*1986*
ISBN paper 0-88132-040-4   371 pp.

Toward Renewed Economic Growth in Latin America
Bela Balassa, Gerardo M. Bueno, Pedro-Pablo Kuczynski,
and Mario Henrique Simonsen/*1986*
(out of stock)   ISBN paper 0-88132-045-5   205 pp.

Capital Flight and Third World Debt
Donald R. Lessard and John Williamson, editors/*1987*
(out of print)   ISBN paper 0-88132-053-6   270 pp.

The Canada-United States Free Trade Agreement:
The Global Impact
Jeffrey J. Schott and Murray G. Smith, editors/*1988*
ISBN paper 0-88132-073-0   211 pp.

World Agricultural Trade: Building a Consensus
William M. Miner and Dale E. Hathaway, editors/*1988*
ISBN paper 0-88132-071-3   226 pp.

Japan in the World Economy
Bela Balassa and Marcus Noland/*1988*
ISBN paper 0-88132-041-2   306 pp.

America in the World Economy: A Strategy for the 1990s
C. Fred Bergsten/*1988*
ISBN cloth 0-88132-089-7   235 pp.
ISBN paper 0-88132-082-X   235 pp.

Managing the Dollar: From the Plaza to the Louvre
Yoichi Funabashi/*1988, 2d ed. 1989*
ISBN paper 0-88132-097-8   307 pp.

United States External Adjustment and the World Economy
William R. Cline/*May 1989*
ISBN paper 0-88132-048-X   392 pp.

Free Trade Areas and U.S. Trade Policy
Jeffrey J. Schott, editor/*May 1989*
ISBN paper 0-88132-094-3   400 pp.

Dollar Politics: Exchange Rate Policymaking in the United States
I. M. Destler and C. Randall Henning/*September 1989*
ISBN paper 0-88132-079-X   192 pp.

Latin American Adjustment: How Much Has Happened?
John Williamson, editor/*April 1990*
ISBN paper 0-88132-125-7   480 pp.

The Future of World Trade in Textiles and Apparel
William R. Cline/*1987, 2d ed. June 1990*
ISBN paper 0-88132-110-9   344 pp.

Completing the Uruguay Round: A Results-Oriented Approach
to the GATT Trade Negotiations
Jeffrey J. Schott, editor/*September 1990*
ISBN paper 0-88132-130-3   256 pp.

Economic Sanctions Reconsidered (in two volumes)
Economic Sanctions Reconsidered: Supplemental Case Histories
Gary Clyde Hufbauer, Jeffrey J. Schott, and Kimberly Ann Elliott/*1985, 2d ed. December 1990*

ISBN cloth 0-88132-115-X	928 pp.
ISBN paper 0-88132-105-2	928 pp.

Economic Sanctions Reconsidered: History and Current Policy
Gary Clyde Hufbauer, Jeffrey J. Schott, and Kimberly Ann Elliott/*December 1990*

ISBN cloth 0-88132-136-2	288 pp.
ISBN paper 0-88132-140-0	288 pp.

Pacific Basin Developing Countries: Prospects for the Future
Marcus Noland/*January 1991*

ISBN cloth 0-88132-141-9	250 pp.
ISBN paper 0-88132-081-1	250 pp.

Currency Convertibility in Eastern Europe
John Williamson, editor/*October 1991*

ISBN cloth 0-88132-144-3	396 pp.
ISBN paper 0-88132-128-1	396 pp.

Foreign Direct Investment in the United States
Edward M. Graham and Paul R. Krugman/*1989, 2d ed. October 1991*

ISBN paper 0-88132-139-7	200 pp.

International Adjustment and Financing: The Lessons of 1985-1991
C. Fred Bergsten, editor/*January 1992*

ISBN paper 0-88132-112-5	336 pp.

North American Free Trade: Issues and Recommendations
Gary Clyde Hufbauer and Jeffrey J. Schott/*April 1992*

ISBN cloth 0-88132-145-1	392 pp.
ISBN paper 0-88132-120-6	392 pp.

American Trade Politics
I. M. Destler/*1986, 2d ed. June 1992*

ISBN cloth 0-88132-164-8	400 pp.
ISBN paper 0-88132-188-5	400 pp.

Narrowing the U.S. Current Account Deficit
Allen J. Lenz/*June 1992*

ISBN cloth 0-88132-148-6	640 pp.
ISBN paper 0-88132-103-6	640 pp.

The Economics of Global Warming
William R. Cline/*June 1992*

ISBN cloth 0-88132-150-8	416 pp.
ISBN paper 0-88132-132-X	416 pp.

U.S. Taxation of International Income: Blueprint for Reform
Gary Clyde Hufbauer, assisted by Joanna M. van Rooij/*October 1992*

ISBN cloth 0-88132-178-8	304 pp.
ISBN paper 0-88132-134-6	304 pp.

Who's Bashing Whom? Trade Conflict in High-Technology Industries
Laura D'Andrea Tyson/*November 1992*

ISBN cloth 0-88132-151-6	352 pp.
ISBN paper 0-88132-106-0	352 pp.

Korea in the World Economy
Il SaKong/*January 1993*

ISBN cloth 0-88132-184-2   328 pp.
ISBN paper 0-88132-106-0   328 pp.

Pacific Dynamism and the International Economic System
C. Fred Bergsten and Marcus Noland, editors/*May 1993*

ISBN paper 0-88132-196-6   424 pp.

Economic Consequences of Soviet Disintegration
John Williamson, editor/*May 1993*

ISBN paper 0-88132-190-7   664 pp.

Reconcilable Differences? United States-Japan Economic Conflict
C. Fred Bergsten and Marcus Noland/*June 1993*

ISBN paper 0-88132-129-X   296 pp.

Does Foreign Exchange Intervention Work?
Kathryn M. Dominguez and Jeffrey A. Frankel/*September 1993*

ISBN paper 0-88132-104-4   192 pp.

Sizing Up U.S. Export Disincentives
J. David Richardson/*September 1993*

ISBN paper 0-88132-107-9   192 pp.

NAFTA: An Assessment
Gary Clyde Hufbauer and Jeffrey J. Schott/*rev. ed. October 1993*

ISBN paper 0-88132-199-0   216 pp.

Adjusting to Volatile Energy Prices
Philip K. Verleger, Jr./*November 1993*

ISBN paper 0-88132-069-2   288 pp.

The Political Economy of Policy Reform
John Williamson, editor/*January 1994*

ISBN paper 0-88132-195-8   624 pp.

Measuring the Costs of Protection in the United States
Gary Clyde Hufbauer and Kimberly Ann Elliott/*January 1994*

ISBN paper 0-88132-108-7   144 pp.

The Dynamics of Korean Economic Development
Cho Soon/*March 1994*

ISBN paper 0-88132-162-1   272 pp.

Reviving the European Union
C. Randall Henning, Eduard Hochreiter and Gary Clyde Hufbauer/*April 1994*

ISBN paper 0-88132-208-3   192 pp.

China in the World Economy
Nicholas R. Lardy/*April 1994*

ISBN paper 0-88132-200-8   176 pp.

Greening the GATT: Trade, Environment, and the Future
Daniel C. Esty/*July 1994*

ISBN paper 0-88132-205-9   344 pp.

Western Hemisphere Economic Integration
Gary Clyde Hufbauer and Jeffrey J. Schott/*July 1994*

ISBN paper 0-88132-159-1   304 pp.